W9-ADP-792

MEDIA
LITERACY

To Molly

MEDIA LITERACY

W. James Potter

SAGE Publications
International Educational and Professional Publisher
Thousand Oaks   London   New Delhi

For information:

SAGE Publications, Inc.
2455 Teller Road
Thousand Oaks, California 91320
E-mail: order@sagepub.com

SAGE Publications Ltd.
6 Bonhill Street
London EC2A 4PU
United Kingdom

SAGE Publications India Pvt. Ltd.
M-32 Market
Greater Kailash I
New Delhi 110 048 India

Printed in the United States of America

Library of Congress Cataloging-in-Publication Data

Potter, W. James.
   Media literacy / by W. James Potter.
     p. cm.
   Includes bibliographical references and index.
   ISBN 0-7619-0926-5 (pbk.: acid-free paper.—ISBN 0-7619-0925-7
(cloth: acid-free paper)
    1. Media literacy. I. Title.
  P96.M4P68 1998
  302.23—dc21   97-33726

This book is printed on acid-free paper.

98 99 00 01 02 03 10 9 8 7 6 5 4 3 2 1

Acquiring Editor:	Margaret Seawell
Editorial Assistant:	Renée Piernot
Production Editor:	Astrid Virding
Production Assistant:	Karen Wiley
Typesetter/Designer:	Rebecca Evans
Indexer:	L. Pilar Wyman
Cover Designer:	Ravi Balasuriya
Print Buyer:	Anna Chin

Contents

PART III   Knowledge

Preface for Faculty

Has this ever happened to you? You're in front of a class of under-graduates giving what you feel is one of your best lectures on media effects, history, economics, or content. A student raises her hand and asks politely, "I'm sorry, but I don't see how this information is important." You get a sinking feeling as you notice that several students nod in agreement.

At first you think that students are so focused on pursuing a career in the media that all they want is some information to help them get their first job as a disc jockey, a camera person, an assistant account executive or the like. There is so much you want to say. You want to tell them that the information you are presenting is more important than directions about which audio buttons to push or how to light a studio set or how to compute a CPM (cost per thousand). You want to make them realize that you are *educating* them for life rather than *training* them for a job. What may seem like irrelevant informa-tion is really part of a knowledge base they will need to draw on every day of their lives as they continuously interact with media, whether they work in one of the media industries or not.

But then you look at the text for the course and notice that it focuses on theories—a word that connotes to students that the information lives in a jar-gon-filled world of abstractions somewhere above them. Or, the text is over-flowing with statistics and charts that glaze the eye and erode students' moti-vation to dig behind the facts to see the organizing perspectives. Or perhaps the text contains many interesting anecdotes that capture the readers' imagi-nations but leave them empty with a "So what?" feeling.

Then it hits you: "What we need is a text that will be broad enough to introduce the important information about the media without wandering off into a lot of detail about historical figures, statistics about content, or formu-las about audience ratings. It should present a broad, well-integrated perspec-tive that would orient students to the key issues, then serve as a foundation for all subsequent media courses. It should be reader friendly with a self-help tone so that students would recognize something on every page that they could use in their day-to-day interactions with the media."

These are the goals for this book, which has been in development over the past 4 years. During that time, it has been pilot tested in four undergraduate classes and undergone several rounds of reviews by multiple reviewers. This process has generated extensive rewriting as a negotiation process between the compelling ideas in the research literatures and the needs of students. This process has been guided by five principles.

First, the book is not written to serve the special needs of a subgroup, such as parents, teachers, or policymakers. Instead, it is written to appeal to a more general audience that wants to think more deeply about the nature of the media, their messages, and their effects on both individuals and society. Also, its focus is not limited to one type of medium or one type of message.

As a college text, this book serves as a broad introduction that spans across many of the boundaries set up in academia to study the media. Some academic programs (such as journalism) focus on newspapers and magazines, whereas others (such as telecommunication and RTV) focus on radio and television. There are film studies programs, programs for recordings in music departments, book publishing in English or literature departments. Also, some programs focus on entertainment, some on information, and others on persuasive messages (marketing/advertising, political science, speech communication, or rhetoric). Some have a social science orientation while others take a cultural/critical approach. Some focus on industry skills (copy editing, reporting, lighting, directing, etc.) while others are more liberal arts programs with an emphasis on theory. Within each of these academic divisions, there is a special set of needs; but across all these divisions, there is the common purpose of educating students to be knowledgeable, well-functioning citizens within our media culture. This book presents an introduction or a kind of "Table of Contents" to the thinking that ties us together in this common goal of educating a media literate generation.

Second, the book is written from a critical perspective. This does not mean that it criticizes everything about the media. Instead, it means that it challenges commonly held beliefs about media effects, how the human mind works, media content, and opinions about the media themselves. The book also lays out arguments about why readers should be more skeptical, and it presents strategies for how readers can get more out of their media exposures. Thus, much of the information is not presented in a purely descriptive tone as is the case with most introductory textbooks. Instead, this book takes a critical perspective and presents arguments in which the information is presented as evidence to advance those arguments. Those arguments are not narrow, prescriptive ones where my purpose is to convince the reader that my perspective on the media is the only one or the best one. Rather, the book advances the arguments broadly to encourage readers to construct their own perspectives. Readers who find themselves disagreeing with my interpretations or extending them (or both) will be best illustrating the principles upon which this book is based.

Third, the arguments in the book are grounded in scientific research. The findings from this type of research cannot answer all our questions, but they can answer many of them. These findings are also useful for filtering out myths and demonstrating support for other speculations. This does not mean that a reader needs to be a statistician, a media theoretician, or a cognitive psychologist. When the book deals with statistics, theory, and psychology, it treats that information in a non-technical manner so that it is accessible to the general reader.

Fourth, in many places the book has a "self-help" tenor in the way it speaks directly to the reader. It presents guidance and practical exercises to help readers develop their own skills for dealing with media messages. Thus the book does not simply present information and leave it up to the students to memorize it or not. Instead, the book tries to sensitize readers to the importance of certain perspectives so that readers will be strongly motivated to explore the value of those perspectives by undertaking exercises. In this way, students have a greater probability of internalizing the key ideas in those perspectives, and that should motivate them to seek out more information in more advanced media courses.

Fifth, the book attempts to keep the focus more on knowledge structures than on individual facts so that readers can get a sense of "the big picture" of the media. Most students seem to be missing this. Their idea of the media is largely informed by their memory of images from television shows. Yet students often arrive at our courses with the belief that they know a great deal about the media because they have spent their lives sitting at an ever-expanding banquet of media channels, personalities, special effects, images, and genres, and they have acquired a great number of unprocessed facts—that is, they have a recognition of a wide variety of names, slogans, plot developments, and sound bites. However, much of this information is not particularly useful in helping them understand the media.

I have found, through knowledge pre-tests administered at the beginning of my courses, that many students lack even a rudimentary understanding of the media industries or their effects. Few students understand the economic nature of businesses or can define "profit." Few have a good idea of how old various media are and of the major influences that shaped their development. Few have any idea about how large the media are in terms of employment or revenue. Students also do not have a broad general understanding of the non-media world. Today, students' knowledge of geography, history, political systems, and economics is very sketchy, while their memory banks are crammed with popular culture images and infobits. More students know exactly what Sandra Bullock's fee for a movie is than know the name of either of the U.S. Senators from their home states. Fewer than half the students have even a close idea of the population of the country or of relative employment sizes of different professions, nor have they developed any strategies to help them make good estimates of these things. Few have a good idea of actual crime rates, per capita expenditures on health care, or the relative costs of different government programs, but they have opinions about crime, health care reform, and government spending. When they form an opinion about something in the media or in society, the opinion is not deeply rooted in reasons; rather it is tethered only to shifting intuitive feelings. If we are serious about educating the next generation to function well in our changing society, we must recognize this challenge.

We have the formidable job of convincing students who have a voluminous knowledge of media and culture that while their knowledge base is miles wide, it is rarely more than an inch deep. That is, we need to help students assemble their knowledge into organized structures so they can see how things fit together and can identify where the gaps are.

As you can see from the five principles above, I am not interested in describing facts to help *train* students for entry-level jobs in a media company. Instead, I am more interested in *educating* students to live in our message saturated culture. Thus, the overriding goal of this book is to help students build their skills and knowledge structures to be more media literate.

But what does "media literacy" mean? This is a term that covers a great deal of conceptual ground. It can refer to the ability to use oral and written language (Maddison, 1971; Scribner & Cole, 1981; Sinatra, 1986), still and moving images (Messaris, 1994; Metallinos, 1994), television (Goodwin & Whannel, 1990), computers (Adams & Hamm, 1989), or to span across many different kinds of media (Silverblatt, 1995). It can be regarded primarily as a skill (Kulleseid & Strickland, 1989; Neuman, 1991) or as an accumulation of knowledge (Bianculli, 1992). It can be treated as a public policy issue (Aufderheide, 1993), a critical cultural issue (Alvarado & Boyd-Barrett, 1992), a set of pedagogical tools for elementary school teachers (Houk & Bogart, 1974), suggestions for parents (DeGaetano & Bander, 1996; Kelly, 1983), McLuhan-esque speculation (Gordon, 1971), or as a topic of scholarly inquiry from a physiological (Messaris, 1994), cognitive psychological (Sinatra, 1986), or anthropological (Scribner & Cole, 1981) point of view. In addition, it can focus primarily on one culture, such as American culture (Manley-Casimir & Luke, 1987; Ploghoft & Anderson, 1981), British culture (Buckingham, 1990; Masterman, 1985), or Chilean culture (Freire, 1985), or on several cultures (Scheunemann, 1996) or span across many countries and cultures (Brown, 1991; Maddison, 1971).

In conducting the research for this book, it became clear that there co-exist several schools of thought held by groups with different but definite ideas about how the term *media literacy* should be used. Four are especially prominent.

One group is composed of scholars who are interested in public policy and who argue for the importance of educating young children and adolescents about the media. The tone of their writings is critical because the authors generally argue that the media are responsible for a range of negative effects on individuals and society—essentially by creating a false consciousness about our world. The audiences for their arguments are educational policymakers and other media scholars. These authors speculate about curriculum changes that need to be implemented in schools in order to address this problem. While some authors discuss particular instructional practices, these are presented as examples of their broad vision rather than as specific suggestions for teachers to implement.

Much of this tradition of thinking about media literacy is traceable to the work of British scholars such as Len Masterman, who wrote *Teaching the Media* (1985); David Buckingham, who edited *Watching Media Learning: Making Sense of Media Education* (1990); Manuel Alvarado and Oliver Boyd-Barrett, editors of *Media Education* (1992); and Andrew Goodwin and Garry Whannel, who edited *Understanding Television* (1990). Other scholars contributing important work to this tradition are Aufderheide (1993); Brown (1991); Freire (1985); Manley-Casimir and Luke (1987); McLaren, Hammer, Sholle, and Reilly (1995); and Ploghoft and Anderson (1981).

A second group includes scholars who are social scientists concerned with how people develop all the skills necessary for literacy with all kinds of media. The writings in this area are primarily intended to help the reader understand the skills involved in processing media messages. Some of these writings take a psychological point of view and focus on processing written and spoken language (Scribner & Cole, 1981) or visual images (Messaris, 1994; Sinatra, 1986). Others take a broader sociological (Silverblatt, 1995) or anthropological approach (Gordon, 1971).

A third group presents its viewpoint in handbooks that provide practical suggestions and exercises for parents (e.g., DeGaetano & Bander, 1996) and teachers (e.g., Houk & Bogart, 1974; Kulleseid & Strickland, 1989). These books are designed to help people work with children to increase their literacy in the various media (Adams & Hamm, 1989), especially television (Kelly, 1983).

A fourth group writes a popular-press type of criticism of the mass media and their effects on society and individuals. The primary targets of criticism are film (Medved, 1992) and television (Mander, 1978; Postman, 1984). However, some of the criticism is against the critics (e.g., *Literacy in the Television Age: The Myth of the TV Effect* by Susan Neuman, 1991, and *Teleliteracy: Taking Television Seriously* by David Bianculli, 1992).

Very important ideas have emerged from each of these groups of thinkers. I have been weaving these ideas together into an integrated whole as I develop my courses, in the belief that students will be able to achieve higher levels of media literacy if they are able to examine this concept from many different perspectives. I therefore try to show students the concept of media literacy from the perspective of a cognitive psychologist in Chapters 3, 4, and 5. Then, in Chapters 6, 7, and 8, the media are examined primarily from the perspective of a critical scholar; of a historian in Chapter 9; of an economist in Chapter 10; of a political economist in Chapter 11; of a marketer in Chapter 12; a social scientist in Chapters 13 and 14; and a sociologist in Chapter 15. The first two and the last two chapters of the book work to integrate the major perspectives in the middle of the book.

The book is composed of 18 chapters that are organized into four parts: Introduction, Skills, Knowledge Structures, and Putting It All Together. Each chapter begins with an outline and a thesis statement, which is the key idea of that chapter. Each chapter includes at least one exercise that students can either do at home to help them apply the ideas in the readings, or do in class as a stimulus to group discussions. At the end of most chapters, there is a short annotated bibliography of several additional readings that students could pursue to extend and deepen their knowledge of the topic of that chapter.

The book has some boundaries that must be acknowledged. First, it is focused entirely on United States media. Second, I do not present the information in this book as the definitive set of all things a person needs to know to be highly media literate. The book is more a table of contents than an encyclopedia. It is a beginning point for getting organized and building substantial knowledge structures. It is also a plan of action to help readers orient themselves in their continuous development of media literacy skills.

Third, and finally, I try to blend the insights from the critical perspective with the social scientific perspective. Social scientists will likely feel uncomfortable with the critical tone of some of the sections, and critical scholars will undoubtedly feel that statistical information is being wrongly privileged in places. However, I feel that taking the risk of attempting a blending of information from the two different worldviews is worthwhile if students (who are largely unaware of this academic distinction) are able to see a broader perspective on the media, their content, and their effects.

References

Adams, D. M., & Hamm, M. E. (1989). *Media and literacy: Learning in an electronic age: Issues, ideas and teaching strategies*. Springfield, IL: Charles C Thomas.

Alvarado, M., & Boyd-Barrett, O. (Eds.). (1992). *Media education: An introduction*. London: BFI Publishing.

Aufderheide, P. (1993). *Media literacy: A report of the national leadership conference on media literacy*. Washington, DC: Aspen Institute.

Bianculli, D. (1992). *Teleliteracy: Taking television seriously*. New York: Continuum.

Brown, J. A. (1991). *Television "critical viewing skills" education: Major media literacy projects in the United States and selected countries*. Hillsdale, NJ: Lawrence Erlbaum.

Buckingham, D. (Ed.). (1990). *Watching media learning: Making sense of media education*. New York: Falmer.

DeGaetano, G., & Bander, K. (1996). *Screen smarts: A family guide to media literacy*. Boston: Houghton Mifflin.

Freire, P. (1985). *The politics of education: Culture, power, and liberation*. South Hadley, MA: Bergin & Garvey.

Goodwin, A., & Whannel, G. (Eds.). (1990). *Understanding television*. New York: Routledge.

Gordon, D. R. (1971). *The new literacy*. Toronto: University of Toronto Press.

Houk, A., & Bogart, C. (1974). *Media literacy: Thinking about*. Dayton, OH: Pflaum/Standard.

Kelly, M. R. (1983). *A parents' guide to television: Making the most of it*. New York: John Wiley.

Kulleseid, E. R., & Strickland, D. S. (1989). *Literature, literacy, and learning*. Chicago: American Library Association.

Maddison, J. (1971). *Radio and television in literacy: A survey of the use of the broadcasting media in combating illiteracy among adults*. Paris: UNESCO.

Mander, J. (1978). *Four arguments for the elimination of television*. New York: William Morrow.

Manley-Casimir, M. E., & Luke, C. (Eds.). (1987). *Children and television: A challenge for education*. New York: Praeger.

Masterman, L. (1985). *Teaching the media*. London: Comedia.

McLaren, P., Hammer, R., Sholle, D., & Reilly, S. S. (Eds.). (1995). *Rethinking media literacy: A critical pedagogy of representation*. New York: Peter Lang.

Medved, M. (1992). *Hollywood vs. America: Popular culture and the war on traditional values*. New York: HarperCollins.

Messaris, P. (1994). *Visual "literacy": Image, mind, and reality*. Boulder, CO: Westview.

Metallinos, N. (Ed.). (1994). *Verbo-visual literacy: Understanding and applying new educational communication media technologies*. Montreal, Canada: 3Dmt Research and Information Center.

Neuman, S. B. (1991). *Literacy in the television age: The myth of the TV effect*. Norwood, NJ: Ablex.

Ploghoft, M. E., & Anderson, J. A. (Eds.). (1981). *Education for the television age*. Springfield, IL: Charles C Thomas.

Postman, N. (1984). *Amusing ourselves to death: Public discourse in the age of show business*. New York: Penguin.

Scheunemann, D. (Ed.). (1996). *Orality, literacy, and modern media*. Columbia, SC: Camden House.

Scribner, S., & Cole, M. (1981). *The psychology of literacy*. Cambridge, MA: Harvard University Press.

Silverblatt, A. (1995). *Media literacy: Keys to interpreting media messages*. Westport, CT: Praeger.

Sinatra, R. (1986). *Visual literacy connections to thinking, reading and writing*. Springfield, IL: Charles C Thomas.

Interesting Reading

Adams, D. M., & Hamm, M. E. (1989). *Media and literacy: Learning in an electronic age: Issues, ideas and teaching strategies*. Springfield, IL: Charles C Thomas. (197 pages)

Adams and Hamm, who come from an educational technology background, offer a very applied approach to media literacy. They lay out some techniques that they suggest teachers can use to increase literacy in their students. The book is scholarly (although on the low end) with its acknowledgment of some of the communication and education literature. There are chapters on teaching mathematics, on computer literacy, and on moral development. There is little factual material or findings from research studies.

Alvarado, M., & Boyd-Barrett, O. (Eds.). (1992). *Media education: An introduction.* London: BFI Publishing. (450 pages with index)

Alvarado and Boyd-Barrett's edited volume contains 63 short essays organized into four sections: Development and Traditions of the Subject of Media Education; Key Aspects of Media Education; Analyzing Classroom Performance; and Practical Issues of Practice, In-Service Training, Strategies, and Media Education Across the Curriculum. All the contributors are British and attention is on how media education should be incorporated into the curriculum in order to educate people between the ages of 4 and 18.

Aufderheide, P. (1993). *Media literacy: A report of the national leadership conference on media literacy.* Washington, DC: Aspen Institute. (37 pages)

This is a report of a meeting held in December 1992 by several dozen Americans concerned about the need for teaching media literacy in the nation's public schools. They derived the following definition of media literacy: "it is the ability of a citizen to access, analyze, and produce information for specific outcomes" (p. v). They recommend that "emphases in media literacy training range widely, including informed citizenship, aesthetic appreciation and expression, social advocacy, self-esteem, and consumer competence" (p. 1).

Brown, J. A. (1991). *Television "critical viewing skills" education: Major media literacy projects in the United States and selected countries.* Hillsdale, NJ: Lawrence Erlbaum. (371 pages including index)

Brown tries to inventory the range of systematic projects that have developed integrated curricula and long-range projects in media education with an emphasis on television. His audience is educators who are trying to design and implement their own media education projects at all levels: grade and high school, college, and adult education, as well as in local, regional, and even national interest groups.

Buckingham, D. (Ed.). (1990). *Watching media learning: Making sense of media education.* New York: Falmer. (234 pages with index)

Buckingham's edited book of 10 chapters deals with various aspects of media education in Britain. The main questions addressed are: What do students already know about the media? How have students learned what they already know? What should students know about the media?

DeGaetano, G., & Bander, K. (1996). *Screen smarts: A family guide to media literacy.* Boston: Houghton Mifflin. (206 pages with appendices and index)

Written by two teachers, this is a book for parents who are concerned about what their children are learning (or not learning) from television. The authors observe that "we are taught how to read and write, but we are not taught about visual images—how they work, how they affect us, and how we can use them for our purposes" (p. xv). The book is full of practical suggestions and exercises for parents and children. There are in-depth treatments of media violence, advertising, and stereotypes, as well as of news and talk shows.

Freire, P. (1985). *The politics of education: Culture, power, and liberation.* South Hadley, MA: Bergin & Garvey. (211 pages including index)

Freire is a Chilean social critic and educator. He treats literacy as a political problem, training teachers to investigate the life and vocabulary of the community. When people can read they are empowered to access more information, but when they read they must have a critical attitude toward the text and not accept it at face value.

Goodwin, A., & Whannel, G. (Eds.). (1990). *Understanding television.* New York: Routledge. (192 pages with index)

Goodwin and Whannel's book contains 12 chapters, primarily by British cultural scholars who teach about television to college students. These essays comprise a text that the authors use to introduce their students to the history, social context, and textual interpretation of television.

Gordon, D. R. (1971). *The new literacy.* Toronto: University of Toronto Press. (190 pages with index)

Gordon argues that the Three Rs are no longer sufficient for literacy in the new media environment. In this rather McLuhan-esque book with its changing type faces, odd graphics and eye-catching use of white space, the author raises issues more than he provides prescriptions or definitions.

Houk, A., & Bogart, C. (1974). *Media literacy: Thinking about.* Dayton, OH: Pflaum/Standard. (115 pages)

Houk and Bogart's book was written for teachers of media literacy in public schools. The authors offer many creative suggestions to teachers.

Kelly, M. R. (1983). *A parents' guide to television: Making the most of it.* New York: John Wiley. (129 pages)

This is a practical handbook. It is very thin on information and research findings with only 17 research studies cited in the entire book. Instead, Kelly focuses on providing parents with lots of suggestions about how to interact with their children while they are watching television.

Masterman, L. (1985). *Teaching the media.* London: Comedia. (341 pages including annotated bibliography and appendices)

Written for teachers of media, this book addresses the questions: Why teach about the media? What are the best ways to teach about the media? Why are media texts the way they are? Masterman seeks to present a set of general principles for teaching about any mass medium.

McLaren, P., Hammer, R., Sholle, D., & Reilly, S. S. (Eds.). (1995). *Rethinking media literacy: A critical pedagogy of representation.* New York: Peter Lang. (259 pages)

This edited volume contains seven chapters by different college professors. It concludes with an discussion among the four authors on the topic of strategies for media literacy. The chapters are critical of the media and argue for an activism.

Medved, M. (1992). *Hollywood vs. America: Popular culture and the war on traditional values.* New York: HarperCollins. (386 pages)

Film critic Medved argues that Hollywood has a value system that is very different from that of mainstream America. He says that Hollywood glorifies the perverse, ridicules all forms of mainstream religion, tears down the image of the family, and glorifies ugliness with violence, bad language, and America-bashing—and then is puzzled by decreasing attendance and increasing criticism.

Messaris, P. (1994). *Visual "literacy": Image, mind, and reality.* Boulder, CO: Westview. (208 pages)

Paul Messaris, a communications professor at the University of Pennsylvania, argues against some commonly held assumptions about visual literacy. For example, he rejects the notion popular among many scholars that there can be no objective standards for judging the reality of visual images. He says that there are generic cognitive skills that people apply when they experience the pictorial media. His notion of training people to be media literate focuses on helping viewers detect unrealistic visual manipulation.

Metallinos, N. (Ed.). (1994). *Verbo-visual literacy: Understanding and applying new educational communication media technologies*. Montreal, Canada: 3Dmt Research and Information Center. (276 pages)

The 38 chapters in Metallinos's volume are from a symposium of the International Visual Literacy Association. The chapters focus on suggestions about how best to use the emerging new technologies to foster verbal and visual literacy.

Postman, N. (1984). *Amusing ourselves to death: Public discourse in the age of show business*. New York: Penguin. (184 pages with index)

Postman presents a strong, well-written argument about how the media, especially television, have conditioned us to expect entertainment. Because our perceptions of ideas are shaped by the form of their expression, we are now image oriented. We respond to pleasure, not thought and reflection.

Sinatra, R. (1986). *Visual literacy connections to thinking, reading and writing*. Springfield, IL: Charles C Thomas. (307 pages)

Richard Sinatra, a professor in human services and counseling at St. John's University, argues that visual literacy is primary to more developed forms of literacy, such as oral language literacy and written language literacy. Many of the arguments in his book are rather technical. For example, he provides an in-depth treatment of the topic of how the human brain processes verbal and visual information.

Preface for Students

H as this ever happened to you? You're sitting in class listening to a professor lecture about the media, and you wonder: How can I memorize all this information? There is so much! How much of this will I be expected to know?

This feeling is a symptom of several needs. Perhaps you need to be convinced that learning the material is worthwhile because it will be useful to you in your life; if you are committed to learning something, it will come much more easily to you. Perhaps you think the information is valuable, but there appears to be too much; in this case, you need some way to organize it all. For example, it is a formidable task to memorize 30 brand new facts, but if you can arrange them into six bundles of five facts each, then they are easier to learn. Better still would be to organize them into a branching structure where the most important idea is regarded as the trunk of a tree and four or five ideas branch off directly from that main idea. Each of those branches has its own four or five extending ideas. Such a structure would be a valuable tool to keep you organized when you are exposed to yet another 30 or even 300 new facts. The structure would orient you to where to place the new information so it could be easily retrieved when you need it for a test, a class discussion, or formulating an opinion years after the class is over. Knowledge structures are very important tools in helping us acquire new information, organize that information, and retrieve that information when we want to use it.

How good are your knowledge structures about the media and the culture they reflect? Let's make a quick assessment and find out. At the end of this Preface, there is a Media Literacy Quiz. This short quiz (it will take you about 10 to 15 minutes) is not a test of the entire extent of your knowledge structures. Instead, it is a small sampling of information that will help you diagnose where your knowledge structures are strongest. Try to answer as many questions as you can, but don't be upset if you leave some blank or get them wrong. Remember, the results are for your eyes only. Okay, turn to the end of the preface, and take the Media Literacy Quiz.

Let's see how you did. In Part I—the Media Industries—you could have earned 29 points. If you earned more than 20 points, you probably have a broad knowledge of the media industries. If you earned fewer than 10 points, you've got some gaps in your knowledge of the size and structure of the media industries.

In Part II—Media Effects—don't focus on how many effects you were able to list. Instead look at the variety of those effects. Are they all negative effects or are there also some positive ones on your list? Are the effects all immediate ones or did you also include effects that take weeks or even years to show up? Are they all effects on your behaviors, or did you also include effects on your attitudes, values, learning of facts, bodily functions, and ability to appreciate art or life? The greater the variety of effects you were able to list, the better your knowledge structure about effects.

In Part III—Media Content—were you surprised by some of the answers? You have watched over 10,000 hours of television programming so far in your life, and you remember lots of specific characters, plots, and show tunes. But are you focusing on the "trees" rather than the "forest"? That is, is your memory so focused on individual characters and shows that you are missing the overall patterns in the television world?

Part IV—Perceptions of the Real World—may seem like a strange component for a media quiz, but much of this information comes to you from the media and may not be very accurate. When this information is good, it gives you a solid foundation for your opinions about education, government, families, health, and crime. If you scored more than 20 points on this section, you probably have a good knowledge base about the real world. More important than the number of points you scored, however, are the patterns of your estimates. Are you able to think logically and construct good estimates even when you don't know the real figures? The patterns of your estimates will show you something about the skills you use. For example, look at your answers to Questions 16 and 17 together. I've had people answer that 60% of the population has not graduated from high school and that 70% of the population has a college degree. That adds up to 130%. The only way this is possible is if millions of high school dropouts also have college degrees. Even though you may not know the answer to either of these questions, it is still possible to be reasonable with estimates. Let's take another example. Look at your estimates for Questions 21 and 28. I've had people estimate that the population of this country was 100 million people, and that the annual birth rate was 50 million. That would mean that over the past 2 years alone, 100 million people were born—which is their estimate of the total U.S. population. Where did all the people over 3 years old come from?

Finally, in Part V—Name Recognition—look at where you earned your points. If you are like most people who take this quiz, you are more familiar with media personalities than with the people who are behind the scenes in the media or with real-world figures.

Now think beyond your scores on the individual sections of the quiz and ask yourself: Could my knowledge base be stronger? If the answer is yes, then read on!

This book is composed of 18 chapters that are organized into four parts: Introduction, Skills, Knowledge Structures, and Putting It All Together. The introductory chapters ask you to confront the questions: *Should* I work on developing my knowledge about the media? Why is this important? How can I get started? In Chapter 1, I present a definition of media literacy that spreads out across a range of skills and knowledge. No one is totally non-media-literate, because everyone has some knowledge and skills. Also, no one is completely media literate, because knowledge continually changes, and our skills can always be improved.

Chapter 2 is designed to show you that media literacy is at a fairly low level in this culture and that this is a problem about which we should be concerned. We live in a media saturated environment where we must filter out almost all of the information that comes to us in order to be able to function in our society. We may be screening out too much, however, which would leave us with a set of faulty beliefs about the media and society.

Part II deals with the skills required for media literacy. Most of you have developed formidable skills for memorizing bits of information so you can do consistently well on exams based on objective knowledge. Yet the skill of memorizing, while useful at times, is less than what you need to be media literate. The higher level skills of analysis, synthesis, evaluation, and problem solving can help you make much more efficient use of your time and can help you see the "big picture."

Chapter 3 reveals how our understanding of the human mind has changed. Psychologists have moved away from mechanical models of logical processing of information toward more open-ended, intuitive models, such as the use of schemas—sets of facts that allow us to organize information. Given the unsystematic, unconscious way we process much of the media information, Chapter 4 makes an argument for more formal processing by developing the skills of analysis, comparison/contrast, evaluation, synthesis, and appreciation.

A developmental perspective on skills is taken in Chapter 5. In psychology, the developmental perspective is generally limited to a focus on children's cognitive development. Chapter 5 expands this focus to look at development into adulthood along the cognitive, emotional, and moral dimensions.

Each of the 11 chapters in Part III helps you build knowledge structures about the media industries, their messages, and their effects. Of course, these chapters cannot give you all the information you need to have well-developed knowledge structures on these topics, but the chapters can orient you to what is important and help you structure your approach to fleshing out your knowledge with additional reading and study. The first three of these chapters examine the essence of different types of messages found across all the media: Chapter 6 examines the news—Is it possible for news to be objective, given all the influences and constraints on journalists? Chapter 7 focuses on advertising messages—How has the increase in the number of advertising messages changed the media industries and other businesses? Chapter 8 examines patterns of entertainment programming—What kinds of characters, portrayals, and themes are most prevalent, and what are the message conventions that shape this content?

The next four chapters will help organize your knowledge structures about the media industries. Chapter 9 helps you see the media industries from an historical perspective. It presents a highlight reel of each medium to show the patterns they have all followed in developing into the powerful giants they are today. An economic perspective is shown in Chapter 10, with each of the mass media industries profiled in terms of its revenues, expenses, and profit margins. Chapter 11 shows patterns of ownership and control of the mass media companies. Each medium is examined separately, then cross-media ownership patterns are explored. Chapter 12 takes a marketing perspective, as the nature of the audience is presented through the eyes of industry decision makers. The view of the audience has changed drastically from the days of seeing it as a mass.

The next three chapters deal with the effects of the media. Chapter 13 will help you expand your vision of what constitutes a media effect. Effects are both long term and immediate. Not only can they affect our behavior, but they also have profound influences on us cognitively, affectively, and physiologically, and these effects are positive as well as negative.

Chapter 14 looks at how the effects processes work on us. These processes are hardly ever simple or direct. More often, the media work in concert with many other factors that each serve to increase the probability that an effect may occur. When we take a broader perspective on effects, we can more accurately assess the influence of the media in our lives.

In Chapter 15, the influences of media are examined in terms of changes in the fundamental institutions of politics, family, religion, and sports. The media, especially television, have forever altered the way these institutions function, which means that the media exert indirect effects on us through these institutions.

Chapter 16 illustrates why a broad knowledge about the real world is as important as a thorough knowledge about the media industries. Real-world knowledge helps us check whether the media are presenting a balanced picture of society. While this chapter cannot present a full inventory of the real-world knowledge a person needs, it presents some examples (such as in the areas of crime, the legal system, and government) to illustrate how real-world knowledge is often at odds with the media picture.

The book concludes with two chapters that lay out some key strategies for improving literacy. Chapter 17 synthesizes the findings in the previous 16 chapters to help build your awareness of your own knowledge structures, awareness about how your mind works, and awareness of the key elements in the effects process. This forms the basis for Chapter 18, which presents perspectives to help you develop your own media strategies at three levels: societal, interpersonal, and personal.

When you read each of these chapters, think in terms of developing your knowledge structures. Begin with the thesis statement, the "key idea" of the chapter. Then look at the outline at the beginning of the chapter. It will show you the major branches and each branch's supporting ideas. Then read the text while continually asking yourself: How does this new information fit in with what I already know? How can I use this? After your first reading, close the book and see how much you can recall. Do you recall only an assortment of facts, or an organized structure? Do the exercises. Continue to think about the ideas as you experience the media in your everyday life. Spontaneously work on parts of the exercise, elaborating and extending your answers. Discuss your growing awareness with others.

This book has a "self-help" tone to it as it presents guidance and practical exercises to help you achieve higher levels of media literacy. I don't want you to memorize any of it. Rather, I prefer that you work with the information and internalize it. This is why I present practical exercises in each chapter. The concepts and lists in the chapters are tools to help you work the exercises. The more you do this, the more you will internalize the information and the longer it will stay with you and the more you will be able to use it. For example, in the chapter on media effects, I present a rather long list of possible effects. If you simply memorize this list, it may help you a bit on a test, but it won't help you become a more empowered consumer of media messages. To develop such power over the effects process, you need to internalize the knowledge about these effects so you can spot them when they occur and protect yourself from the effects you don't want and amplify the effects you do want. The more you practice spotting and naming these effects, the more you will be internalizing the information and learning about a tool that will be useful for the rest of your life. That's why the concepts are presented as tools to help you achieve a better life.

In summary, the purpose of this book is to help you develop strong knowledge structures about the media. Will the book provide you with all the information you need? No. There is simply too much information for one course; you will need to take other courses and read other books. What this book will do is give you the broad perspective you need to get started efficiently. It will introduce you to the big picture of knowledge and alert you to the skills you will need to navigate through all the media information and to make better sense of it.

It is important to get started now. The world is rapidly changing because of the media. VCRs, computers, the Internet, and other media channels are substantially revising the way the media industries do business and the way we receive information and entertainment.

I hope you will have fun reading the book, and I hope it will give you a new perspective from which to view the media. If it does, you will be gaining new insights about your old habits and interpretations. If this happens, I hope you will share your insights with me. Much of this book was written to reflect some of the problems and insights my students have had in the media literacy courses I have taught. I have learned much from them. I'd like to learn even more from you. So let me know what you think—send me a message at: potter@sscf.ucsb.edu.

See you on the journey!

Acknowledgments

This book project has traveled a very long distance from the time it initially rippled across my brain as a fascinating but unformed idea. Since that time hundreds of students in six COM 113 classes here at the University of California at Santa Barbara have helped me form the idea into something useful for a broad range of undergraduates. I thank them for every question, every puzzled look, every expression of frustration, and especially for the smiles when they saw the knowledge come together into something meaningful.

I thank the very large number of reviewers hired by Sage to critique early, mid, and near final drafts of this project. In the early stages those critics compared the draft to many interesting things ranging from a valuable handbook all the way to lower forms of livestock wearing bad make-up. I thank these critics for making me understand in a profoundly emotional way what I had long understood in a purely cognitive way—that people bring deeply ingrained agendas to their readings. Because this book is focused on helping people read the media, I thank all the reviewers for helping—in their own ways—to keep me sensitive to this essential point. Therefore, I thank the early reviewers for making me wrestle with the fundamental questions of interpretation; I thank the mid process reviewers for helping me with the structure and completeness of my arguments; and I thank the tail end reviewers for their valuable—and numerous—suggestions for making the book reader friendly.

Margaret Seawell is an acquisitions editor extraordinaire. Her early excitement over the proposal made me believe that I could write this book. During the rough reviews, she kept my spirits up with her one-of-a-kind sense of humor. And during the great reviews, she was always able to shrink my head back down to proper size so it could continue to fit in front of my word processor. And in the meantime she would buy me crème brûlées every six months to keep me manic enough to finish all the writing, rewriting, and editing on time. She is the consummate professional you wish everyone could be.

There are three other people at Sage who are responsible in large part for the quality in this book. In the production of this book, Astrid Virding made it look easy, although her production flow charts look like the corporate tax code. Kristin Bergstad, who from her editor's nest in the hills of New Hampshire sent me over 400 questions, which gave structure and fiber to my summer vacation. And thanks also to Kassie Gavrilis who undertook some major promotional efforts early.

If you like this book, then I share the credit of success with all the people I mentioned above. If you find a mistake, a shortcoming, or a misinterpretation, then it is my fault for not fully assimilating all the high quality help I have been privileged to experience.

Media Literacy Quiz

This is a short exercise to test your knowledge base of the media industries and of some areas of real-world knowledge.

 Part I: The Media Industries

1. In which decade were each of the following media industries introduced into this country?

   a. Broadcast television: _____

   b. Magazines: _____

   c. Film: _____

   d. Radio: _____

   e. Cable television: _____

   f. Personal computers: _____

2. Which of the mass media is most dominant today? _____

3. What is meant by "profit"? _____

4. How much money did consumers spend directly on the media last year?

   _____

5. How much money was spent supporting the media indirectly through advertising? _____

6. Which are the most economically concentrated media industries?

   _____

7. What is the largest media company? _____

8. List the top five highest paid entertainers between 1995 and 1997.

   a. _____

   b. _____

   c. _____

   d. _____

   e. _____

9. What is the largest cable television company in this country? _____

   What percentage of America's households are its customers? _____

10. How many theatrical movie screens are there in this country? _____

11. What is the profit margin averaged across all industries in this country?

   _____

   What is the average profit margin in the following media industries?

   a. Book publishing: _____

   b. Magazine publishing: _____

   c. Newspaper publishing: _____

   d. Broadcast television: _____

   e. Cable television: _____

   f. Radio: _____

12. What percentage of the labor force works in some form of the media? ___

Part II: Media Effects

13. Has the media had any effects on you? If so, list them. _____

   _____

   _____

   _____

   _____

   _____

   _____

   _____

   _____

Part III: Media Content

14. On prime-time television, what percentage of all characters are:

   a. Male: _____

   b. African American: _____

   c. 65 years old or older: _____

   d. Overweight: _____

   e. Handicapped: _____

Part IV: Perceptions of the Real World

For questions in this section (15 through 41) think only about this country when making your estimates.

Education

15. Percentage of adults who have not completed high school: _____

16. Percentage of adults who have a 4-year college degree: _____

17. Percentage of college graduates who have earned their degree in 4 years or less: _____

Government Expenditures

18. What percentage of the total U.S. economy (Gross Domestic Product) is due to expenditures of the federal government? _____%

19. Of the total expenditures of the federal government, what percentage is spent on each of the following:

   a. % spent on national defense _____

   b. % spent on physical resources (transportation, commerce, housing, etc.)_____

   c. % spent on human resources (social security, Medicare, health, education, veterans' benefits, etc.)_____

   d. % spent for interest on the national debt_____

Demographics

20. What is the population of this country? _____ people

21. What percentage of the U.S. population is 60 years old or older? _____%

22. What is the median age of the population? years old _____

23. How many immigrants will come to the United States this year? _____

24. What percentage of the immigrant total will come from Mexico? _____%

Families

25. How many marriages this year: _____

26. How many divorces this year: _____

27. How many people will be born this year in this country: _____

28. What percentage of these births will be to unmarried mothers: _____%

29. What is the median household income: $ _____

Health

30. What is the per capita spending on health in this country? $ _____

31. What percentage of health care is paid for by Medicare? _____%

32. What percentage of the working force is employed in health care? ____%

33. What percentage of medical doctors are male? _____%

34. What percentage of the U.S. population has a disability that limits their ability to function? _____%

Crime

35. Number of crimes reported to police last year: _____

36. Percentage of crimes cleared by arrest: _____%

37. Percentage of crimes that are violent: _____%

38. Number of prisoners on death row: _____

39. Average number of prisoners executed each year since 1930: _____

Legal System

40. Percentage of lawyers who are female: _____%

41. Number of cases filed in U.S. Supreme Court last year: _____

 Part V: Name Recognition

Who are these people? For each of the following names (42 through 71) that you recognize, write a brief, one-sentence description of who that person is.

42. Roone Arledge: _____

43. Sandra Bullock: _____

44. Jim Carrey: _____

45. Marcy Carsey: _____

46. Dan Conner: _____

47. Patricia Cornwell: _____

48. George Costanza: _____

49. Kevin Costner: _____

50. Michael Crichton: _____

51. Michael Eisner: _____

52. Sandra Day O'Conner: _____

53. Stephen Hawking: _____

54. Dean Koontz: _____

55. Michael Irvin: _____

56. Alan Greenspan: _____

57. Gerald Levin: _____

58. Heather Locklear: _____

59. Courtney Love: _____

60. Nelson Mandela: _____

61. John Malone: _____

62. Reed Hundt: _____

63. William Rehnquist: _____

64. Janet Reno: _____

65. Geraldo Rivera: _____

66. Dennis Rodman: _____

67. Bernard Shaw: _____

68. James Waller: _____

69. Who is the president of your college/university? _____

70. Name one of the U.S. Senators from your state. _____

71. Name the U.S. Congressperson from your home district. _____

PART I

Introduction

CHAPTER 1

What Is Media Literacy?

KEY IDEA *Media literacy is a perspective from which we expose ourselves to the media and interpret the meaning of the messages we encounter. We build our perspective from knowledge structures.*

Most of us think we are fairly media literate. After all, we have graduated from high school and reached adulthood. We know the lyrics and melodies of many songs. We recognize the names and faces of celebrities. We know how to read. We can easily follow plots in movies and television shows. We know what flashbacks mean, and we know enough to get scared when the soft background music builds to a shattering crescendo as a character steps into danger. We might even know how to play games on a computer and program a VCR. Clearly we know how to expose ourselves to the media, we know how to absorb information from them, and we know how to be entertained by them.

Are we media literate? Yes, of course. We have acquired a great deal of information and developed remarkable skills. The ability to speak a language, to read, and to understand photographs is an achievement that we too often take for granted. Language literacy means that we have acquired an abstract linguistic system of symbols and syntax rules that allows us to share meaning about hypothetical ideas as well as tangible objects. Reading means that we are able to recognize written symbols individually and in combinations. Picture literacy is the ability to look at lines and shapes on a flat surface and to perceive three-dimensional patterns. Even when the drawings lack color, realistic detail, and dimension, we can fill in these gaps and see things beyond what is literally there. Being literate about moving images is an even greater achievement. Film and television are complex modes of communication involving the interplay of pictures, speech, music, graphics, and special effects. To make sense of all these stimuli, we need a wide range of abilities.

We should not overlook what we have accomplished, but it is also important to acknowledge that we all can be much more media literate. So while it is good to celebrate the abilities we have developed, we must also recognize that there is considerable room for improvement.

Improvement in what way? A starting place for thinking about improvement is a broad definition of what it means to be media literate.

What Is Media Literacy?

In the minds of most people, the term *literacy* is most associated with the print media, meaning the ability to read (Scribner & Cole, 1981; Sinatra, 1986). Some people expand the term to *visual literacy* as they think about other media such as film and television (Goodwin & Whannel, 1990; Messaris, 1994). Other writers have modified the term to *computer literacy* (Adams & Hamm, 1989). In this book, the term is stretched to apply to all media.

Of course, messages change if they are translated from one medium to another. A candidate's political position will appear different if we read about it in a newspaper than if we hear her tell us her position on the radio or if we see her give a speech on television. We need different sets of skills to process messages from different types of channels, but there is also a generic set of skills that underlies our ability to process any type of media message—this is the focus of media literacy.

The Definition

Media literacy is a perspective from which we expose ourselves to the media and interpret the meanings of the messages we encounter. We build this perspective from knowledge structures. To build our knowledge structures, we need tools and raw material. The tools are our skills; the raw material is information from the media and from the real world.

People operating with a high level of media literacy have a strong, broad perspective. They actively use a set of highly developed skills to place a media message inside the context of a well-elaborated knowledge structure and so are able to interpret any message along many different dimensions. This gives them more choices of meaning. Are all choices of meaning equally good? The answer is no. Highly literate people know how to sort through all the choices of meaning and select the one that is most useful from several points of view—cognitive, emotional, moral, and aesthetic. Thus, media literate people have greater control over media messages.

In contrast, people operating at lower levels of media literacy have a weak, limited perspective on the media. They have a smaller, more superficial, and less organized knowledge structure that gives them an inadequate and confusing contextual background to use for interpreting the meaning of a media message. These people are also habitually reluctant or unwilling to use their skills, which remain underdeveloped and therefore more difficult to employ successfully. As a result, it is unlikely that people at lower levels of media literacy will construct multiple meanings from a media message, so they are much more likely to accept the surface meaning in the message itself. Thus, low literacy people are much less able to identify inaccuracies, to sort through controversies, to appreciate irony or satire, or to develop a broad, yet personal view of the world.

In short, it is better to perform at higher levels of media literacy, because doing so gives you many more options. These options translate into more power by giving you more control over your beliefs and behaviors. With few or no choices, much of the world is closed, and you are forced to accept unquestioningly the dominant themes, values, beliefs, and interpretations presented in the media.

Foundational Ideas

This definition of media literacy rests on five fundamental ideas. Each of these is explained below.

Media Literacy Is a Continuum, Not a Category. Media literacy is not a categorical condition, like being a high school graduate or being an American. With categorical conditions, either you are something or you are not. In contrast, media literacy is best regarded as a continuum in which there are degrees.

We all occupy some position on the media literacy continuum. There is no point below which we could say that someone has no literacy, and there is no point at the high end where we can say that someone is fully literate—there is always room for improvement.

Media Literacy Needs to Be Developed. Your position on the media literacy continuum can improve to higher levels. Some of this change occurs through a process of maturation, and some of it can only be accomplished by conscious practice. As for maturation, our capacities grow from when we are infants through adolescence. When we are very young, our minds are not developed enough to allow for an understanding of abstract thoughts, such as required by mathematical reasoning, for example. Our minds mature as we grow through childhood (Smith & Cowie, 1988). A task of reasoning (such as multiplying 4×5) is very difficult for us when we are 4 years old but very easy for us a few years later. We also mature emotionally (Goleman, 1995) and morally (Kohlberg, 1981). As we reach higher levels of maturation intellectually, emotionally, and morally we are able to perceive more in the media messages.

Maturation raises our potential, but we must actively develop our skills and knowledge structures in order to deliver on that potential. Merely exposing ourselves to media messages will not help us develop to higher levels, unless we actively process those messages. If we are passive, we can still pick up a good deal of information in our media saturated culture, but that information will be neither balanced nor complete. To illustrate this point, let's say a person needs 100 facts to have a commanding knowledge base in a particular area. Passive exposure to the media might result in the person being exposed to maybe a dozen facts. When this small sub-set of 12 facts is repeated over and over again, the repetition can give the person a sense that the information is developing into a strong knowledge structure. In this case, however, the continual flow of messages does not broaden the person's knowledge structure. Instead the constant flow of the same messages serves to reinforce a narrow, unbalanced set of facts. Unless the person actively seeks a wider variety of sources of information, this knowledge structure will not expand, even though the person will think that he or she is keeping informed and learning more because of the constant exposure to information.

People operating at the lowest levels of media literacy are in a relatively mindless state during exposure; that is, they are not concentrating on the messages, nor are they actively thinking about the meaning of those messages. Instead, they accept the surface intentions of the message designers. If they watch an ad and acquire a positive attitude about the product, they have accepted the surface interpretation of the ad's designer. In the long term, as they watch thousands of ads for all sorts of products, they accept unquestioningly the interpretation that all problems are immediately solvable by buying something.

People operating at a slightly higher level of media literacy are often active in processing messages and constructing their own interpretations. Yet because they do not have a well-developed knowledge structure, they have fewer options of meaning available to them. Their choices are limited, because they do not have a wide enough range of experience and knowledge to allow them to see most messages from many different perspectives. Also, they either don't have well-developed skills or they are reluctant to use the skills they do have. When skills are weak, it takes a lot of effort to use them.

People operating at high levels of media literacy are mindful during exposure. They are skeptical of the interpretations they see and actively process those messages. This process frequently ends with them constructing their own meanings. Sometimes they do accept an interpretation from the media, but this acceptance is not mindless; instead it is the result of a reasoned, conscious process in which they realize the media interpretation is the best among all available alternatives.

Unless we stay active in processing messages, our position on the media literacy continuum can degrade to lower levels. Without continually practicing skills, they will deteriorate. Without continually updating and adjusting our knowledge structures, they quickly become out of date and cluttered with unprocessed information. For example, the ownership, control, economic, and organizational patterns of the media industries change every year. Every week brings a flood of new messages. Every year, social scientists conduct hundreds of important studies that require us to expand as well as alter the way we think about effects. If we don't keep up, we will slide behind.

Media Literacy Is Multi-Dimensional. There are four inter-related dimensions of media literacy: the cognitive, emotional, aesthetic, and moral dimensions.

Each of these is a continuum—persons' abilities range along each of them. These domains can be independent of one another; for example, a person might be high on only one and low on all others. Someone who is highly media literate realizes that there is a synergy among the four; that is, developing to a very high level on one usually requires significant development on the other three.

The *cognitive domain* refers to mental processes and thinking. Cognitive abilities range from simple awareness of symbols to a complex understanding of how a message was produced and why it was fashioned in the way it was. This is the intellectual dimension. It relies heavily on strong knowledge structures to provide a rich context in the construction of meaning.

The *emotional domain* is the dimension of feeling. Some people have very little ability to experience an emotion during exposure to the media, while others are very sensitive to cues that generate all sorts of feelings in them. Some emotions are associated with negative effects. For example, young children who see very violent horror films experience an extreme amount of fear that can incapacitate them for hours and even leave lasting emotional scars. Emotional reactions can also be positive. Feeling a character's depth of grief over the loss of a loved one requires a relatively high degree of literacy in the emotional domain.

Emotions need not be only the strong ones like rage, fear, lust, hate, and others. Producers have easy-to-recognize symbols to trigger these, so it does not require a high degree of literacy to perceive and understand these emotions. There are also more subtle emotions, such as ambivalence, confusion, wariness, and so on. Crafting messages about these emotions requires more production skill, and a higher degree of literacy is required of the audience if it is to recognize the symbols that signal these emotions and to feel the emotion the producer is trying to elicit.

The *aesthetic domain* refers to the ability to enjoy, understand, and appreciate media content from an artistic point of view. This appreciation requires an awareness of the skills used in the craft of producing messages in the various media—including an ability to detect the difference between art and artificiality. It also includes the ability to spot the unique artistic style of a writer, producer, or director.

The *moral domain* refers to the ability to infer the values underlying the messages. In situation comedies, the values portrayed in the messages are usually that humor is an important tool in dealing with problems; wit is power; problems are never serious and all are solvable in a half hour. In action dramas, the values portrayed in the messages are that violence is usually a successful means to get what you want and that the world is a dangerous place.

It takes a highly media literate person to perceive moral themes well. You must be able to think past individual characters in order to focus your meaning-making at the overall narrative level. You separate characters from their actions—you might not like a particular character but you like his or her actions in terms of fitting in with (or reinforcing) your values. You do not focus your viewing on only one character's point of view, but try to empathize with many characters so you can vicariously experience the various consequences of actions through the course of the narrative.

Like the other dimensions, this one is also a continuum. At the lower end of this continuum is the tendency to perceive all the elements in the show as an undifferentiated mass or blur. Higher on the continuum, you are aware of the values on the surface of the messages. At the highest levels, you perceive patterns of values underlying messages across different vehicles, and you take a clear moral position in favor of or in opposition to those values.

The Purpose of Media Literacy Is to Give Us More Control Over Interpretations. All media messages are interpretations. Journalists tell us their interpretation of what is important and who is important. Entertainment storytellers show us their interpretation of what it means to be human, to develop relationships, to engage in conflict, and to achieve happiness. Advertisers try to convince us that we have problems and that their products can help us quickly overcome those problems. Also, as audience members we can construct our own interpretations of those messages.

A key to media literacy is *not* to engage in the impossible quest for truthful or objective messages. They don't exist. Instead, we need to be aware of the interpretive process and to be vigilant in looking for patterns in interpretations within media messages. This means avoiding mindless exposure to the media, which results in uncritically accepting the media interpretations by default.

The process of media effects continues whether we are aware of it or not. When we can gain greater control over the media (not just through exposure but also through interpretation), we can amplify the effects we want to have and discount those we want to avoid.

In order to achieve this purpose, we need to be able to recognize the full range of media effects and how they exercise their influence on us. This is not an easy task. Most media effects are subtle; they happen very gradually; and most of the effects take a long time to show up. By the time they reach a high enough profile to be easily recognized, they have grown deep roots in our subconscious and are very hard to change.

Media effects also often exert their influence indirectly, through other people or institutions. Even if we somehow avoided all direct exposure to media messages, we would be influenced indirectly by the messages that have influenced our institutions of government, family, education, and religion. The only way to be completely free of all media influence is to remove yourself completely from society and its institutions. But, ironically, this might potentially be the greatest media influence of all—to force you to alter your lifestyle radically and to give up all the many benefits of being part of our culture.

The reasonable response to the flood of media messages is to be more active in processing them in order to get the information and experiences you want and value. By developing a higher level of media literacy, you gain control over the media influence process. You know how to spot those subtle yet important effects as they occur, and you know how to intervene in that effects process in order to shape the effects you want.

Building Strong Knowledge Structures

To build our knowledge structures, we need tools and raw material. The tools are our skills. The raw material is information from the media and from the real world. If we have a great deal of information but weak skills, we will not be able to make much sense of the information. If we have strong skills but don't expose ourselves to a wide enough range of media messages or real-world experiences, our knowledge structures will be very limited and unbalanced.

The Importance of Information

Information is the essential ingredient in knowledge structures, but having a great deal of superficial information about television shows or popular music does not in itself make a person media literate. If all we have is the recognition of surface information such as lyrics to television show theme songs, names of characters and actors, settings for shows, and the like, we are operating at a low level of media literacy. In order to move up the continuum to higher levels of literacy, we need to organize the information well into a useful knowledge structure. In undertaking such an organization, we need to be mindful of concerns for both depth and breadth of information. As for depth, we need to get below the surface of superficial information and look for patterns and trends, differences and similarities. We need to seek answers to the questions of "How" and "Why" in order to understand the values operating in the media industries, the themes and patterns in the content, and the wide range of subtle effects those messages exert on us over time.

Our knowledge structure also needs breadth. What are the important components of our knowledge structure when it comes to media literacy? First, we need knowledge about the message conventions used by media producers and the patterns of content these conventions produce. Second, we need knowledge about the media industries: origins, patterns of development, economic bases, and structural contexts (ownership patterns and governmental regulation). Third, we need to understand how the media view us as audiences. Fourth, and perhaps most important, we need a broader perspective on media effects. This means recognizing long-term as well as short-term effects; recognizing effects on society as well as on individuals; and recognizing that effects can be cognitive, attitudinal, behavioral, and physiological.

We also need to have a strong knowledge structure about the real world—both factual information and social information. *Factual information* refers to characteristics about the world that are usually not in dispute (not open to individual interpretation). Examples include the size of the population of this country, names of political leaders, final scores of sporting contests, the distance between cities, and so on. In contrast, *social information* refers to our shared understandings about human interactions. Examples include the moral themes within a culture or institution, as well as the way people should behave in certain roles (such as student, romantic partner, friend, stranger, family member, job applicant, athletic team member, etc.).

People who have had a wider range of experiences in the real world have a broader base from which to appreciate and analyze media messages. For example, those who have helped someone run for political office can understand and analyze press coverage of campaigns to a greater depth than those who have not had any real-world experience with political campaigns. People who have played sports will be able to appreciate the athletic accomplishments they see on television to a greater depth than those who have not physically tested themselves on those challenges. People who have had a wide range of relationships and family experiences will have a higher degree of understanding and more in-depth emotional reactions to those portrayals in the media.

Information is the raw material on which our skills work to build knowledge structures. In order to get good raw material, we need to expose ourselves to a wide variety of messages to expand our base. We also need to search out more in-depth information on areas where we have some superficial knowledge so as to deepen our understanding. Although most of this information comes from media sources, we also need to search out information from primary sources in real life.

The Importance of Skills

When thinking about media literacy, many scholars focus on skills (Brown, 1991; DeGaetano & Bander, 1996; McLaren, Hammer, Sholle, & Reilly, 1995), and there are many different kinds of skills mentioned. This range of skills can be categorized into rudimentary skills that are basic to media use and those that are more advanced.

The *rudimentary skills* are the ones we use to govern our exposure to the media, recognize symbols, and match meaning. For media exposure, we need to know what vehicles are available and how we can gain access to them.

When we have access, we need to recognize the symbols presented. Some symbols are words, so we need to know what a word is compared to a letter, or a sentence, or a line of type, and so on. Some symbols are elements in pictures, so we need to be able to recognize form, dimension, perspective, and the like. Some symbols are audio, so we need to be able to recognize voice, music, sound effects, and more. Some symbols are movements on a screen; we need to be able to recognize a cut, dissolve, pan, zoom in, and so on.

When we recognize the existence of a symbol, we need to attach meaning to it. For example, we memorize the definitions of words and the conventions of grammar and expression to be able to read. From our experience of listening to radio, we know that certain sounds signal the lead-in to news, certain voices convey humor or seriousness, and certain sounds convey danger or silliness. With television and film, we learn the meaning of a flashback, an extreme close-up on a character's face, character stereotypes, and what to expect in the unfolding sequence of a detective show.

As young children, we practice using these rudimentary skills and continually improve. By early adolescence, we are fairly proficient, and additional practice no longer serves to improve those skills by much. Their use becomes automatic; that is, we do not need to think consciously as we apply them. For example, when we are very young, our minds are not mature enough for us to recognize written symbols and to associate meaning with them. When our minds mature, we reach a point where we have the potential to read, but we must work to deliver on that potential. Try to think back to when you were about 5 years old and first learning how to read the written word. You probably had to expend a good deal of effort to concentrate on each word and recognize its meaning and how it sounded when pronounced. Then you needed to work through the struggle of putting words together into sentences and recognize a larger chunk of meaning. The act of reading a page of a book took a long time and was exhausting. Now, after years of practice, you take the skill of reading for granted. Your eyes fly over the words, barely "seeing" them. Instead your mind is "seeing" the ideas and images evoked by the words. The little black lines that form the letters and words are transparent— you see right through them as if they were dust on a window that looks into the rooms of the author's mind—rooms arranged with the furniture of ideas.

The benefit of being proficient in the rudimentary skills is that our exposures are more efficient—we no longer struggle when reading a newspaper

article or following a plot in a TV show or film. The danger of this proficiency is that our exposures require very little concentration, and this leads to mindless exposure where we accept the surface meanings in the messages. When we simply match a meaning to a symbol, we accept that meaning without challenge, and each time we mindlessly match, that meaning is reinforced.

Once these rudimentary skills have been acquired, it could be tempting for us to think we are media literate and to stay on this plateau, practicing these lower level skills the rest of our lives. There is another set of more *advanced skills* that gives us the opportunity to develop greater control over the media messages. These are the skills that allow us to move the interpretive control away from the media messages and much more into our own realm of control.

Applying advanced skills requires concentrated thinking. This means that with the advanced skills, we do not take messages for granted. Instead, we have a skepticism that guides our interaction. We critically challenge messages and the meaning they imply. These advance skills are analysis, comparison/contrast, evaluation, synthesis, and appreciation.

Putting It All Together

Remember that media literacy is a continuum. People are positioned along that continuum based on the skills and knowledge they bring to bear (cognitively, emotionally, aesthetically, and morally) for the purpose of gaining control over the meaning process. Along that continuum, we can identify some key positions (see Table 1.1).

The lower three levels shown in the table are stages we go through as young children. Acquiring Fundamentals happens during the first year of life; Language Acquisition occurs during years 2 and 3, and Narrative Acquisition during years 3, 4, and 5. These are stages that children leave behind as they age into adolescence and adulthood.

The Developing Skepticism stage occurs between about ages 5 to 9, and the Intensive Development stage follows shortly after. Many people stay in the Intensive Development stage the rest of their lives, because this stage is fully functional—that is, people in this stage feel they are getting exposure to the messages they want and getting the meaning they want out of those messages. They feel they are fully media literate and that there is nothing more they need to learn.

The next three stages shown in Table 1.1 can be regarded as advanced, because they require the continual use of higher level skills and the active development of elaborate knowledge structures. People in the Experiential Exploring stage feel that their media exposure has been very narrow, and they

Table 1.1 Typology of Media Literacy

Stage	Characteristics
Acquiring Fundamentals	Learn that there are human beings and other physical things apart from one's self; these things look different and serve different functions
	Learn the meaning of facial expressions and natural sounds
	Recognize shapes, form, size, color, movement, and spatial relations
	Learn rudimentary concept of time—regular patterns
Language Acquisition	Recognize speech sounds and attach meaning to them
	Be able to reproduce speech sounds
	Orient to visual and audio media
	Make emotional and behavior responses to music and sounds
	Recognize certain characters in visual media and follow their movement
Narrative Acquisition	Develop understanding of differences:
	Fiction vs. non-fiction
	Ads vs. entertainment
	Real vs. make-believe
	Understand how to connect plot elements
	By time sequencing
	By motive-action-consequence
Developing Skepticism	Discount claims made in ads
	Sharpen differences between likes and dislikes for shows, characters, and actions
	Make fun of certain characters even through those characters are not presented as foils in their shows
Intensive Development	Strong motivation to seek out information on certain topics
	Develop a detailed set of information on particular topics (sports, politics, etc.)
	High awareness of utility of information and quick facility in processing information judged to be useful

Table 1.1 Continued

Stage	Characteristics
Experiential Exploring	Seek out different forms of content and narratives
	Focus on searching for surprises and new emotional, moral, and aesthetic reactions
Critical Appreciation	Accept messages on their own terms, then evaluate them within that sphere
	Develop very broad and detailed understanding of the historical, economic, political, and artistic contexts of message systems
	Develop ability to make subtle comparisons and contrasts among many different message elements simultaneously
	Develop ability to construct a summary judgment about the overall strengths and weaknesses of a message
Social Responsibility	Take a moral stand that certain messages are more constructive for society than others; this is a multi-dimensional perspective based on a thorough analysis of the media landscape
	Recognize that one's own individual decisions impact society—no matter how minutely
	Recognize that there are some actions an individual can take to make a constructive impact on society

seek exposure to a much wider range of messages. For example, people who have watched only prime-time action/adventure and situation comedy programs will begin to watch news, PBS documentaries, travelogues, MTV, science fiction, offbeat sports, and more. They will pick up niche magazines and books about unusual topics. The thrill for these people is to see something they have never seen before. This makes them think about the variety of human experience.

People in the Critical Appreciation stage see themselves as connoisseurs of the media. They seek out messages that are better cognitively, emotionally, aesthetically, and morally. They have strongly held opinions about who the best writers are, the best producers, the best news reporters, and so on, and they have lots of evidence to support their well-reasoned opinions. They can talk fluently and at length about what makes a good writer and how these elements are exhibited in a particular writer's body of work.

Social Responsibility is characterized by people who have a critical appreciation of all kinds of media messages, but instead of having a primarily internal perspective (as with the Critical Appreciation stage), the perspective here is external. The person at this stage not only asks, "What is best from my point of view and why?" but is also concerned with such questions as, "What types of messages are best for others and for society?"

Be careful not to think of these positions as fixed, distinct stages. Instead, think of them as overlapping stages in a fluid process. They are offered here more for purposes of illustration than as definitive positions. You have a typical position on the continuum, but that position is not static. You move up and down depending on the medium you are interacting with, depending on the message, and depending on your motive for the exposure. For example, when you are reading a book that is considered a classic novel for a college course, you may be able to reach up to the Critical Appreciation level. But when you flick on the television and watch *MTV Beach Party* to relax, you might sink down to the Intensive Development level. There is nothing wrong with this moving around. There are times when we just want to "veg out" and don't want to spend the effort to stay at the highest stages. Just remember that there is a difference between people who stay at the lower stages because they are unable or unwilling to operate at higher stages and people who are able to operate at all stages but occasionally choose to take it easy at the lower stages.

We all have a stage at which we feel generally at home. This is where we are most comfortable in our interactions with the media. We are usually able to move up a stage or two from this home base, but moving up a stage requires a conscious effort and we must expend more energy to apply higher level skills, so we don't move up unless we are strongly motivated to do so.

Summary

In this book, media literacy is treated very broadly. It is not limited to reading or to any other single skill, and it is not limited to children. Media literacy is regarded as a perspective from which we view media messages. There are many different perspectives available to us, depending on our level of skill and our knowledge structures. We have all developed the basic skills for exposing ourselves to media messages and for making some rudimentary meaning of them. Having more highly developed literacy means that we actively apply more advanced skills and a larger, more elaborate knowledge structure in being able to perceive multiple meanings in any media message.

This greater awareness gives us more options of meaning to select from, and more options translate into more control in constructing the cognitive, emotional, aesthetic, and moral effects we want.

Developing media literacy can be illustrated by an eight-stage continuum of Acquiring Fundamentals, Language Acquisition, Narrative Acquisition, Developing Skepticism, Intensive Development, Experiential Exploring, Critical Appreciation, and Social Responsibility. Our movement from lower to higher stages requires the active application of more sophisticated skills and the development of more elaborated knowledge structures. Because the strength of our knowledge structures varies from topic to topic, we will find ourselves moving around from stage to stage as we continue to expose ourselves to media messages.

References

Adams, D. M., & Hamm, M. E. (1989). *Media and literacy: Learning in an electronic age: Issues, ideas and teaching strategies.* Springfield, IL: Charles C Thomas.

Brown, J. A. (1991). *Television "critical viewing skills" education: Major media literacy projects in the United States and selected countries.* Hillsdale, NJ: Lawrence Erlbaum.

DeGaetano, G., & Bander, K. (1996). *Screen smarts: A family guide to media literacy.* Boston: Houghton Mifflin.

Goleman, D. (1995). *Emotional intelligence.* New York: Bantam.

Goodwin, A., & Whannel, G. (Eds.). (1990). *Understanding television.* New York: Routledge.

Kohlberg, L. (1981). *The philosophy of moral development: Moral stages and the idea of justice.* New York: Harper & Row.

McLaren, P., Hammer, R., Sholle, D., & Reilly, S. S. (Eds.). (1995). *Rethinking media literacy: A critical pedagogy of representation.* New York: Peter Lang.

Messaris, P. (1994). *Visual "literacy": Image, mind, and reality.* Boulder, CO: Westview.

Scribner, S., & Cole, M. (1981). *The psychology of literacy.* Cambridge, MA: Harvard University Press.

Sinatra, R. (1986). *Visual literacy connections to thinking, reading and writing.* Springfield, IL: Charles C Thomas.

Smith, P. K., & Cowie, H. (1988). *Understanding children's development.* Oxford, UK: Basil Blackwell.

Further Reading

Bianculli, D. (1992). *Teleliteracy: Taking television seriously.* New York: Continuum. (315 pages with indices)

David Bianculli was a TV critic/columnist for 15 years before writing this book, which is a defense of television. Admitting that 90% of TV content is "crap," he feels that there is nevertheless a great deal of value. He presents a manifesto of 10 points, all intended to increase respect for television. The first section is the most interesting part of the book. Here, he presents a 150-question literacy quiz (75 questions about TV and 75 about classic literature and music). The TV questions are very easy to answer and the other questions are very difficult. His point is that the population is very TV literate. He also presents a fascinating history of criticism of various forms of literature and music dating back to Plato; this clearly shows that some people think every new piece of art is bad and every new medium is dangerous.

Silverblatt, A. (1995). *Media literacy: Keys to interpreting media messages.* Westport, CT: Praeger. (340 pages including index)

Silverblatt's mass media book has the feel of a textbook for an introductory-level course, and presents many photographs and student exercises. In some chapters, the author gives information about what is needed as far as knowledge about the media is concerned. The first section of the book, Keys to Interpreting Media Messages, lays out a method for critically analyzing the process, context, framework, and production values of the mass media. The second section, Media Formats, presents exercises to show readers how to analyze print journalism, advertising, and American political communications. The third section—the smallest at under 40 pages—briefly raises some critical issues, such as violence in the media, children, social change, and global communications.

Exercise 1.1 Analyzing Your Degree of Literacy in Reading a Magazine Article

1. Think about the last magazine article you read. Write the name of the article and the name of the magazine on the worksheet on the following page.

2. Notice that the worksheet has two columns (Skills and Knowledge) and four rows (Cognitive, Emotional, Aesthetic, and Moral), making eight blocks.

3. Think about the experience you had while reading that article. What skills did you use when reading and thinking about the article? Write those skills in the appropriate blocks, depending on whether the skills were cognitive, emotional, aesthetic, or moral.

4. Now think about the knowledge you needed before reading the article in order to make sense of it. What facts and opinions did you bring to the reading experience? Write those elements in the appropriate blocks.

5. Take a look at the pattern of your responses. Are some blocks full of writing while other blocks are empty? Think about why there is a difference in the amount of detail across the different blocks. Is it because you are not used to thinking about certain components? Or is it because the experiences you had within certain components were occurring without your conscious knowledge?

6. Compare the results of your exercise with those of a friend. Did your friend have more details in certain blocks compared to yours? If so, did that additional detail extend your thinking? The more people's work you compare, the more you can see a range of differences.

Exercise 1.1 Worksheet

Article Title: _____

Name of Magazine: _____

	Skills	*Knowledge*
COGNITIVE		
EMOTIONAL		
AESTHETIC		
MORAL		

CHAPTER 2

The Importance of Media Literacy

KEY IDEA *Our environment is saturated with media messages that blur the line between reality and fantasy. Because much of our exposure is passive, we develop faulty beliefs about the world.*

In 1964, Sherwood Schwartz produced a television show called *Gilligan's Island*. This was a farcical comedy about seven characters who had been on a pleasure cruise and encountered a storm that left them shipwrecked on an island somewhere in the Pacific Ocean. After about six episodes had aired, Schwartz was contacted by the Coast Guard and told they had received several dozen telegrams from people who were complaining that the military hadn't sent a ship to rescue these people. These telegrams were serious. Schwartz (1984) was dumbfounded, calling this the "most extreme case of suspension of belief I ever heard of." He wondered, "Who did these viewers think was filming the castaways on that island? There was even a laugh track on the show. Who was laughing at the survivors of the wreck of the S.S. Minnow? It boggled the mind" (p. 2).

Hearing a story like this, we are likely to smile and think that those people must be extremely media illiterate to be so influenced by the media that they could not tell the difference between reality and fantasy. We smugly feel that we don't have that problem—but remember that media literacy is a continuum. We are constantly faced with the challenge of controlling the media's influence on us, and the difference between us and the viewers who contacted the Coast Guard is only a matter of degree. All of us must continually decide how closely media messages reflect real life. Sometimes these decisions are relatively easy: It is simple for most of us to realize that there is nothing in real life at all like *Gilligan's Island*. Other decisions are harder to make accurately—especially when they are subtly shaped over a long period of time by the accumulation of hundreds of slightly misleading messages. The following story, which will illustrate this point, happened to me; perhaps something similar has happened to you.

One night when I was out jogging, I saw my neighbor out walking her new dog—a Doberman with a nasty face.

"That's a pretty big dog, Rene," I said as I slowed down—being careful not to get too close to the muscular dog straining at the leash.

"Yes, this is Spike," she replied.

"Hi, Spike. Good boy, Spike." I smiled weakly, wondering whether I should hold out my hand to pet his jet black head, from which his beady eyes fixed on my jugular.

"I got him for protection."

"Protection from what?"

"Protection from muggers," she said to me as if she were a kindergarten teacher and I were a 5-year-old.

I looked around. In our peaceful upscale suburban neighborhood, the only people stirring were a few home owners walking their very large dogs. "Rene, there are no muggers in this neighborhood. And in the five years I've lived here, there has never been a mugging."

"See? It pays to have a big dog."

I was puzzled by this logic, but decided to probe. "Rene, if you're really that concerned about crime, have you also put extra locks on your doors or bought a home alarm system?"

"Don't be silly. Criminals rarely break into houses. The danger is from the muggers."

I felt like telling her that if she were familiar with real-life crime statistics, she would know that there is a much higher likelihood that her house would be burglarized than that she would be mugged—even if she walked around all night without her dog. Also, it was very unlikely that her house would be burglarized, especially in this neighborhood, and that the risk of burglary had been going down over the past decade as property crime rates have been dropping.

"Don't you watch the news?" she said. "There is so much crime, and every day some poor soul is getting knifed or killed!"

Then it became clear to me. She was getting her information about risks in her neighborhood not from her neighborhood but from the media. Newspapers and television shows were telling her that crime was taking place every day. The media were scaring her to get her attention, and they certainly had her attention. They also had shaped her beliefs about crime, stimulated her to spend money on a guard dog, and altered the way she spent her evening—taking care of the none-too-affectionate Spike.

When I suggested that she was being influenced by the media, she laughed and told me I was naive not to realize the risk I was taking. I felt the same way about her.

As these examples illustrate, the media can blur the distinction between reality and fantasy. Their power to do this rests on two conditions: a culture saturated with media messages, and our inability to process all the messages, which leads us to form faulty beliefs.

Message Saturation

The mass media bombard us with thousands of messages every day. We are completely unaware of most of these messages. Consider the following scenario: As you drive down the street glancing at messages on billboards, news and advertising messages come out of your car radio. A taxi passes with a reminder to watch a certain television show. At the dentist's office, you read a magazine. In the background, music from an FM radio station soothes and relaxes you before the sharp objects enter your mouth. As you leave the office, the news of your cavity is already in a computer and moving at the speed of light through fiber-optic cable into your insurance company's database in another city across the country. On your way home, you stop at a grocery store where you scan a display of coupons from yesterday's newspaper. In the background, recorded music puts you in an active, spending mood as you walk aisles jammed with 30,000 products that attempt to reach into your mind and stir up memories of their million-dollar advertising campaigns. Your shopping cart is covered with ads, and so is your cash register receipt. At home, you turn on the TV for company while you put your groceries away. Then you pop a tape into your Walkman and go out for some exercise, wearing clothes emblazoned with logos of sports teams, your college, and several soft drinks. You run by the movie theater and look at its big bright posters of coming attractions. Back home again, you pick the newspaper up from the porch and toss it onto the coffee table—noticing a picture of a car wreck and a burning building on the front page.

Suddenly the phone rings and a voice asks you to be part of a survey on media usage habits.

You say, "I really don't have time for the media."

The surveyor asks, "Can you remember any media messages from the past day or so?"

You are peeved. "Like I said, I don't have time to expose myself to the media. I'm too busy."

"One last question. Can you think of any way that the media have affected you?"

Trying to be helpful, you say, "Well, I did listen to the weather report on the radio yesterday, so I took an umbrella with me to school."

Because much of our exposure to media messages is not planned by us, it is easy to discount it or to forget that it even occurred. Thus, we don't realize how much we are exposed to the media. We tend to think in terms of the exposure we seek out, rather than all the exposures that happen to us. Our culture is saturated with media messages, and we have to work hard to avoid them.

Availability

Think about the opportunities for exposure you have during any given day. If you live in a large city, you can receive about 50 radio stations. Even if you live in a relatively small market, you can still get about a dozen. Your cable company provides more than 40 channels offering a total of more than 1,000 hours of television *per day*. As for print, you have a choice of several daily and weekly newspapers, more than 10,000 magazines that issue copies weekly or monthly, and 1,000 brand new book titles every week. Hollywood studios release about 350 film vehicles each year, and other filmmakers produce untold thousands of educational and corporate training films. What's more, if you have a computer, there are thousands of games and programs available to you, or you could get on the Internet where there are more than 12,000 electronic information services that offer consumers everything from complex electronic legal libraries to reports on local surfing conditions, and almost everything imaginable in between (Black, 1992). With such a connection, a person can communicate point-to-point through e-mail; get together with others in chat rooms for interactive conversations; exchange information on bulletin boards; share software; undertake electronic publishing; engage in entertainment by participating in clubs and contests; and buy products and services.

We truly live in a media saturated culture. Every year, the number of messages greatly expands as new technological channels (such as cable television, computers, the Internet, etc.) come on line and grow stronger and as old channels find creative new ways to put more messages in front of us.

Active Exposure

We spend large amounts of money and time seeking out particular messages in the media. One of the most expensive items in your apartment or dorm room is your television set, which you (or your parents) gladly paid for—along with the electricity to run it—in order to get "free" television. More than 99% of all households in this country have at least one television and one radio. To put this percentage in perspective, only 94% of all households have a telephone and only 92% have indoor plumbing. Television and radio are only two of the many media that are constantly bringing you entertainment, information, and advertising messages (see Table 2.1).

Every day, you actively seek out certain messages to fulfill particular needs for information or entertainment, and you probably actively avoid other media messages, such as ads that interrupt your favorite shows or songs that you hate. When you are active you are aware of your decision making, and you are in control of your exposures.

Passive Exposure

As the number of messages expands, we reach a limit of how active we can be in deciding what to expose ourselves to and what to avoid. We cannot always be active, so we put our minds on automatic pilot and let the messages happen to us passively without paying much attention. When a message comes along that we particularly like or particularly hate, it captures our

Table 2.1 Exposure to the Media

Television

- Over 99% of all households in this country have at least one television set.
- Even among this country's poor people, 95% have at least one television set and 40% have more than one.
- While they are away at school, about 70% of college students have TV sets and 29% have VCRs.
- Four out of every five households have a VCR, and 90% have access to cable or satellite TV, although 20% choose not to subscribe.
- The average American watches television for more than 1,500 hours each year, and 75% say they watch every day.

Radio

- 99% of all households own at least one radio.
- The average household has more than five radios.
- 95% of all automobiles have a radio.
- 61% of all adults have a radio at work.
- Americans listen to an average of 3 hours of radio a day.
- 66% of all American adults listen to radio on an average day.
- 80% of the population listens to radio on the weekend for an average of 5 hours.
- The weekly cumulative radio audience is 95% of all Americans 12 and older.

Books

- More than 50,000 book titles are now published each year, compared to 11,000 in 1950.
- Since 1950, the number of bookstores has more than doubled, and so have per capita book sales and library circulation.

Magazines

- About 83% of U.S. households subscribe to at least one magazine, and magazine circulation has been growing faster than the population since the late 1950s.

Film

- The major Hollywood studios release about 350 feature films annually.
- 40% of Americans go out to movies regularly

Table 2.1 Continued

Computers

■ In 83% of households with computers, people say they use their PCs more than 5 hours a week.

■ By 1997, 9.5 million people were using the Internet—including more than a million children under 18. The average session lasts about 68 minutes and about two thirds of users look for information weekly, and a quarter search daily.

SOURCES: A. C. Nielsen, 1990; Audits & Surveys, 1991; Austin, 1989; Donnelly, 1986; Jeffres, 1994; Kantrowitz, 1993; Miller, 1989; Newspaper Advertising Bureau, 1988; Radio Advertising Bureau, 1991, 1993; Shapiro, 1992; Standard & Poor, 1996, p. L32.

attention and we deal with it—then we return to automatic pilot. This means that our exposure to media messages is constantly taking place, even if we are unaware of it.

Even if you do not own a TV set or a radio, you still are exposed passively to broadcast messages from sets down the hall, in the student union, or at friends' homes. You are passively exposed to messages on billboards, buses, taxis, and in public bathrooms. You will see references to media products and messages on T-shirts, hats, notebooks, cups, and other places.

Even if you avoid all media, you will still be exposed to media messages. You will hear people talking about messages they heard from the media (scores of sporting contests, weather reports, actions of characters on their favorite TV shows, the lyrics of popular songs heard on the radio or on CDs). Your exposure can thus be directly from the media or indirectly through other people.

To illustrate the prevalence of media messages in your own life, turn to Exercise 2.1. This exercise is designed to sensitize you to how much you are personally exposed to the media—actively and passively, directly and indirectly.

 Faulty Beliefs

Because much of our contact with media messages is passive, our exposure does not necessarily translate into higher knowledge and more insights about our world. On the contrary, habitual passive exposure to this constant flow can serve to reduce our literacy if we merely float along in the stream of messages. If we accept unquestioningly the images in these messages, we can end up with faulty beliefs about both the world and ourselves.

An interesting place to observe faulty beliefs in the general population is in the results of public opinion polls. Here beliefs appear faulty either because they are not accurate reflections of reality or because they are logically inconsistent. Both types of faulty beliefs can be traced to the effect of certain images prevalent in media messages. When people accept these media images without challenging them, the opinions they build on these images are likely to be faulty. In this section, we examine four such general beliefs, then we examine an example of a specific belief that gives an illustration of how all these general beliefs work in combination.

General Faulty Beliefs

Exaggerated Problems in Society. In a wide range of public opinion polls, we find that people exaggerate the problems of crime, health care, education, religion, and family—believing that all are serious, growing problems. We know that these faulty beliefs are effects created by the media, because of a combination of three reasons. First, people do not see these as problems in their personal lives—only in society. For example, in surveys about crime, only 17% of people think crime is a big problem in their own community but 83% of Americans think crime is a big problem in society (Whitman & Loftus, 1996). Thus, most people do not experience crime in their own lives and therefore do not think it is a big problem where they live. They are convinced, however, that it is a big problem in society. Where could they get such an idea? From the media's fixation on crime in the news with its ethic of "if it bleeds, it leads."

Second, the media present pessimistic messages about crime and the failure of institutions both in newscasts and in entertainment programming. The media present high-profile events such as the O. J. trial or Susan Smith buckling her two toddlers into car seats and running the car into a pond to drown them. These high-profile images are reinforced by constant stories about other crimes every day.

Third, these pessimistic messages are exaggerations. For example, watching evening newscasts with their fixation on crime and violence leads us to infer that there must be a high rate of crime and that most of it is violent assaults. In reality, however, the overall crime rate in this country has been declining for the past 5 years, both in terms of crimes reported to the police and of actual victimization rates; for instance, home burglary rates dropped by 50% between the mid-1970s and the mid-1990s. Moreover, less than 20% of all crime is violent. More than 80% of all crime is property crime with the victim not even present (*U.S. Statistical Abstracts,* 1996), but in a recent poll only 7% of Americans believed that violent crime had declined in the past 5 years (Whitman & Loftus, 1996).

There are other examples of how people in surveys exaggerate problems in society. With health care, 90% of adults think that the health care system is in crisis, but at the same time, almost 90% feel that their own health care is of good quality. About 63% of people think other people's doctors are too interested in making money, but only 20% think their own doctor is too interested in making money. As for education, 64% give the nation's schools a grade of C or D, but at the same time, 66% give their local public school a grade of A or B. As for religion, 65% say that religion is losing its influence on American life, while 62% say religion is becoming a stronger influence in their lives. As for responsibility, almost 90% believe that a major problem with society is that people don't live up to their commitments, but more than 75% say they meet their commitments to families, kids, and employers. Nearly half of the population believes it is impossible for most families to achieve the American Dream, while 63% believe they have achieved or are close to achieving the American Dream. Between 40% and 50% think the nation is currently moving in the wrong direction, while 88% of Americans think their own lives and families are moving in the right direction (Whitman, 1996).

Beliefs Are Polarized. Most people think that the media, especially television, have either a very strong effect or absolutely no effect—there is very little middle ground. Almost half (49%) of all Americans believe the media have too much power (Parisot, 1988). This figure is higher than that found in other countries, such as Germany (where 32% held this feeling) and France (29%). For example, people fear that TV has a strong effect that transforms viewers into zombies who begin to behave like the characters they watch. This attitude is seen most clearly in the topic of violence on television. Some people believe that others, after watching crime and violence, will go out right after the show and commit violent crimes. There are also people who believe that if PSAs (Public Service Announcements) about using condoms are allowed on TV, these PSAs will teach children that it is permissible and even a good thing to have sex. This is clearly an overestimation; the media do not turn people into zombies by taking over their minds and completely transforming their personalities and forcing them to do things against their will.

Contradictorily, people also *under*-estimate the influence the media have on them. When they are asked if they think the media have any effect on them personally, only 12% say yes. These people argue that because the media are primarily channels of entertainment and diversion, they have no negative effect on them. The people who believe this say that they have watched thousands of hours of crime shows and have never shot anyone or robbed a bank. Though this may be true, this argument does not fully support the claim that the media have no effect on them; this argument is based on the false premise that the media trigger only high-profile, negative behavioral effects that are easy to recognize.

This schizophrenic attitude is also in evidence in the media industries. For example, the media take in more than $270 million from advertisers *every day* by convincing them that the public is strongly influenced by commercial messages. When such huge sums of money are being spent, there is strong reason to believe that many people in the industry are convinced that advertising works. Yet these same media people do not feel that violence, sex, or bad language have any effect on their audiences.

This polarized belief regards the media as a kind of light switch. Either it is turned on—in which case people are helpless in the face of an overwhelming effect; or the media effect is turned off—in which case people are subject to no influence at all. This is the wrong way to think of media effects. Instead, we should envision a continuum with a powerful effect at one end and no influence at the other; in between, there are miles of room for all sorts of harder-to-recognize intermediate media effects.

Although most people know what to look for at the extreme ends of this continuum, they don't know how to recognize the many effects that occur between those poles. Their perspective is limited to looking for direct effects, so they do not see the effects that influence them indirectly through other people or through the institutions of government, religion, education, and family. They look for changes and do not see the effects that maintain the status quo. They look for short-term effects and ignore effects that build up over months and years. They look mostly for behaviors and don't consider cognitive, attitudinal, or physiological effects. Many everyday effects *are* cognitive—people do learn something, like today's weather, a sports score, or that a sale is taking place at their favorite store. People can also learn these things indirectly by listening to their friends talk about what they have read in a newspaper, for example. Many effects are on attitudes—people change their opinions about the day, or a sports team, or a product. People can also maintain the same positive opinion about a product over years of advertising so that their opinion gains so much weight and importance that it can never be changed. An effect can also be physiological. People might become excited by watching something, or be calmed by listening to peaceful music.

These are all effects. When you expand your perspective on what a media effect is, you can see that hardly an hour goes by in your life without your experiencing some kind of media effect. With a broader perspective, you can avoid the prevalent myth that "the media exert no effect on me!"

Focus Is on Negative Effects. When it comes to media effects, the public thinks primarily in terms of the negative influence of sexual suggestiveness; bad language; and high-profile, gruesome, violent acts. A *U.S. News & World Report* poll reported in April 1996 found that more than two thirds of Americans believe television contributes to violence, erodes family values, and fosters a destruction of government. Also, 84% of the public said it was concerned about the relationship of extramarital sex on TV with real-life problems. Even 80% of Hollywood executives questioned in a mail survey agreed that there was a link between TV violence and violence in real life.

Fear of the mass media and their negative effects has been around a long time. David Bianculli (1992), a TV critic and columnist, presents a fascinating history of the criticism of various forms of literature and music dating back to Plato. He shows that throughout history there have been people who thought every new piece of art was bad and every new medium was dangerous. One example he cites is a magazine article published in 1885 that complained about Mark Twain's *Huckleberry Finn*. The article's author was concerned about Huck's behavior of faking his own death by killing a pig and smearing its blood, along with some of his own hair, on an axe. The author complained that boys who read this in the book would repeat this behavior.

At the end of the 19th century, the fear was that newspapers that printed gruesome and sensational stories would debase the morals of their readers. In the 1920s and 1930s, the most popular question was, "What effect does propaganda have on newspaper readers and radio listeners?" With the advent of television, the most important and enduring question has been, "What effect does viewing TV content, especially violence and sex, have on children?"

Even college professors think that the influence of television is mostly negative. A poll of 500 college-level teachers and communication scholars found that 84% believed TV led to increased buying behavior; 80% believed it led to decreased physical activity; 80% said it decreased reading time; 76% argued that it increased desire for immediate gratification; 66% said it increased aggressive behavior; 66% believed it increased ethnic stereotyping; 58% said it decreased attention span; 58%, increased interest in sex; 58%, increased distortion of political perceptions; 47%, increased alienation; 45%, increased sexual stereotyping; and 42%, decreased social values (Bybee, Robinson, & Turow, 1982). Some positive effects were also mentioned: 91% said TV led to increased world knowledge; 66%, increased verbal ability; and 52%, increased pro-social behavior. Notice how many more negative things there are in this list.

The media are responsible for many negative effects, but it is a myth that they are not also responsible for many positive effects. People who are highly media literate have a broad enough perspective on effects to be sensitive to perceiving all kinds of media influences. They also know how to tell the difference between the positive and the negative.

The Media Are at Fault—Not Me. Often, when people see a problem and are not sure why it exists, they look around for easy targets to blame, and the media are easy targets because they are so pervasive and so visible. By producing so many messages on so many topics, the media present many examples of content that could trigger a negative effect. For example, when people hear that a terrible crime has taken place, they often feel that the media are to blame, because they present so much information about crime. If people think that sexual mores have relaxed, they feel that the media are to blame, because the media constantly present portrayals of all forms of sexual behaviors to keep us thinking about it.

Often, people will complain but do nothing. The advantage of blaming someone else absolves us from doing something about the problem. For example, in surveys, 56% of people say that movies are getting worse over time (Medved, 1992). People complain about the increasing use of bad language, explicit sex, and graphic violence, yet the movies with many of these elements seem to make the most money. Also, if the public really does believe that movies in general are getting worse each year, then we should expect the number of movie attendances to drop—especially since the price of tickets keeps going up—but the number of movie attendances keeps rising. We see the same contradictory pattern in television, where public opinion polls show that people think the quality of television is steadily going down, but viewing rates steadily climb. Reviewing these patterns, Comstock (1989) concludes that public opinion about television is not a particularly strong predictor of television consumption; many people complain about TV but still watch it a great deal.

Skepticism about the media can be a good thing if it is informed and active. Informed skeptics are people who read a great deal (Whitney, 1985) and who are more highly educated, wealthier, and who have more knowledge (Gaziano & McGrath, 1987). Informed skepticism is triggered by finding discrepancies between media messages and what people personally experience in their lives (Cozzens & Contractor, 1987). These people have good reason to be skeptical of the media when they see inaccuracies and misleading, superficial coverage of complex issues.

Uninformed skepticism, however, is part of the problem. Uniformed skeptics usually have lower education, lower incomes, and less knowledge of the media (Gaziano & McGrath, 1987). They blame the media because it is the easy thing to do. They can develop righteous anger and vent without having to do anything constructive. The problem with this thinking is that it ignores personal responsibility, and instead blames something else. This is a clear mark of a person who is not very media literate.

There are many more faulty beliefs than those listed here. You may be able to think of some more now. If not, keep this topic in mind as you continue to expose yourself to media messages. Continually ask yourself: "What are my beliefs about the media?" As you do, you will be surprised at what you find. You may feel very comfortable with some of your beliefs, but others may puzzle you as you wonder where they came from.

There are critics who warn us about certain beliefs, but sometimes they create new beliefs that are also faulty. For example, in 1978, Jerry Mander published a book titled *Four Arguments for the Elimination of Television.* Some of the evidence for his arguments is convincing, such as his argument that television partitions viewers off from real life. Other of his arguments are fairly weak, such as that light waves coming off the TV screen cause cancer. The most damaging aspect of his argument is its simple-minded condemnation of an entire channel of communication. This is like the bumper stickers that say "Kill Your Television." Did you ever wonder about the people who have those stickers on their cars? Do those people also think that books should be burned, because some of them contain violence, sex, bad language, or ideas with which they disagree? Do those people also think they should kill the people around them, because some people exert negative effects?

Television is a tool. It is a sign of media illiteracy to fear a tool that can be used for all sorts of purposes—good as well as bad. Instead of fearing TV, we should demand that the people in charge (such as producers and programmers) use the tool responsibly. Most important, we need to learn how we as individuals can use this tool in our everyday lives to enhance the effects we want.

An Example of Faulty Beliefs at Work

In the late 1970s, the National PTA appointed a Television Commission to hold hearings on the negative impact that TV was having on the education of the nation's youth. Teachers testified that TV had shortened children's attention spans and that they had to create spectacular signals to get the attention of pupils. Parents complained about the loss of adult-child interactions and felt that this contributed to the loss of a strong family relationship. Television was also blamed for fostering passive behavior in the form of requiring viewers to exercise less judgment and independent thinking (National PTA Television Commission, 1977).

Since that time, reports have continued about how poorly this nation's youth do on learning compared to youths in other countries. For example, the

Third International Mathematics and Science Study, which is administered to eighth graders in 41 countries, revealed that American students rank 28th in math and 17th in science in the world ("The Learning Lag," 1996). Reports like this lead critics to complain that children in this country watch too much television. Yet the same report says that students in Japan rank 3rd on both tests, although they watch as much television as do American kids—so the blame cannot be placed solely on television.

Still, the criticism persists that television is a cause of lowered academic achievement. Many conscientious parents believe that it is bad for their young children to watch television. They believe that TV will somehow make their children's minds lazy, reduce their creativity, and turn them into lethargic entertainment junkies. They worry that if this happens, their children will not value achievement and will not do well in school.

This type of attitude clearly puts blame on the media, not the child or the parent, for poor academic performance. It also focuses on only the negative effect and gives the media no credit for potentially positive effects. Young children (especially those with higher IQs) have strong appetites for all kinds of stimulation and information. It is therefore good to allow them to have access to all sources of information—including television—so their natural curiosity and subsequent growth is not impeded. Active children will not turn into television zombies. If television messages are dull, the children will become bored and do something more challenging. For passive children, however, television is likely to reinforce that passivity. Again, the point is that television is a tool. It can be used to strengthen some children and weaken others. To predict its effect, we need to have a broad perspective on media effects (positive as well as negative) and to place the blame or credit with the child who uses the tool, rather than on the tool itself.

There has been a good deal of criticism focusing on how the rise of television has hurt the development of print literacy and scholastic achievement among children. Several studies have reported a negative relationship between amount of television viewing and scholastic achievement (California Assessment Program, 1981; Morgan & Gross, 1980), and some have gone as far as to say that watching television can hamper the acquisition of reading skills (Hornick, 1978; Williams, 1986). Other scholars have found that there is a positive correlation (Schramm, Lyle, & Parker, 1961) or no correlation (Roberts, Bachen, Hornby, & Hernandez-Ramos, 1984).

This mixture of results is confusing to parents. Typically, people will resolve this controversy by choosing to believe one side and rejecting the other. However, on this issue, like most issues, both sides have some truth to them, but neither side is completely right. The best understanding of the issue lies somewhere in between the two positions. To understand the nature of this "middle ground," we must analyze the evidence more closely.

At first, the evidence seems to support the claim that there is a negative relationship between the amount of TV viewing and academic achievement (Potter, 1987), but this is a spurious relationship; that is, it is attributable to a person's IQ. Children with lower IQs watch more television and they have lower achievement. Studies that account for IQ and that control for its effect in the analysis find that the negative relationship disappears and something else appears—a threshold effect. What is a *threshold effect?* It is an effect that does not show up until we get beyond a certain point or a threshold. In this case, the threshold is about 30 hours of television viewing per week. To illustrate: Among children who view less than 30 hours of television per week, there are no negative effects on classroom performance—the children still have enough time to do their homework and to play with their friends. The children who view more than 30 hours of television per week begin to show a negative effect, however, and that effect gets stronger, the more hours they watch beyond that threshold.

Neuman (1991) provides a well-reasoned treatment of this topic in her book *Literacy in the Television Age,* in which she organizes her criticism into four categories: displacement of time and energy, information-processing ability, uses and gratifications, and interest stimulation. After carefully reviewing the research, she concludes that there is no support for any of these criticisms. She says, "While television is clearly not an educational panacea, the charges against the medium have been unwarranted. Television viewing has replaced neither book reading nor homework, and has not lessened the desire for achievement. Rather the medium is used selectively by children to serve their functional needs" (pp. 158-159). She also says that reading and writing activities are perceived as serving a different set of needs and gratifications from television viewing. In conclusion she says, "Most children, watching between 2-3 hours daily, are successfully achieving and are developing higher-level literacy skills than previous generations. In homes where literacy is prized, television becomes another resource to enhance children's knowledge and critical thinking" (p. 159).

As for displacement, the average child does watch about 20 hours of television a week, but this does not displace activities that are more positive. Furthermore, "the amount of leisure reading has remained amazingly stable over time: In 1945, children were reading about 15 minutes a day, and today, they are still reading approximately the same amount of time" (Norman, 1991, p. 192).

As for short-term gratifications, there is a fear that television viewing is "creating a generation of spectators who rely more on vicarious experience than on active involvement in learning" (Norman, 1991, p. 193). Some think that this could lessen a person's attention span, but again there is no support for this fear.

When we pose the question, "What effect does viewing television have on a child's academic performance?" we could give the simple, popular answer: "There is a negative effect." Now, however, you can see that this answer is too simple-minded. It is also misleading, because it reinforces the limited belief that media effects are negative and polarized, and that the media are to blame. Instead, we all need to build stronger knowledge structures so that we can formulate more accurate, well-reasoned opinions about the media. As long as our beliefs are faulty, we cannot exercise adequate control over the media's effects on us.

Why the Faulty Beliefs?

Why do we hold these faulty beliefs? There are many reasons. Notice that many of the arguments above were based on the results of public opinion surveys. Some people criticize public opinion surveys, because the surveys often produce inaccurate data. To illustrate this, imagine that you answer your telephone and someone asks you to participate in a public opinion survey. You are curious, so you agree. Then the caller asks you the following questions: "Last Tuesday, what articles of clothing did you wear? Did you brush your teeth? If so, how many brush strokes? Who did you talk to during the day? Exactly what did you say to those people?" These sound like silly questions, because they force us to remember the mundane, trivial things we do each day. Our media behaviors are also mundane activities. For example, did you read the newspaper last Tuesday? If so, did you skip any pages? How many lines of type did you actually read? Did you watch television? For how long? Did you change the channel? How often? And what exactly did you watch— count all the pauses as you channel surfed. Was the radio on in your car? What songs played and what ads aired?

These questions are impossible to answer accurately, because they ask about mundane behaviors—things we do every day but do not think much about and therefore do not remember in detail. Most of what occupies our time each day is mundane. We cannot keep all this detail in our minds; we must continually dump the mundane details of our day from our memories to make room for thinking about more important things. If we didn't, our minds would very quickly become clogged with these minutia and keep us from functioning. However, this continuous, automatic process of clearing our memories leaves us with little recall of how we actually spend our time, especially when it comes to the media. An interesting example of this point comes from a study by Ferguson (1994), who had people watch an hour of television while he monitored how often they changed the channel with a remote control. Immediately after the viewing session, he asked people to recall how many times they had changed channels. Most people had already erased those memories and had no idea of how often they performed the mundane behavior of channel changing a few minutes earlier. More than 20% under-reported their changing by a factor of more than 8. For example, a person who changed the channel 80 times but estimated the number of changes at 10 would be under-reporting by a factor of 8. One person changed the channel 122 times but estimated 3; another changed channels 396 times and estimated 20; and another made 181 changes and estimated 300. The point is that these people could not remember back a few minutes and make a good estimate of a mundane behavior during media exposure. Most of us would have the same trouble. This is why it is difficult for people to recall all the small media effects that occur all the time.

Surveys of media use have highly suspect results because much of our media use is mundane. Also, the results of surveys about our opinions are often suspect. For example, imagine a survey researcher calling you and asking you for your opinion about something you care little about—such as whether you support the planting of elm trees rather than oak trees in your city parks. You might say "Elm trees" just to be cooperative, even though you could care less. The next day you see a headline in the local newspaper—"Controversy Brews—55% of Residents Favor Oak Trees"—and read that the city council is taking action to plant oak trees. You remember that you voted for elm trees and you become angry that your opinion is being ignored.

The point here is not so much that public opinion surveys can be faulty as it is that our opinions can get started in all sorts of strange ways, and often they are not based on sound reasoning or on in-depth knowledge of a situation. They can spontaneously spring forth, in surveys or conversations, without much thought or foundation.

When it comes to the media, we often create opinions on intuition or on partial, anecdotal information. We might look for high-profile anecdotes in the media and in our real lives. When we see these instances (especially in the media), we assume a powerful effect. When we do not see them (especially in our real lives), we assume no effect. Finding media effects is very difficult, because the evidence often lies in the mundane details of our everyday lives, and we simply do not pay much attention to these details.

Another reason we hold faulty beliefs is that we, as humans, need to simplify the complexity in our world, so we continually construct explanations for things. Yet in constructing such explanations, we are not very rigorous about collecting all possible data. Instead, we latch on to a few examples and generalize from them. We are also not very systematic in logically inferring a conclusion from examples. Instead, we take intuitive shortcuts to arrive quickly at what seems like a reasonable explanation.

When certain explanations gain widespread acceptance, they become operating principles that define our culture. If these operating principles are fanciful or faulty explanations, they can get us into trouble by making us believe the wrong things or focus on false issues.

We need to monitor our beliefs continually and try to determine why we hold them. If we do not do this, then it is not possible to challenge ourselves to think more deeply about something that has a strong, continual influence on our knowledge, attitudes, and behaviors. When we think more deeply and more systematically about this, we can get control of those influences. If we don't, we will continue to accumulate knowledge very haphazardly and put those elements of information sloppily together into opinions that we will come to hold more dearly over time—thus firmly entrenching faulty beliefs.

Summary

Because the media make so many messages so easily accessible, they give us the impression that we are seeing the world in all its variety, and the more exposure we have, the more we begin to feel we are in a superior position to understand how the world operates. But, are we really learning things of value? Knowing all the words and tunes of a genre of popular music does not translate into expertise about the recording industry or radio broadcasting. Knowing a lot about current events presented by news organizations does not necessarily mean we know what the problems in the world are—or how to deal with them.

Our constant exposure to media messages influences the way we think about the world and ourselves. It influences our beliefs about crime, education, religion, families, and the world in general. If our exposure is mostly passive, then the mundane details in those messages exert their effect without our awareness. It is from this massive base of misleading or inaccurate images that we infer our beliefs about the world.

How can we gain control over the development of our knowledge structures, over the formulation of our opinions and the shaping of our fundamental values? How can we be more careful in the formulation of our opinions and thus reduce faulty beliefs? We need to increase our media literacy.

References

A. C. Nielsen Co. (1990). *1990 report on television.* Northbrook, IL: Author.

Audits & Surveys. (1991). *The study of magazine buying patterns.* New York: Publishers Clearing House.

Austin, B. A. (1989). *Immediate seating: A look at movie audiences.* Belmont, CA: Wadsworth.

Bianculli, D. (1992). *Teleliteracy: Taking television seriously.* New York: Continuum.

Black, C. (1992, January). Fair and equal access. *Link,* p. 43.

Bybee, C., Robinson, D., & Turow, J. (1982). *Mass media scholar's perceptions of television's effects on children.* Paper presented at the Annual Convention of the American Association for Public Opinion Research, Hunt Valley, MD.

California Assessment Program. (1981). *Student achievement in California schools, 1979-80 annual report: Television and student achievement.* Sacramento: California State Department of Education. (ERIC Document No. ED 195 559)

Comstock, G. (1989). *The evolution of American television.* Newbury Park, CA: Sage.

Cozzens, M. D., & Contractor, N. S. (1987). The effect of conflicting information on media skepticism. *Communication Research, 14,* 437-451.

Donnelly, W. J. (1986). *The confetti generation: How the new communications technology is fragmenting America.* New York: Henry Holt.

Ferguson, D. A. (1994). Measurement of mundane TV behaviors: Remote control device flipping frequency. *Journal of Broadcasting & Electronic Media, 38,* 35-47.

Gaziano, C., & McGrath, K. (1987). Newspaper credibility and relationships of newspaper journalists to communities. *Journalism Quarterly, 64,* 317-318.

Hornick, R. (1978). Television access and the slowing of cognitive growth. *American Educational Research Journal, 15,* 1-5.

Jeffres, L. W. (1994). *Mass media processes* (2nd ed.). Prospect Heights, IL: Waveland.

Kantrowitz, B. (1993, May 31). An interactive life. *Newsweek,* pp. 42-44.

The learning lag: You can't blame TV. (1996, December 2). *U.S. News & World Report,* p. 16.

Mander, J. (1978). *Four arguments for the elimination of television.* New York: William Morrow.

Medved, M. (1992). *Hollywood vs. America: Popular culture and the war on traditional values.* New York: HarperCollins.

Miller, S. (Ed.). (1989). *America's watching: 30th anniversary 1959-1989.* New York: Roper Organization.

Morgan, M., & Gross, L. (1980). Television viewing and academic achievement. *Journal of Broadcasting, 24,* 117-132.

National Parent Teacher Association. (1977). *Television's impact on the education of the nation's youth.* Chicago: National PTA.

Neuman, S. B. (1991). *Literacy in the television age: The myth of the TV effect.* Norwood, NJ: Ablex.

Newspaper Advertising Bureau. (1988). *News and newspaper reading habits: Results from a national survey.* New York: Author.

Parisot, L. (1988, January/February). Attitudes about the media: A five country comparison. *Public Opinion,* pp. 18-19, 60.

Potter, W. J. (1987). Does television viewing hinder academic achievement among adolescents? *Human Communication Research, 14*(1), 27-46.

Radio Advertising Bureau. (1991). *Radio facts for advertisers 1990.* New York: Author.

Radio Advertising Bureau. (1993). *Why radio?* New York: Author.

Roberts, D. F., Bachen, C. M., Hornby, M. C., & Hernandez-Ramos, P. (1984). Reading and television: Predictors of reading achievement at different age levels. *Communication Research, 11*(1), 9-49.

Schramm, W., Lyle, J., & Parker, E. B. (1961). *Television in the lives of our children.* Stanford, CA: Stanford University Press.

Schwartz, S. (1984, Winter). Send help before it's too late. *Parent's Choice,* p. 2.

Shapiro, E. (1992, February 27). New marketing specialists tap collegiate consumers. *New York Times,* p. 16C.

Standard & Poor. (1996, July). *Index to surveys.* New York: Author.

U.S. Statistical Abstracts. (1996). Washington, DC: Department of Commerce.

Whitman, D. (1996, December 16). I'm OK, you're not. *U.S. News & World Report,* pp. 24-30.

Whitman, D., & Loftus, M. (1996, December 16). Things are getting better? Who knew? *U.S. News & World Report,* pp. 30, 32.

Whitney, D. C. (1985). *The media and the people: America's experience with the news media—A fifty year review.* New York: Columbia University, Gannett Center for Media Studies.

Williams, T. M. (Ed.). (1986). *The impact of television: A social psychological analysis of the changing screen.* Hillsdale, NJ: Lawrence Erlbaum.

 ## Further Reading

Mander, J. (1978). *Four arguments for the elimination of television.* New York: William Morrow. (371 pages)

Mander presents a blanket criticism of television, very anecdotal and casual, not scientific or compelling. His arguments are: (a) TV mediates experience and this removes viewers from experiencing real life, (b) TV colonizes experience, that is, a few people control the content and this perspective is imposed on all viewers, (c) TV makes us sick physically (ingesting artificial light) and mentally (dims the mind, hypnotizes, suppresses imagination), and (d) it has inherent biases against subtlety (away from the sensory, toward the extraordinary).

Neuman, S. B. (1991). *Literacy in the television age: The myth of the TV effect.* Norwood, NJ: Ablex. (230 pages)

Neuman treats literacy mainly as a print skill then lays out the arguments that TV has reduced literacy. These fall under four theories: displacement, information processing, short-term gratification, and interest stimulation. She shows that the empirical evidence does not support any of these theories, that is, the criticism that the media has hindered literacy is unwarranted.

Exercise 2.1   Becoming Sensitized to Media Message Saturation

Part I: Estimate Your Exposure

Right now, try to estimate how many minutes and hours you spend with each of the following media during a typical week:

____ Watching television (cable, broadcast, movies played on a VCR, etc.)

____ Watching films at a theater

____ Listening to radio (at home, in your car, etc.)

____ Listening to recordings (CDs and tapes)

____ Reading newspapers

____ Reading magazines of all kinds

____ Reading books (texts for class, novels for pleasure, etc.)

____ Using the computer (games, word processing, surfing the Internet, etc.)

____ TOTAL

Part II: Track Your Exposures

Keep a Media Exposure Diary for 1 week. Get a small notebook—one you can carry with you wherever you go for 7 days. Every time you are exposed to a message from the media, either directly or indirectly, make an entry of the time and what the message was.

Direct exposures are those in which you come in contact with a medium and experience a message during that contact. For example, if you watch *Melrose Place* then write: "Message: *Melrose Place*; Time: Monday 8-9." Listening to KXXX for 30 minutes in the car is also direct exposure.

Indirect exposures are those in which you see a reminder of a media message, such as seeing a title of a movie on the marquee of a theater or at a bus stop. You don't see the film itself (that would be a direct exposure) but you see something that reminds you of it. Also, listen to conversations. If people talk about something they heard on the media, then you have been exposed to that media message indirectly. For example, if you heard your friends talk about *Melrose Place* then write: "Message: Talked with friends about *Melrose Place*; Time: Tuesday morning 10-11:30." If you happened to hear your roommate humming a popular song that is played often on the radio, then write: "Message: Room-mate hummed X song; Time: Wednesday all day."

At the end of the week, analyze the entries in your diary to answer the following questions:

1. What was the total time were you exposed to media messages?
2. How many exposures did you experience during the week?
3. What proportion of the exposures were direct and what proportion indirect?
4. What proportion of media exposures were initiated by you (active) and what proportion just happened (passive)?
5. How do your diary data compare to your estimates from Part I?
6. What kind of messages were most prevalent?

Part III: Avoiding Exposure

Choose a day as Media Message Avoidance Day. When you get up in the morning, do not turn on your radio, television, or stereo. See how long you can go without exposing yourself to a message from the media. Also, how long can you go without accidently seeing or hearing an actual media message or a reference to a media message?

PART II

Skills

CHAPTER 3

How Does the
Human Mind Work?

KEY IDEA *We have pictures (schemas) in our minds about how characters should look and how stories should be told. We use these schemas to help us make sense of the many messages we get from the media and from real life.*

The human mind is incredibly complex and is capable of wonderful things. It can create great music, new worlds, complicated bureaucracies, sad stories, and even silliness. It can also comprehend these things in the creations of other human beings. How does it comprehend such things?

For centuries, philosophers and poets have speculated about the boundaries of the mind and its inner workings. More recently, psychologists and neuro-scientists have added their speculations to the wide array of explanations. We still do not have any definitive answers; perhaps we never will. What we do have is a series of conceptualizations about how we as humans comprehend our social experience. Most of these ideas have been developed to explain how we process information from our everyday contacts with other people. These explanations can also be applied to how we make sense of the messages that come from the media.

In this chapter, you'll learn to think like a cognitive psychologist, someone whose career is spent trying to understand how humans process information and make sense of their worlds. Cognitive psychologists come up with explanations—theories—about how the human mind works. Over time, as they learn more about how we think, they change their explanations.

The knowledge structure you will build from this chapter will help you understand how your mind processes messages from the media; this will allow you to exercise greater control over that process. It is also important for you to know how explanations about thinking have changed so that you can avoid traps of faulty thinking about how your mind works.

Changes in Thinking About Thinking

Early Conceptualizations

Cognitive psychologists used to view our minds as responders to media stimuli. Under this stimulus-response theory, people were thought to make simple associations whenever they saw a word or symbol. For example, it was believed that when readers saw the printed word *dog,* they automatically associated this three-letter combination with a certain type of four-legged furry animal. Thus, the human mind was regarded as a large dictionary of learned definitions. Every time the mind perceived a symbol, it would work like a machine to match that symbol with its meaning in the mental dictionary.

Researchers soon realized that this rather simple perspective could not account for much of the meanings people were deriving from the media. Reading a book requires more than simply recognizing words and matching individual meanings. What if a word in our mental dictionary has more than one meaning? For example, *bad* can mean "not good" but it can also mean "very good." *Cool* can mean "a low temperature," "a chilly demeanor," "a laid back attitude," or "very good." Which meaning do we match? It depends on the context of the sentence in which it is used. Matching by itself is therefore not enough: We often must understand the meaning of the sentence before we can figure out the meaning of some of the words in the sentence, but how do we understand the meaning of the sentence without first understanding the meaning of the words? Are you beginning to see how complex this issue is?

Now consider this: The idea conveyed by a sentence has more to it than the simple sum of the meanings of each of the words. The arrangement of words and the grammar as well as the punctuation is important. For example, if two characters are kissing and one says, "Don't! Stop!!!" that conveys a very different meaning than if the character says, "Don't stop." What's more, the way sentences are arranged into paragraphs and stories conveys more meaning than the simple sum of the idea conveyed in each sentence. If you read about a mother saying, "You are so smart" to her child, the meaning can change given the overall story. If the mother has just seen her child brag that he can take his bicycle apart and fix it but in the process he destroys it, her comment is sarcastic. If she has just looked at her child's report card and seen only excellent grades, her comment is one of pride and happiness. Determining the meaning of words, sentences, and stories is a complex process.

Cognitive psychologists realized they needed to develop more sophisticated approaches to understanding how we process information. One such approach, called *social learning theory,* focuses on the importance of contextual cues in determining meaning (Bandura, 1973). With social learning theory, the mind is regarded as more complex than a machine that simply makes associations between symbols and dictionary meanings. Everyone's mind does not process each symbol in the same way. Each of us draws from our own experiences as well as from contextual elements in each message. We take clumps of stimuli together: When we see an action, we do not simply associate a conditioned meaning to that action. Instead, we examine the context of that action.

With television portrayals, we examine who it is that performs the action. We assess how much we identify with that character. We examine whether the action is successful and what happens to the character after performing the action, and we also consider what other characters in the plot think about the action. We use all of these elements to determine the meaning of that single action. Because we all make decisions differently, we arrive at a great many unique meanings for that one action. Thus social learning theory is quite different from the more simple stimulus-response theory that says we all recognize the same symbols and have all been conditioned to associate the same meaning with a particular symbol.

By the 1970s, psychologists had found substantial differences across individuals in the way they selected and processed information. Psychologists therefore shifted their focus to explaining the differences in how people selected elements and assembled them into conclusions. They found that people were not rational and scientific but instead were subject to all sorts of distortions. Often, people fail to consider all, or even most, of the available information when making judgments about other people. Research showed that humans tend to favor concrete over abstract information; that is, people are more comfortable thinking about specific people rather than society in general. People also like to regard isolated anecdotes rather than broad principles of human behavior. They would rather simplify their world by ignoring multiple cases and concentrating on only one or two when making up their minds. People are severely limited in their ability to combine different sources of information, so they will most often select the event with the highest profile or the idea they are most comfortable with and simply go with that. Finally, research found that people are usually biased in their decision making simply by the natural and necessary use of procedures that make putting things into categories easier (Bargh, 1984).

Think about how this explanation has been used by television journalists who must construct easy-to-understand stories on complex issues, such as the federal health care policy. The journalist will try to make the issue less abstract by translating it into more concrete human terms. He may find a family that is not covered by health insurance and show how helpless children suffer from their parents' inability to find jobs with companies that offer health care. The camera shows us the caring parents on the verge of tears holding their feverish children. We have strong emotional reactions of sympathy for the family and of rage against a government that cannot deal with this serious problem. However, we are not told how serious the problem is, how widespread it is, whether the government can do anything to help, or any of the other hundreds of details that are necessary for us to develop a full, reasoned appreciation of the problem. Instead, we jump from one media anecdote to a strongly held, emotional opinion.

If we do not seek out a broader range of information and work on developing a stronger knowledge structure, we are stuck with our emotionally derived attitude about the entire health care system. This attitude then guides our future exposures to messages about health care. We will seek out messages that confirm our attitude, and we will avoid messages that go against our attitude, because they will be much more difficult to reconcile with our existing opinion. Thus, attitudes play a key role in how we process information.

Cognitive-Attitudinal Models

The first attitudinal models of opinion formation and change were based on the assumption that we strive to make our world consistent, that we seek balance between our opinions and those of our friends. Let's say, for example, that your best friend is a big fan of the shock jock Howard Stern. If you are also a big fan of Howard Stern, then your attitude is in balance with your friend's—you both like the same entertainer. But let's say you hate Howard Stern; in this case things are out of balance. You will strive to get things back into balance. Either you will try to listen to Howard Stern's show, trying to find things to appreciate so you can become a fan and share this experience with your friend, or you will begin questioning your friend's judgment or sanity; eventually your friend's reverence for Howard Stern will drive you crazy and you'll feel you have to get another best friend.

An explanation focusing on consistency of attitudes is useful with simple examples, but the world is much more complex. Think about what your best friend believes. Do you agree with all of his or her opinions? We don't drop our friends because one (or even several) of their opinions don't match our own—we don't need perfect balance. Instead, we act less than purely rational and we accommodate differences of opinion.

Cognitive psychologists developed some newer explanations of attitude formation and change: the heuristic-systematic model, the elaboration likelihood model, and the attitude accessibility approach. Each of these places a person's attitude about something at the heart of information processing. If you have a positive attitude about something, you will look for different information, process that information differently, and arrive at a different conclusion than if you have a negative attitude.

Heuristic-Systematic Model. Attitudes are often changed by heuristics, which are shortcuts in thinking. Heuristics are simple rules that allow us to circumvent the need to process every element in a message. Examples include: Experts can be trusted; long arguments are strong arguments; attractive people are right. These rules provide shortcuts around more complete processing of messages that would take a great deal more effort. They save us a lot of effort. The rules are learned from experience, so they are usually accurate enough for use in our everyday lives.

One kind of heuristic is called the "availability heuristic." This is a shortcut that people use to estimate the likelihood of something by noticing how quickly instances or associations can be brought to mind. If they can quickly think of an example of something, they conclude that that thing is more likely to occur. For example, if you think of risks of death, you will be much more likely to think of homicide than pneumonia, because the media in news and entertainment programs contain many more images of homicides than pneumonia sufferers. Because you can remember an image of a homicide much more quickly than of someone with pneumonia, you are likely to estimate that more people die from homicides. In reality, however, five times as many people die of pneumonia each day as die of homicides. Also, if someone asks you for your attitude about minorities in our culture you are much more likely to think of African Americans than of Mongolian Americans, who are much more in the minority. Because the media have far more images about African Americans, these images are much more accessible to you.

Shortcuts are easy to use and they save us time. Sometimes, when we want to be very careful in formulating an opinion about something very important to us, we avoid these heuristics and instead go to the trouble of undertaking a much more complete and systematic processing of information. For example, when you first meet someone, you use heuristics to decide quickly whether you like her or not. You look for a few keys, such as physical appearance, the manner of dress, the smile, and the way she speaks. That is usually enough for you to make up your mind whether you like her. But if you were faced with the decision about whether to move in with this person, you would be much more systematic in processing all the information about her before you would be persuaded to share your personal space.

Elaboration Likelihood Model. According to this model, attitudes can be changed by two routes. The central route of information processing involves a thorough consideration of the merits of the arguments given. People must be highly motivated to use this route, because it requires more time and effort to think through all the merits of each argument. As people think through an argument, they elaborate it by making relevant associations, scrutinizing the evidence, inferring its value, and evaluating the overall message.

In contrast, the more automatic peripheral route includes attitude change that occurs with little thought or elaboration. This route relies on a variety of superficial strategies, all of which share the feature of ignoring message quality; that is, people do not evaluate the credibility of sources or carefully analyze their claims.

Think of typical advertisements on the radio or television. Do these ads usually give you a lot of information and ask you to evaluate their claims systematically? No. Instead, they give you an image or a simple idea to make you feel good about the product and then hope that you will let the message in through the peripheral route so that you don't challenge any of the claims.

Attitude Accessibility Approach. This model regards an attitude as an association between a given object and a person's evaluation of that object. The stronger the association, the more accessible a person's attitude. Attitudes are more easily activated when they have been recently or frequently activated.

People who are more attuned to their attitudes are referred to as "low self-monitors." These people typically have more accessible attitudes than other people do. Already existing attitudes strongly determine what these people think. In contrast, "high self-monitors" are continually modifying their attitudes as new information becomes available. Thus their attitudes are more complex and harder to access.

Think of your attitude about some issue important to you. Are you a low self-monitor, that is, can you easily express your attitude in one simple sentence, and has this attitude remained the same for years without modification? Or are you a high self-monitor, that is, it is difficult to express your opinion without a lot of conditions and qualifiers, and it is an opinion with which you are continually tinkering as you get new information?

All of the models presented thus far have limitations in their abilities to explain how we think and how we create our attitudes, but each model has also made a valuable contribution to moving our understanding forward bit by bit. Today, cognitive psychologists have moved on to a schema-based explanation about how we make sense of our world.

Schemas

Think of *schemas* as knowledge structures. Schemas are sets of facts that each of us assembles in order to be able to organize the information we hold in our minds (Graesser, Millis, & Long, 1986).

These sets of facts are organized by categories. A *category* is defined as "a set of features that serve as bases for inferring membership in it" (Wyer & Gordon, 1984, p. 79). For example, we all have a schema for animals; it contains some rules for what we should include and what we should exclude. Inside this schema we have a sub-schema for dogs, one for cats, and so forth. Each of these has rules that tell us what should be included and how one set is different from another.

Perhaps it is useful to think of schemas as slides in a projector. When we are confronted by something—let's say an animal—we pull up a slide and project it onto the animal. If the animal we see conforms to the sketch on our slide (information in our schema), we say it fits and we call the animal by the name of the schema. If the animal does not fit, we usually look for other schema until we find one that the animal does fit. If we can't find a schema that fits, we either give up and say, "I have no idea what that is!" or we find the schema with the closest fit and modify it, while thinking, "I believe that is a dog, but I have never seen one that color or size before."

Types of Schemas

As we grow older we develop thousands of schemas to cover all possible people, events, ideas, and things in our experience. These schemas can be arranged in several meaningful groups as follows:

Self Schemas. These are all the images you have of yourself. Most people have more schemas and more elaborate schemas about themselves than about anything else.

Person Schemas. You have a schema for every person you know. Each of these schemas includes the physical characteristics and personality traits of that person. The schemas are very sketchy for acquaintances, but for your closest, long-time friends, your schemas are highly elaborate.

Role Schemas. These are your expectations for how people should behave in certain situations. You have a role schema for behaving as a student in the classroom, one for behavior at a family reunion, one for a job interview, one for a party with friends your age, and so on. Each of these roles is very different, because each has a different goal and requires a different set of attitudes and behaviors.

Event Schemas. These are expectations you have that unfold over time, and as such they can be regarded as scripts. In the long term, you have a script that tells you what you should be doing in the next few years and what you should be doing in 10 or 20 years with your imagined career and family. In the short term, you have scripts that guide what you should say in conversations; that is, if someone is funny, you respond one way, but if the person is a bore you respond another way.

Using Schemas With Media Information

The conception of schemas was developed to explain how people interact interpersonally. This conception also works as an explanation for how people make sense of messages from the media. However, there are three major differences in how schemas are used in the two different settings. First, the media provide a wider range of messages than does a person's real social life. People need a wider range of schemas to deal with the types of people they see in the media but do not encounter in their interpersonal interactions—people such as national political figures, major entertainers, professional athletes, psychopathic killers, the very rich, and others. People also need a wider range of event schemas to understand what it means to play a sport professionally, to be a person living in Bosnia, to be a knight looking for the Holy Grail in Medieval times, or to be an astronaut on a futuristic voyage to another galaxy.

Second, the media have a sense of authoritarianism about them. Thus when we read something in the media, we feel it has been written by an expert so we should believe the claims in the message. Because cameras have recorded images of actual events presented as news, we are likely to believe those images. The repetitiveness of messages also contributes to this expert effect.

Third, in conversations your level of involvement is fairly high, but with the media, involvement is usually very low. People are more active in searching for schemas and modifying them in interpersonal situations, because there is usually more of a negotiation process in which we are more likely to modify our schemas. When we expose ourselves to the media, we search out a schema that fits the media messages early on in our exposure, then stick with that schema.

For all these reasons, we must regard the use of schemas as being different with media messages than it is with interpersonal communication. This means that when people view a television program, watch a film, or read a story, they use different types of schemas. The primary examples of these types of schemas are: narrative, character, setting, thematic, and rhetorical.

Narrative Schemas. We have learned the formulas of storytelling. In order for stories to make sense, they must have a social logic to them. We apply that logic to determine if a character's behavior seems reasonable to us (Black, Galambos, & Read, 1984). When we experience a "story" we must make sense of all the elements in it, so we make conscious selections from among story elements. We make our selections on the basis of how central to the story certain elements are and how distinctive certain portrayals and actions are.

We have schemas for fantasy, for news, for serious drama, for farce, and more. In each of these schemas we have sketched out the elements that generate action, what heightens action and intensifies interest, and how conflict is resolved. We have schemas for flashbacks, dream sequences, and projections into the future.

In television, there are easily recognizable formulas. Simple shows follow these formulas closely, so you don't have to think much about plot. In contrast, more complex shows will signal a recognizable formula early in the program, but break with the formula in order to surprise you emotionally or to get you more involved cognitively. This requires that you search continually for new schemas to make sense of the action. When viewers don't want to work that hard, they turn off these complex programs and instead choose to watch the easy formula programs.

Character Schemas. The media deal in stock characters (i.e., stereotypes) that we can easily recognize. Our character schemas are what make it possible for us to have such a sense of recognition. Examples of stereotypes include the following:

- the strong self-reliant police-detective who uses unconventional methods to deal with the scum on the street. He is irritated by his authoritarian bosses but always gets the job done using his own unorthodox methods.
- the nurturing mother who has kooky kids and an idiot husband.
- the sexy young female actress/model/nurse/secretary who becomes a romantic interest of a male hero.
- the young street punk who commits petty and violent crimes, usually for drugs. He is tough and sassy until police intimidate him into making a plea bargain.
- the doofus male adolescent who displays hilariously dysfunctional social skills. Though he is very sensitive, he never learns from his social mistakes.

Stereotypes can be both good and bad. They are good in that they are a necessary mode of processing information, especially in highly differentiated societies—an inescapable way of creating order out of "the great blooming, buzzing confusion of reality" (Lippmann, 1922, p. 96). They are bad in that they are often inadequate as well as biased; they often serve as obstacles to rational assessment; and they are resistant to social change.

We use stereotypes to deal with real-world information, not just media portrayals. For example, when we meet people for the first time, we try to "type" them based on the characteristics we can immediately notice, such as age, gender, appearance, how they talk, and so on. Once we have typed someone (chosen a person schema), we have a set of expectations that governs our behavior. For example, if we see a 5-year-old girl in a fancy dress playing with a doll on the steps of a church, we would immediately call up a specific set of expectations. In contrast, if we see a middle-aged man with a beer belly straining his dirty T-shirt, who is chewing tobacco and cleaning a rifle, we would call up a very different set of expectations. Stereotypes provide us with a set of expectations that we can access quickly as we encounter people and events.

Setting Schemas. Settings influence our expectations. If an armed robbery takes place in a liquor store in a poor urban neighborhood, the meaning of that crime can be different from a robbery that takes place in the bedroom of an upper-middle-class family home in a small rural community.

Thematic Schemas. Thematic schemas help us recognize the moral of a story. This knowledge structure is of a higher order than the previous three, because they are used in inferring this one. Viewers observe how certain characters perform in the quest of their goals, and they observe what happens to those characters. For example, if a bad character is punished for his behavior, the theme is usually that "crime doesn't pay" or that "honesty is the best policy." But if a good character is continually punished, the theme can be something quite different, such as "the world is unfair" or "good guys finish last."

Rhetorical Schemas. A rhetorical schema is your inference about the story-teller's purpose. Is the primary contribution of the story to provide information or to entertain? Is the story trying to teach a moral lesson or to provide a fantasy escape? Is the story meant to be humorous, and if so, how—with slapstick? satire? irony?

Let's consider an example to illustrate the use of schemas while viewing a detective program. Two African American male youths go into a liquor store, pull out their guns, and demand that the owner give them all his cash. While the owner empties the cash register, the youths are observed by a customer in the back of the store. The customer, an off-duty policewoman not in uniform, sneaks around to the entranceway and gets ready to confront the thieves. The youths grab the money and back away from the owner toward the entranceway. As they turn to flee the store, the policewoman points a gun at them and tells them to stop. One youth spins around and fires his gun in her direction. She fires back, killing him. The other youth runs by her and gets away. She is frozen in shock as she realizes she has just killed a human being.

In order to comprehend this story, viewers must infer the roles and traits of the characters. The gun, the dress, and demeanor of the youths would signal to viewers that they are dangerous criminals. When the woman is identified as a policewoman, viewers pull up their law enforcement schema. Viewers must also infer the goals of the characters: The youths want money for their own personal gain; the policewoman, off duty and at considerable risk to her own life, tries to apprehend the criminals.

Not all viewers activate the same schemas. For example, some viewers might pull up a schema about the youths that sketches them as victims of society, because they were forced into a criminal life. When using this schema, the inference becomes that it is wrong for the white power structure to punish one of the disadvantaged youths with immediate death. The theme is interpreted to be that the social structure will crush certain powerless people without taking the time to understand their situation. Other viewers, in contrast, might pull up a feminist schema that criticizes this narrative for showing women as weak, because the policewoman was paralyzed with remorse and not able to pursue the second criminal as men would do.

Schemas are very useful in processing information from the media. If a viewer had to construct all these structures from scratch for each exposure to programs, it would be a staggering amount of work. People do not want to work this hard, especially when they simply want to be entertained. Instead, they simplify by using the schemas they have developed in past viewing. As people watch a new program, they can make adjustments to their schemas; with formulaic television programs, however, the adjustments are very minor. If a new show requires too great an adjustment, viewers will find it unpleasant and reject the program.

Origin of Schemas

Where do schemas come from? We are not born with them. In essence, schemas represent the creation of reality, and reality can be constructed in two forms. First, society can create a reality, and individuals can learn the lessons of society by learning those schemas. Second, individuals can construct their own realities by designing schemas that either create brand new schemas or elaborate and extend society's general ones.

Learning the Schemas of Society. Institutions must transmit their meaning to each new generation through a process called *socialization.* There are three main processes in socialization: externalization, objectivation, and internalization (Berger & Luckmann, 1966).

Externalization is the process of typifying behavior on either a small scale or a large scale. On a small scale, people express attitudes and behaviors as they interact with one another in a social world. Particular attitudes and behaviors become common in certain situations; that is, people develop habits. For example, let's say you are in an interpersonal conversation that is heating up and developing into an argument. You have a high value for peace and harmony, so you switch into a polite mode to try to calm down the other person. Also, you tell the person that the argument is your fault, and this serves to make the other person less defensive. You find that the argument stops and harmony is restored. The next time an argument begins, you become overly polite and start blaming yourself for the argument. Over time this particular strategy becomes a habit in argument situations. You have learned a useful tactic in dealing with a particular social situation.

On a large scale, we can see that certain behavioral patterns are continually exhibited by a wide range of people. Let's say that in a culture most people become very polite when a conversation starts to become contentious. This common behavioral pattern might be traceable to a value of harmony that is taught by the institutions of religion and family. These institutions have passed their values down to generation after generation so that the behaviors serve as external reminders of the institutional values.

Objectivation is the process by which the externalized products of human activity attain the character of objectivity; that is, they become legitimate. When these typified patterns are used by others, the patterns can become an institution. Once an institution becomes established, it serves to control human conduct with its previously defined patterns of conduct. As people conform to these patterns, the institution gains credibility and acceptance. Over time, institutions are regarded as having a reality of their own. When this happens, they are said to have been "objectified."

Internalization is the process by which people learn about their social world and so become a product of it. People learn to observe the rules and lessons of society.

Berger and Luckmann (1966) say that the most important vehicle of reality maintenance is conversation—not so much the explicit words as the implicit meanings. In other words, the content does not define the world as much as the assumptions behind the conversation define the background of a world that is silently taken for granted. That which is never talked about comes to be shaky or forgotten. That which is talked about becomes clearer as reality. Conversations can thus alter behavior when they are supported by significant others with whom we have established a strongly emotional identification. These significant others are the guides into a new reality. The journey into a new reality is accomplished when it is supported by what is called a legitimating apparatus, something that reinforces the new interpretations at each stage of change and forces old realities to be abandoned.

Berger and Luckmann (1966) draw an interesting contrast between primitive and complex societies. In primitive societies there is a high proportion of institutionalized activity, because most problems are held in common by all members of that society. In contrast, complex societies have very few problems held in common by all people, and therefore there is almost no common stock of knowledge. The United States is a highly complex society, so we would ordinarily expect very little sharing of a common stock of knowledge. We have very highly developed mass media, however, especially television, which can serve as an institution that conveys a common experience to all members of our complex society and thus brings us together. The media give us all the same ability to witness the same conversations and to participate vicariously in many actions with surrogate significant others.

Construction of Schemas by Individuals. When you are exposed to the media, you are continually forming impressions. This impression formation is guided by your goals for the exposure. If you don't have any clear goals, you have little psychological involvement, and your impressions are very superficial. When you do have clear goals, you become more involved during an exposure session, and you expend more mental energy in processing the images and encoding them into more elaborate knowledge structures.

When we organize information into knowledge structures, we are driven by two goals: accuracy and efficiency. Accuracy means to "get it right," so when we need to fit a new bit of information into an already existing knowledge structure, we try to fit that information into several places until we find one where it fits well. Efficiency is important to people who want to process a great deal of information as quickly as possible—which is most of us, most of the time. When our goal is efficiency, we put a new bit of information quickly into the first place that makes sense. If we have highly developed skills of thinking, the two goals go together—that is, we are able quickly and efficiently to make accurate decisions in adjusting our knowledge structures. If our thinking skills are not very good, however, in our attempt to be efficient we often place new knowledge in the wrong place in our knowledge structures, which then become cluttered and less usable over time.

Using Schemas

The use of schemas brings three important tasks into play: matching, bridging, and pruning. Matching is the sorting through of schemas until the one that best fits the situation is found. Bridging refers to the linking together of several schemas, such as linking a several-character schema with a plot-and-theme schema. Pruning is the process of removing specific elements from schemas over time to make them more general and thus better able to fit a wider set of examples.

Matching. When you are exposed to a media message, you first need to find a schema that could fit the situation and thus provide you with a road map to make sense of the unfolding message. You do this by picking a schema that seems reasonable, matching the key elements in the schema with the key elements in the message, and deciding whether the schema is a good match or not. If it isn't, you look for a schema that is a better match.

How do we know which elements in a message are the "key elements" we should focus our attention on in matching? We activate filters that screen out most of the detail in a message and screen in those elements that are either central or distinctive. An element is central if it is essential to the plot; it is distinctive if it is rare or unusual.

We are quick to pull up our most easily accessible schemas, and we tend to stay with them until the new information conflicts too strongly. We favor the primacy effect, that is, we favor the first-used schema over chosen ones later. Schemas that are easily accessible are used first; this means we use schemas that fit our moods.

When the costs of being wrong are high, we gather more data and change our schemas; the goal is accuracy. When speed and closure are the goals, we seek efficiency.

Bridging. When we are exposed to a media message, we must typically use several schemas at the same time. For example, when watching a movie we pull up a schema for each major character, one for plot, and one for theme—at minimum. Bridging refers to the linking together of several schemas.

How does this linking occur? Black, Galambos, and Read (1984) use the metaphor of a chemical filter as an explanation. Chemical filters (used by Black et al. to represent knowledge structures and associated concepts) in a solution (the internal representation) interact, or bind, with other substances introduced into the system (input from the sentences in a story). These concepts from the story enter the system and begin to interact with the filters. When a new idea is encountered, we try to apply a filter (a knowledge framework) to it so it makes sense. Keep in mind that these filters are not static— they change as they evoke other filters.

Pruning. Over time, a particular schema might become too specific if we have added a lot of detail to it. For example, let's say we are introduced to Harry, who is visiting from England where he is enrolled in an exclusive prep school. We pull up our "English prep school" schema, which is fairly sketchy and has only a few details, such as rich, privileged, snotty, and the like. As we get to know Harry, we find him to have a lot of positive qualities. He is hardworking, intelligent, witty, athletic, and socially concerned. We add these details to our "English prep school" schema. Because many of these qualities are special to Harry and do not fit the general schema of "English prep school," we must prune away the specific qualities and leave only the general ones so that the schema can serve as a useful template for that *kind* of person rather that *specific* person.

Schemas change as they are used. With more usage, schemas become more organized, thus becoming more efficient. With more usage they also become more accurate as they assimilate more information. They also often become less general, so we must construct new schemas so we have a set that ranges from the specific to the general.

Media Alter the Human Mind

As can be seen from the information above, psychologists and researchers have changed the way we think about the human mind. However, there are also people who argue that the human mind itself has changed over the past few decades, and that this change is due to the influence of the media.

Healy (1990), in her book *Endangered Minds,* argues that children's minds are being altered by exposure to the visual media, especially computer games. Recent studies suggest that intensive game playing actually redraws the brain's neural maps, and that children who play a lot of computer games have cognitive strategies that are parallel—not sequential. This could make it more difficult for them when they must learn sequential tasks like reading and mathematical reasoning—both of which are very linear and analytical.

Healy says that children who enter elementary school are smarter in some ways each year, but that they are less able to handle school and its requirements. Children are less able to pay attention and to listen. This could be because many children either have information overload from the constant bombardment of media messages, so they shut down when they get to school, or because they have become accustomed to a level of stimulation much higher than a teacher can provide, so they become bored. Healy says that the visual media (especially television and video games) are responsible for this condition of over-stimulation, because those media strongly stimulate the right side of the brain while ignoring the left side. The left side of the brain is used less and therefore develops more slowly, leading children to have trouble with reading, arithmetic, and other traditional academic subjects.

Instead, the right side is stimulated by the fast-changing scenes on TV, as well as by video games with lots of novelty and movement. The visual media are very spatially oriented. This is especially the case with computers, which require a different form of skill. By playing computer games, children

acquire new ways of learning. They're honing special graphics and motor skills. They can process huge amounts of visual information in parallel. On a daily basis, they scope out new games, grasp the operating rules, navigate bewildering 3-D geographies, and jump through abstract mental hoops with concentration usually reserved for competitive test taking. (Gross, 1996, p. 64)

So far, we do not know for sure whether the media are causing changes in the way people think or whether the way people think is responsible for their seeking out certain kinds of media and making those media so popular. There is likely to be an element of truth in both explanations.

Summary

Cognitive psychologists developed some simple models to explain how the human mind works. These models are useful to get us started thinking about the workings of our minds, but they are too simple to serve as useful explanations in many situations, especially with the media. Meaning making is a complex and dynamic process. We do not simply match our memorized meanings to individual symbols.

People are not very systematic or complete in processing information about their world, because they are not always motivated to achieve accuracy. Many times they are more interested in efficiency, so they favor concrete over abstract information; become severely limited in their ability to combine different sources of information; fail to consider all or even most of the available information when making social judgments; and are biased simply by the natural and necessary use of simplifying categorization procedures.

Cognitive psychologists have moved beyond the simple models and now tend to favor schemas as an explanation for how humans construct meaning from complex messages. People rely on schemas to help them identify symbols and make sense of them. There are many different kinds of schemas for social situations: self, person, role, and event. Also, there are schemas for dealing with media: narrative, setting, thematic, rhetorical, and character.

We learn general schemas of society through a process of socialization as institutions pass their versions of culture down to us. Also, we construct our own schemas for our special needs, then elaborate and refine those schemas through processes of matching, bridging, and pruning. We continually update our set of schemas as we encounter new experiences. Over time, our set of schemas grows and becomes more useful in helping us make sense of any kind of real-world or media message.

References

Bandura, A. (1973). *Aggression: A social learning analysis.* Englewood Cliffs, NJ: Prentice Hall.

Bargh, J. A. (1984). Automatic and conscious processing of social information. In R. S. Wyer, Jr., & T. K. Srull (Eds.), *Handbook of social cognition* (Vol. 3, pp. 1-44). Hillsdale, NJ: Lawrence Erlbaum.

Berger, P. L., & Luckmann, T. (1966). *The social construction of reality.* Garden City, NY: Doubleday.

Black, J. B., Galambos, J. A., & Read, S. J. (1984). Comprehending stories and social situations. In R. S. Wyer, Jr., & T. K. Srull (Eds.), *Handbook of social cognition* (Vol. 3, pp. 45-86). Hillsdale, NJ: Lawrence Erlbaum.

Graesser, A. C., Millis, K. K., & Long, D. L. (1986). The construction of knowledge-based inferences during story comprehension. In N. E. Sharkey (Ed.), *Advances in cognitive science 1* (pp. 125-157). New York: John Wiley.

Gross, N. (1996, December 23). Zap! Splat! Smarts? *Newsweek,* pp. 64-71.

Healy, J. M. (1990). *Endangered minds: Why children don't think and what we can do about it.* New York: Simon & Schuster.

Lippmann, W. (1922). *Public opinion.* New York: Harcourt, Brace.

Wyer, R. S., Jr., & Gordon, S. E. (1984). The cognitive representation of social information. In R. S. Wyer, Jr., & T. K. Srull (Eds.), *Handbook of social cognition* (pp. 73-150). Hillsdale, NJ: Lawrence Erlbaum.

Further Reading

Berger, P. L., & Luckmann, T. (1966). *The social construction of reality.* Garden City, NY: Doubleday. (219 pages with index)

This is a classic book about how people come to know their world. Written by two sociologists, this short but dense book carefully lays out a theory about how certain information gains prominence in a society and how that information is then internalized by members of that society.

Fiske, S. T., & Taylor, S. E. (1991). *Social cognition* (2nd ed.). New York: McGraw-Hill. (718 pages with index)

This is an excellent book that lays out clearly the cognitive perspective on how the human mind works in social situations. It also serves as a strong reference with over 140 pages of references.

Healy, J. M. (1990). *Endangered minds: Why children don't think and what we can do about it.* New York: Simon & Schuster. (382 pages with index)

Healy argues that we are unwittingly rearing a generation of "different brains." Her point is that our brains have changed physiologically due to massive exposure to visual messages in the media, so that what it means to be intelligent has changed. The old skills of reading the written word and of mathematical reasoning are much lower than before because our attention spans are so much shorter.

Exercise 3.1 Examining How People Make Sense of Their World

1. Test your understanding of models of thinking.
   a. Next time you are in a conversation with a friend and your friend expresses an opinion, try expressing an opposite opinion. Observe what your friend does. Does she or he ignore the disagreement? Or does she or he try to put things back into balance by either (a) trying to change your mind or (b) changing her or his mind to agree with you?

   How important was that opinion to your friend? Do you think the level of importance of your friend's attitude was related to how your friend reacted?

   Try this with several friends. Do their reactions vary across different types of people?

   b. Find several topics on which your friend does not have an opinion. On one topic, try to get your friend to form an opinion by giving him or her lots of information and a systematic argument—thus forcing the use of the central route to processing information. Later, on another topic, try to get your friend to form an opinion by providing one anecdote or an emotional reason. Several days later, get your friend into a conversation about these topics and see if your friend has an opinion. If so, can she or he remember where the opinion started?

2. Become more sensitive to the way you use schemas.
   a. Watch an episode of a situation comedy. Take notes about schemas:

   Narrative: Write down the important events in the plot.

   Characters: List each of the important characters and describe them in one sentence each.

   Setting: List two things that typically happen in that setting, then list two things that would never happen in that setting.

   Thematic: What is the moral of this story?

   Rhetorical: What is the storyteller's purpose? Is it to provide you with information, to entertain you, or a combination?

   If the purpose is entertainment, what kind of entertainment?

   b. Now watch episodes of several other situation comedies. If you watched *Coach* above, watch something totally different, such as *Saved By the Bell* and *Taxi*. Again, make notes on schemas.

   c. How many schematic elements can you list that are common to all of these situation comedies?

   What elements made the comedies different from one another?

   d. Choose another genre (such as action/adventure, comedy cartoons, real-life crime, family drama, etc.) and repeat the exercise.

CHAPTER 4

The Skills of Media Literacy

KEY IDEA *Exercising high levels of media literacy requires the usage of two types of skills: Rudimentary skills are those acquired during childhood that bring us up to a functional level of literacy. Advanced skills are those that we must continually exercise to expand our understanding and appreciation of media messages.*

The setting is a kitchen table where two mothers are having coffee while their 6-year-old sons watch Saturday morning television in the adjoining family room.

"I don't know what I would do without television," says Janet. "I can tell Harley to watch and he is perfectly happy for hours. Meanwhile, I get some time to myself."

"But don't you think that all that TV viewing may be hurting him?" Marilyn is wary as she looks into the family room and sees little Harley kneeling in front of the TV set, staring passively, while her son Julian fidgets in a nearby chair.

"It doesn't hurt him a bit. Look at him. He's perfectly happy." Janet sips her coffee. "Besides, it's the only time I can keep him quiet. Otherwise he's all over me, wanting me to entertain him."

Julian comes into the kitchen, saying, "Mom, I'm bored. Can you read me a book?"

Marilyn reaches into her handbag to pull out a book and thinks, "I'm so glad Julian is not addicted to television and likes to read." Julian snuggles in his mother's lap as Marilyn begins to read to him.

Harley suddenly runs into the kitchen, making car-like noises, screeching around the table, then crashing into his mother. "Mom, I'm watching this really cool show." He proceeds to tell her all about the plot and his favorite characters in stunning detail. Janet thinks, "I don't know how he keeps all that action straight in his mind. And so many characters! It makes no sense to me."

Harley then spins around to Julian. "What is your story about?"

Julian shrugs his shoulders.

"Hey Julian. Tell me about your story."

Julian shrugs again and waves Harley away.

"That's not very nice, Julian," says Marilyn. "Tell your friend what this story is about."

"Mom, it's just a story. Read some more."

This short scene illustrates that some of the preconceptions we have about media literacy should be challenged. For example, one preconception is that people who watch a lot of TV are less media literate than those who prefer reading. In the scenario, Harley loves TV and he gets a lot out of it. He follows the plot and characters closely. He remembers the information and can tell others about the show. In contrast, Julian prefers reading, but he is passive and seems to like reading only so he can be held by his mother, apparently getting little information out of the reading.

Another preconception is that all children are lower in media literacy than adults. In the scene above, Harley seems to get more out of the TV messages than his mother, so in some ways it is possible for children to be more media literate than some adults. Literacy also varies across types of messages. As you can see, the idea of media literacy is complex.

To clarify the reasons for this complexity, we need to understand that media literacy is not a single skill. Instead, people build media literacy by mastering and continually applying a variety of skills. Some of these are rudimentary skills that we develop throughout our childhood as we mature cognitively, emotionally, and morally. As young children, we practiced using these rudimentary skills and continually improved until we reached a basic level of functional literacy. By early adolescence, we were fairly proficient with these rudimentary skills. Some people stay primarily at this functional level the rest of their lives, being able to continue their exposure to media messages and receiving some meaning from the messages.

A second set of skills is more advanced. Their use requires that we have first mastered the rudimentary skills then continue to improve our interactions with the media so we can get deeper levels of meaning and a wider range of experiences from the media. These advanced skills are what provide us with much more power over the media in terms of giving us more latitude in constructing our own meanings from messages rather than having to accept the surface meaning provided in the messages.

 ## Rudimentary Skills

The rudimentary skills can be examined in two ways. One way is to look at skills such as reading, listening, and viewing as processes. In order to talk about these processes, however, we must examine the steps or components in the processes. In this section, we will examine the rudimentary skills in both ways, starting with the component skills, then building to the process skills.

Component Skills

When we break process skills down into steps or components, we can identify four: exposure skills, the ability to recognize symbols, the ability to recognize patterns, and the skill of matching meaning. With exposure, we need to know what vehicles are available and how we can gain access to them. Once we have access, we need to be able to recognize the symbols presented. The individual symbols are the micro-units in a message—a word, a figure in a photograph, a note in a melody. When a mass of symbols occur together, which is almost always, we need to see connections among the individual elements. Words form sentences, then paragraphs, chapters, and books. A visual shape is part of the overall composition of a photograph. A musical note played against other notes can be part of a chord, and when the note is played as part of a sequence of notes, it can form the pattern of a melody. Recognizing the meaning of a sentence, a picture, or a melody requires us to have had the experience of previously associating that pattern with a meaning. Let's take a closer look at each of these rudimentary skills.

Exposure. Exposure is usually regarded in a technological sense, but there is more to it. Let's say you want to find out if the New York Jets football team won its game yesterday. You could turn on your television and tune in to the sports station—a skill requiring some technological expertise—but you would need to know something about which channel the sports station was on and when it broadcasts its football updates. You would also need to know if the Jets played a game yesterday and whether it is football season. If you tune in to the correct sports update show in April, you have the technological expertise for the exposure you want, but your knowledge base is so weak that you don't realize that football season has been over for more than 3 months and there is no chance for you to be exposed to a score of a Jets game. The technological skill of knowing how to turn on a machine works together with knowledge structures to create the exposures you want. If either is missing, you will be frustrated.

At your current stage of development, the technological skills might seem pretty simple to you. You may be able to operate a remote control device (RCD), program your video-cassette recorder (VCR), and to navigate your computer onto the Internet, but these are things you had to learn, and not everyone has learned them. Unlike the other rudimentary skills, the ability to access technology is not usually higher with children than with adults. Think about the people in your family. Who is more likely to be able to program the VCR or the buttons on the car radio or to set up the components of a stereo system—your parents or your younger brothers and sisters?

Deciding what to expose yourself to is part of this exposure skill, and this judgment grows with experience (DeGaetano & Bander, 1996). For example, who in your family would be more likely to give a better answer to the following questions: What kinds of authors should you read when you want to be entertained by a humorous detective novel? Which movie directors should you seek out when you want to see an epic film? Which magazines have the strongest political orientations? Which vehicle has the most credible news reports?

Notice that the application of this skill, like other skills, relies on good knowledge structures. The more information you have about media channels, vehicles, and messages, the higher your potential for exercising this skill. However, if this information is not structured effectively, then you will not be able to access it efficiently. This skill is therefore not the same as information; rather, it is your ability to add information to your knowledge structure and to access it quickly when you want to make a decision.

Recognizing Symbols. Some symbols are words, so we need to know what a word is compared to a letter, a sentence, a line of type, and so forth. Some symbols are elements in pictures, so we need to be able to recognize form, dimension, and perspective. Some symbols are audio, so we need to be able to recognize voice, music, and sound effects. Other symbols are movements on a screen; we need to be able to recognize a cut, a dissolve, a pan, a zoom in, and more.

All media users must first go through a process of extracting elements from the mass of stimuli in any message. Without this step in the process, no meaning can be perceived. This point may seem trite to you, but it is enormously important. You have mastered this so well that you take this accomplishment for granted. To help you realize this, do the following short exercise. Turn on your television set and get very close to the screen so that your nose is touching the glass. Squint your eyes until they are almost closed and try to focus on an area of about one quarter of an inch. What do you see?

The television picture screen is really individual dots arranged in a grid of 525 lines. Every $\frac{1}{30}$ of a second the dots change color. The hue of the dots is limited to three primary colors, but when you move back a few feet from the screen you can see the blending of those three primary hues into an entire rainbow of colors. Also, you no longer see the dots or even the lines; instead you see images. The dots on the screen do not move, but it appears that the images of people and objects are moving on the screen. How is this possible? Your mind blends the individual primary colors into combinations. The blinking off and on of different colored dots leads your mind to perceive that there are objects on the screen and that they are moving.

You take this skill for granted, because you have been practicing it so well for so many years. Even so, this is a skill you had to learn as a child. Very young children watch television in an exploratory mode, because they do not yet have a strong command of symbols and conventions. They pay most attention to perceptually important formal features (such as loud sounds, unique voices, special effects, etc.) and struggle to figure out what they mean. As children develop cognitively, they shift out of the exploratory mode and into a search mode; this happens as early as 3 to 4 years of age. By kindergarten, a continuous story line holds children's attention better than disconnected segments in a magazine format. They still use formal features (interesting visual and audio cues such as animation, children's voices, special effects) to decide what is important to attend to—for example, a laugh track signals that a program is a comedy. With experience, young children become much more adept at recognizing the traditional symbols.

With newspapers, young children will look at the front page and will "see" the same thing an adult sees, but will not be able to extract many elements. They will recognize that certain things are pictures, but they will not be able to extract any of the words or graphics; that is, they will not be able to distinguish the boundaries of the symbols there. With radio, children will "hear" the sounds but not be able to recognize the boundaries between the songs, jingles, happy chat, serious news, and ads.

Recognizing Patterns. Once you have recognized a symbol, you must put it together with other symbols to form a pattern. Within media messages, there are various types of guidance that provide help. With print, for example, the letter or word is the basic symbol unit. The words are not arranged randomly; instead, the author arranges the words in a special pattern to evoke a particular meaning in all readers. The larger the assortment of symbols, the more interpretation is required. For example, with smaller assortments (such as letters into words and words into sentences), there are fairly well accepted formal rules that most of us use without thinking. When reading, we carefully follow the construction rules of grammar and sentence syntax with little interpretation. As symbol sets become much larger and complex (such as plot development and narrative conventions), we must exercise much more interpretation.

We must also recognize patterns in the visual media. Messaris (1994) argues that children first need to learn to interpret still images, because of their two dimensionality, lack of color, and reduced detail. Then the issue of literacy moves to the more complex task of interpreting the interplay of pictures, speech, music, graphics, and special effects, such as required for film and television. At each of these levels, we must know how to spot patterns among the symbols. Production techniques can help us identify these patterns, but we must learn how production techniques themselves cluster into patterns. For example, there are formulas for the way a camera frames something to reveal its image as a coherent object, action, or space through the successive presentation of partial views. We must learn how production techniques tell us what a character is feeling and thinking through the juxtaposition of facial close-ups and appropriate contextual cues. Also, production techniques regulate emphasis and emotional tone in a scene through variation in camera positioning vis-à-vis the scene's action, but we must learn these conventions so we can spot the patterns.

We also have to be able to spot patterns in narratives. We must be able to link a character's motives with his or her actions; to link actions with consequences; to understand the unities of time and place; and to infer themes. If we cannot make these linkages, we will not be able to see the patterns among the symbols.

Matching Meaning. After we have isolated a symbol, we must interpret it; that is, match the symbol with a meaning we have already learned. For example, we memorize the definitions of words and the conventions of grammar and expression to be able to read. From our experience of listening to radio, we know that certain sounds signal the lead-in to news, certain voices convey humor or seriousness, certain other sounds convey danger or silliness. With television and film, we learn the meaning of a flashback, an extreme close-up of a character's face, character stereotypes, and what to expect in the unfolding sequence of a detective show. We have learned to connect certain symbols with certain meanings.

The same type of matching process takes place with patterns of symbols, although it is more complex because there are more elements involved. Messaris (1994), to illustrate this point using the media of film and television, reminds us that we must pay attention to all of the information coming to us from pictures, speech, music, graphics, and special effects, and that the way to construct meaning from those complex modes of communication is to focus on the interplay among them. One strategy is to focus on patterns in *changes* across time, place, or both. For example, when we see a sequence of shots of two people talking in a living room, followed immediately by a sequence of shots of the same two people talking in a car, we infer that some time has passed between the conversation in the living room and the conversation in the car. We use the audio and visual cues of setting to notice that there has been a change in location (even when the conversation continues on the same topic), and that this change in location must also mean that some time has passed. We might also look at whether the two characters are dressed the same in both sequences for more information about how much time might have passed.

The other strategy focuses on a pattern of *unity* of time and place. In this strategy, there are three conventions: First, we use the convention of trying to assemble the pieces of a scene (or of an object, an action, or a space) into a coherent whole in our minds. For example, a scene in a television show might consist of several different shots of people talking to each other at a party, but we are never shown a full shot of the entire room in which the party is taking place. In our minds, we construct the overall geography of the room from the pieces we are given, and we use this construction to keep straight where all the characters are and who is likely to talk to whom. A second convention is to infer what characters are thinking about from their unverbalized thoughts and feelings. To do this, we pay attention to the juxtaposition of facial close-ups and appropriate contextual cues. One character may be telling another that he does not care for her, but his body language and facial cues tell us that he really is in love with her. A third convention is to infer the emotional tone of a scene by "reading" the production cues. For example, a scene that consists of long shots of a solitary character walking in wide, open spaces, accompanied by slow, sad music leads us to infer loneliness. Fast, close-up shots of guns blasting, special effects of bodies blowing up, and a sound track of loud music and screams leads us to infer excitement and perhaps fear.

Process Skills

When we exercise the skills described above, we rarely use them individually or in isolation. Instead, we use a combination of them to achieve the goal of understanding the meaning of large sets of symbols. The media application skills of reading, listening, and viewing are really combinations of the components just described.

For example, when we read a novel, we choose which one to expose ourselves to, look at each word and associate its dictionary meaning with it, see the pattern of words arranged in a grammar, and try to track the meaning of that sentence. Our ultimate goal, however, is to read the book and follow the story all the way through. Thus the task of reading a novel also requires the understanding of the symbols of story and narrative, not just the symbols of letters, words, and sentences.

The understanding of narratives is important to all these media application skills. We make sense of information by attempting to arrange elements into "stories." In order for stories to make sense, they must have a social logic to them; we apply this logic to determine if a character's behavior seems reasonable to us (Black, Galambos, & Read, 1984). When we experience a "story" we must make sense of all the elements in it, so we make conscious selections from among story elements on the basis of distinctiveness and centrality.

When a story is ambiguous, we look for some clue (such as the title) to use as a guide in understanding the story. Once we have a guide, we use it to set up expectations for what should be happening and it will determine which elements (which characters and happenings) are important and which should be backgrounded. These guides (or schemas) will not only determine how much of the text we remember, but which parts will be likely to be recalled. The more knowledge we have in a particular area, the easier it will be to process new information and the more likely that it will be remembered. In addition, facts that can be organized by well-known schemas will be more tightly connected in memory than facts that cannot be so well organized.

By early adolescence, we are fairly proficient with all of these rudimentary skills, and although additional practice does little to improve them, continual use has the effect of reinforcing the skills. Their use becomes automatic; that is, we do not need to think consciously as we apply one or more of the skills. The good side of this condition is that our exposures are more efficient—we no longer struggle when reading a newspaper article or following a plot in a TV show or film. The dangerous side of this condition is that our exposures require very little concentration, and this leads to mindless exposure where we accept the surface meanings in the messages. When we simply match a meaning to a symbol, we accept that meaning without challenge, and the meaning is reinforced.

These skills are refined through practice during repeated exposure to the print and visual media. Once people acquire these rudimentary skills to the point that they are comfortable with them (usually during the early elementary school years), they may think they are media literate and stay on this plateau, practicing these rudimentary skills the rest of their lives. But there is another set of skills—advanced skills—that gives us the opportunity to develop control over media messages. The advanced skills require more effort and concentration. Using advanced skills, we do not take messages for granted. Instead, we develop a skepticism that guides our interaction. We critically challenge messages and the meanings they imply on the surface.

Advanced Skills

While being able to extract some rudimentary meaning from a wide range of media messages is an accomplishment, there is more to media literacy. This something more is often referred to as "critical viewing" (Messaris, 1994), or "critical thinking" (Brown, 1991), or just "critical" (McLaren, Hammer, Sholle, & Reilly, 1995; Silverblatt, 1995). This extra "critical" level is defined in several different ways. To illustrate, McLaren and colleagues (1995) conceptualize critical literacy as giving individuals power over their culture and thus enabling them to create their own meanings, identities, and to shape and transform the material. Brown (1991) says that critical thinking includes "understanding the process of valid inferences, abstracting, generalizing, syllogistic reasoning, propaganda analysis, and various forms of problem-solving traditionally exercised in language and mathematics studies" (p. 12).

In this section, we will deal with three families of advanced skills: skills that help with message focused sense making, those that extend the sense making beyond the messages, and the skills of appreciation.

Message-Focused Skills

When we stay within the bounds of a message or set of messages, we use four skills to interpret meaning: analysis, comparison/contrast, evaluation, and abstraction. Analysis refers to breaking the message down into meaningful elements. Next, we compare and contrast those elements to the elements in our existing knowledge base. Where the elements are the same (compared), the new elements reinforce the existing ones. But where there is a difference (contrasted), a controversy arises. Which elements are to have greater credence? We must evaluate the new elements from the media message and the old elements in our existing knowledge base. This process serves to discount certain elements and amplify others. Abstracting is the ability to assemble a clear accurate description of the media message. Each of these is developed in more detail below.

Analysis. Analysis refers to the breaking down of a message into meaningful elements. It is possible, of course, to read an entire newspaper or watch an entire movie without analyzing it—that is, we could experience it as a monolithic whole and have some kind of overall impression of it. Typically, such an impression is so general (e.g., "It was good") that we do not think about the reasons why—that would require us to analyze it and to identify the parts we liked the best.

Being good at analysis requires a highly developed knowledge base, because there are many different ways to analyze a news story, or a movie, or a novel. The more context we have (about narrative forms, industry motives, message conventions, etc.) the more dimensions we will be able to use in the analysis, and the more literate the analysis will be.

The task of analysis is to break messages down into meaningful components so that we can understand what the message was composed of and how those elements fit together. This is especially important with statistics. If we don't analyze statistics, then it is likely that we could be misled. Most of the statistics we see in the media are percentages. A percentage is an expression of the relationship between two numbers.

Let's look at an example to see why it is important to analyze media messages, especially those presenting statistics. All of us have probably seen at least one story that talks about how high the divorce rate has become in this country. Often these stories will say the divorce rate is now 50%, but what does this really mean? Let's analyze it. This figure is a percentage computed from two numbers. What are those numbers? If we compare the number of marriages with the number of divorces in any given year, we get a ratio of 2 to 1. In other words, there were twice as many marriages last year as there were divorces; or, expressed another way, the number of divorces last year was 50% of the number of marriages. But this makes it sound like half the married people get divorced each year; this interpretation is wrong. If we change the base number of the comparison, we get a very different number. Let's compare the number of divorces last year with the number of total existing marriages at the beginning of that year. When we make this comparison, we get a figure of about 1%. This means that last year, 1% of all existing marriages ended in divorce by the end of that year. Which is the correct divorce rate: 50% or 1%? They both are. The difference is not attributable to an inaccuracy; it is attributable to a difference in the base of comparison, and both bases of comparison are legitimate.

See how statistics can be misleading? It is important that you always analyze numbers in media messages to make sure you understand how they were computed. If you do not do this, you are in danger of interpreting the wrong meaning from accurate figures.

People at lower levels of media literacy accept the claims made in media messages at face value, even though these claims are often wrong or misleading. Unless we analyze the claims, we have no way of protecting ourselves from faulty information or opinions. When we do analyze the claims, we need to look for traps in reasoning. Five of these traps are illuminated below.

One trap is to become so skeptical of statistics that you don't believe any of them. Not all statistics are equally credible—or faulty. If you know what to look for, you can separate the good from the bad.

A second problem is the ecological fallacy in which a message shows you that there is a causal relationship between two things merely because they occur together. For example, in the 1950s it was found that crime rates were highest in neighborhoods where immigrants were most numerous. Some people used this co-occurrence to "prove" that immigrants were a cause of crime. A closer look at the numbers, however, revealed that immigrants were forced to live in neighborhoods where crime rates were high, because they could not afford more expensive housing in safer neighborhoods. Immigrants themselves committed very few of the crimes (Strauss, 1996). Unless you analyzed the claim carefully, you would misinterpret the relationship.

A third problem is the so-called butterfly effect. This is named for the belief that if a butterfly flaps its wings today in the Amazon basin, it will trigger a chain of events that will eventually lead to rain in your hometown next week. The problem with this "connection" is that there are too many simultaneous effects occurring, any one of which could account for the rain. You would have to analyze each link along the causal chain to see if there were any faulty links that would invalidate the jumping from a particular cause to a far-removed effect.

A fourth problem is the halo effect: This occurs when we believe someone else's explanation merely because we believe that person to be an expert or because we trust the person. Yet even experts are sometimes wrong because of faulty reasoning. We must analyze their claims to see if this is one of the times they are right.

A fifth problem is believing false predictors. Economists are continually developing sophisticated mathematical models to predict facets of the stock market or the economy. Meteorologists use supercomputers to predict weather trends, yet are often wrong. At any given time there are many different predictive outcomes, and almost all of them will be wrong. If you accept one of these unquestioningly, you will probably select a wrong one. To protect yourself, look carefully across all the predictions at a given time to see what the majority say, or look at the history of a particular model to see what its track record is. Some models are better at predicting the performance of certain stocks; however, be careful to understand that "better" is not perfection. My predictive model may be better than any of the others, but I may be right only 35% of the time. If you invest with me, you'll be better off than using other models, but you'll still lose money most of the time with me.

Comparison/Contrast. After we have broken a media message down into its component parts, we need to compare those elements with the elements in our existing knowledge structure. Elements that match are compared; elements that differ are contrasted. If all of the elements match, then the message adds nothing new to our existing knowledge base; it merely adds weight to it through reinforcement. If some elements are different, then we need to move on to the next skill, evaluation.

Let's consider an example. Imagine that I show you three objects: a red ball, a pear, and a knife. Then I show you an apple and ask you which of the three objects is related to the apple. You could pick the red ball, saying that the ball and the apple share the same shape and color. Or you could pick the pear, reasoning that the apple and the pear are both examples of fruit. Or you could pick the knife, thinking that you always use a knife to pare an apple before eating it. Which of these three is correct? They all are, because each is related to the apple in some way. Making good comparisons is not a rudimentary skill, because it is not simply memorizing the one best pairing for every object or concept. Instead, comparisons rely on your ability to see reasonable connections among objects. The more connections you can see and articulate, the stronger is your skill of comparison. Thus you are more media literate when you can see a given object from many different perspectives—each of which relates the object to something else.

Let's do this exercise with a television character by considering George on the *Seinfeld* show and pose the question: Is George a stereotypical character or is this character fresh and original? First, we must analyze George to identify key characteristics. We find that George is a 30-something, balding, white male. These particular characteristics tie him to many other characters on television. At this point, we might conclude that he is a stereotype. But let's go deeper and examine his personality. He is neurotically insecure—unable to sustain a romantic relationship with a woman despite his constant questing. He takes great pleasure in small achievements and is proud of his ability to fail. As we perceive more in the character, we have more points of comparison and contrast. Thus, the more detail we see, the more we can appreciate George as a fresh, original, unique character. Of course, with some characters, there is not much beyond the surface traits, so analyzing and comparing/contrasting do not yield much. The important idea is that we exercise the more advanced skills to determine for ourselves whether a character is truly superficial or whether all we see is the superficial. This is a key difference. In the first case, we are more highly media literate, and the conclusion of superficiality is our decision. In the latter case, we simply accept the surface characteristics as determined by the message producers.

On what points can we make comparisons/contrasts in the media? One point of comparison is to look across media. How is a message changed as it is freed from the constraints of one medium and becomes subject to the constraints of another? Some elements do not change, but others do.

Another point of comparison is to look across vehicles. Within any medium, there is a variety of vehicles. Making comparisons across vehicles reveals the editorial perspectives, business constraints, and vision of the audience of the decision makers. To see that not all magazines are alike, compare a non-fiction story in *Newsweek, Cosmopolitan,* and *Soldier of Fortune.*

Other points of comparison are across episodes of a show to see character development or across performances of a particular artist to assess his or her range. There are many possibilities for points of comparison. Not all of them are equally useful. A key to using these advanced skills is to have an agenda for assessing a deeper and broader set of meaning in the messages, then apply the skills consciously in working toward that goal.

Evaluation. Evaluation is assessing the value of an element. If we find an element in a media message that does not conform to our existing knowledge structure, we must decide whether to give high value to the new element and therefore change our knowledge structure, or to value more highly our existing knowledge structure and disregard the new element. In essence, we are cross-checking facts or perceptions. For example, let's say you hear a very damaging claim against a political candidate whom you favor. Your existing knowledge base has a great deal of positive elements and very few negative elements about this candidate. The new claim does not fit into your existing knowledge base, because your knowledge base is favorably constructed for the candidate. You must decide whether to believe the new claim and incorporate it into your knowledge base, which would require substantial alterations, or to disregard the new claim.

There are several strategies you could use to make the evaluation. You could examine the credibility of the claim, that is, what is the source of the accusation and does it seem plausible? Another strategy is to "weight" the claim. If the claim sits out there by itself with no additional people coming forth to support it, then the claim has little weight, especially compared to the weight of favorable knowledge you already have about the candidate.

People who operate at higher levels of media literacy will be more careful, reasonable, diligent, and logical when working through the evaluation problem. People at lower levels of media literacy will feel the task is not worth the effort and quickly make an intuitive judgment.

Making good evaluations requires the use of cognitive and emotional skills. The cognitive skills of objective, logical reasoning can order our alternatives according to how useful they are in achieving some goal, but what happens when this logical process results in several good alternatives? What can we do at that point? This is where emotions become important. Goleman (1995) warns us that emotions are an important part of evaluation. Unless we factor in how we feel about something, we will be paralyzed and unable to make a decision. The purely logical route might take us to a place where several options are viable or possible. Which do we choose? We need to have enough self-awareness about our emotions to determine where our preferences lie. Goleman says that many decisions "cannot be made well through sheer rationality; they require gut feeling, and the emotional wisdom garnered through past experiences" (p. 53).

There is a difference between using our emotions and letting our emotions use us. When we are highly media literate, we use our emotions—we don't ignore them. If we try to ignore them, they can influence us subconsciously. Emotions that stay at the subconscious level can still exert influences on our decisions and behaviors, but they do so without us being aware of it. Even without our awareness, decisions are being made, attitudes shaped, and behaviors acted. Goleman (1995) reminds us, "as Freud made clear, much of emotional life is unconscious; feelings that stir within us do not always cross the threshold into awareness" (p. 54). Being media literate requires us to develop greater self-awareness about our emotions so we can use them in the evaluation process.

Abstraction. Abstracting is the ability to assemble a clear, accurate description of the media message. This requires us first to analyze the message and identify all its component parts. Then we must evaluate the components to select those that are most important to the message. Finally, we must assemble a short description of the message from the results of our evaluation of components.

Abstracting is what you do when you tell a friend about a book you read or a show you saw. Some of us are able to abstract better than others. For example, let's say you ask your friend to tell you what happened on the last episode of *ER.* Your friend says, "A bunch of doctors helped some sick people." Your friend has captured the essence of the show but you haven't learned anything about that particular episode. If instead your friend says, "This mugging victim covered with blood was brought in by an ambulance and the medical team went to work checking his vital signs, then Dr. Greene put a tube down his throat so he could breathe," this provides a lot more vivid detail, but it covers only a few minutes of the hour-long show. A good abstract is one that is detailed enough to convey the feeling of the important events in the show but also broad enough so that all the essential happenings are covered. It requires that we break the show down into parts, evaluate the importance of the different elements as to their centrality to the action, then report the most important parts in a narrative that flows without raising any unanswered questions.

Message-Extending Skills

The advanced skills described above limit our focus to the meaning within messages or sets of messages, but there is more to media literacy skills. Some skills, such as generalization and synthesis, take us well beyond those messages. Generalization refers to the ability to perceive one or a few concrete examples and use them to construct a conclusion or opinion about a general trend. Synthesis is the ability to reassemble elements into a new structure.

Generalization. We generalize all the time. For example, let's say you watch a movie where a young child throws a temper tantrum then think: "All children are so spoiled these days!" You have seen the portrayal of only one child and from this very limited contact you have fashioned a belief about all children.

The key to media literacy is that we make good generalizations from our limited contact with messages and not fall into the trap of making faulty generalizations. In this trap, people focus on an isolated incident and conclude that it represents the typical. For example, people who read a news story about a criminal who copies an unusual bank robbery shown in a popular recent movie might conclude that all movies are bad or that certain movies are responsible for the high rate of crime in society. Concluding that all movies are bad because one person copies a particular action from one movie is a faulty generalization. No one movie can represent the incredible variety of all movies. Also, concluding that movies alone are responsible for crime in society is also a faulty generalization, because this conclusion fails to consider the many factors that lead a particular person to commit a crime.

This generalization trap is also frequently in evidence when we try to assess risk in our personal lives. Often, the media will present a story—either a news story or fiction—of an airplane mishap, a stalker, or something that makes us fearful. We then use this one incident to overestimate the risk to ourselves from this type of occurrence while ignoring other things (that the media do not talk about) that may pose a much higher risk to us. For example, in 1987 many news reports told about the danger of asbestos in older school buildings and the risk to children. Fear spread as people generalized a belief that all schools had problems and that their children were at risk. Almost overnight the asbestos removal industry more than doubled its revenue. However, the actual risk of a premature death from exposure to asbestos is 1 in 100,000. Compare this to the rate of premature death due to being struck by lightning at 3 in 100,000. There is also a generalized belief by many in the population that exposure to X rays in dentists' and doctors' offices is risky. It is, but the risk of premature death due to smoking cigarettes is 2,920 *times* greater than premature death due to exposure to diagnostic X rays (Matthews, 1992). Even so, many people calmly accept the risk of smoking but feel gravely at risk when a dentist x-rays their teeth once a year.

How can we avoid the trap of making false generalizations? There are two strategies. One is to get general information so you don't have to construct a wild guess about what everybody does or thinks from watching one person or one news program. Look up the actual rates of divorce, risk, governmental expenditures, and so on.

Unfortunately, not all information is in books or accessible. What do you do when you want to generalize in areas where no authoritative general information exists—such as what is the best way to end a romantic relationship? In this situation, you must use another strategy. Try to examine several dozen specific cases rather than only one. Don't look at romantic relationships just in the media, look at romantic relationships in real life. If a pattern consistently shows up in these many cases, then it is a better bet that the pattern may be common to all instances. Also, in collecting your observations, try to find cases that are able to represent the norm. Don't focus all your attention on how Beavis or Butthead would end a romantic relationship. Even if you observe 100 freaks, you still can't use the patterns you see there to make a case that all normal people behave a certain way.

Synthesis. This is the skill of reassembling all the valuable elements into a new knowledge structure, opinion, or fresh perspective. Doing this well requires creativity and a willingness to break the old rules.

Unless we are able to reassemble all the facts on an issue into a new structure, we cannot generate new opinions. Unless we can reassemble emotional, aesthetic, and moral interpretations into a fresh perspective on a film, novel, or television show, we are forced to accept the insights of others.

Like with the other advanced skills, synthesis can be conducted over a range of challenges from a quick micro-level synthesis to a very-large-scale creation. For example, on the micro level, when a television program breaks for a commercial, sometimes we reassemble the characters and elements in the plot line to imagine what is coming next or to imagine ourselves in the teleplay. This type of synthesis can take only a few seconds and be more emotionally guided than intellectually complete. On a larger scale, we may one day become inspired to write an episode of our favorite show. In order to do this we need a deep knowledge about all the elements in the previous episodes. We need to know all the quirks about each character and have an intimate sense of what each would do or say in any situation. Then, in writing our script, we would need to evaluate the appropriateness of dialogue, plotting points, character interactions, and more. The final product depends on our complete command of all these elements assembled in a new, creative manner.

Appreciation

Being media literate does not mean that we react to media messages purely in an intellectual manner. Media literacy also depends on quality reactions of an emotional, moral, and aesthetic nature.

At the more rudimentary level of media literacy, appreciation is simply an overall global reaction to a message. At a more advanced level, you can have a multifaceted reaction that is based on an acute awareness of how different facets of a message can affect you not just emotionally, but also morally and aesthetically. For example, you might hate a movie for manipulating your emotions but really admire the artistry of the director; or you might greatly admire the moral position of a book but feel the author was not a good writer and not able to evoke any strong emotions.

This appreciation skill is an important element to some scholars (Messaris, 1994; Silverblatt, 1995; Wulff, 1997). For example, Messaris argues that viewers who are visually literate should have an awareness of artistry and visual manipulation. By this, he means an awareness of the processes that create meaning through the visual media. What is expected of sophisticated viewers is some degree of self-awareness about their role as interpreters. This includes the ability to detect artifice (in staged behavior and editing) and to spot authorial presence (the style of the producer/director).

When you watch a movie, in how many different ways are you able to appreciate the film? For most of us, appreciation is usually focused on the overall plot and the acting. We appreciate the film's ability to keep us interested and excited. We also admire how certain actors are able to project an interesting character. There are many other things going on in the film, too, many of which we take for granted unless they appear as really unusual. For example, think about the last film you saw. Did you notice the editing—were there dissolves, flashbacks, cuts on dialogue, pacing that excited you in places? Was there music under the entire film or just in places? Can you remember how certain scenes were lighted to change colors or to bring about a certain mood? Can you remember how the characters were dressed in all scenes? How were the rooms furnished to convey information about the background of the action and characters? The more of these questions you can answer with confidence and with vivid detail, the more you have applied the advanced skill of appreciation while being exposed to that movie.

Summary

The knowledge structure presented in this chapter divides media literacy skills into rudimentary and advanced. The rudimentary skills are those we develop through maturation and practice during the early years of our lives. By adolescence, we have gained a great deal of experience with the media and we have matured cognitively, emotionally, and morally to a point where we have developed a good facility for exposing ourselves to the media messages we want; for recognizing symbols and patterns among symbols; and for matching learned meaning with those patterns. When we enact these skills in combination, we are able to read, listen to, and view media messages fairly easily. Because the application of these skills becomes easy, we often use them without thinking, that is, our minds are on automatic pilot.

The advanced skills require conscious effort and a critical perspective throughout exposure. They require the active processing of messages through the skills of message-focused sense making (analysis, comparison/contrast, evaluation, and abstraction), as well as through the skills of message-extending sense making (generalization and synthesis). The skill of appreciation is also important.

Operating at higher levels of media literacy requires the active use of these skills, and it also requires a highly developed knowledge base. It is important that the two components of skills and knowledge do not merely co-exist, but that there is an active interplay between the two. Skills are only useful when they have raw material—knowledge—on which to work. Remember that a knowledge base is more strongly formulated when it has been constructed with a wide range of skills that have been more highly developed.

References

Black, J. B., Galambos, J. A., & Read, S. J. (1984). Comprehending stories and social situations. In R. S. Wyer, Jr., & T. K. Srull (Eds.), *Handbook of social cognition* (Vol. 3, pp. 45-86). Hillsdale, NJ: Lawrence Erlbaum.

Brown, J. A. (1991). *Television "critical viewing skills" education: Major media literacy projects in the United States and selected countries.* Hillsdale, NJ: Lawrence Erlbaum.

DeGaetano, G., & Bander, K. (1996). *Screen smarts: A family guide to media literacy.* Boston: Houghton Mifflin.

Goleman, D. (1995). *Emotional intelligence.* New York: Bantam.

Matthews, J. (1992, April 13). To yank or not to yank? *Newsweek,* p. 59.

McLaren, P., Hammer, R., Sholle, D., & Reilly, S. S. (Eds.). (1995). *Rethinking media literacy: A critical pedagogy of representation.* New York: Peter Lang.

Messaris, P. (1994). *Visual "literacy": Image, mind, and reality.* Boulder, CO: Westview.

Silverblatt, A. (1995). *Media literacy: Keys to interpreting media messages.* Westport, CT: Praeger.

Strauss, R. (1996, November 29). The numbers game. *Los Angeles Times,* p. E4.

Wulff, S. (1997). Media literacy. In W. G. Christ (Ed.), *Media education assessment handbook* (pp. 123-142). Mahway, NJ: Lawrence Erlbaum.

Exercise 4.1   Becoming Sensitive to Rudimentary Skills

By the time you have reached college age, you have been practicing rudimentary skills for well over a decade. You are so proficient at using these skills that you take them for granted. The purpose of this exercise is to help you experience what it felt like before you were so proficient at these skills.

Exposure

1. Buy a piece of sophisticated electronic equipment and try to hook it up and operate it without any help and without reading the directions.

2. Sit down in front of a computer and try to boot up an application (such as a word processing, spreadsheet, or communications program) that you have never run. Today, many of these are very user friendly with lots of menus and help screens. Try to find a program from at least 10 years ago and run that.

3. Try to play a video game you have never played before. These are usually user friendly at the very beginning so you can begin playing, but most of them have many challenges that you must figure out. See how long it takes you to progress to various points in the game. Then find a child to play the game and watch how long it takes him or her to learn it.

4. Think up three topics that you know absolutely nothing about. Go to a library. Without using computer searches, the card catalog, or a librarian, see how much information you can find on each topic.

Recognizing Symbols

5. To sensitize yourself to how much you have learned about recognizing patterns, turn on your television set but leave the sound off. Now get very close to the screen so that your nose touches the glass and try watching television for one minute. Can you recognize any patterns? Probably not—you have not learned how to spot individual symbols that are that close.

Recognizing Patterns

6. Take a magazine article on something you do not know much about. Cut the article apart so that each paragraph is separate from all the others. Randomly order the paragraphs. Now read the newly arranged article and see if you can follow a progression of thought.

Matching Meaning

7. Find a book written in a language you do not understand, such as French, Italian, Spanish, or German. Begin reading aloud. You will be able to recognize individual letters and groupings of letters, or words, and although you probably will be able to pronounce these words to some extent, you will not be able to match any meaning to most of them.

Exercise 4.2   Exercising Advanced Skills

1. Think of some current event of interest to you. Now find a newspaper article on that topic and analyze it—break it down into its main components.
   a. What was the main point of the story?
   b. Were quotations used?
   c. What sources were interviewed?
   d. What are the key facts and figures?
   e. Are there important visuals—graphics or photographs?
2. Find a story in a recent magazine on the same topic and analyze it.
3. Find this story covered on television and videotape it, then analyze it.
4. Compare across the three stories: Which elements appeared in all three versions?
5. Contrast the stories: What are the really noticeable differences?
6. Evaluate the set of elements: Which of the elements are the most valuable in terms of informing the audience about the current event?
7. Synthesis: Take the elements you valued highly in #6 and assemble them into a magazine story. What information would you present first? What would the following sequence of information be? As you assemble the flow, is something missing—that is, do you need to put in something that was not in any of the three stories you analyzed? Why do you need this extra element: to help the balance of the story; to help it flow more smoothly; to help make it more interesting?
8. Synthesis: Repeat the process in #7, but instead of assembling the elements for a magazine story, assemble them for a television news story.

CHAPTER 5

The Developmental Perspective

KEY IDEA *Media literacy must be developed. It cannot simply be switched on all of a sudden. Instead, it is a life-long path toward higher understanding of media messages and their fit with one's own social world.*

Two fathers are proudly discussing how smart their children are. One of the fathers says, "Robert, my five-year-old, already knows how to read."

"So does my four-year-old, Jeremy," says the other father.

"When I say Robert can read, I don't mean simple preschool books. I mean he can read books that my older children read in the fourth and fifth grade."

"Jeremy reads at a sixth-grade level."

"Is that so? Well, Robert reads the newspaper—every night, and we discuss the news. He really understands everything."

"We had to get Jeremy a subscription to the *New York Times.* He just pestered us so."

"Well, Robert saved up his own money and bought his own subscriptions to *The Atlantic Monthly* and *Forbes.*"

"That's great! Then your Robert must have read the article that my Jeremy had published in *The Atlantic Monthly*—it was only a short article but then Jeremy is only four years old."

Sometimes proud parents tend to overestimate their children's abilities to understand media messages. Some parents work very hard with young children in an attempt to accelerate their abilities. They try to give their children lots of experience with the media and work actively with their children to build their skills. These two elements—experience and conscious application of skills—are important. A third element, maturation, is also important.

Let's examine maturation first. Along the path to higher media literacy there are some gates—especially along the early part of that path. When we encounter one of these gates, we must wait behind it until we mature to a certain level, then the gate opens and we can proceed. There are a series of cognitive gates, emotional gates, and moral gates. These gates occur every few years throughout childhood and hold us back in the early stages of media literacy. For example, most humans are not capable of acquiring the skill of reading until they are beyond the age of 4 or 5, because their minds have not matured to a point where such learning is possible. Trying to teach reading to 2-year-old children is very frustrating. No matter how hard you work or how hard the children work, their minds have not matured enough to be able to use the skills required for reading a book. Once the child's mind matures to the point where he or she can use those skills, however, the practice of reading begins to pay off.

This is why children's exposure cannot be compared to that of adults. Children are not people who differ from adults simply because they have less experience. They also have less ability to make sense of their experiences. As they mature cognitively, emotionally, and morally, they are able to apply the rudimentary skills better by perceiving more symbols in their exposures, recognizing patterns better, and associating meaning more efficiently. As they reach adolescence, they have passed through the last maturation gates and are capable of applying the advanced skills of analysis, comparison/contrast, evaluation, abstraction, generalization, synthesis, and appreciation. Whether they actually do apply these skills or how well they apply them is no longer a matter of maturation—it depends on their experiences and whether they concentrate during exposures.

Second, as people age they acquire more experience with the media and with real life. This greater experience helps them build stronger knowledge structures. Age does not automatically translate into experience, however. As we travel down the media literacy path, some people pick up a thousand different experiences while others stay in one place and re-live the same experience a thousand times. People who are stuck in one place along the path (repetitive exposure to only one kind of medium, vehicle, or message) are not broadening their knowledge structures.

Third, we need to practice our skills consciously during exposures to all kinds of media. The advanced skills do not develop through maturation; they must be developed through work and continual practice. With mindful exposures, we monitor the application of advanced skills and make adjustments to strengthen them.

These three factors work together. For example, a young girl of 7 will be able to read, because she has passed through the gate of cognitive maturity and her mind has developed to a point where she can learn to read. If she reads a simple book on gardening, she will be able to recognize most words and be able to recognize how the words are assembled into sentences to convey an idea. She has a rudimentary reading skill. If she also has a good deal of experience in gardening, this experience along with her reading skill will combine to allow her to read the book more quickly and to acquire a good deal more meaning from it than a child who has not had any experience in gardening. As her experience with gardening increases, her need for more information will also increase. She will subscribe to gardening magazines, listen to tapes on gardening, and seek out television programs on the subject. As her knowledge base grows, she will seek out information from related areas—perhaps botany and landscape architecture. If she carefully analyzes the messages as she is exposed to them, she will be comparing and contrasting the new information with what she already knows. Some of that new information will be valued and therefore retained, but other bits of information will be discarded. Over time, she will have to restructure her knowledge base through synthesis to make it more organized and efficient. If she does this consciously and self-reflexively, she will be in control of her decisions and guide the restructuring of her knowledge. She will also be strengthening her advanced skills along the way. Finally, she will be developing a better "eye" for the artistry of gardening, and her ability to appreciate will be increased. Thus the combining of experiences from the media along with real-life experiences and the conscious application of advanced skills along the way moves her farther down both the gardening path and the media literacy path.

Now let's look at how a person develops in the cognitive, emotional, and moral areas. Remember, development takes place simultaneously across these three areas, but for purposes of clarifying the nature of each, they will be explored individually below. Notice that with each one, development is influenced by a combination of maturation, experience, and conscious application of skills.

 ## Cognitive Development

Cognitive development refers to mental processes. From a media literacy perspective, the more developed a person's mental abilities are, the more literate the person is. This means that people with higher media literacy have an easier time applying a full range of mental skills, such as the rudimentary skills of being able to seek out media messages and to pay consistent attention to them. It also means having the advanced skills of being able to analyze the messages to extract a full range of symbols; to perceive the context surrounding each symbol and to assimilate that information into an interpretation of what the symbol means by making comparisons and contrasts in order to recognize alternative interpretations; to evaluate the different elements in a message for accuracy and utility; to abstract the key ideas in the message; to make appropriate generalizations; and to synthesize creative, more useful interpretations.

In addition, the stronger a person's knowledge structure is, the more literate that person is. This means having an in-depth understanding of the media across a broad range of topics, such as production techniques, narrative structures, character patterns, and thematic indicators; knowledge about industry practices, motivations, and perceptions of audiences; knowledge about the full range of media effects; and a self-monitoring awareness about the variety of ways the human mind can process information from the media.

With cognitive development, children generally differ from adults in three ways. First, children have a less developed knowledge structure, because their experience with the media and life is less. Second, children are weaker in their skills, again because they have had less practice than adults. Third, at young ages, children have a low ceiling of ability, that is, additional practice and experience won't help until the mind matures to a point where it is able to handle higher level skills. This third difference has been the focus of a great deal of research by developmental psychologists.

The most influential thinker in this area is the Swiss psychologist Jean Piaget. He shows that a child's mind matures from birth to about 12 years of age, during which time it goes through several identifiable stages (Smith & Cowie, 1988). Until age 2, children are in the sensori-motor stage, then advance to the pre-operational stage from 2 to 7 years of age. Then they progress to the concrete operational stage, and by 12 they move into the formal operational stage, where they are regarded as having matured cognitively into adulthood. In each of these stages, children's minds mature to a point where they can accomplish a new set of cognitive tasks. For example, in the concrete operational stage (between 7 and 12) children are able to organize objects into series. If you try to teach this skill to a child of age 3, you will fail—no matter how organized and clear your lessons are. Another skill that is developed throughout childhood is conservation, which is the ability to realize that certain attributes of an object are constant, even though that object is transformed in appearance (Pulaski, 1980). For example, ask a child to make two balls of clay the same size. Then roll one of them out into a long, thin shape like a snake, and ask the child which of the two pieces of clay is bigger. A young child will say the snake is bigger than the ball, because the snake is longer. The child does not have the ability to understand that the same amount of clay has been conserved, that only the shape (not the quantity) has been changed. Children's minds have matured enough to understand the idea of conservation by the time they reach about age 7.

When children interact with the media, we can see these cognitive stages in operation. Sometimes children's lower cognitive abilities will make them more susceptible to media effects, but there are other times when a "switched-off ability" actually serves as protection.

Infants and Toddlers

Children begin paying attention to the TV screen as early as 6 months of age (Hollenbeck & Slaby, 1979), and by the age of 3 years many children have developed regular patterns of viewing for about an hour or two per day (Huston et al., 1983). Nielsen data indicate that by ages 2 through 11, children are viewing between 28 and 30 hours per week, and this exposure amount is fairly stable over these years.

When watching television, young children are in a primarily exploratory mode. This means they monitor the TV set not for unfolding stories but for individual actions that have a very high profile. They look for action rather than dialogue or conversation. They look for motion, color, music, sound effects, and unusual voices. They have great difficulty in following the elements in a plot and in understanding character development and motivations for actions (Wartella, 1981). The reason for this is that young children, who have not developed very sophisticated narrative schemas, have trouble following stories unless the stories are very simple and short. Children must also learn about the principles of narrative progression (Meadowcroft & Reeves, 1989).

Even very young children are able to pay attention to television commercials. Attention depends on several factors. Attention is greater with commercials for products relevant to children and to commercials with higher levels of audio complexity or physical action. Attention is also enhanced by audio elements such as lively music, singing, rhyming, and sound effects. In addition, attention is enhanced by visual elements such as active movement, animation, and visual changes in general.

Children

By about age 4, children shift out of the exploratory mode and into a search mode. This means that they begin developing an agenda of what to look for; their attention does not simply bounce haphazardly around from one high-profile action to another. By kindergarten, a continuous story line holds their attention. They focus their attention on formal features (such as interesting visual and audio cues like animation, children's voices, or special effects) in making their decisions about what is important in the shows. For example, they interpret that a laugh track signals that a program is a comedy.

Also by age 4, children begin trying to distinguish between ads and programs. At first this is difficult, until they develop the skills of perceptual discrimination. During this trial-and-error learning, children either express confusion about the difference or use superficial perceptual or emotional cues as the basis for the distinction. With practice, they become better at separating ads from program content.

Children must also acquire the knowledge that ads are paid messages that are designed to get them to buy something—or to get them to ask their parents to buy something. Only 10% of children 5 to 7 years of age have a clear understanding of the profit-seeking motives of commercials; 55% are totally unaware of the nature of ads and believe commercials are purely for entertainment. For example, Wilson and Weiss (1992) found that compared to older children (7 to 11), younger children (4 to 6) were less able to recognize an ad for a particular toy and comprehend its intent when it was shown in a cartoon program, even when the product "spokesperson" was a character from a different cartoon program.

Disclaimers placed before ads to alert children to the fact that the program is being interrupted and an ad is about to be shown do not generally work well with children younger than 7, because they do not fully understand what an ad is. When disclaimers are in both the audio and video tracks, children are better able to perceive them. Also, when disclaimers are reworded into the language of children, their comprehension dramatically increases. At this young age, heavy viewing of TV seems neither to retard nor accelerate children's understanding of commercials, although it does seem to produce more favorable attitudes toward advertising and advertised products.

Parents overestimate their children's understanding of TV commercials. In most households there is relatively little mediation of children's exposure and reactions to commercials. Children's responsiveness to and understanding of commercial messages in the media can be influenced by parental and family influences. Even young children (kindergarten age) can be trained to understand the persuasive nature and techniques of commercials. This understanding will lead to increased skepticism.

By the second or third grade, most children have overcome their difficulty distinguishing between programs and commercials. With the combination of cognitive maturation, experience, and stronger knowledge structures, children really understand the nature and purpose of ads. This understanding leads to a drop in attention to the ads. In fact, attention is inversely related to the knowledge and experience necessary for critically evaluating ads. By the fourth grade, children have developed a critical and skeptical attitude toward advertising. They are also cynical about the credibility of commercials and begin to feel that advertisers have lied to them in an effort to get them to buy products that are not as desirable as the commercials' portrayal.

Can you remember back to when you were in early elementary school and you saw an ad for some fantastic toy that you just had to have? If you are male, the toy was probably a GI Joe or some sort of action toy like a truck or helicopter. In the ad, the thing moved and made action noises and did really cool things. But when you got the toy, it just sat there like the inert piece of plastic that it was. You felt betrayed, but at the same time you learned something about advertising.

Even after developing your skepticism about advertising, you still pay attention to ads somewhat and acquire information from them. In homes where consumption of goods is made important through conversation and expression of materialistic attitudes, more favorable attitudes toward commercials develop.

The ability to recall brand names and product attributes increases with age, especially between kindergarten and third grade. Simplified wording significantly affects comprehension and recall, but even for older children there is still some difficulty in understanding certain types of claims, such as superlative, comparative, and parity claims. For example, a parity claim is something like, "Buy Brand X, because it is as good as Brand Y." Children are confused by this type of claim if they don't use Brand Y. Also, children get confused about how Brand X and Brand Y can be so similar, unless the ad clearly shows the similarity across brands on the product attributes that are most important to children.

By ages 10 to 12, children have a well-developed idea of the economic nature of TV—that is, its profit-making motive—and most children this age and older are very skeptical of ads. This skepticism is usually limited to their experience with products. For example, their skepticism is high with ads for familiar toys. Presumably, they have had real-world experiences with these toys and have learned that the ads contain exaggerated claims. Children are much less skeptical of ads for medical or nutritional products; understandably, they have much less technical knowledge about these products and have less of a basis for skepticism. Among older children, skepticism about advertising can be overwhelmed by a steady diet of commercials. Heavy viewers of ads are more likely to believe them than are light viewers.

By the time they are 10 or 12 years old, children have also developed an understanding of motives of characters and how motives influence action. With this comes a greater ability to distinguish among characters along more dimensions. Children of this age are not limited to understanding characters based on only their physical traits but can also infer personality characteristics.

Adults

Although most of the research has focused on how our minds develop, there is a growing literature on adult cognitive development, showing that our intelligence and other mental skills change throughout the course of our lives. For example, Sternberg and Berg (1987) argue that there are changes throughout adulthood in two kinds of intelligences: crystalline, which is the ability to memorize facts, and fluid, which is the ability to be creative and to see patterns in complex sets of facts. They point out that research has shown that "whereas crystallized ability seems to increase throughout the life span, although at a decreasing rate in later years, fluid ability seems first to increase and later to decrease" (p. 4). They say that "crystallized ability is best measured by tests requiring knowledge of the cultural milieu in which one lives, for example, vocabulary and general information, whereas fluid ability is best measured by tests requiring mental manipulation of abstract symbols, for example, figural analogies and number series completions" (p. 4). Think back to the Pre-Quiz in the Preface of this book. The Pre-Quiz questions measured your crystalline intelligence. If you had acquired a large number of individual facts (like crystals), then you probably answered a lot of questions correctly. Being media literate requires you to develop your crystalline intelligence so as to acquire many facts, but you also need to develop your fluid intelligence in order to assemble those facts creatively into useful knowledge structures.

Although there is evidence that our minds continue to mature throughout adulthood, the substantial gains in media literacy come not so much through maturation but through experience and consciously working on developing higher order skills. Unfortunately, few people continue to work at this consciously. This can be seen in figures that indicate that most people do not even process most of the information they are exposed to—rather, they screen it out and do not remember it even a short time after exposure. Most people remember only about 10% of what they hear and 40% of what they see (Adams & Hamm, 1989).

Continuing to develop media literacy throughout adulthood requires the continual expansion of our experiences and knowledge structures through the more sophisticated use of the higher order skills of analysis, comparison/contrast, evaluation, abstracting, generalization, and synthesis. Not all adults do this. What is the difference between those who do and those who don't? The answer is a person's cognitive style. A cognitive style is a person's approach to organizing and processing information (Hashway & Duke, 1992). People vary in their cognitive styles along several key dimensions that are described below.

Field Dependency. Perhaps the most important dimension in cognitive styles is the degree to which a person is field dependent. Think of a continuum from dependent to independent. People are positioned along this dimension in terms of their abilities to distinguish between signal and noise in any message. Noise is the chaos of symbols and images; signal is the information that emerges from that chaos. People who are highly field dependent get stuck in the field of chaos—seeing all the details but missing the big picture, which is the signal. Field independent people are able to sort quickly through the field to identify the elements that are important and then ignore the distracting elements (Witkin & Goodenough, 1977).

For example, when watching a story in a television news show, field-independent people will be able to identify the key information of the who, what, when, where, and why of the story. They will quickly sort through what is said, the graphics, and the visuals to focus on the essence of the event being covered. People who are field dependent will perceive the same key elements in the story but also pay attention to how the news anchor is dressed, the hair, the makeup; the color of the graphics; the background people walking around the scene; and other details. To the field-dependent person, all of these elements are of equal importance, so field-dependent people are as likely to remember trivia as they are the main point of the story.

No one is purely field dependent; that is, no one perceives every micro element in every message and is totally incapable of sorting the signal from the noise. People vary by degrees. To estimate your position on the continuum, try this mini-exercise. Close this book. Then, on a piece of paper, jot down the main idea in this chapter and three subsidiary ideas that amplify that main idea. If you were able to do this quickly, you are an active reader and field independent. Before reading this chapter, you probably looked carefully at the chapter's first page with its key idea and outline, then you scanned through the chapter to get a feel for its structure and main points. Then, with that structure in mind, you were able to navigate your way efficiently through the reading—adding detail to your structure at appropriate places. So, when I asked you to close the book and write down the main idea, you had a picture of the entire chapter and were able to do this exercise easily. If you instead struggled with this mini-exercise, you are less field independent: You did not have the "big picture" of this chapter clearly in your mind. As you read through the chapter, you may have given each sentence and each idea equal weight. When I asked you to write down the most important ideas, you probably listed the most recent ideas you encountered, or perhaps you were able to list 10 or 12 points but were not able to decide which were more important, that is, which were superordinate to others. Perhaps you could not list any points, in which case you were forcing your eyes on each line of type but your mind was not distinguishing the ideas (the signal) from the lines of type (the noise). Developing field-independent strategies requires a little more work up front when beginning to read a chapter, but it is a much more efficient way to acquire and organize information.

We live in a culture that is highly saturated with media messages. Much of this is noise—that is, it does not provide us with the information or emotional reactions we want. Field-dependent people are passive and float along in this stream of messages, unable to do much of the conscious filtering that would help them focus on the signal and ignore the noise.

Tolerance for Ambiguity. Every day we encounter people and situations that are unfamiliar to us. To prepare ourselves for such situations, we have developed sets of expectations (schemas) for people and events. What do we do when our expectations are not met and we are surprised? People who have a low tolerance for ambiguity filter those messages. In contrast, people who are willing to follow observations into unfamiliar territory that goes beyond their preconceptions have a high tolerance for ambiguity.

During media exposures, people with a low tolerance for ambiguity encounter messages on the surface. If the surface meaning fits their preconceptions, then it is filed away as a reinforcement of their preconceptions. If it does not meet them, it is ignored. In short, there is no analysis. There is also no formal or systematic comparing or contrasting of the message elements with those of other messages, because these people seldom recall any of the discordant elements that would be required for making a contrast. These people are also not in a position to synthesize, because they are not motivated to create new perspectives.

People with a high tolerance for ambiguity do not have a barrier to analysis. They are willing to break any message down into components and to make comparisons and evaluations in a quest to understand the nature of the message and why their own expectations were wrong. People who consistently attempt to verify their observations and judgments are called scanners, because they are perpetually looking for more information (Gardner, 1968).

Conceptual Differentiation. People who classify objects into a large number of mutually exclusive categories exhibit a high degree of conceptual differentiation (Gardner, 1968). In contrast, people who use a small number of categories have a low degree of conceptual differentiation.

Related to the number of categories is category width (Bruner, Goodnow, & Austin, 1956). People who have few categories to classify something usually have broad categories so as to contain all types of messages. For example, if a person has only three categories for all media messages (news, entertainment, and ads), then each of these categories contains a wide variety of things. In contrast, someone who has a great many categories would have narrow ones. For them, all entertainment is not the same—some is comedy and some drama. Within comedy there is situation comedy, stand-up comedy, cartoon comedy, and more.

When people see a new stimulus, they must categorize it. Levelers tend to categorize new stimuli with previous types; they look for similarities, then match on them. They try to build cohesive cognitive schemas, but they fail to recognize small differences and gradual changes over time. In contrast, sharpeners focus on differences and try to maintain a high degree of separation between new stimuli and older stimuli (Pritchard, 1975).

What do people focus on when they make their conceptual differentiations in the sorting process? There are two broad types of sorting strategies: descriptive and inferential. The descriptive strategy relies on easily observable physical characteristics on which everyone would agree. For example, if you were shown pictures of a dozen people and asked to sort them into groups, you might choose the criteria of gender, ethnicity, or age. These are characteristics that are usually observable in pictures, and all sorters are likely to observe the same thing. An inferential strategy is one that requires you to make a judgment on abstract characteristics. For example, you might judge some of the people in the pictures to be sad and others to be happy and make your categorization on this judgmental criterion. We cannot "see" sadness, or any other emotion, motive, thought, or personality characteristics directly; instead, we infer these when we see some surface cues, though surface cues are not the thing itself.

Reflection-Impulsivity. This is a dimension that separates people in terms of how quickly they make decisions about messages and about how accurate those decisions are (Kagen, Rosman, Day, Albert, & Phillips, 1964). People who take a long time and make many errors are regarded as slow/inaccurate; those who are quick and make few errors are fast/accurate; those who take a long time and make few errors are reflective; and those who are quick and make many errors are impulsive.

In sum, cognitive development is an important component of media literacy. Children's minds mature, thus making it possible for them to understand important characteristics about the media. For adults, the potential is in place. Adults can use that potential by practicing higher order skills with the media. That practice will be more fruitful if we work on adjusting our cognitive styles by becoming more field independent through learning to focus more on signal and less on noise; by developing a higher tolerance for ambiguity and being willing to scan more messages and in greater depth; by developing knowledge structures with more categories of varying widths and being comfortable with inferential as well as descriptive sorting strategies; and by moving away from making impulsive sorting decisions.

 ## Emotional Development

Media messages can arouse emotions in people of all ages. Emotions do not have to be learned in the sense that we learn to recognize words in order to read. Instead, emotions are hardwired into our brains (Goleman, 1995). Regardless of the culture in which we are raised, we all can recognize in ourselves and in others the basic emotions of anger, sadness, fear, enjoyment, love, surprise, disgust, and shame.

We develop higher levels of emotional literacy by gaining experience with emotions and by paying close attention to our feelings as we interact with the media. With greater experience with emotions, we are able to make finer discriminations. For example, we are all familiar with anger, because that is one of the basic emotions, but it takes experience with this emotion to be able to tell the difference between hatred, outrage, fury, wrath, animosity, hostility, resentment, indignation, acrimony, annoyance, irritability, and exasperation.

Relation to Cognitive Development

A lack of cognitive development can prevent emotional reactions. For example, very young children cannot follow the interconnected elements in a continuing plot; instead, they focus on individual elements. Therefore they cannot understand suspense, and without such an understanding, they cannot become emotionally aroused as the suspense builds. This means that a child's ability to have an emotional reaction to media messages is low not because of a lack of ability to feel emotions, but because of a lack of ability to understand what is going on in certain narratives.

By adolescence, children have reached cognitive maturity, and all the gates are open to a full understanding of all kinds of narratives. Even so, some adolescents and adults still do not have much of an emotional reaction to media stories. Some people can be very highly developed cognitively but very under-developed emotionally. Goleman (1995) argues that a person's emotional intelligence interacts with IQ. He says, "we have two brains, two minds—and two different kinds of intelligence: rational and emotional. How we do in life is determined by both—it is not just IQ, but emotional intelligence that matters. Indeed, intellect cannot work at is best without emotional intelligence" (p. 28).

How can we develop our emotional intelligence? Salovey and Mayer (1990) say that we can develop emotional literacy by working in five areas: reading emotions (empathy), developing emotional self-awareness, harnessing emotions productively, managing emotions, and handling relationships. The first three of these have relevance to media interactions and how we deal with those messages. First, we need to develop greater empathy, which refers to our ability to see the world from another person's perspective. Second, we need to be aware of our own emotions as well as to understand what causes and alters them. Third, we need to be less impulsive and to exercise more self-control in concentrating on the task at hand, rather than becoming distracted by peripheral emotions.

Being emotionally literate requires an understanding of how emotions are evoked by the media and how we can control those effects when we are confronted with different types of messages. We can use the media to achieve the emotional effects we want if we are conscious of what we are doing and aware of how the effects work. For example, if we are having an inappropriate emotion, like an unreasonable fear of dogs—or snakes, dentists, heights, or flying—the media can help reduce the degree of that emotion. We could read about dogs and learn more about their likes and dislikes. We could watch videos and films of harmless puppies frolicking. These exposures could gradually build to show larger and larger dogs. Over time, we could feel our fear being greatly reduced to the point that we could be around real dogs without panicking.

When we are unaware of emotional effects, the media can exercise unwanted influences, such as reducing our sensitivity to things that we should care about. For example, people who watch a great deal of violence on television become desensitized to the suffering of victims both on television and in the real world. Viewing violence that gradually increases in severity becomes less and less anxiety provoking, especially if the viewing is done in relaxing conditions.

How a message evokes an emotional response rests with the combination of the message itself and the way the viewer/reader interprets it. The sequencing of elements in a message fosters a mood that affects emotional responsiveness. A message element is assigned meaning only in the context given by the perceived pattern and themes of the entire message. Viewers and readers develop interpretative schemas to use in giving meaning to individual parts of a communication. The schema can function as an aid and basis for recalling the substance of the story: Particularly important items are remembered. The schema constitutes a basis for perceiving similarity in communication experiences that differ in details.

Interpreting Media Messages

The task of interpreting emotions well from media messages requires us to be able to read the verbal and nonverbal cues from characters, the situational cues, and then properly coordinate the interpretation of both sets of cues. Adults give precedence to situational cues if cues are not coordinated. Children give precedence to verbal and nonverbal cues.

What are the kinds of cues that can trigger our emotions? The beginning point for this understanding is how media narratives can evoke emotions. Below are four findings.

First, we are more likely to have stronger emotional reactions when we are exposed to realistic narratives in realistic settings. Realistic elements draw us more strongly into the narrative by reminding us of our real lives and actual experiences. Thus the narrative will resonate more with our personal experience. This serves to engage our remembrance and imagination to a higher degree. On the other hand, desensitization is enhanced when we believe the action we are viewing is fantasy and when we believe that everything will work out all right in the end.

Second, we will have a stronger emotional reaction with narratives that feature characters with whom we can identify. Some of us tend to identify with characters who are most like us. Others of us identify most strongly with fantasy characters, usually those who are stronger, richer, smarter, or more physically attractive than we are.

Third, narratives that follow a conventional pattern will be easy for us to follow and can evoke some standard emotions. Yet in order to evoke really strong emotions, the narrative has to surprise us by changing the formula or bending the rules to take us "over the edge" of what we expect.

Fourth, massive exposure to arousing stimuli, especially sex and violence, can substantially diminish our emotional reactions to such stimuli. This is called "excitatory inhibition" (Zillmann, 1991). We can recover from this desensitized condition. For example, if we look at erotic pictures in a magazine we will become aroused. If we continue to look, the pictures will gradually lose their exciting nature and, after many hours of exposure, we might become bored with looking at the pictures. If we come back to the pictures several weeks later, however, we will find that we are still sensitive to their ability to arouse us.

In sum, emotional literacy is tied to cognitive development. The emotional reactions of children who cannot read or follow visual narratives will be limited to reactions to micro-elements in messages. As people mature to a point of mastering the lower order skills, there is still a range of emotional abilities. Some people are better able to "read" emotions in themselves and others, because they have a higher degree of empathy and greater self-awareness. In contrast, people with lower literacy are not able to experience emotions vicariously through characters, and they may be desensitized to many emotions by constant exposure to superficial treatments of news stories and formulaic fictional plots.

Moral Development

Like Piaget, Lawrence Kohlberg has studied the development of children. Piaget was concerned with cognitive development; Kohlberg focused on moral development. He suggested that there are three levels of moral development: pre-conventional, conventional, and post-conventional. The centerpiece is "conventional," which stands for fair, honest, concerned, and well regarded—characteristics of the typically good person (Kohlberg, 1966, 1981).

The pre-conventional stage begins at about age 2 and runs to about age 7 or 8. During this time children are dependent on authority, because their inner controls are weak. Young children depend on their parents and other adults to tell them what is right and to filter the world for them. A child's conscience is external, that is, a child must be told by others what is right. The pre-conventional stage has two sub-stages.

■ *Sub-stage 1:* Children are motivated by avoiding punishment, and this guides their reasoning. They do not distinguish between accidents and intentional behaviors. If a child spills milk or steals a cookie and both are punished, both are regarded as equally bad.

■ *Sub-stage 2:* Children are guided by self-satisfaction as expressed in the attitude: You do me a favor and I'll do one for you. What brings pleasure to a child is felt as a reward.

During the conventional stage, children develop a conscience for themselves as they internalize what is right and wrong. They distinguish between truth and lies. The threat of punishment is still a strong motivator.

■ *Sub-stage 3:* Children are motivated to get the approval of others—peers, parents, and other people. This is the "good-boy, good-girl" orientation.

■ *Sub-stage 4:* Children's motivation shifts to a sense of duty and obedience to authority. They become concerned with avoiding harm to others and dishonor to themselves. They have an orientation toward law and order. Many people stop developing at this point; this may be the highest level they ever exhibit.

The post-conventional stage begins in mid-adolescence when some people are able to transcend conventional notions of right and wrong as they focus on fundamental principles. This requires the ability to think abstractly and thereby recognize the ideals behind society's laws. Thus the stages in the post-conventional level are characterized by a sense that being socially conscious is more important than adhering to legal principles.

■ *Sub-stage 5:* In this stage, there is a focus on the social contract. Individuals consent to do certain things even if they do not agree with them. In return, those individuals get to live in a society where things run harmoniously. Correct action is defined in terms of general rights, usually with legalistic or utilitarian underpinnings that are agreed upon by society.

■ *Sub-stage 6:* People are motivated to make ethical decisions according to their own conscience. They focus on universal principles of justice and respect for human dignity. The rules of society are integrated with a person's conscience in the creation of that person's hierarchy of moral values. Thus there are times when the demands of society are most important; at other times, the dictates of the person's conscience must be obeyed. To an individual at this stage, external punishments are much less important than is feeling internally right about his or her decisions.

Kohlberg's stages are not fixed steps that everyone follows in sequence. People can move around among the steps depending on particular problems and moods. Each stage is very different, however, and they are hierarchically ordered such that the more evolved person is one who operates most consistently at the highest levels.

Gilligan (1993) has extended Kohlberg's ideas by arguing that there is a gender difference in moral development. Men base their moral judgments on rights and rules, while women tend to think in terms of care and cooperation. In a conflict situation, therefore, women are likely to try to preserve relationships; men are likely to search for a moral rule and try to apply it.

Let's examine these stages using a media example. Bobby is a young child whose family uses the television as a baby-sitter. Bobby watches a great deal of television unsupervised; there is no parent or authority figure to help him process the messages or to give him a countervailing perspective on the real world. Therefore his moral development during the pre-conventional stages is shaped by the themes in the television messages, mainly cartoons, action/adventure shows, and situation comedies. From this steady exposure, Bobby is likely to learn the following moral lessons: Aggression (both physical and verbal) is an acceptable and successful way to solve problems; with a little hard work, everyone can be successful—that is, be wealthy, powerful, and famous; family relationships are full of conflict and deceit but family members still love each other; and romantic relationships are exciting, but superficial and temporary.

As Bobby moves into the conventional stages, much of his behavior will be governed by these moral lessons. He feels that the best way to get approval from others is to be funny, live dangerously, and have lots of peer relationships filled with conflict—that makes an active, interesting life. Finally, as Bobby reaches late adolescence and confronts the post-conventional stages, he must begin asking such questions as: "How can I live my life so as to benefit society in general?" "How can I resolve moral dilemmas so that I don't make decisions on a purely selfish basis?" Given Bobby's moral development and the lessons he has learned, it is unlikely that he will be interested by these post-conventional questions. It is probable that he will stay at the conventional stage and continue to make decisions based on these moral principles of which he is not fully aware.

Summary

Development is a key idea of media literacy. We evolve gradually through stages of development, and we are unaware of passing from one to another. This development occurs simultaneously in the areas of cognitions, emotions, and moral perspective.

When we are children, we pass through many stages relatively quickly. This maturation process opens gates and allows us to practice new skills and gain greater experience. By adolescence we have mastered the lower order skills, but this does not mean that the developmental process is over. Rather, at this point we gain more control over the process, because we do not have to wait for maturation steps to occur; instead, we can practice the set of higher order skills as we gain more experience with both media messages and the real world and thus build stronger and more elaborate knowledge structures. As long as we actively process media messages, we increase our media literacy and gain greater control over media effects.

References

Adams, D. M., & Hamm, M. E. (1989). *Media and literacy: Learning in an electronic age: Issues, ideas and teaching strategies.* Springfield, IL: Charles C Thomas.

Bruner, J. S., Goodnow, J., & Austin, G. A. (1956). *A study of thinking.* New York: John Wiley.

Gardner, R. W. (1968). *Personality development at preadolescence.* Seattle: University of Washington Press.

Gilligan, C. (1993). *In a different voice.* Cambridge, MA: Harvard University Press.

Goleman, D. (1995). *Emotional intelligence.* New York: Bantam.

Hashway, R. M., & Duke, L. I. (1992). *Cognitive styles: A primer to the literature.* Lewiston, NY: Edwin Mellen.

Hollenbeck, A., & Slaby, R. (1979). Infant visual and vocal responses to television. *Child Development, 50,* 41-45.

Huston, A., Wright, J. C., Rice, M. L., Kerkman, D., Seigle, J., & Bremer, M. (1983). *Family environment and television use by preschool children.* Paper presented at the Biennial Meeting of the Society for Research on Child Development, Detroit, MI. (Eric Document No. ED 230 293)

Kagen, J., Rosman, D., Day, D., Albert, J., & Phillips, W. (1964). Information processing in the child: Significance of analytic and reflective attitudes. *Psychological Monographs, 78,* 1.

Kohlberg, L. (1966). Moral education in the schools: A developmental view. *School Review, 74,* 1-30.

Kohlberg, L. (1981). *The philosophy of moral development: Moral stages and the idea of justice.* New York: Harper & Row.

Meadowcroft, J., & Reeves, B. (1989). Influence of story schema development on children's attention to television. *Communication Research, 16,* 353-374.

Pritchard, D. A. (1975). Leveling-sharpening revised. *Perceptual and Motor Skills, 40,* 111-117.

Pulaski, M. A. S. (1980). *Understanding Piaget: An introduction to children's cognitive development* (Rev. & expanded ed.). New York: Harper & Row.

Salovey, P., & Mayer, J. D. (1990). Emotional intelligence. *Imagination, Cognition, and Personality, 9,* 185-211.

Smith, P. K., & Cowie, H. (1988). *Understanding children's development.* Oxford, UK: Basil Blackwell.

Sternberg, R. J., & Berg, C. A. (1987). What are theories of adult intellectual development theories of? In C. Schooler & K. W. Schaie (Eds.), *Cognitive functioning and social structure over the life course* (pp. 3-23). Norwood, NJ: Ablex.

Wartella, E. (1981). The child as viewer. In M. E. Ploghoft & J. A. Anderson (Eds.), *Education for the television age* (pp. 28-17). Springfield, IL: Charles C Thomas.

Wilson, B. J., & Weiss, A. J. (1992). Developmental differences in children's reactions to a toy advertisement linked to a toy-based cartoon. *Journal of Broadcasting & Electronic Media, 36,* 371-394.

Witkin, H. A., & Goodenough, D. R. (1977). Field dependence and interpersonal behavior. *Psychological Bulletin, 84,* 661-689.

Zillmann, D. (1991). Television viewing and physiological arousal. In J. Bryant & D. Zillmann (Eds.), *Responding to the screen: Reception and reaction processes* (pp. 103-133). Hillsdale, NJ: Lawrence Erlbaum.

Further Reading

Goleman, D. (1995). *Emotional intelligence.* New York: Bantam Books. (352 pages with index)

In this readable best seller, Goleman argues that there is an emotional IQ as well as an intellectual one. He challenges the long held belief that a person's intelligence, as measured by a narrow IQ test, is an adequate predictor of success or ability. First, he broadens the conception of intelligence, then shows how a person's emotional development interacts with a broad range of cognitive abilities. He cites physiological data to show that emotions are part of the brain and are triggered by the capacity of the body.

Kohlberg, L. (1981). *The philosophy of moral development: Moral stages and the idea of justice.* New York: Harper & Row. (441 pages)

Kohlberg lays out his moral development scheme of three stages, each with two sub-stages. There are many examples relating this structure to how people come to understand the concept of justice.

Pulaski, M. A. S. (1980). *Understanding Piaget: An introduction to children's cognitive development* (Rev. & expanded ed.). New York: Harper & Row. (248 pages with index)

This is a very clear, well-organized description of most of Piaget's thinking and research. There are many drawings to illustrate key concepts.

Exercise 5.1 Being Aware of Your Development

The Questions

Cognitive Development

1. Think of your favorite television series, then answer the following two questions:

   a. Make a list of all important characters and describe each in detail.

   b. Write out a plot for what will happen on a future show.

Emotional Development

2. All emotions have a range of sub-emotions or sub-types. For example, the emotion of fear includes the sub-emotions of terror, panic, fright, dread, consternation, apprehension, anxiety, nervousness, wariness, edginess, concern, and qualm or misgiving. Each of these is a type of fear, but each indicates a different feeling of fear. How many sub-emotions can you list for love? How many sub-emotions can you list for sadness?

3. Watch a television show and count how many times you see the emotions of fear, love, and sadness.

   a. When you see one of these emotions, can you classify which type (sub-emotion) it is?

   b. Watch several different kinds of television programs and notice which emotions are most prevalent and which emotions are hardly ever portrayed.

Moral Development

4. Watch several action/adventure television shows or movies in which there are a good deal of antisocial behaviors, such as crime, violence, and lying. Notice how the characters justify these acts to themselves and to others. Think about those justifications and try to place those characters on Kohlberg's levels of moral development.

   a. Now think about the show as a whole and try to infer the intentions of the writers and producers. To which moral level of viewers are they trying to appeal?

   b. If you were producing this show and you wanted to appeal to viewers who were several sub-levels *higher*, what would you change in the scripts?

   c. If you were producing this show and you wanted to appeal to viewers who were several sub-levels *lower*, what would you change in the scripts?

Thinking About Your Answers

Cognitive Development

1. Your answers to the first part (a) reflect your degree of crystalline intelligence. Look at how many characters you listed. For each character, how many adjectives or descriptive phrases did you list? Notice the variety in the descriptors: Were they all physical attributes, or did you also list other attributes such as personality, dress, career, favorite gestures/mannerisms, and so on? The more detail you have in your answer, the more information you can access about that show.

   Your answers to the second part (b) reflect your degree of fluid intelligence. If you had a difficult time thinking of any plot developments, you are probably low on fluid intelligence. If you wrote down lots of events, look at how your events tie into the past action on the show. Is your plot more of the same events or does your plot really push the characters well beyond where they are now? If you have exhibited a lot of imagination and creativity, you are high on fluid intelligence.

   Compare your performance on (a) and (b). If you did much better on (a), then your profile is more crystalline, and you have a strong ability to gather facts. If you did much better on (b), then your profile is more fluid, and you favor imagination and searching for new perspectives. Developing to a high level of media literacy asks you to increase both of these types of intelligence.

Emotional Development

2. The more sub-emotions you can list, the more you are attuned to subtle variations in emotions and the more emotionally literate you are.

3. It takes skill in empathy to be able to spot emotions in others, especially to make fine distinctions among sub-emotions. Television shows and movies are packed with emotions. Many of these are very easy to spot, but some of the sub-emotions are more difficult to perceive. Can you think of examples of the emotions that are more difficult to perceive? How does the expression of emotions (and types of emotions) differ in situation comedies compared to action/adventure shows?

Moral Development

4. Can you make any generalizations about where most television characters would be on Kohlberg's levels of moral development? If you can see a clear pattern and can argue your conclusion with lots of examples, you are fairly morally literate. Your moral literacy is also high if you can understand how scripts could be changed to appeal to a different level of viewer.

PART III

Knowledge

CHAPTER 6

What Is News?

KEY IDEA *News is not a reflection of actual events; it is a construction by journalists who are subjected to many influences and constraints.*

Is News a Reflection or a Construction?
Influences and Constraints
    Commercialism
    Story Formulas
    Resource Constraints
    Organizational Forces
    Advertisers
    Use of Sources
    Deviance
    Geographical Focus
News Perspective
    Advantage
    Disadvantage
    Values of Journalists
    Changes

The Issue of Bias
Objectivity
Balance
Context

Is News a Reflection or a Construction?

If you were to ask someone how the news differs from entertainment programming, most people would say that entertainment is fiction and therefore made up by writers, while news presents actual events that have happened. We think of news as a reflection of the events of the day; that the media are merely holding a mirror up to reality or that the media are a magic window on the world.

Yet when we take a close look at the news, it becomes clear that news does not *reflect* reality. Instead, it is a construction by journalists. While news coverage is triggered by actual occurrences, the coverage of those occurrences is influenced by processes and constraints much like fiction is. News is a creation resulting from the active selecting and interweaving of images into a processed reality. In constructing their stories, journalists rely on the facts in the event being covered, but they are also strongly influenced by elements outside the event, such as their deadlines, space limitations, and their own news sense.

The construction process essentially encompasses three tasks: (a) Selecting what gets covered, (b) deciding what will become the focus of the story, and (c) determining how the story gets told. As for what gets covered, only a minute sliver of human activity is selected from all the possible stories that could be reported. Think of all the things you did last week. How many of those events were covered as news? Probably none. Why? Journalists don't think of you as a newsworthy person. Your week was filled with all sorts of things that interested and even excited you, but none of these things met journalists' particular definition of newsworthiness.

Deciding what the focus of the story will be is what is known as looking for the "hook" to get people interested in the story. Journalists then write the lead (the first sentence) to set the hook. With any event, there are many different elements that could be chosen as the hook of the story. As an example, let's say a journalist covers a speech by a political candidate running for office. The journalist could decide that the story should be: (a) that the candidate gave a speech; or (b) that the candidate looked tired giving the speech because of a hectic day of campaigning; or (c) that the candidate is trying to make up ground in the polls where she now trails her opponent by only 5%; or (d) that the candidate introduced a new position in the speech; or (e) that the candidate's new position is at odds with the position of the leaders of her party, and some controversy might be brewing. These are only five of many different ways a journalist could decide what the focus of the story should be. Each of these would result in a very different story about what happened, and each story would require a different hook to gain people's interest.

The journalist also decides how the story should be told. Following through with the example of the political candidate's speech, let's say that the journalist chose as the hook option: (e) the candidate's new position is at odds with the position of the leaders of her party, and some controversy might be brewing. The TV journalist can decide to talk about the speech or to show the candidate laying out the controversial position. There could be reaction shots from audience members—either happy or shocked. The journalist could interview people in the audience, or party leaders, or the candidate's handlers, or the opposition candidate for a reaction. These are all choices the journalist must make. Then, after these elements are selected, the journalist must decide how to sequence them in the story.

Thus, news is not something that happens; instead, news is what gets presented. We almost never see news events as they happen. Instead, we are shown the media's manufactured construction of the events.

Influences and Constraints

What influences the construction process? There are many factors, including commercialism, story formulas, resource constraints, organizational forces, advertisers, use of sources, deviance, and geographical focus.

Commercialism. Arguably the strongest influence on the construction of news is its commercial nature (Altheide, 1976). News organizations are businesses that compete with each other for audiences and advertisers. Success is often viewed in terms of which competitor appeals to the largest audience and thereby generates the greatest revenue from advertisers.

The pressures of commercialism set up a conflict between two perspectives on news. In one perspective, professional responsibility, journalists regard themselves as having a responsibility to inform the public about the most important and significant events of the day so that people can use the information to make better decisions as citizens of their society. For example, journalists operating within this perspective would strive to provide in-depth information on candidates and issues during a campaign so that voters could make more informed decisions. These journalists would also try to present clear explanations about economic conditions, implications of government policies, the patterns of changes in society, and other broad-scale issues so the public is exposed to the context behind individual issues.

In contrast is the marketing perspective, where news workers pay careful attention to what kinds of stories and presentation formats generate the largest audience. Journalists operating under the marketing perspective, for example, would try to produce stories that grab the attention of large audiences by shocking them or by highlighting the unusual.

Marketers must also be careful not to alienate potential audience members. For this reason, newspapers have become less political, even to the point of rarely endorsing candidates. For example, in 1940 about 87% of the country's newspapers clearly endorsed one of the candidates for president; by 1992, the figure had dropped to 37%. Newspaper managers fear that an endorsement could alienate many readers and therefore cost the newspaper revenue. Radio and television stations almost never endorse candidates.

The influence of commercialism has moved the news away from the professional responsibility perspective and placed it squarely under the marketing perspective. This means that there is a growing commitment to entertainment in order to attract large audiences. Postman and Powers (1992) illustrate this when they argue that what television news says it is presenting and what it actually presents are two different things. Journalists want us to believe that they are presenting the important happenings of the day that all citizens should know about, but what they really present are superficial constructions designed to attract large audiences for advertisers.

The shift to commercialism is seen most clearly in the way some news programs are themselves turning into ads. For example, Kaniss (1996) criticized news shows in the Philadelphia area by pointing out that during the November 1996 sweeps month, the local CBS affiliate on its evening news show ran nine stories about the *Titanic,* a ship that sank 84 years ago but was the subject of a CBS mini-series. The local ABC affiliate frequently ran news stories about Mickey Mouse; the ABC network is owned by Disney. Local affiliates also frequently ran news stories about stars on their network series, and they often ran soft news stories on topics of made-for-TV movies appearing that night on the network.

Story Formulas. Journalists are very busy people. Their days are filled with an incredible amount of detail that must be processed on short deadlines. A reporter at a daily newspaper may have to write several dozen stories every day. Do reporters spend hours thinking about the best way to communicate the essence of each story, then several more hours polishing up draft after draft? Rarely do they have this luxury. Instead, they must assemble the facts of a story in a matter of minutes, then move on to the next story. How do they do this? They use formulas.

One of these formulas is the inverted pyramid, which involves putting the most important information at the beginning then moving down the list of important information until it is all included in the story. Another formula involves constructing a lead sentence with something (such as a gruesome event or an unusual quote) that will grab the reader's attention, then telling the story using a narrative format. A third formula provides descriptive information about the who, what, when, where, why, and how of an event. Journalists use these formulas—and others—so they don't have to invent new methods of reporting the world every time they confront it (Fishman, 1980).

The use of these formulas is widespread across journalism; in a given locale, if a story is covered by one news vehicle, it is likely to be covered by them all. With minor variations, the information in (and structure of) a story in a small newspaper is the same as in a story in a very large newspaper or on television or radio news.

Resource Constraints. Though the news gathering departments of the major broadcast networks and the major daily newspapers are very large and have considerable resources, there are limits. There are never enough resources to allow covering all the events that happen in a given day. Choices must be made because of these constraints of time, place, space, and talent (Tuchman, 1978). As for time, organizations create deadlines and rhythms of work so they can produce a product every day. As for place, certain institutions and sources are appropriate locations for news while others are not. All media vehicles have space limitations, either in the form of column inches in print vehicles or of seconds in broadcasts. Talent is also a constraint, with journalists' varying abilities to ferret out information, organize it, and present it clearly.

Organizational Forces. Factors about the organization/corporation influence the content of a newscast. The two primary components of this are organizational structure and ownership/control.

Organizational structures vary. Small companies are more flexible and entrepreneurial. They search out new needs and quickly adapt. In contrast, large companies are compartmentalized, with each division having a special function and its own staff of technical people. These large bureaucracies are more resistant to change, but also more resistant to outside pressure, because the business and editorial departments are separated.

Ownership patterns can also influence news content. For example, the *New York Times* has remained in the hands of one family for more than 100 years. There is a very high potential for the members of that family to have a strong influence on that newspaper. In contrast, other newspapers might be owned by a large media conglomerate with thousands of shareholders, each with a very low potential for influence.

While there are some examples of newspapers changing their editorial stance because of pressure from an owner, they are rare. What is more typical is that the newspaper is pressured by the owner(s) to make a larger profit, which means giving more attention to the marketing perspective.

Advertisers. Some advertisers pressure the media, and some do this more successfully than others. For example, compare the performance of two drug companies. In 1981, 124 people died from taking Oraflex, an anti-arthritis pill marketed by the Eli Lily drug company. The Food and Drug Administration had allowed the drug to go on sale in April 1981 despite an FDA investigator's warning that Eli Lily had withheld data on the dangerous side effects of the drug. This event received almost no coverage.

In October 1982 several people died from taking Tylenol capsules that were poisoned on store shelves, and this event received major continuing coverage. The Johnson & Johnson Company appeared to be less skilled in controlling stories about the poisoning of Tylenol capsules than was the Eli Lily Company in controlling the situation around Oraflex.

Use of Sources. News is shaped by the sources of information that are used to construct the stories. The dominant sources of news are institutions, such as governments and public relations groups. Most companies and institutions have public relations departments whose only job is to establish themselves as experts and feed information to journalists. Once a person is established as an expert source on an issue, he or she is called by journalists when they want an expert opinion on that particular issue.

How do journalists know who is an expert? Most journalists don't have the experience or education to evaluate the credentials of many people who could serve as experts in news stories, so they choose people not on the basis of knowledge but on their appearance of expertise and their willingness to tell a good story. This point is illustrated by Steele (1995), who examined how television news organizations selected and used expert sources to interpret the news. She found that news organizations chose expert sources that reflected journalists' understanding of expertise. Experts were selected according to how well their specialized knowledge conformed with television's "operational bias," which places its emphasis on players, policies, and predictions of what will happen next. Steele concluded that these processes undermine the ideals of balance and objectivity, as well as severely limit how news is framed.

Deviance. The media are interested in presenting deviance (Shoemaker, 1987; Shoemaker, Danielian, & Brendlinger, 1991). Deviance covers those things that are out of the ordinary, and the more they differ from reality, the more they are considered newsworthy.

With news coverage, there are two types of deviance (Shoemaker & Reese, 1996). One is statistical deviance, which "causes things that are unusual (either good or bad) to be considered more newsworthy than commonplace events" (p. 47). For example, if a woman gives birth to a child, that is not news, but if a woman gives birth to quadruplets, that is unusual and therefore is newsworthy. The statistical probability of giving birth to four children at once is very low, so this gets covered.

The other type is normative deviance, which refers to ideas or events that break norms or laws. For example, if a person goes to a bank and puts money into his account, that is normal and will not be covered. If a person goes to a bank and withdraws money from other people's accounts at gunpoint, however, that breaks the law and gets covered. Thus the media focus on crime. Within crime news, there is a preference for violent action (Antunes & Hurley, 1977; Windhauser, Seiter, & Winfree, 1990) and crimes against people (Ammons, Dimmick, & Pilotta, 1982; Fedler & Jordan, 1982), which are rarer and more deviant than property crimes. Deaths due to violence are also more likely to be reported than deaths due to disease (Combs & Slovic, 1979). This over-reporting of crime is also found in other countries, such as England (Roshier, 1981).

Geographical Focus. Important things happen every day, all over the world, but the American news media give the most coverage to events in this country—which is only to be expected. There is also a fair amount of coverage of the industrialized countries, but little coverage of Third World countries. For example, Larson (1983) examined international news coverage on television and found that events in the Third World were covered less than events in industrialized countries and that what coverage there was of the Third World was crisis oriented (Larson, 1983). The same pattern was found by Potter (1987) in newspapers. Kim and Barnett (1996) show clearly that the news flow of information around the world is dominated by the Western industrialized countries. This power is associated with the degree of economic development.

Even within this country, the news coverage is not balanced geographically. Instead, events occurring in the Northeast and along the Pacific Coast are covered the most, while events happening in the rest of the country are under-covered (Graber, 1988).

News Perspective

All of the above influences shape how journalists select which events to cover and how they construct their stories. These selection and construction decisions are made from what is called the "news perspective." Learning to be a journalist means being socialized into this news perspective.

Advantage. The advantage of the news perspective is that it helps journalists simplify and organize the overwhelming amount of material they must sift through on a daily basis. The use of this perspective can be seen in "the routines of news detection, interpretation, investigation, and assembly" (Fishman,

1980, p. 18). Because this news perspective is shared among news workers of all levels (reporters and editors) as well as across different media, it serves as a kind of code of professionalism because it legitimates the "intertwining of political and corporate activity" (Tuchman, 1978, p. 14).

The news perspective is not something that is consciously imposed by powerful elites, such as the owners of the media. Instead, it grows naturally out of the traditional procedures used by news workers and leads us to ask: How could the news be any way else?

Reporters and editors are socialized over time to accept this news perspective. For example, there is a considerable overlap in news stories at local television stations in the same market. Davie and Lee (1993) found that 56% of stories were the same, with stories from network sources having more similarity. The non-overlapping stories were more likely to be from local sources. Davie and Lee (1995) also analyzed local television newscasts and found that there is a distinct preference for sensational stories that feature acts of sex and violence and are easy to explain. There was little differentiation among the stations, leading to the conclusion that the news sense of all local producers is almost the same. Hudson (1992) ran an experiment on over 100 news directors and executive producers from all sizes of markets, all over the country. He showed them a violent incident and asked them how much of the incident they would show in a newscast. Most considered the shooting and the victim falling to the floor acceptable, but excluded images of the dead body. This same news judgment was found in all market sizes and across all kinds of stations—which supports the news perspective theory.

All news is relatively homogeneous across all kinds of outlets. The news content presented in the different mass media tends to be the same; that is, the content of news presented by a television station is the same as the content of news presented by a radio station, a newspaper, or a magazine. The particular medium does not strongly influence the content of news stories. Differences among media do have some effect, but not much, in changing the news. For example, television journalists look for stories with high visual impact, but if a story is important, all media will cover it whether it is visual or not.

Disadvantage. The disadvantage of the news perspective is that its limited vision results in a very narrow view of what is news. It also leads journalists to treat those selected stories superficially, thus distorting reality. Altheide (1976) argues that "the organizational, practical, and other mundane features of news work promote a way of looking at events which fundamentally distorts them. . . . In order to make events news, news reporting decontextualizes and thereby changes them" (p. 24-25).

Values of Journalists. A set of values is at the base of the news perspective. Shoemaker and Reese (1996) argue that journalists exhibit eight mainstream American values. Notice how similar these are to your own values.

■ Individualism: people who do things their own way, even against powerful odds
■ Moderatism: fanaticism of any kind arouses skepticism
■ Social order: peace and order are valued; people who deviate from this are labeled wrongdoers
■ Leadership: there are high expectations of leaders; those who are found to be weak, dishonest, or immoral are investigated
■ Ethnocentrism: other countries are judged against American standards
■ Altruistic democracy: there is a democratic ideal of efficient government and participation by all citizens; deviations from this are news
■ Responsible capitalism: fair competition without unreasonable profits or exploitation of workers
■ Small-town pastoralism: small towns and rural areas are the font of virtue

Changes. The news perspective has changed over time from social responsibility to marketing. Many editors used to hold the perspective that they were charged with selecting what was important and presenting that information to their readers. They then used the criteria of significance, proximity, and timeliness. These are the classic journalism school criteria. The purpose behind this social responsibility perspective is to build an informed public, which is essential in a democracy.

With increasing competition among television news programs over the past two decades, the news perspective has been changing to one of marketing. The primary job of editors now is to attract and maintain as large an audience as possible, so editors are charged with guessing what readers would find most arousing and entertaining. The most important news criteria now are conflict, appeal to emotions, and visualization. Given these criteria, it is not surprising that the news has become much more sensational. To illustrate this, Slattery and Hakanen (1994) compared local television newscasts from 1976 and 1992. They found a dramatic decline in hard news coverage of the government, from 64% down to 19%, while coverage of human interest stories and sensationalism climbed from 10% to 41%. During the same time, there was a shrinkage in the news hole of the late evening newscasts from 13 minutes to 11.8 minutes, thus allowing more time for advertising. This is the classic pattern of the marketing perspective.

The Issue of Bias

The public is generally happy with news coverage, with about 60% to 67% saying that the news media are not biased (Bower, 1985; Hickey, 1972). This belief is held equally across the political spectrum. But what is meant by bias? Does it mean lack of objectivity? Or imbalance? Or a superficial context?

Objectivity

There is a strong ethic of objectivity in journalism (Parenti, 1986). But what does this mean? Editors may be objective in the sense that they don't want to publish a "slanted" story. They are very subjective, however, in which stories get assigned, which stories get written by the best reporters, which stories get edited down, and which stories get printed on the front page.

It is difficult to understand what journalists mean by objectivity. This will be illustrated by the following story. In the summer of 1995, Allan Little, a veteran foreign correspondent for the British Broadcasting Corporation, was covering the war in Bosnia. One day, as the Serb soldiers were approaching a Muslim town, he wanted to tell the story of an impending massacre but his editor told him that such reporting would not be objective. Little was told to report just the facts of the day with no background and no interpretation, which he did. Although Little knew that it was the practice of the Serb forces to slaughter all the Muslims they could and that the town was unprotected and would soon fall into Serb hands, he could not put that context into his news story. On July 11th, the Serb soldiers captured the town, rounded up the thousands of men and boys in the village, and killed them all. Little says, "I still to this day feel sullied and tainted that I pulled my punches on that one" (Randolph, 1997). The accurate or complete story would have been to report the event in the context of Serbian goals and past behaviors during the war. In that way, viewers could see the true horror of the aggression and get a much better understanding of what was taking place. Instead, in the guise of "objectivity," reporters could convey only the details of how far the Serb army advanced each day. Which way of reporting would have been more meaningful to readers? Which would have been more interesting? In situations such as this one, it is difficult to understand what journalists mean by "objectivity." Perhaps this is not a useful term.

Balance

Many journalists prefer the criterion of balance, which is the recognition that there is more than one side to any story, and journalists should attempt to present all sides. This has been the criterion of journalists who realize it is impossible to be completely objective. In order to be fair, they attempt to achieve balance in their stories. This means including the viewpoint of more than one side in the story, and with some stories there are many sides.

Are news stories balanced? Fico and Soffin (1995) looked at balance in newspaper coverage of controversial issues such as abortion, condoms in schools, and various governmental bills. Balance was assessed by examining whether both sides of an issue were illuminated in terms of sources interviewed for both sides, whether assertions for both sides were in the headline, first paragraph, and graphics. They found that 48% of stories analyzed were one-sided, that is, the other side was not covered at all. They counted the number of story elements that illuminated the different sides of each issue and found that on average one side received three more elements compared to the other side—therefore the average story is imbalanced. Only 7% of stories were completely balanced. The authors concluded that professional capability, ethical self-consciousness, or both, are lacking in many journalists.

If journalists are unable to provide us with balance, then we must construct it for ourselves if we are to be media literate. This means we must seek out information from all sides of an issue. But how can we know how many sides there are? We can't. Instead, we must develop a skepticism about all issues and never be confident we have all the information from all sides.

Context

The so-called new journalists take the perspective that the facts do not convey the importance of any story—readers need context. Without context, the story has ambiguous meaning. For example, a story could report that Mr. Jones was arrested for murder this morning. That fact can have very different meanings if we vary the context. Let's say that the journalist puts in some historical context—that Mr. Jones had murdered several people a decade ago, was caught, convicted, served time in prison but was recently released be-cause of a ruling of an inexperienced and liberal judge. In contrast, let's say that Mr. Jones, one of the candidates running for mayor, was arrested despite the fact that police had in custody another man who possessed the probable murder weapon and who had confessed. The fact of the arrest takes on a very different meaning within different contexts.

Contextual material is very important. Many stories are fairly formulaic and mostly bland, however (Parenti, 1986). The stories that are limited to the basic facts of an event do not help audience members construct the meaning of that event.

Asking journalists to build more context into their stories presents two problems. First, journalists vary widely in talent, and it takes a very talented and experienced journalist to be able to dig out a great deal of relevant con-textual information on deadline. Second, when journalists have the responsi-bility of constructing the context, they are given a lot of power to define the meaning of the event for the readers. Journalists can substantially change the meaning if they leave out (whether intentionally or through an oversight) an important contextual element.

Exposure and Learning

Access to news is now easier than ever, and there is more of it available. There are almost 9,000 newspapers (daily and weekly) and more than 10,000 magazines covering almost every topic imaginable. There are television cable networks and radio stations that are "all news," and almost all broadcast television stations have newscasts, most of which have grown in length over time. In 1950, the television networks presented 15 minutes and local stations presented another 15 minutes of evening news. In early 1960, the networks increased to 30 minutes and so did local news broadcasts. In the 1980s, many local stations went to an hour of evening news, realizing that it was a money-maker for the station. Once a news department has a good crew, it doesn't cost the station any more to go from a 30-minute to a 60-minute newscast, and it gives the station the potential to double its revenues by selling twice as many minutes of advertising.

Exposure

Despite the availability of more news, exposure to news and information is down. People are not seeking out the news as they once did. A recent poll ("Fewer Adults Reading Papers, Watching News," 1995) shows that only 45% of American adults read newspapers regularly, and only 61% watch television news. Furthermore, there is reason to believe that news exposure will continue to dwindle. About 55% of people over 50 years of age are regular readers of newspapers, but this figure drops to only 28% for people under 30. Younger people are not developing the news habit, and as they age and replace older people who do follow the news, the overall rates of news exposure will drop.

Learning

What do we learn from exposure to news messages? This question has two very different answers. In the short term, we learn facts, but in the long term, we may be learning something much more significant—that is, we learn what is important in our society.

Learning Facts. Americans regard television as their main source of news (Robinson & Levy, 1986), but research shows that people do not remember much from television news stories (Gunter, 1987). American children who watch a lot of television are less informed about the world than their counterparts who watch little television (Lee & Solomon, 1990). Meisler (1994) reports that in a recent poll of eight countries, Americans knew less about current events than did citizens in the other seven nations.

This problem can be traced to three factors: (a) Most news stories on television or radio do not contain much information, (b) people who rely primarily on television news do not also get news from other sources, and (c) most stories are presented with little context that would help viewers make sense out of the story and place it in their existing knowledge structures.

Learning What Is Important. The mass media exert a powerful influence by making us believe that certain things (events, issues, and people) are important while others are not. This is called agenda setting. Media are more effective at telling people what is important to think *about* than they are at telling people what to think. For example, the media, through a continual stream of stories about social welfare programs, are effective at telling us that this is something worth thinking about; but the media are not effective in convincing people that they should support or reject social welfare programs. The agenda-setting function of the mass media is quite powerful, especially when there is an overlap in coverage among the various media.

Parenti (1986) extends this point by arguing that

> even more than manipulating actual opinions, the media have a great deal of power in controlling *opinion visibility.* They create a media image of public opinion that often plays a more crucial role in setting the issue agenda than does actual public opinion and which has a feedback effect on actual opinion. (p. 89)

> As Senator McCarthy discovered, if the press is cooperative enough, the charges don't have to be true, no more than the claims made by a Geritol or Pepsi advertisement. Factual rebuttals mean less than we would suppose because facts are not really what are being treated. The specific facts of the matter are less important than the cumulative, residual effects that remain long after the specifics are forgotten or never learned. (p. 168)

Criticisms of News

Bias in Ignoring Stories

In his book *Censored: The News That Didn't Make the News—and Why,* Jensen (1995) argues that every year the news media in this country ignore many important stories. He defines censorship as "the suppression of information, whether purposeful or not, by any method—including bias, omission, under-reporting, or self-censorship—which prevents the public from fully knowing what is happening in the world" (p. 16). Jensen explains that there is not a consciously evil conspiracy that controls which stories get covered. Instead, stories are sometimes overlooked because they don't fit the traditional news frame or because they are potentially libelous. The main reason a story will not get coverage, however, is due to a fear that the coverage might cost the media company revenue: "Corporate media executives perceive their primary, and often sole, responsibility to be the need to maximize profits, not, as some would have it, to inform the public" (pp. 17-18).

Jensen argues that the number one censored story in 1995 concerned the National Institute for Occupational Safety and Health (NIOSH), which is the part of the National Centers for Disease Control and Prevention that is entrusted with the job of monitoring the safety of the workplace. NIOSH must inform workers when they are in serious danger of contracting life-threatening diseases from exposure to chemicals and other hazardous materials in the workplace. Jensen says that 10 years ago, over 240,000 people were found to be in danger in 258 work sites around the country, yet less than 30% of these people have been notified so far, leaving 170,000 people working at risk for the past decade with the government's knowledge and inaction.

When a critic of the news is bothered that a certain story is not covered, an editor can always say: "We can't cover everything; I must draw the line somewhere." But sometimes this constraint excuse is used to cover up a decision that can be traced to the editor's news perspective—not the resource limitations. In this case, the critic is not arguing that every event should be covered; instead, the criticism is a questioning of the editor's judgment for deciding that certain stories were more important than others that did not get covered. This selection process has the effect of moving other happenings to a lower priority and pushing many below the line that must be drawn.

This lack-of-resources argument becomes even more spurious when we see how much overlap there is in allocating these "limited" resources. For example, the Associated Press news service has more than 100 reporters in Washington, D.C., alone, and all of them are trying to develop the same contacts at the White House. During the presidential nominating conventions in 1996, more than 16,000 news people covered those non-events; that is, everyone knew who the candidates were going to be well before the conventions.

The major news organizations have all had their budgets expand greatly over decades without providing an expansion in the amount of news. For example, the annual budget of the ABC network news department grew from about $1 million in the early 1960s to over $300 million in the late 1980s, but with that enormous growth in resources, the amount and quality of news did not increase 300 times during that period.

Also, CNN and all-news radio shows have significant budgets and a very large newshole, but the number of stories they cover is very small compared to the space they have. Their news judgment has not been to provide a greatly expanded breadth of stories. Instead, they maintain a narrow vision of what is important and present those same stories over and over all day.

Bias Toward Particular Political Views

In an analysis of Gallup Poll public opinion data, it was found that more than half of Americans felt that the media were influenced by advertisers, business corporations, Democrats, the federal government, liberals, the military, and Republicans (Becker, Kosicki, & Jones, 1992). The newspaper industry itself finds the same thing in its own surveys. For example, a survey by the American Society of Newspaper Editors found that a majority of people believed the media have political leanings (Jeffres, 1994).

What is interesting is that conservatives feel that the media has a generally liberal leaning, while liberals feel that the media are conservative. Conservatives complain that most news reporters are liberal in their own views and that they show this bias when they present their stories. In contrast, liberals feel that conservative commentators have too much power and have redefined the American agenda to stigmatize liberals.

In the early days of this country, most newspapers were founded by people who had a clear political viewpoint that they wanted to promote. Towns had multiple newspapers, each one appealing to a different niche of political thinking. By the late 1800s, newspapers had shifted from a political focus to a business focus with the goal of building the largest circulation. In order to do this, newspapers lost their political edge so as to avoid offending potential readers. This model still underlies the mass media. Decisions are made to build audiences, not to espouse a political point of view. Sometimes arguing for a particular political point of view can be used as a tool to build an audience, but these instances are found only within media that have a niche orientation. Instead, the large national news organizations, such as the television networks and the large newspapers, try to present both sides of any political issue so as to appear objective and balanced.

Too Much Bad News

In surveys, most people will complain about the amount of bad or negative news and ask for more good news, saying that is what they prefer (Galician, 1986), that bad news is not necessarily more interesting. Yet the news organizations predominantly feature bad news (such as crime, scandal, and controversy). There are two ways to look at this anomaly: On the industry side, news programmers believe that these portrayals are what the public wants. Their job is to create the largest audiences, so why would they program something that would not attract the most people? On the consumer side, people say that if they are not given alternatives, they cannot show the industry what they really want.

Superficial Information

The news media are often criticized for providing only superficial information and little or no context for important stories. Thus the news media are not providing the public with enough guidance to reach sound opinions about the important issues of the day. We can see evidence of this in public opinion polls that reveal that the public is missing key information. For example, according to public opinion polls, only 17% of people think crime is a big problem in their own community, while 83% of Americans think crime is a big problem in society (Whitman & Loftus, 1996). That is, most people do not experience crime in their own lives and therefore do not think it is a big problem where they live, even though they hold the opinion that the country is in bad shape.

Where do they get the idea that crime is a problem when they don't experience any in real life? From the media. The media constantly present stories about crime. Some of those stories are very high-profile events, like the O. J. Simpson arrest and trials; Susan Smith buckling her two toddlers into car seats and running the car into a pond to drown them; Lorena Bobbit cutting off her husband's penis; or the Menendez brothers killing their parents. These high-profile crimes are repeatedly played out in the media and their images stay with viewers. In addition, the media present through the news a constant stream of crime news that reinforces the impression that there is a great deal of terrible crime.

What is the reality about crime? The crime rate has been falling, in terms of both crimes reported to the police and actual victimization rates. Also, home burglary rates have dropped 50% over the past two decades, but in a recent poll only 7% of Americans believed that violent crime had declined in the past 5 years (Whitman & Loftus, 1996). The news does not give us an accurate picture of crime in society; instead, it continually tries to shock us with coverage of untypical events.

The media also do a poor job informing us about the major issues of the day—such as the federal deficit. A recent poll found that most people do not understand what is happening with federal deficits. About 70% thought that the deficit had increased over the past 5 years, 17% thought that it stayed the same, and only 12% picked the correct answer—that it was decreasing. The deficit has decreased from 4.7% of the gross domestic product in 1991 to 1.5% in 1996—the lowest level in 22 years (Dentzer, 1996). Apparently, people are either buying the political argument that we have a serious problem with an increasing deficit or they do not understand the difference between *deficit* and *national debt.* The deficit is the difference between what the federal government takes in and what it spends in a given year. The national debt is what the federal government owes, which is now about $5.2 trillion and growing each year. Either way, the news media have failed to inform people adequately. This is additional evidence that the news industry is not primarily focused on informing people.

Bagdikian (1992) argues that the most significant form of bias in journalism appears when a story is reported with a lack of context. The fear is that context would be only the journalist's opinion, and opinion must be avoided in "objective reporting." There is a difference between partisanship and placing facts in a reasonably informed context of history and social circumstance. "American journalism has not made a workable distinction between them" (p. 214). Bagdikian says that "there are powerful commercial pressures to remove social significance from standard American news. Informed social-economic context has unavoidable political implications which may disturb some in the audience whose world view differs" (p. 214). The media report undisputed facts about things, but ignore the meaning behind the facts and in so doing severely limit our ability to see that underlying meaning.

Becoming Literate About News

How can we protect ourselves from the illusion that we are being informed about the important events of the day when we faithfully expose ourselves to news messages in the media? The key is to develop higher media literacy with more elaborated knowledge structures and stronger higher order skills. There are four strategies that can help us achieve this: (a) Analyze the news perspective, (b) search for context, (c) develop alternative sources of information, and (d) be skeptical about public opinion. To apply these strategies in a balanced way, remember that both skills and knowledge can be developed cognitively, emotionally, aesthetically, and morally (see Table 6.1).

Analyze the News Perspective

Remember, news is a construction by editors and journalists. They make their selections and decisions based on their news perspective. When we watch a news program on TV or read a newspaper, we are learning as

Table 6.1 Examples of Different Kinds of Media Literacy Skills and Knowledge

	Skill	Knowledge
COGNITIVE	Ability to analyze a news story to identify important points	Knowledge of this topic from previous news stories
	Ability to use information base to determine if this news story presents a balanced set of facts or if key elements are left out	Knowledge of this topic from real-world sources and experiences
EMOTIONAL	Ability to put one's self into the position of different people in the story	Recalling from personal experience how it would feel to be in the situation in the story
	Ability to extend empathy to other people contiguous to the news story	
AESTHETIC	Ability to analyze visual syntax used to tell the story	Knowing the visual and audio elements that are available to TV news producers
	Ability to analyze the narrative structure	Knowing what kinds of narratives are available and the challenges in using them
	Ability to compare and contrast the artistry used to tell this story with that used to tell other stories	
MORAL	Ability to identify your personal moral stance in reacting to the people and events in the story	Accessing information about histories of the featured people in order to help explain their current actions
	Ability to separate people from actions	Having information about similar events to use as a template for this story
	Ability to determine relative responsibilities for the actions	
	Ability to consider extenuating circumstances	

much (or more) about those news organizations as we are about the events in the story. By keeping this in mind, we will be learning a great deal about news values while at the same time protecting ourselves from accepting the false belief that the news is a complete, accurate, and balanced picture of our world. Getting that kind of a picture should be our goal, but to achieve that goal, we must seek out many sources and be actively critical of their information.

Search for Context

Often we hear the phrase "news and information" and read this as a single concept rather than two, but it is important to make a distinction between news and information. News is that which is "new" in some sense. If it is something we already know, it is not news. News, therefore, must be out of the ordinary, that is, deviant. It must make us think, "This is very strange!" It must entertain or excite us in some way. In contrast, information tells us something of value about our world. It makes us think, "That is something important that I should know; that is something I can use."

Of course, this is not a neat, categorical distinction; that is, something can be both news and information. Sometimes the elements of news and of information are clearly identifiable. For example, a news story might begin with the announcement that J. J. Jones was arrested for jumping out of a tree and mugging an old woman as she walked through the city park. This is highly unusual and deviant, so it would be covered as news. People watching this story would say "Gee whiz. What is the world coming to?" If the story ends at this point, it is merely news. If it continues by putting the arrest in context, then it would most likely contain information, such as changes in the rate of crime in the park, reasons for the changes, the police department's success rate of solving those crimes, and the like. This context provides readers with something they can use—not just a fleeting emotional reaction. At higher levels of media literacy, people can more clearly see this distinction between news and information—and demand more information.

Develop Alternative Sources of Information

In their book *How to Watch TV News,* Postman and Powers (1992) say that before watching television news, people should prepare their minds through extensive reading about the world. In short, if individual messages in the media do not provide much context, then you need to search out the context for yourself. With important social, political, and economic issues, this usually means reading books and magazines. When you do this, make sure you read a variety of viewpoints. Context is more than getting exposure to one perspective on a problem—no matter how deep that may be. A fully developed knowledge structure requires in-depth exposure to the issue from as many different points of view as possible. If you find a detailed article on a topic in a conservative magazine, try to find the same topic treated in liberal, middle-of-the-road, and non-political magazines. Following this strategy will result in your knowledge structure on this topic being much more elaborate, and your resulting opinion will be much more sound.

Be Skeptical About Public Opinion

The problem with public opinion is not with measuring it accurately. There is a good technology that can do this well when opinions exist. The problem is that people often don't have an opinion about something, or they are not sure what their opinion is—they are ambivalent. To illustrate this, take your own informal opinion poll. Ask several of your friends for their opinions on the deficit, health care reform, campaign finance reform, capital punishment, and some local issues of concern to you. Notice that most respondents will feel that they should have opinions, and they will give them to you. Then ask them why they hold those opinions. Do they quote many facts in a logical, well-reasoned argument that provides a strong foundation for their opinions? Or do they act kind of embarrassed and defensive? Are their opinions deeply held and of strong value to them? Or are their opinions superficial and based on a few random facts? How do you feel about national policy being formulated on the basis of these opinions?

Summary

News is not a reflection of actual events; it is a construction by journalists who are subjected to many influences and constraints. Each day journalists must select from all of human activity those things that they feel should be reported. For each event selected, journalists must decide what the focus of the story should be so that it will hook an audience. Finally, news workers must assemble the news elements into a structure that will tell the story. In performing these tasks, journalists cannot be objective, so they try for the goal of being balanced. However, careful analyses of the news indicate that most stories are not balanced.

Formulas guide the construction process. The purpose of these formulas is to build the largest audience and thereby make the maximum revenue with the minimum expense for the industry. This has led to a focus on the trivial, the sensational, and the superficial. News now asks only for our eyeballs, not our gray matter. Of course there are exceptions, because the industry displays a range of practices; but when we look at the mainstream of news messages, these are the patterns we see most clearly.

Most of us feel we have a good understanding of current events, because we read newspapers and magazines and keep up with news on radio and television. Yet without a complete knowledge of the day's events themselves, we cannot tell if the news coverage is complete, balanced, or accurate. Instead, we must trust the media to give us the full picture; however, the media do not give us the full picture.

Being media literate requires us to search out a wide range of sources and to build stronger knowledge structures that give us the context that mainstream news programs do not provide. We, as the audience for news, need to demand more context from the media so that we can develop a fuller understanding of current events. We need to view news with skepticism, realizing it is a construction by journalists using their news frame to decide what is important. We must also be skeptical of public opinion. In short, we need to be more active and to be conscious in using higher order skills to process news messages.

 ## References

Altheide, D. L. (1976). *Creating reality: How TV news distorts events.* Beverly Hills, CA: Sage.

Ammons, L., Dimmick, J., & Pilotta, J. (1982). Crime news reporting in a black weekly. *Journalism Quarterly, 59,* 310-313.

Antunes, G., & Hurley, P. (1977). The representation of criminal events in Houston's two daily newspapers. *Journalism Quarterly, 54,* 756-760.

Bagdikian, B. (1992). *The media monopoly* (4th ed.). Boston: Beacon.

Becker, L. B., Kosicki, G. M., & Jones, F. (1992). Racial differences in evaluation of the mass media. *Journalism Quarterly, 69,* 124-134.

Bower, R. T. (1985). *The changing television audience in America.* New York: Columbia University Press.

Combs, B., & Slovic, P. (1979). Newspaper coverage of causes of death. *Journalism Quarterly, 56,* 837-843, 849.

Davie, W. R., & Lee, J.-S. (1993). Television news technology: Do more sources mean less diversity? *Journal of Broadcasting & Electronic Media, 39,* 453-464.

Davie, W. R., & Lee, J.-S. (1995). Sex, violence, and consonance/differentiation: An analysis of local TV news values. *Journalism & Mass Communication Quarterly, 72,* 128-138.

Dentzer, S. (1996, November 4). Delusions about deficits—and debt. *U. S. News & World Report,* p. 59.

Fedler, F., & Jordan, D. (1982). How emphasis on people affects coverage of crime. *Journalism Quarterly, 59,* 474-478.

Fewer adults reading newspapers, watching news. (1995, April 6). *Santa Barbara News-Press,* p. A5.

Fico, F., & Soffin, S. (1995). Fairness and balance of selected newspaper coverage of controversial national, state, and local issues. *Journalism & Mass Communication Quarterly, 72,* 621-633.

Fishman, M. (1980). *Manufacturing the news.* Austin: University of Texas Press.

Galician, M. L. (1986). Perceptions of good news and bad news on television. *Journalism Quarterly, 63,* 611-616.

Graber, D. A. (1988). *Processing the news: How people tame the information tide* (2nd ed.). New York: Longman.

Gunter, B. (1987). *Poor reception: Misunderstanding and forgetting broadcast news.* Hillsdale, NJ: Lawrence Erlbaum.

Hickey, J. (1972, April 8). What America thinks of TV's political coverage. *TV Guide,* pp. 6-11.

Hudson, T. J. (1992). Consonance in depiction of violent material in television news. *Journal of Broadcasting & Electronic Media, 36,* 411-425.

Jeffres, L. W. (1994). *Mass media processes* (2nd ed.). Prospect Heights, IL: Waveland.

Jensen, C. (1995). *Censored: The news that didn't make the news—and why.* New York: Four Walls Eight Windows.

Kaniss, P. (1996, December 19). Bad news: How electronic media muddle the message. *Philadelphia Inquirer,* p. A35.

Kim, K., & Barnett, G. A. (1996). The determinants of international news flow: A network analysis. *Communication Research, 23,* 323-352.

Larson, J. (1983). *Television's window on the world.* Norwood, NJ: Ablex.

Lee, M., & Solomon, N. (1990). *Unreliable sources: A guide to detecting bias in news media.* New York: Carol Publishing Group.

Meisler, S. (1994, March 16). Poll: News media outclass churches. *Seattle Times,* p. A5.

Parenti, M. (1986). *Inventing reality: The politics of the mass media.* New York: St. Martin's.

Postman, N., & Powers, S. (1992). *How to watch TV news.* New York: Penguin.

Potter, W. J. (1987). News from three worlds in prestige U.S. newspapers. *Journalism Quarterly, 64,* 73-79.

Randolph, E. (1997, April 22). Journalists find little neutrality over objective reporting. *Los Angeles Times,* p. A5.

Robinson, J. P., & Levy, M. R. (1986). *The main source.* Newbury Park, CA: Sage.

Roshier, B. (1981). The selection of crime news by the press. In S. Cohen & J. Young (Eds.), *The manufacture of news: Deviance, social problems and the mass media* (pp. 40-51). Beverly Hills, CA: Sage.

Shoemaker, P. J. (1987). The communication of deviance. In B. Dervin (Ed.), *Progress in communication science* (Vol. 8, pp. 151-175). Norwood, NJ: Ablex.

Shoemaker, P. J., Danielian, L. H., & Brendlinger, N. (1991). Deviant acts, risky business, and U.S. interest: The newsworthiness of world events. *Journalism Quarterly, 68,* 781-795.

Shoemaker, P. J., & Reese, S. D. (1996). *Mediating the message: Theories of influences on mass media content* (2nd ed.). White Plains, NY: Longman.

Slattery, K. L., & Hakanen, E. A. (1994). Sensationalism versus public affairs content of local TV news: Pennsylvania revisited. *Journal of Broadcasting & Electronic Media, 38,* 205-216.

Steele, J. E. (1995). Experts and the operational bias of television news: The case of the Persian Gulf war. *Journalism & Mass Communication Quarterly, 72,* 799-812.

Tuchman, G. (1978). *Making news: A study in the construction of reality.* New York: Free Press.

Windhauser, J. W., Seiter, J., & Winfree, L. T. (1990). Crime news in the Louisiana press, 1980 vs. 1985. *Journalism Quarterly, 67,* 72-78.

Whitman, D., & Loftus, M. (1996, December 16). Things are getting better? Who knew? *U.S. News & World Report,* pp. 30, 32.

 **Further Reading**

Altheide, D. L. (1976). *Creating reality: How TV news distorts events.* Beverly Hills, CA: Sage. (220 pages)

Altheide's ethnography is about how people in the news room create a community to get their news work done. His central thesis is that "events become news when transformed by the news perspective, and not because of their objective characteristics" (p. 173). He develops a construct called "news perspective" to explain how the staff select and treat the news. News perspective is a sort of bias that helps journalists simplify and organize the overwhelming amount of material they must sift through. This news bias is influenced by the constraints of commercialism, scheduling, technology, and competition. Altheide argues that "the organizational, practical, and other mundane features of news work promote a way of looking at events which fundamentally distorts them" (p. 24). "In order to make events news, news reporting decontextualizes and thereby changes them" (p. 25). The biggest influences on the news scene are commercialism (ratings and the drive for profit), competition (from other media), and the community context (especially political ties).

Fishman, M. (1980). *Manufacturing the news.* Austin: University of Texas Press. (180 pages, with index)

Fishman argues that journalists construct social reality for audiences. To do this, journalists develop routines so they don't have to invent new methods of reporting the world on every occasion they confront it. He makes a distinction between routine journalism and manipulated journalism. Routine journalism is the "good, plain, solid, honest, professional news reporting" that is produced through the "daily methods and standard practices of journalists" (p. 15). In contrast, manipulated journalism is the product of a political game in which the news is produced to service certain interests. Even routine journalism displays an ideological hegemony that can be traced to "the routines of news detection, interpretation, investigation, and assembly" (p. 18).

Jensen, C. (1995). *Censored: The news that didn't make the news—and why.* New York: Four Walls Eight Windows. (332 pages, with index)

Begun by Jensen in 1976, Project Censored invites journalists, scholars, librarians, and the general public to nominate stories they feel were not reported adequately during that year. From the hundreds of submissions, the list is reduced to 25 based on "the amount of coverage the story received, the national or international importance of the issue, the reliability of the source, and the potential impact the story may have" (p. 15). A blue ribbon panel of judges then selects the top 10 censored stories for the year.

Postman, N., & Powers, S. (1992). *How to watch TV news.* New York: Penguin. (178 pages, with index)

Postman and Powers argue that what television news says it is presenting and what it actually presents are two different things. Television claims to present the important happenings of the day that all citizens should know about, but what it really presents are superficial constructions designed to create large audiences for advertisers. The authors say that in order for people to prepare themselves to watch television news, they need to prepare their minds through extensive reading about the world.

Shoemaker, P. J., & Reese, S. D. (1996). *Mediating the message: Theories of influences on mass media content* (2nd ed.). White Plains, NY: Longman. (312 pages, with index)

Shoemaker and Reese review research on media content and build toward a theory with assumptions, propositions, and hypotheses. The first two chapters lay the foundation for studying media content. Chapter 3 presents what is known about media content. The heart of the book is the next six chapters, which review all the different types of influences on media content. In Chapter 10, the authors lay out an organization that shows how effects and content can be studied together. In the last chapter, they present their theory, which is really a list of assumptions, propositions, and hypotheses, in about 10 pages.

Tuchman, G. (1978). *Making news: A study in the construction of reality.* New York: Free Press. (244 pages)

Tuchman hung out in news rooms over a 10-year period in order to find out how news workers construct reality. She found that news workers developed a code of professionalism that was based on the interests of the organizations they worked for and that the central concept of this professionalism is the "news frame." The news frame is what news workers use to determine whether events "fit" as news.

Exercise 6.1   Practicing Analyzing the News

1. On a blank sheet of paper, draw the structure of Table 6.1. That is, create two columns: label one "Skills" and the other "Knowledge." Now create four rows, labeling them Cognitive, Emotional, Aesthetic, and Moral. Your table should have eight blocks. Make a copy of this table so you have two of them.

2. Now watch a news story on television. If you can, videotape the news story so you can watch it more than once.

3. After a single viewing, write down the skills and knowledge you needed to achieve a basic minimal understanding of what the story is about. Think in terms of your everyday viewing of news where you just want to monitor the surface facts in order to keep up with the day's major events.

4. Now think about the skills and knowledge you would need to achieve a much more complete understanding of the meaning of the event in the news story and write these on the second sheet. Think in terms of what it would take for you to be an expert on the event. This may require that you view the tape several times.

5. Look at what you have written in response to #4. Does it differ much from what you have written in response to #3? How much detail do you have in each of the eight blocks? With which blocks did you struggle the most? Why do you think you struggled there?

6. Compare the results of your tables with those of a friend. Did your friend have more details in certain blocks compared to yours? If so, did that additional detail extend your thinking? The more people's work you compare, the more you can see a range of differences.

Exercise 6.2   Inferring News Workers' Decisions

Gather together three or four newspapers for the same day—the more the better.

1. Look at the composition of the first page across those newspapers, and think about the differences and similarities of news perspectives.

   a. What are the major stories in terms of placement and size?

   b. What pictures and graphics are used? Are they used to present substance or are they used merely to make the page more appealing to the eye?

   c. How much of the front page is composed of non-news matter?

2. Read the major news stories.

   a. What criteria were used to select them?

   b. What type of element is emphasized in the stories—are the facts primary or is the context primary?

   c. Is the story balanced or are there obvious viewpoints ignored?

3. Look at the sections of the newspapers.

   a. Which sections are there? (such as sports, women, business, etc.)

   b. Look at how the space is allocated. How much space is given to ads? How much to hard news? How much to soft, entertainment-type news?

4. What happened within the past 24 hours that is not covered?

5. In summary, which of these newspapers do you think is the best and why?

6. Later today, listen to some news on the radio and watch some on television. How is the news different in these media compared to newspapers?

Exercise 6.3   Exercising Higher Order Skills

Think of some current event of interest to you. Now pretend you are an editor of a newspaper. What elements would you want to have in the story?

1. What sources would you want to interview?
2. What facts and figures would you want to have?
3. What historical contextual factors would you want?
4. Would you want visuals—graphics or photographs?

CHAPTER 7

Commercial Advertising

KEY IDEA *There is strong competition in markets that have only small differences among products, so advertising must create the illusion that the products have major differences and that the products will solve our problems. Over time, advertising has created a huge industry of dream makers who have an enormous influence on our economy, our society, and us.*

Economic Effects of Advertising
Price Levels
Distribution Costs
Market Entry
Value of Products
Consumer Demand
Consumer Choice

Effects on Individuals
Immediate Effects
Reinforcement
Opinion Creation
Opinion Conversion
Canalization
Inoculation
Purchase Behavior
Socialization
Over Time, Advertising Serves to Make Us Feel Insecure
Advertising Makes Us Believe in Unreality
Advertising Creates a Consumer-Focused Society
Subliminal Persuasion
Side Effects
Nutrition
Beauty
Drugs
Friendships
Effects on Children

Summary

W̲e live in an economy with a plethora of consumer products. For example, the average American supermarket offers more than 30,000 products for sale. Without advertising, most of those products would never get our attention. Even with advertising, many products do not break through all the clutter and make an impression on us as potential customers. More than 200 items are introduced every month, but despite all the research and testing, less than 10% of new products make it. Advertising is the means by which marketers get our attention, create favorable attitudes, stimulate us to buy their products or services, then reinforce that buying behavior.

Advertising Is Pervasive

How much advertising is there in this country? America is saturated with advertising. The United States has less than 10% of the world's population, but almost half of all the money spent for advertising is for ads to people in this country, and the amount continues to grow. In 1940 the industry spent $16 on each person in the country; by 1980 it was $260, and now it is over $600. This means that the number of ads also continues to grow. Between 1967 and 1982, the number of print and broadcast ads doubled. Between 1982 and 1997, the number doubled again.

We are literally constantly surrounded by ads. It has been estimated that the average American sees anywhere from 300 (McCarthy, 1991) to 1,600 (Clark, 1988) ad messages each day. Even if we take the low end of this range, that is about 110,000 messages each year or almost 20 ads for every waking hour. The number of ads competing for our attention continues to grow in all media and even in other outlets (see Table 7.1).

The Business of Advertising

The cost of doing business in the United States has increased greatly as advertising becomes a continually stronger economic force. In 1900, about $500 million was spent on all forms of advertising. By 1940, the amount was $2 billion; it took 40 years to multiply four times. In 1980 the amount was $60 billion, or a growth of 30 times in those 40 years. In 1997, the amount was close to $170 billion. It is difficult to comprehend how much money this is, so let's compare it to the expenditures of the federal government (see Table 7.2).

Advertisers pay huge sums to get their messages out in front of their target audiences. The cost of a 15-second ad in a high-rated prime-time network program can cost as much as $300,000, and a one-minute ad in the Super-bowl costs well over $1 million. Even with its outrageously high bid for the

139

Table 7.1 Pervasiveness of Advertising in America

- *Sixty percent of the typical newspaper is advertising.* Newspapers are now primarily vehicles for ads rather than for news. For example, the *New York Times* Sunday edition contains 350 pages of ads.

- *Movie theaters bombard viewers with ads.* A series of ads is projected on movie screens while the audience waits for the film to begin, and ads are embedded in the film itself because various companies pay to have their products prominently displayed throughout the plot: for example, Lays potato chips in *Poltergeist,* Wheaties in *Rocky III,* Budweiser beer in *Tootsie,* Milk Duds and Zagnut in *48 Hours.* There are 30 companies in Hollywood that place products within movies and TV shows. In *Santa Claus—The Movie,* McDonald's paid $1 million to the filmmakers to have a scene set in a specially constructed McDonald's restaurant; McDonald's also spent $18 million on promotion and network advertising for that film.

- *Some radio stations present 40 minutes of ads per hour.*

- *Ad clutter on television continues to grow.* Most television stations now present at least 40 ads per hour. During prime time, the Big Four (ABC, CBS, Fox, and NBC) aired an average of 14 minutes 15 seconds of ads and promos during every hour, and in daytime the time is even greater, with the average across all channels being almost 19 minutes per hour (Standard & Poor, 1996, p. M38).

- *Ads are embedded in some TV shows.* CBS's *The Price Is Right* gets $1 million in payments from product producers each year; this is in addition to the prizes the manufacturers give away on the show.

- *Children's TV programs contain a high proportion of ads.* Cable networks have the least amount (10:38 per hour on average) compared to broadcast networks (12:09) and independents (13:29) (Kunkel & Gantz, 1992).

- *Many children's shows are really non-stop advertising.* Some Hollywood films and television programs are nothing more than continuous advertising for themselves and the products that are associated with them. For example, the producers of the film *Superman* marketed more than 1,000 Superman-related products. They promoted the movie and the products with $6.5 billion of messages through radio, TV, magazines, and newspapers.

- *Now advertisers are creating their own shows, often naming them after their products.* For example, Nissan helped create a show to reach the target audience for its Pathfinder—a target of men and women with a median age of 40 and a median income of $75,000 (Matzer, 1996). Nissan's show, called *Pathfinder: Exotic Journeys,* is a half-hour travel adventure show hosted by model Cheryl Tiegs. Subaru is developing a competing travel series named after its vehicle Outback. Dodge has its action-adventure series called *Viper.* Dodge told producers it did not want sex or foul language so as to provide a "good, healthy family show that provides a showcase for our product" (p. D4). Dodge plans to develop Viper-related merchandise, much of it intended for children.

Table 7.1 Continued

- *Sporting events are themselves vehicles for ads.* Even the Olympics are advertising events. The 1984 Olympic Games in Los Angeles were the first to be supported entirely by commercial sponsorship, and they made a big profit. VISA alone spent $25 million on rights and promotions. One by one, all major sporting events are turning to sponsorships for funding.

- *Ads are in public schools.* Whittle Communications gives to all participating public schools the equipment needed to receive satellite programming and provides them with a 12-minute news program daily. Inserted in the programs are 2 minutes of ads paid for by companies interested in getting their ad messages in front of youngsters. About 65% of the public in national polls objected to this, but Whittle went ahead in the schools that did not object (Turow, 1992).

- *Ads appear everywhere.*

  Ads are on the sides of buildings, on taxis, busses, and even on the clothing of people walking in the streets.

  Talking billboards are fitted with a low-power radio transmitter that tells motorists where to tune for more information about the product advertised on the billboard (Horowitz, 1996).

  Ads have even moved into public rest rooms. Chicago's United Center sports arena charges advertisers $1,000 a year for an 8- by 11-inch space on its bathroom walls (Horowitz, 1996).

  Ads will also appear on police cars in Oxnard, California, where the City Council approved a money-raising plan to sell advertising space on police cruisers ("Police Cars," 1995).

  Pepsi-Cola has produced the first TV commercial in space by paying Russia to have their cosmonauts aboard the space station Mir display a can of Pepsi into space (Horowitz, 1996).

Table 7.2 Comparing Advertising Expenditures to Federal Spending in 1996

Medicaid (health care for the poor)	$39 billion
Education, job training and social services	$37 billion
Transportation (highways, airports, trains)	$28 billion
Agriculture	$17 billion
Science, space, and technology	$13 billion
Foreign aid	$10 billion

This totals "only" $144 billion or considerably less than what was spent on all forms of advertising in 1996.

broadcast rights to the 1996 Summer Olympics, NBC easily sold $600 million in ads to cover all the costs and make a profit (Standard & Poor, 1996, p. M38).

The two media that account for most of this ad revenue are newspapers and television (see Table 7.3). Newspapers have always accounted for the biggest share of the advertising dollar, but the television share has been growing. With cable television becoming more aggressive in the advertising market, it is likely that television ad revenues will surpass newspaper ad revenues in the near future.

While the saturation of advertising is mostly an American phenomenon, it has also spread to other countries. For example, in Italy the number of commercials rose from 45,000 to 400,000 in 2 years (Clark, 1988, p. 17). The money spent on ads as well as the number of ad messages is increasing rapidly in the rest of the world. In 1994, for the first time the amount of money spent on advertising in the United States ($150 billion) was less than the amount spent in the rest of the world combined ($178.4 billion) (Standard & Poor, 1996, p. M17).

The advertising business is made up of four components: the advertisers of products and services, the advertising agencies, the companies in the advertising research industry, and the media.

Advertisers

The top 100 leading advertisers account for 24% of all advertising placed in this country. These are the huge marketing companies. For example, in 1996 Procter & Gamble spent $8.3 billion on marketing to generate sales of $33 billion, which means that about 25% of the cost of those products goes into marketing ("Procter & Gamble," 1996).

Agencies

There are more than 10,000 advertising agencies in the United States. Most of these (about three quarters) are small, with fewer than five employees. These small agencies compete for local business. The national ads are almost totally controlled by several hundred very large agencies—some of which employ a thousand or more people, such as McCann Erikson Worldwide, Young and Rubicam, and J. Walter Thompson.

Advertising Research Industry

Marketing research has mushroomed in size and importance since the 1960s as we have shifted to an information society. Now the industry gener-

Table 7.3 Share of Total Advertising Expenditures by Medium in 1995

Share (%)	Medium
21.5	Newspapers
21.4	Television
18.6	Direct mail
6.6	Radio
5.9	Yellow pages
4.9	Magazines
0.8	Outdoor (billboards, posters, etc.)
20.3	Other (event sponsorships, in-store displays, etc.)

SOURCE: 1995 data from Standard & Poor's *Index to Surveys,* 1995, p. M17.

ates $6 billion a year by selling information to all kinds of advertisers, agencies, and media organizations. The industry is all over the world with over 40 countries that each generate at least $1 million in research sales every year. Even countries such as Yugoslavia, Kenya, and the Ivory Coast *each* have more than 14 firms doing research. Of the total amount of money spent on research in the entire world, 46% will be spent in the United States. In this country there are thousands of research firms, 200 of which are considered to be large national firms; the top 5 are very, very large.

Researchers have provided advertisers with a great deal of information about how people perceive things and what they like. Research has shown that time-compressed ads are better. In an effort to get more speech into commercials, devices have been developed to time compress them. People prefer a speech rate 25% faster than normal. When broadcast, viewers cannot tell the difference. The effect on recall is dramatic—about 35% better than non-time-compressed ads. Also, it has been found that when the human voice is most effective when it is pitched in the frequency range between 2 and 6 kilohertz, so engineers adjust voices to fit into this range. In headlines, 8 to 10 words are optimal in terms of recall. In mail order advertising, headlines between 6 and 12 words get the most coupon returns. Back pages of publications pull 150% better than inside pages.

Researchers have become very sophisticated. Some researchers measure brain waves by attaching electrodes to our scalps to monitor brain activity. Left-side brain activity indicates analytical thinking, right-side activity indicates emotions. Women have a great deal of right-side activity when a product spokesperson is too handsome—which means the spokesperson is distracting the viewer from processing the information, and he must be fired. Researchers look for CEP (Cortical Evoked Potential), which is the degree of attention the person is paying. People's brain waves don't lie, even though people will tell you lies for purposes of social desirability. For example, Cher rates very high on CEP as a TV personality with both men and women, but most women will say they do not want to see "that tramp" on television.

Media

Advertising is the principal source of revenue for most of the commercial media throughout the world. Media vehicles therefore try to construct audiences and then rent them out to advertisers.

One type of desirable audience is the quantity audience. This is what the commercial television networks strive to construct, especially for their prime-time period (8 p.m. to 11 p.m. each night). A prime-time show that gets a rating of 11 will be regarded as absolutely terrible. This means that only 11% of all households—"only" 19 million people—watched it. Even though this is more than all the people who saw the Broadway smash hit *Chorus Line* in its extraordinarily long 10-year run, the television networks are not satisfied with such a small audience.

Things are getting worse for the television networks, because they have been losing viewership. Until the late 1970s, they got a 95 share but their share has been shrinking each year. A difference of 1 rating point for a show over the course of a single season could mean almost $100 million to the network, so networks are strongly motivated to increase the size of their audiences as much as possible.

A second type of desirable audience is the niche audience, which is composed of a certain type of person that particular advertisers want to reach. For example, a company marketing sporting goods wants to reach adolescents and younger adults who like to participate in sports. Such a company would not want to incur the cost of advertising to a general audience on prime-time television, preferring instead to concentrate its ads on ESPN, in magazines like *Sports Illustrated,* and in the sports pages of local newspapers.

Advertising has also moved onto the World Wide Web. As of late 1996, 200 Web sites were already generating ad revenue, with the top 10 accounting for 60% of the total of $130 million (Greenstein, 1996). Companies marketing computer and telecommunication services were the largest advertisers.

There is a problem in determining exposures to the ad messages. Web sites record how many visits they receive each day, but don't know who those visitors are or whether 1,000 visits means 1,000 different people or only 100 people who each visit 10 times. Also, the brand new industry is trying to determine how to price ad space and whether the size of ads should be standardized. These problems will be worked out in the next few years, and advertisers will spend billions of dollars getting their messages in front of us as we navigate through the Internet.

Social Criticisms

The pervasiveness of advertising has become a concern of social critics. Some of them regard advertisers as unscrupulous manipulators who will do or say anything to get you to give them your money. Others regard advertisers as American heroes who are responsible for keeping the economy fired up by creatively encouraging more and more consumption. They see advertising as a glamorous profession for creative people—a fast track to a rewarding career.

Who is right? Is advertising good or is it bad? To think through the issue and arrive at your own answer, think past individual ads you might remember. Instead, focus on advertising as a dynamic and ambiguous field of stimuli, and think about how advertising might be affecting you in particular and society in general.

Remember also to keep in mind that when we think about the social effects of advertising, there are many perspectives. Determining who is right is difficult, because the arguments are based much less on facts than they are on different philosophies. Two differing philosophies are presented below.

Social Philosophers

John Kenneth Galbraith, Harvard economist and advisor to presidents, views advertising as primarily a negative force on society. He argues that a good deal of the consumption in high-production economies such as ours is unnecessary. Manufacturers produce much more than Americans need to consume. If it weren't for advertising, consumers would buy much less. Because the management of companies is under a great deal of pressure to increase production (in order to increase profits and to beat last year's goals), they use advertising heavily. They must create and control demand. Second, Galbraith believes that consumers can be persuaded. The minimum needs of consumers (food, clothing, and shelter) are affected little by advertising, but as a consumer's needs become psychological, advertising has a more powerful effect. Third, Galbraith believes this artificial demand—which is driven by advertising—leads to a misallocation of resources in society.

In contrast to Galbraith, historian David Potter regards advertising as a positive force on society. He sees advertising as a social institution comparable to the school and the church in its power to convey information and to teach values. An important value in America is the transforming of natural resources into abundance. Advertising supports this value and reinforces

Americans' inherent need to consume and to enjoy that consumption. However, Potter does express some concern that, unlike other institutions, advertising has no overriding responsibility to society. It has no motivation to seek the improvement of the individual or to impart qualities of social usefulness. Its only responsibility is to serve the marketing objectives of the company that pays for it.

Popular Criticisms

Over the years, there has been public criticism of advertising for all sorts of reasons. Seven of these issues are presented below. Notice that each criticism is controversial, that is, it is easy to see that there are people who would agree and others who would disagree with each of these types of criticisms. Notice that the difference of opinion in each of these seven issues can be traced to underlying philosophies about things other than advertising.

Advertising Debases the Language. Some people complain that advertising slogans misspell words, use poor grammar, and glorify slang. Whether you are bothered by this or not depends on your conception of what language is. Some people feel there is a proper way to speak, that not speaking properly is a sign of ignorance, and that it is offensive.

Other people view language as something that is organic and growing to meet the changing needs of a culture. They feel that bending and breaking the rules of grammar, spelling, and expression are signs of creativity and should be valued.

Advertising Makes Us Too Materialistic. How much is *too* much? Some people believe we should conserve natural resources and live at a lower level of consumption. Other people believe that we should always strive for more of everything; when it looks like we might run short of resources, we will be able to figure out a way to solve the problem.

Advertising Manipulates Us Into Buying Things We Don't Need. How do we define a need? If we stick to basic survival needs, then yes, advertisers ask us to buy many things beyond our absolutely basic needs for survival. Yet as the psychologist Abraham Maslow has pointed out, there are levels of needs beyond survival; these additional needs include safety needs, social needs, self-esteem needs, and self-actualization needs.

Advertising Is Offensive or in Bad Taste. Who is to determine what bad taste is? This is a personal judgment. Some people are offended when they see ads for condoms or feminine hygiene products, but others appreciate being exposed to this information.

Advertising Is Excessive. The average person is exposed to between 300 to 1,600 ads per day. Whether this is excessive or not is a matter of opinion. For example, when people are asked, "Do you think there is too much advertising on television?" about 70% of people say yes. But if they are asked, "Do you think that your being shown all this advertising is a fair price for you to pay to be able to see 'free' television?" again 70% will say yes (Miller, 1989).

Advertising Perpetuates Stereotypes. If advertisers are trying to sell to a wide audience, they must use stereotypes. You see a wider range of characters when looking at ads aimed at specialized targets, but even there, advertisers must develop the idea and not the person, and do it very quickly. A 15-second ad cannot develop a character in all the rich detail needed to make us feel that it is not a two-dimensional stereotype.

Advertisers Should Be More Socially Responsible. Advertisers depend on the goodwill of the public, so they should act socially responsible in order to maintain that goodwill. Advertisers, however, are often so motivated by the marketing perspective that they completely ignore their social responsibility. For example, for 50 years liquor manufacturers have not used television to advertise their products because of a sense of social responsibility, in a voluntary attempt to protect children and teenagers from seeing liquor ads. During the fall of 1996, however, Joseph E. Seagram & Sons began airing spots for two whisky brands on independent TV stations around the country. The company was motivated to begin using the powerful advertising medium in order to increase sales. In defense of his company's move, Tod Rodriguez, general sales manager, said, "There are a lot worse things than alcohol ads on TV" (Gellene, 1996). Many people found this incident very upsetting and the Seagram Company's reasoning very self-serving. Incidents like this illustrate the shift away from social responsibility and toward marketing.

Deception

Perhaps the most damaging criticism of advertising is that it is generally deceptive. In this sense, deception does not refer to the truthfulness of the claims in individual ads. Advertisers rarely present a blatant falsehood in their ads, because such lies are easy to spot and advertisers don't want to be fined for lying. Yet if an ad does not make a strong claim for its product, the ad has no persuasive value; if it does make a strong claim, it may be deemed as false or misleading. So what do advertisers do? They use puffery, that is, they puff up their product with exaggerations that are expressions of opinion rather than claims of some objective quality or characteristic of the product. Puffery gives viewers the illusion that they are being given important information about the product, but this illusion evaporates when we look more closely at the ad. For example, have you ever seen an ad where any of the following claims were made: "the best of its kind," "the most beautiful," or "the finest." These slogans at first seem to be telling us something, but upon closer examination, the claims turn out to be empty, because they cannot be tested.

Also, some ads present implied superiority claims, such as "Nothing beats a great pair of L'eggs" (pantyhose), "The ones to beat" (Chrysler K cars), and "Nobody does it better" (Winston Lights cigarettes). On the surface, these slogans imply that their products are superior, but when we examine them more closely we realize that they are not really making a clear comparison with another product.

Another element of puffery is when an ad tells the truth—but not the whole truth. For example, many brands that are labeled as a fruit juice drink contain only 10% fruit juice; the ad contains an element of truth, but it is misleading. Also, ads for many cereals show a brand as "part of this complete breakfast," which features several nutritious foods such as fruit, bread, and milk. This statement is literally truthful, but almost none of the nutrition in the claim comes from the cereal.

One of the most insightful criticisms about advertising deception has been advanced by Preston (1994), who points out that while most advertising is not technically false, it cannot be considered true, because most ads make implicit claims that cannot be tested. Advertisers know that explicit claims can be checked for truth and are therefore regulated, so they cannot make strong explicit claims. However, they can make very strong implicit claims. Preston says that this condition arises from a market of many brands with no real differences across them.

How do advertisers use puffery to suppress the truth? Jamieson and Campbell (1988) list the following tactics:

- Pseudo claims: An example of this is "X fights cavities," but we are not told how. Is it a chemical in the toothpaste, the movement of the brush on the teeth, or the habit of brushing?
- Comparison with an unidentified other: "X has better cleaning action." Better than what? Better than another brand? Better than not cleaning? There is an implied comparison that makes the product sound superior, but the claim really is meaningless.
- Comparison of the product to its earlier form: "X is new and improved!" Again, on the surface this seems like a good thing—until we start thinking about it.

What was wrong with the old version? What is wrong with this current version that will end up being new and improved again next year?

■ Irrelevant comparisons: "X is the best selling product of its kind." What kind? Maybe "kind" is defined so narrowly that there is only one brand of its kind. Maybe it is the best seller because it is the cheapest or because it wears out so fast.

■ Pseudo survey: "Four out of five dentists surveyed said they recommend X." Who are these four? Maybe they were paid to recommend the product.

■ Juxtaposition: A smiling person holds a product so that viewers associate happiness with the product. The ad makes no explicit claim, but implicitly it is telling you that the product will make you happy.

Advertising messages are thus designed to trick us into believing there is more to the product than there really is. They give us the illusion of making a strong claim when in fact the claims are weak or non-existent.

There are screening boards within the industry to filter out certain ads. Each network screens the ads it considers airing, over 50,000 each year (Jamieson & Campbell, 1988). However, the criterion for filtering out an ad is not whether it could potentially mislead the audience or not; instead, the filter is whether the ad could potentially offend the audience.

Public Opinion

With less than 10% of the world's population, the United States consumes nearly 30% of the planet's resources. Americans can choose from more than 30,000 supermarket items, including 200 kinds of cereal. Do we really need all these material products?

Americans say they are dissatisfied with materialism despite all the abundance. In a recent survey, 82% of Americans agreed that most of us buy and consume far more than we need, and 67% agreed that Americans cause many of the world's environmental problems, because we consume more resources and produce more waste than anyone else in the world (Koenenn, 1996).

Still, Americans have positive beliefs and attitudes about advertising. About 45% say they have a generally favorable attitude toward advertising, while only 15% have an unfavorable attitude. The rest have mixed opinions or are indifferent. Only 10% associate advertising with manipulation or propaganda.

Nevertheless, 80% of people feel that television advertising offers primarily deceptive persuasion, and only 17% regard TV advertising as a source of information (Norris, 1983; Soley & Reid, 1983).

When we look across the information on public opinion in this section, we can see that Americans have an almost schizophrenic attitude about advertising. We believe we are too materialistic but keep asking for more products. Despite the huge amount of advertising, which continues to grow each year, and despite the fact that most of us think advertising is deceptive, few of us hold a negative attitude about advertising.

Economic Effects of Advertising

If it weren't for advertising, most of us would base our purchasing decisions primarily on differences of quality and price among products, but advertising gives marketers more options in the ways they can appeal to consumers. Advertising has the ability to create all sorts of lifestyle images to surround the product and its usage. Over time, certain industries (home care, personal care, and over-the-counter drug products) have shifted away from competing over quality. Laundry detergents, for example, show very little difference in price or quality across different advertised brands; that is, there isn't much difference between the chemicals in the containers of different brands. However, there is fierce competition among those brands. Advertising campaigns have been very successful in making consumers believe there are enormous differences. This type of competition is not unique to laundry detergents—it is found with almost all products in supermarkets, drug stores, and even department stores. If price were the only (or primary) issue, then advertising would not be very interesting. Advertisers would not need creative agencies; they would only need to lower the price to compete more strongly.

Although most people say that price is the most important element in deciding which products to buy, large marketers do not want to compete on price. They don't want to differentiate on price, because they fear this could lead to a downward spiral of prices, and if that were to happen, many companies would lose money. Instead, they use advertising to create the illusion that differences exist in the products themselves so price will become irrelevant to the purchase decision. They attempt to make their products distinctive both in name and in function and assign some sort of consumer value to these distinctions. To do this, they use the tools of advertising and product promotion.

Given this type of competition in most industries, we need to consider a set of questions that probes the economic value of advertising. The answers to these questions are not always simple. It is a very complex, but important, endeavor to determine the influence of advertising on the economy. The answers are most usefully presented in a debate format, because we are not absolutely sure of the effect or because there are several simultaneous effects that often cancel each other out.

We now take a closer look at the effects of advertising on six issues for which it has been criticized: (a) price levels are maintained at artificially high levels when there is little price competition, (b) distribution costs rise with so many brands, (c) non-price competition makes market entry more difficult, (d) advertising inhibits innovation that would lead to greater value of products, (e) advertising artificially increases consumer demand, and (f) it decreases consumer choice.

Price Levels

Does non-price competition support artificially high prices? The answer appears to be no. For example, in the analgesic product category, there are about 225 brands, including Bayer, Bufferin, Tylenol, Advil, and others. The major brands are heavily advertised and compete well with the house (or generic) brands that do no advertising and thus have lower prices. The non-advertised brands account for only about one third of all tablets sold. Since two thirds of the units sold are at much higher prices, it cannot be said that those prices are "artificially high," because most consumers are willing to pay them. Thus, the prices of advertised brands are higher, but not "artificially" higher.

Distribution Costs

With so many products flooding the markets, is the cost of distribution higher than it would be if there were fewer brands? The opposite seems to be true. At the beginning of the 20th century, products were distributed through wholesale distributors, but now most products are distributed directly to discount mass merchandisers such as supermarkets and chain drug stores. Since the middleman is cut out, there is less handling of the product, and the distribution costs are reduced.

Market Entry

Does non-price competition make it more difficult for a new product to enter the market? This question is complex and sets up a debate in which both sides present convincing arguments.

One side says that market entry might be difficult but it is certainly not impossible. As evidence, it cites the fact that thousands of new products are introduced each year. Successful marketing companies consistently develop new products that invade markets of well-established brand franchises. Notable successes include Toyota and Datsun, Lite beer, and Aquafresh toothpaste. So while the costs to entry are raised by advertising, the barriers are not prohibitive. Costs for plants and machinery are far higher than the costs of advertising.

The other side of the debate says that new products require major advertising campaigns to break through the clutter and let potential customers know the product is available for purchase. Advertising costs can be very high, sometimes requiring $50 million to launch a new brand. Advertising costs have risen so high that even established marketers have become extremely conservative, and this has stifled innovation. Many companies are therefore going to low-budget, low-risk product spin-offs. For example, in 1989, there were 5,779 packaged goods introduced into the marketplace; two thirds of these were nothing more than improved formulations, new sizes, or new packages for existing brands.

An example of this is product extensions, which are less risky than new product introductions. LifeSavers introduced LifeSavers Holes; a package sells for the same price as a package of regular LifeSavers but it contains only half the amount of candy. The sweetest part of the deal is that the company saved millions of dollars on research, development, and marketing. In addition, there is Son of Snickers (peanut butter version), Arm & Hammer's carpet deodorizer and oven cleaner, Jell-O brand cake mixes, Band-Aids with pictures of the Cookie Monster and the Ninja Turtles, Double Stuff Oreos, Low Salt Ritz crackers, and Apple Newtons, to name a few.

Some critics see this as a dangerous trend. The short-term-perspective managers of the 1980s were too afraid to take a real risk, favoring instead surefire, low-cost product introductions, with the profits going right to the bottom line, making them look like heroes. However, the market place becomes less vital with the loss of genuine innovations.

Value of Products

Does advertising have an effect on the value of products? Advertising hasn't been shown to have much effect on changing the products themselves, that is, making the composition of the actual product more valuable. However, advertising does add value to a product by attaching a special image to it. People decide on products for many emotional and psychological reasons, and advertising creates the images to give consumers those reasons to use the product.

Advertising can also suggest additional ways of using the product, and this makes the product more valuable to the consumer without changing the product. For example, Arm & Hammer wanted to stimulate sales of its baking soda, so it told customers to use it to freshen the air in their refrigerators, as a toothpaste, and as a rug cleaner.

Consumer Demand

Does advertising have an effect on consumer demand? The answer is not a simple one. Our needs drive the development of new products, such as vehicles, computers, health aids, and even taste treats. Marketers then advertise these new products to let us know they exist. We then consume these new products, which leads to our becoming dependent on them, and our need for them becoming stronger. Each of these four is a link in the chain of influence. If one of the links is missing, the cycle is not completed. For example, if advertising fails to reach the intended targets, there will not be much consumption; or if a company recognizes a need but develops a poor product, people will not consume it. Only when all links are working is the cycle complete, and the demand grows. You can see that advertising is an important link in the cycle of increasing demand, but it is not responsible for this effect by itself. Advertising by itself serves not so much to increase demand for a product as to speed up the expansion of a demand that would come from favoring conditions.

Need → Product Development → Advertising → Consumption

Consumer Choice

Does advertising increase the number of product choices for consumers? There are two opposing answers to this question depending on how you define choice. On the one hand, we can argue that there is an enormous variety of choices. Just look in any store. The growth of advertising has made it possible for all these products to claim a position in the marketplace and to compete successfully. For example, in 1975 the average American supermarket offered an average of 9,000 items; by 1985 it offered 22,000; now there are more than 30,000 products.

On the other hand, we can argue that most of the different brands in a product category are the same. As new brands are added, we are not really given more choices; instead we are being offered more of the same old thing. For example, are LifeSavers Holes really a different choice than LifeSavers?

Effects on Individuals

Does advertising have a persuasive effect? The answer is, very definitely, yes. Advertising messages in the mass media have been found to have persuasive effects immediately after exposure as well as over the long term. They also have unintended as well as intended effects.

Immediate Effects

The mass media have been found to be influential in creating, shaping, and changing attitudes. Their main influence, however, is in reinforcing already held attitudes and behaviors.

Reinforcement. Advertising's most powerful effect is not in changing people's minds; instead, its power rests in reinforcing already held attitudes and behaviors. Reinforcement of attitudes consists of providing confirmatory information to make people feel that they believe the right thing. Advertising's main role is to reinforce our feelings of satisfaction for brands we already use.

Opinion Creation. The mass media are effective in creating opinions among people who were not previously inclined one way or another on an issue. If an issue is really new, people are less predisposed to moderate the influence of the advertising message.

Opinion Conversion. Conversion of opinion can, but rarely does, occur as an effect of an advertising message. When conversion does occur, the conditions that ordinarily prevent conversion are less active, or are non-existent, or actually encourage change themselves. Groups and group norms are usually weak or non-existent if conversion occurs. Group norms may also change in an effort to get to a more fundamental norm. Persons under cross-pressures are particularly susceptible to conversion, because their opinions are unstable.

The influence of interpersonal sources is more powerful than the influence of the mass media. Interpersonal sources are not necessary for conversion, however, and if they are not present or if a person has low influence, then the mass media are effective. Mass media are most effective in reaching opinion leaders, who in turn influence other persons.

Canalization. Advertisers use the media not to create a new need so much as to build a canal between a person's existing needs and that person's perception of the advertised product. For example, let's say you feel a high need to be popular. You see an ad in which a character who looks and acts like you is surrounded by the kinds of people you want to be your friends. The character is respected and admired because of drinking a certain cola or wearing a certain brand of jeans. The designer of this ad has built a psychological canal between your existing need to be popular and a particular product.

Inoculation. Medical doctors inoculate us against disease by exposing us to a mild form of the disease so that our bodies can build up an immunity; when we are later exposed to that disease, we are not susceptible and do not get sick. Sometimes advertisers try to inoculate their target audience to an upcoming claim about to be made by their competitors. In this case, advertisers design a message to belittle the competitors' claim, so that the target audience will think the claim is false or silly. Later, when the audience is exposed to the competitor's claim, they will not believe it.

Purchase Behavior. Advertising does, of course, have an effect on our purchasing behaviors. After all, this is the ultimate goal of all advertising campaigns. Ad campaigns try to lead us to this effect in steps. For example, first a company lets us know it is in business, then it builds a positive attitude toward its products, and eventually it triggers our behavior to try a product.

Socialization

Some effects of advertising show up only after thousands of exposures. As we are exposed to advertising messages, there is a great deal of subconscious processing as we assimilate the underlying meaning behind the ads. This is known as socialization. There are many socialization effects of advertising. Let's consider three such examples.

Over Time, Advertising Serves to Make Us Feel Insecure. One of the goals of advertising is to turn our critical perception away from the product—and toward ourselves. We are made to feel that there is something wrong with us or our lifestyles and that the product can change our life; seldom are the actual attributes or ingredients of the product mentioned. The world of mass advertising teaches us that want and frustration are caused by our own deficiencies and that the goods that will fix everything are within easy reach, before our eyes in dazzling abundance, available not only to the rich but to millions of ordinary citizens (Parenti, 1986).

Advertising Makes Us Believe in Unreality. Its glittering images present a world that is unreal—one in which problems are fairly simple and can be solved in 30 seconds or less. To have access to those solutions and hence a happy life, all we have to do is go to a store and buy something.

Advertising Creates a Consumer-Focused Society. Advertising turns everything into a product. Today, advertising is the product. It doesn't just sell the product, it becomes the product; that is, it becomes the sole reason why people buy and use certain products.

Advertising not only urges products on us, we become one of its products. Commercials sell products on the surface, but the more important and more long-term effect is to sell an entire way of life—a way of experiencing social reality that is compatible with the needs of a mass-production, mass-consumption, capitalist society (Parenti, 1986).

Subliminal Persuasion

Is there such a thing as subliminal persuasion through the mass media? There may be such an effect, but not in the way most people believe. The popularized version of subliminal persuasion reflects a conscious effort on the part of the sender to deceive viewers by adding something to a message that is not consciously perceivable by a person—though the person's unconscious mind "sees" that "extra message." For example, in the 1950s, James Vickery inserted messages of "Eat Popcorn" and "Drink Coke" into a theatrical film, and claimed that the theater audience bought much more popcorn and Coke, even though no one reported seeing the ads because they were projected too quickly. Later it was found that Vickery's results were a hoax. Even so, this story has entered our folklore, and many people believe that unscrupulous advertisers are inserting messages in ads in a way that those messages are below our threshold to perceive them consciously.

In the millions of ad messages produced each year some subliminal elements may be embedded, but there is a serious question about their effect. If an element is truly subliminal, it means that it is below our threshold of perception, that is, we cannot perceive it. If we can't perceive it, then it has no way to make an impression on our mind, either consciously or subconsciously.

There is a great deal of information that is perceived, then processed subconsciously rather than consciously—this is where we should place our concern. To illustrate, let's consider an example of an ad for Crest toothpaste. On the surface it is only an ad for a particular toothpaste, but it comes with several layers of deeper meaning embedded in the message that cannot be removed. At a deeper level, the ad is a message about the importance of health. At an even deeper level, it conveys a message about consumerism, that is, you need to buy something to clean your teeth; you cannot simply use water to brush your teeth. At a deeper level still is an implied endorsement of eating foods that contribute to tooth decay, but by using toothpaste you remove the risk— so a quick fix is possible, that is, you can have it both ways. You can see that a "simple" ad for a toothpaste carries with it several layers of meaning, some of which are consciously processed (buy Crest), and some of which are unconsciously processed (how to solve problems, the nature of health, etc.)

Side Effects

Commercial advertising is moderately successful in achieving its intended effects of creating positive attitudes toward products and a desire to use those products. Advertising can also have unintended side effects, such as shaping our beliefs about nutrition, beauty, drugs, and friendships, to name a few.

Nutrition. Children's beliefs about the nutritional values of various foods are shaped by advertising. Children are not critical evaluators of claims made in food advertising; they tend to accept advertising claims as being truthful, even when those claims are exaggerated. Later, when they find out that the advertised products are not as large or exciting or tasty, they are surprised and disappointed. Children's conceptions of what constitutes appropriate breakfast and snack food as well as their actual consumption patterns may be influenced by the products they see advertised. Also, Public Service Announcements (PSAs) have been shown to be effective in influencing children's attitudes and behaviors regarding nutrition and food consumption.

Beauty. Exposure to ads about beauty products causes adolescent girls to place more importance on beauty-related characteristics in their real-life personal roles. In addition, women who watch ads featuring thin models can have their perceptions of their own bodies altered (Myers & Biocca, 1992).

Drugs. Children's exposure to non-prescription drug advertising has no influence on their attitudes toward non-prescription medicines, their actual use of OTC (over-the-counter) drugs, or the use of illicit drugs. Also, there is no relationship between exposure to televised medicine advertising and use of illicit drugs.

The findings are different with cigarette advertising, however. Pollay and his colleagues (1996) conducted a study that tracked 20 years of cigarette ads and found that teenagers are three times as likely as adults to respond to cigarette ads. He also found that certain ad campaigns were particularly effective with children and adolescents; 79% of teen smokers use the brands depicted by the Marlboro Man, Joe Camel, and the fun couples of Newport.

Friendships. Viewers often become involved in a kind of parasocial interaction with celebrities who appear in television ads (Alperstein, 1991). Even when viewers are skeptical of the advertisement, they still feel a strong interaction. Thus the use of celebrities serves to capture attention and hold it long enough to create uncertainty in the mind of the viewer who does not like the product.

Effects on Children

Children are regarded as an important market by advertisers. American kids (4 to 18) have a combined annual allowance of $70 billion, the same amount as Finland's total gross domestic product ("Material Kids on the March," 1994). Younger children are targeted with ads on Saturday mornings when almost all the ads are for toys or food. Among the food ads, 90% are for junk food, such as sugary cereals, candy bars, potato chips, and fast foods (Wharton, 1991).

This leads parents and social critics to be concerned about children when it comes to advertising. Recall from Chapter 5 that young children have not developed to a point where they can understand certain elements about ads and therefore cannot protect themselves. Unfortunately, parents rarely view ads with their children and discuss them; they become mediators only when children are disappointed with a product or when they are frustrated that their parents won't buy it (Adler et al., 1980).

 ## Summary

Some people regard advertisers as unscrupulous manipulators who will do or say anything to get you to give them your money. They think advertising has changed the culture for the worse by making us too materialistic—creating a throw-away society of products, ideas, and people.

Other people regard advertisers as American heroes who are responsible for keeping the economy fired up by creatively encouraging more and more consumption. They claim that this has produced the richest society ever—one with the highest standard of living and the most variety in everything. They see advertising as a glamorous profession for creative people—a fast track to a rewarding career.

Who is right? Is advertising good or is it bad? What is the myth and what is the truth? You must decide for yourself. In making such a decision, it is risky to base it on a few intuitive impressions. Instead, it is much better to base your decision on a strong knowledge structure. Building such a knowledge structure requires you to be sensitive to the issues of how advertising influences businesses, the economy, critics, the public, language, and individuals—especially children. On almost all of these issues, there is a range of opinion. When you understand that range and the philosophies motivating different positions, you are better able to construct a well-reasoned opinion for yourself.

References

Adler, R. P., Lesser, G. S., Meringoff, L. K., Robertson, T. S., Rossiter, J. R., & Ward, S. (1980). *The effects of television advertising on children: Review and recommendations.* Lexington, MA: Lexington Books.

Alperstein, N. M. (1991). Imaginary social relationships with celebrities appearing in television commercials. *Journal of Broadcasting & Electronic Media, 35,* 43-58.

Clark, E. (1988). *The want makers.* New York: Penguin.

Gellene, D. (1996, September 24). Seagram plans more TV ads for whiskey. *Los Angeles Times,* p. D2.

Greenstein, J. (1996, December 2). Advertisers still trying to get a line on net users. *Los Angeles Times,* p. D5.

Horowitz, D. (1996, June 24). Nowhere to hide from advertisers. *Santa Barbara News-Press,* p. B7.

Jamieson, K. H., & Campbell, K. K. (1988)). *The interplay of influence* (2nd ed.). Belmont, CA: Wadsworth.

Koenenn, C. (1996, May 14). Let's get simple. *Los Angeles Times,* p. E1.

Kunkel, D., & Gantz, W. (1992). Children's television advertising in the multichannel environment. *Journal of Communication, 42*(3), 134-152.

Material kids are on the march. (1994, April). *NEA Today,* p. 10.

Matzer, M. (1996, November 26). TV sponsors find more visible outlets for their plugs. *Los Angeles Times,* pp. D1, D4.

McCarthy, M. J. (1991, March 22). Mind probe. *Wall Street Journal,* Sec. B, p. 3.

Miller, S. (Ed.). (1989). *America's watching: 30th anniversary 1959-1989.* New York: The Roper Organization.

Myers, P. N., Jr., & Biocca, F. A. (1992). The elastic body image: The effect of television advertising and programming on body image distortions in young women. *Journal of Communication, 42*(3), 108-133.

Norris, V. P. (1983). Consumer valuation of national ads. *Journalism Quarterly, 60,* 262-268.

Parenti, M. (1986). *Inventing reality: The politics of the mass media.* New York: St. Martin's.

Police cars to add advertisements. (1995, July 13). *Santa Barbara News-Press,* p. A4.

Pollay, R. W., Siddarth, S., Siegel, M., Haddix, A., Merritt, R. K., Giovino, G. A., & Eriksen, M. P. (1996). The last straw? Cigarette advertising and realized market shares among youths and adults, 1979-1993. *Journal of Marketing, 60,* 1-16.

Preston, I. (1994). *The tangled web they weave: Truth, falsity, & advertisers.* Madison: University of Wisconsin Press.

Procter & Gamble to cut advertising expenditures. (1996, February 19). *Santa Barbara News-Press,* p. B5.

Soley, L. C., & Reid, L. N. (1983). Satisfaction with the information value of magazine and television advertising. *Journal of Advertising, 12*(3), 27-31.

Standard & Poor. (1996, July). *Index to surveys.* New York: Author.

Turow, J. (1992). *Media systems in society.* New York: Longman.

Wharton, D. (1991, June 10). Let 'em eat junk? Fat chance, Solon says. *Variety,* p. 33.

Exercise 7.1   Becoming Sensitized to Advertising

1. How much advertising are you exposed to on a daily basis?

   For one day, carry around a sheet of paper in your pocket and every time you are exposed to an advertising message write down the following information: Record the time, the product advertised, and the channel. Remember, channels can be media (newspapers, television, radio, etc.) or they can be non-media such as posters (on walls, cars, kiosks, sidewalks, etc.), ads on clothing (sweatshirts, hats, footwear, etc.), and more.

   How many ads were you exposed to in one day? How many different channels were used? How many of these exposures did you seek out?

2. Watch one hour of television and write down each ad. Remember, a promo for a station or a television show counts as an advertisement.

   How many did you record? Were you surprised at the number?

3. Go through your local newspaper page by page and count the ads.

   Are you surprised at how many ads there are? Does this amount bother you? If so, would you be willing to pay more for the newspaper if all ads were eliminated? About 80% of a newspaper's revenue comes from advertising, so if your newspaper currently costs 50 cents, that cost would increase to about $4.00 per issue if subscribers like you had to contribute all of the newspaper's revenue.

4. On a piece of paper make two lists. On one side, list all the breakfast cereals you can remember. Then turn the paper over and list all the shampoos you can remember.

   Go to a supermarket and count how many different cereals and shampoos are on the shelves. Were you able to name them all? What percentage were you able to name? Of those you did not have on your list, can you recall anything about their advertising campaigns? If so, why do you think you could not remember them when you made your list?

5. Next time you go to the drugstore or the supermarket to shop, try buying as many non-advertised products as you can instead of the advertised brands you usually buy.

   How much money did you save? Is the savings worth it or do you feel that you have made a big mistake?

6. Run a taste test for your friends. Buy several brands of advertised cola and some obscure brands. Pour each brand into its own cup. Ask your friends to taste each and tell you which cola is in which cup. Could your friends guess the brands? Were they sure of their choices or were they making wild guesses?

CHAPTER 8

What Is Entertainment?

KEY IDEA *It is very important that we clearly see the major differences between the world of television entertainment and the real world, so that we can prevent the attractive fantasy on television from influencing our expectations about the world in which we must live.*

The World of Television Entertainment
Characters
Demographics in the Aggregate
Stereotypical Portrayals
Families
Plot Elements
Sex
Violence
Health
Themes

Entertainment Conventions
Marketing Perspective
Collaboration
Degree of Realism
Paradoxes

Summary

M ost of us feel we have a good understanding of media content, because we recognize the names and faces of movie stars. We know the words and melodies of popular songs. We can tell our friends about what happened in detail on our favorite television shows.

How much *do* we know about the patterns of characters, actions, and themes across the media entertainment landscape? For example, do you know what the themes are that underlie most of media entertainment? What *types* of characters are most prevalent in entertainment? Do you understand why media entertainment follows certain conventions? These are important questions.

These questions are addressed in this chapter, where the focus is on television entertainment. Why television? Because television is the most pervasive medium for entertainment. Almost all of us get most of our entertainment from television compared to any other medium. Because we take this exposure for granted, we are not conscious of the broad patterns of characterization and plot that we constantly see. Yet these patterns—even though they are fictional—can influence what we think about the real world.

The World of Television Entertainment

There is a wide variety of portrayals across the television landscape—all sorts of people, some heroic, some despicable, some mysterious, some simple. All kinds of settings—contemporary, historic, futuristic. All kinds of narratives, images, and messages. In this chapter, we are not concerned with the range and all the uniqueness. Instead, we are concerned with what is typical in the world of television entertainment. Why place the focus on the typical? Because the unusual stands out, but the typical is often overlooked. To test to see if you are aware of the typical patterns, turn to the end of the chapter and take the Quiz: Patterns in Television Entertainment.

To find out how you did on the Quiz, read on through this chapter to see what the answers are.

Characters

The characters on television are very different from people in real life. This is not to say that there are not types of people in real life like almost every character on television. Instead, in the aggregate, the world of television is different than the real world. The differences can be seen most clearly in two ways. First, when we look at patterns in the aggregate, we see that the demographic balance is very different in the television world compared to the real world. Second, we see that the characters are presented as stereotypes.

Demographics in the Aggregate. In this section we will examine the areas of gender balance, ethnicity, age, marital status, social class, and occupations.

As for gender, there are far more males than females portrayed on TV. When all roles on television are considered, males outnumber females three to one, but this imbalance varies by type of program. In soap operas there is a balance among the genders. In situation comedies and family dramas there is also almost a balance, but in police/detective shows males outnumber females five to one.

As for ethnicity, 80% of all characters are white Americans. Until the late 1960s, only 2% of television characters were African American; the figure climbed to about 10% and has stayed there ever since. Hispanics have not fared as well. Although Hispanics make up about 9% of the U.S. population, only 1.5% of all television characters are Hispanic.

As for age, young children and the elderly are under-represented on television. Fictional characters under 19 years of age make up only 10% of the total television population even though they make up one third of the U.S. population. Also, characters over 50 years of age account for about 15% of all television characters. Thus, three quarters of all television characters are between the ages of 20 and 50, while in the real world, only one third of the population is between these ages. The most dramatic imbalance is in the over-65 age group. Barely more than 2% of television characters are at least 65 years old, but 11% of our real-life population is in this age bracket.

The marital status of women on television is known more often than that of men. The marital status is obvious for about 80% of the women; it is obvious for about 45% of the men. Of those characters whose marital status you can tell, more than 50% of the females are married while less than one third of the males are married. Though divorce is more common on television now than it was in the early in 1970s, most females on television are still married.

As for socio-economic status (SES), almost half the characters on television are wealthy or ultra-wealthy, and very few (less than 10%) are lower class. As a character grows older, he or she is shown with a higher SES.

The higher prestige occupations are over-represented on fictional television. Nearly one third of the television labor force is professional and managerial, while in real life the figure is only 11%. Working class people are greatly under-represented, except for a few television-world professions. For example, prostitutes outnumber machinists by 12 to 1 on TV; there are twice as many doctors as welfare workers; eight times more butlers than miners; and 12 times more private detectives than production line workers.

The world of work may be changing a bit. Vande Berg and Streckfuss (1992) analyzed occupations in prime-time television and found that there was a slight increase in the representation of women and the heterogeneity (variety) of their occupational portrayals. Still, women remain under-represented and limited in their depictions in organizational settings. Males outnumbered females 2 to 1 in the workplace.

What can account for this dominance of males, whites, and youthful adults? Perhaps it is due to the demographics of the people who are television writers. Turow (1992) says that according to the Writers Guild of America, during the 1980s white males accounted for more than three quarters of the writers employed in film and TV. Minorities accounted for 2% of all writers. Writers under 40 account for over half of employment, and the share going to older writers is declining.

Stereotypical Portrayals. Characters in the television world are developed as stereotypes according to certain formulas that make the characters easily and quickly recognizable to viewers.

There is a good deal of gender stereotyping for both males and females. The main character, who is typically a white, middle-class youthful male, is usually portrayed with positive personality characteristics such as competency, leadership, and bravery. Women and minorities suffer by comparison. Male stereotyping has three main characteristics: First, males are portrayed in a greater variety of roles than are women. Males are usually shown on television as being more professionally oriented to business issues. Second, males are stereotyped as ambitious, competitive, smart, dominant, powerful, and violent. They are portrayed as being logical and rational. They successfully solve problems, usually without help. They are portrayed as being stable and not showing emotions except anger. They are more likely to share and cooperate with others, to sympathize and explain feelings to others, repair damage caused by others, and to resist the temptation to break societal rules. Third, males are shown doing typically male things, such as driving, participating in sports, using firearms, and conducting business. Emphasis on the male body is on strength, performance, and skill development.

As for females, there are two primary stereotypes. If a woman is single, she is often portrayed as a sex object; emphasis on the female body is on attractiveness, desirability, and youth. If a woman is a mother, she is usually portrayed as wise and nurturing.

Older characters, especially males, tend to be cast in comic roles. The elderly are likely to be treated with disrespect and are often shown as stubborn, eccentric, and foolish.

Families. There have been some changes in the way families are portrayed on television. On domestic comedies, the adult members of families are now more likely to interact more openly, and there is more expression of feelings in spousal relationships (Douglas & Olson, 1995). Adults are also shown as having more conflicts with children. As a result, the relational environment has become more conflictual and less cohesive in modern TV families than in TV families from earlier decades. Also, modern TV families are less able to manage day-to-day life and less able to socialize children effectively (Douglas & Olson, 1996).

Plot Elements

What narrative elements do entertainment programs present to move the plot along? Two of the most popular are sex and violence, because they serve the function of arousing the audience and getting viewers interested in following the action. Narrative elements about health tend to be more in the background of most plots.

Sex. Sexual activity on television has been prevalent since the 1970s (Buerkel-Rothfuss, 1993; Cassata & Skill, 1983). If we limit our definition of sex to visual depictions of intercourse, the rate fluctuates around one (Greenberg et al., 1993) or two (Fernandez-Collado, Greenberg, Korzenny, & Atkin, 1978) acts per hour of prime time. In soap operas, the rate is even higher.

If we expand the definition to include all visual depictions of sexual activity, such as kissing, petting, homosexuality, prostitution, and rape, the hourly rates go up to about 3 acts on prime time and 3.7 acts per hour on soap operas (Greenberg et al., 1993). When the definition is expanded further to include talk about sex as well as sexual imagery, the rate climbs to 16 instances per hour on prime time (Sapolsky & Tabarlet, 1990). Most of this talk about sex is on situation comedies in the early evening when it is presented in a humorous context.

Most of the sex is not presented responsibly from a health point of view. Schrag (1990) reports that American children and teens view an average of 14,000 sexual references and innuendos on television each year. Of these, less than 150 refer to the use of birth control, so that the rate of unprotected TV sex is very high, but there is a very low incidence of sexually transmitted diseases (STDs) or of pregnancies.

Violence. Scholars have been monitoring the amount of violence on television ever since the early 1950s. Depending on the definition of violence, it has been found on from 57% to 80% of all entertainment programs (Columbia Broadcasting System, 1980; Greenberg, Edison, Korzenny, Fernandez-Collado, & Atkin, 1980; Lichter & Lichter, 1983; "NCTV Says," 1983; Potter & Ware, 1987; Schramm, Lyle, & Parker, 1961; Signorielli, 1990; Smythe, 1954; Williams, Zabrack, & Joy, 1982).

The most consistent examination of television violence has been conducted by Gerbner and his associates (e.g., see Gerbner, Gross, Morgan, & Signorielli, 1980). Since the late 1960s, they have documented the frequency of violent acts that fit the following definition: the overt expression of physical force (with or without a weapon) against self or other, compelling action against one's will with the threat of being hurt or killed, or actually hurting or killing. Signorielli (1990) reports that from 1967 to 1985, the hourly rate has fluctuated between four and seven violent acts, with peaks occurring about every 4 years.

The most comprehensive analysis of violence on television has been conducted in the National Television Violence Study (1996), which analyzed the content of a total of 3,185 programs across 23 television channels from 6 a.m. until 11 p.m., 7 days a week, for the course of a television season. The researchers report that 57% of all programs analyzed had some violence and that one third of programs presented nine or more violent interactions. This study also examined the context within which the violence was presented and found that rarely was the violence punished and rarely were victims shown as suffering any harmful consequences. Also, 37% of the perpetrators of violence were portrayed as being attractive, and 44% of the acts were shown as being justified. These patterns led the researchers to conclude that not only was violence prevalent throughout the entire television landscape, but that it was typically shown as sanitized and glamorized.

Although the focus of most of the research about violence on television has been on physical forms, there is a growing awareness that verbal forms should also be examined. While it is possible that viewers might imitate the murders and physical assaults they see on television, it is far more probable that they would imitate the verbal acts of deception and insults. Granted, physical violence is almost always more harmful to its victims, but when the issue is the probability of imitation, then verbal forms of violence must also be seriously considered.

The research shows that verbal violence is at least as prevalent as physical violence. For example, Williams and colleagues (1982) report a rate of 9.5 acts of verbal violence as well as 9 acts of physical violence per hour on North American (U.S. and Canadian) television. Potter and Ware (1987) found about 8 acts of physical violence per hour and an additional 12 acts of verbal violence on American television. Also, Greenberg and his colleagues report that an average prime-time hour of television contains 22 acts of verbal aggression and 12 acts of physical aggression (Greenberg et al., 1980).

Health. Almost all television characters are portrayed as being healthy and active. Only 6% to 7% of major characters are portrayed as having had injuries or illnesses that require treatment. Pain, suffering, or medical help rarely follow violent activity. In children's programs, despite greater mayhem, only 3% of characters are shown receiving medical treatment.

When medical problems and help are portrayed, this is not in a preventative or therapeutic manner, but in a dramatic and social way. Physical illness and injury affect heroes and villains, males and females, and other groups, alike.

Illness and health are the most important problems on soap operas. About one half of all characters are involved in some health-related occurrence. Hardly anyone dies a natural death on television; but death is dealt with openly and realistically in soap operas.

Prime-time characters are not only healthy, they are also relatively safe from accidents, even though they rarely wear seat belts when they drive cars. What's more, they are rarely portrayed as suffering from impairments of any kind as a result of an accident.

Eating and drinking are frequent activities on entertainment programs. About 75% of all shows display this activity, but the eating is usually unhealthy. The traditional meals of breakfast, lunch, and dinner combined account for only about half of the eating; snacking accounts for the rest. Fruit is the snack in only 4% to 5% of the episodes.

Between 25% and 45% of the American population is overweight, but on television, only 6% of the males and 2% of the females are. Furthermore, TV characters do not gain weight from their high-calorie diets.

The use of alcohol, tobacco, and illegal drugs on television has dramatically declined over the years. Smoking was a frequent activity until the mid-1980s, when it almost completely disappeared except in reruns of old movies.

Alcohol use has also substantially declined. When it is presented now, it is frequently shown with negative consequences. Until the mid-1980s, alcohol consumption was common on television. The drinking of alcohol was shown twice as often as the drinking of coffee and tea, and 14 times that of soft drinks, 15 times that of water. It was shown as sociable, happy, and problem free. Also, alcohol use was rarely portrayed with any negative consequences. When negative consequences were shown, they were usually very slight, such as a temporary hangover. Despite high rates of consumption across many characters, only 1% of television drinkers were portrayed as having a drinking problem.

Prime-time characters are not shown with any kind of physical impairments. Rarely does a character even wear glasses—even in old age only one out of four characters wears them. Only 2% of characters on prime-time shows are physically handicapped. When they do appear, they tend to be older, less positively presented, and more likely to be victimized. Almost none appear on children's shows.

Estimates of the number of shows portraying a character as being mentally ill range from 11% to 17%, and characters portrayed as being mentally ill are shown in a negative stereotype. Almost half have no specified occupation and 75% have no family connections. They are shown to be active, confused, aggressive, dangerous, and unpredictable. In real life, mentally ill people are usually passive and withdrawn, frightened, and avoidant. On television they tend to be males, but in real life there is a balance between males and females.

As a group, the mentally ill on television are more likely to commit violence and to be victimized. For every 10 normal male victims of violence, there are 17 mentally ill victims of violence. Mentally ill people are not treated sympathetically; they are shown as the bad guys, that is, the crazed criminals who are very dangerous.

Doctors are greatly over-represented on television compared to their numbers in real life. Health care professionals dominate the ranks of professionals, despite the paucity of sick characters on television. There are proportionally five times as many doctors on TV as in real life. Only criminals or law enforcers are more numerous. Doctors are largely absent from children's programs.

Themes

Television is essentially a conservative medium; that is, it reflects what it believes are mainstream American values. Television programs do this so as not to offend people whom they want in their audiences. While television entertainment is substantially conservative, it continually tests the line of acceptability, especially in the areas of sex, violence, and language. Over time, that line changes as the public criticizes certain shows or portrayals or as the public remains silent and indicates its consent.

When we look at the broad patterns of characterization and plots over a long period of time, it becomes clear that television entertainment has some favorite themes (Comstock, 1989). Among these are the following:

1. *Material consumption is very satisfying.* It is obvious that advertisements tell us that material possessions bring happiness and confer status, but the entertainment programs present the same theme. Comstock says, "It is not solely that

so many stories revolve around the rich, but that in so many instances dwellings and their furnishings are beyond the means of those portrayed as occupying them" (p. 172). For example, the popular situation comedy *Friends* features Monica, a part-time cook, and Rachel, a waitress in a coffee house, who are shown supporting themselves in a well-furnished two-bedroom apartment in downtown Manhattan.

2. *The world is a mean and risky place.* There is a great deal of crime and violence throughout the television world.

3. *The TV world has turned the social pyramid upside down* by showing most characters as wealthy and powerful and very few of them as working class.

4. *Males are more powerful than females in terms of income, job status, and decision making.* This is slowly changing, but we are still far from a balance of power.

5. *Occupational status is highly valued.* Professional occupations are depicted as worthwhile and manual work as uninteresting. People attain the status of a worthwhile profession through upward mobility from the middle class. This upward mobility is accomplished through self-confidence and toughness; goodness of character alone is not enough. The movement upward is usually quick and painless.

6. *There are a few privileged professions where the people there are almost always shown as doing good and helping others.* Most businesspeople, however, are shady. Businesspeople are frequently shown cheating, embezzling, and even murdering. Businesses are frequently portrayed as polluting, abusing their power, and taking advantage of the gullible public.

7. *Law enforcers are over-represented as being successful, strong, and justified.* Private eyes are almost always shown as better than the police.

8. *There is a belief in the occult, life on other planets, life after death, and hidden, malevolent purposes behind the inexplicable.*

9. *A person's self-interest is very important.* People are motivated to get what they want regardless of the feelings of others. Examples include extramarital affairs, crime, hard-driving businesspeople, and police who disregard the rights of others to achieve their goals.

10. *There are often truly heroic acts portrayed* where there are daring rescues, selflessness, loyalty to others, and the struggle against difficult odds to do the right thing.

Entertainment Conventions

Now that we have seen some of the major patterns of entertainment content in the aggregate, let's explore some reasons why it appears the way it does.

Marketing Perspective

Over the years, the media have shifted from a product orientation to a marketing orientation. This means they no longer begin with developing what they think are the best products, then try to develop a need in the audience for the products. Instead, they begin with a focus on audiences and determine what audiences want. Then they develop products to fulfill those already existing needs. In the book industry, for example, editors used to search out those they thought were the best writers and publish them, assuming that the public would buy what the editors regarded as the best writing. Now book publishers have divided the reading public into niches (such as readers of romance, detective fiction, exposés, self-help, etc.), each with its own special tastes. Publishers conduct a great deal of research about what the people in each of these niches want to buy, then look for products that can satisfy those needs. This is the marketing perspective.

The same is true of television. Programmers spend their time developing a finely tuned sense of what kinds of entertainment the public wants to see. When a certain kind of story does very well, programmers commission sequels, spin-offs, and clones of that story, thinking that these new shows will also do very well. When the work of a particular writer, producer, director, or actor does well, demand for that person becomes high, and the price for his or her services increases dramatically.

People who work in the media "abide in a world where talent is a commodity whose value depends only in small part on brilliance and in large part on the revenues associated with popularity" (Comstock, 1989, p. 162). Therefore, talent becomes the ability to produce shows that will be popular.

What makes a show popular? This is the key question for producers and programmers. In general, popularity is achieved with creativity within a formula. All stories must have a quick beginning in which a problem is established, and conflict among attractive characters is continually heightened in order to keep viewers interested. At the end of each episode, the conflicts must be cleanly resolved to the satisfaction of the audience—unless the show is a continuing drama, in which case viewers must be left with some major unresolved conflicts so they will want to tune in to the next episode. All of this action must ebb and flow around breaks for commercials. In addition, each genre (situation comedies, action/adventures, soap operas, etc.) has its own special conventions. Also, producers must distort social reality on behalf of telling a good story. This means making characters bigger than life; telescoping time so that events happen much faster than in real life; and making conflicts more dramatic, leading to a climax that neatly resolves the action.

There is a need for creativity, diversity, and departures from the commonplace—but only within the established formulas. This means making stereotypical characters appear fresh and giving the traditional plots new twists. It also means pushing the envelope of what is considered acceptable. As Comstock (1989) points out,

> Much of what is on television today would not have been considered acceptable by broadcasters or the public 20 or even 10 years ago. Public tastes and social standards have changed, and television has made some contribution to these changes by probing the borders of convention accompanying each season. . . . These conventions of popular entertainment provide television, as they do other media, with rules that minimize the possibility of public offense. (p. 182)

Collaboration

The production of television entertainment is a collaborative process; that is, there are no shows that are the sole creation of a single person. Cantor (1980) shows that "the television drama is a product of exchange and struggle among several different organizations and groups" (p. 14). One of these groups is composed of the program creators, which includes writers, producers, directors, and actors. These people want the autonomy to create the shows they want. Another group consists of the programmers, who are the decision makers at the television networks. They want to build the largest audiences possible. A third group is the advertisers, who want to get their messages to their target audiences but they don't want to place those messages in programs that have content that might offend their target consumers. Fourth is the public, which consists of citizen action groups and federal regulators. The process of producing and programming television entertainment is influenced by social relationships, political agendas, and economic goals among these groups.

Degree of Realism

The television world may often appear like the real world, but it is very different. In the real world, most of life is fairly routine and uneventful, but on television, life is very arousing—full of strong emotion, high drama, and fast-paced action. Television ignores things that are not visually interesting, such as thinking by ourselves, reading, walking, and other quiet activities that make up much of our lives. Activities such as housework, running errands, and small talk with neighbors are vastly under-represented. Instead of ennobling our ordinary experiences, television suggests that they are not of sufficient interest to document.

The mythical world portrayed by television is characterized by an over-representation of the wealthy and an under-representation of the lower class, a lack of social problems, and the triumph of rigid middle-class morality. The demographic characteristics of television characters are highly skewed. Gender stereotyping is strong. Most characters appear very healthy but they rarely perform activities that contribute to their health or safety, and the settings are highly artificial.

Producers are under no obligation to present an accurate account of the mundane world. Their task is to build as large an audience as possible. To do this they must rely on all their creative powers to achieve a dramatic effect; they deliberately distort the world to surprise and startle, to make us examine things in new ways. Some creative types produce fantasy, which by definition is totally unlike real life—they do this to allow us to escape our lives and to see imaginative occurrences. Other producers, who try to capture real life, must do so in an intriguing manner. That is, they avoid presenting the mundane mainstream of real life and instead highlight the occurrences at the margins where there are particularly interesting people or events. This is real life in the sense that it could happen or even did happen.

The danger, of course, is that if our exposure is exclusively fantasy programming, we will only see the unusual, and that if we take those entertainment messages at face value without thinking deeper into the themes and lessons they are attempting to convey, we will come to believe the real world is like that fantasy world.

Television producers will never move to the mundane center of life. If they did, their audience would evaporate. This means that the way to deal with the unrealistic picture presented by television entertainment is *not* to pressure producers to make their world of fiction more realistic. That would be silly. Instead, it is to educate viewers about the patterns they are seeing but not recognizing in the world of television entertainment.

The world of television entertainment differs from the real world in many ways. As we move to cable and into the multi-channeled environment, it appears that the same content is spreading out over those channels rather than new forms of content emerging. For example, Kubey, Shifflet, Weerakkody, and Ukeiley (1996) analyzed content across 32 channels on a typical cable system and found the same patterns of gender, race, and age across all channels.

Paradoxes

The entertainment conventions just discussed are interesting, because they present some paradoxes. One of these paradoxes is that most media, especially television, are very conservative; that is, they do not want to offend anyone and lose audience members. Yet they continually take on controversial issues and push the envelope on violence, language, and sex. Many critics complain about television portrayals, especially those in the early evening when children are viewing, yet each year producers keep presenting language that is a bit more outrageous and sexually suggestive behaviors that leave less and less to the imagination.

Another paradox is the high amount of crime and violence on television and in the movies. People continually complain about this. Viewing a great deal of this type of content makes viewers feel more fearful of the real world, yet people continue to view it and to demand these types of programs.

A third paradox is with our mixed perceptions of the way violence is portrayed. The formula for violence tells us that it is okay for criminals to behave violently throughout a program as long as they are caught at the end of the show. This restores a sense of peace—at least until the commercials are over and the next show begins. We as viewers somehow feel comforted by all this violence. We also feel that it is permissible for police officers, private eyes, and good-guy vigilantes to break the law and to use violence as long as it is used successfully against the bad guys. We do not take an absolute position that violence is good or that it is bad; instead our position is situational: Violence is good if the people we like use it, and it is bad if other people use it.

Summary

The world of television entertainment differs from the real world in many ways. The television world contains fewer women, minorities, poor people, and blue-collar workers. Television plots are often driven by sex and violence, with unrealistic messages about health in the background. The television world is based on certain themes that continually appear.

The people who create this world must be creative within a rigid formula. Viewers want formulaic characters and plots so the entertainment is easy to follow, but they also want excitement and surprise. Producers who have the ability to create programs that fulfill these audience needs have a talent that is in high demand. Talent in this case is not defined in terms of artistic ability; rather, this talent is the ability to meet the needs of audiences.

References

Buerkel-Rothfuss, N. L. (1993). Background: What prior research shows. In B. S. Greenberg, J. D. Brown, & N. Buerkel-Rothfuss (Eds.), *Media, sex and the adolescent* (pp. 5-18). Cresskill, NJ: Hampton.
Cantor, M. G. (1980). *Prime-time television.* Beverly Hills, CA: Sage.

Cassata, M., & Skill, T. (1983). *Life on daytime television.* Norwood, NJ: Ablex.

Columbia Broadcasting System. (1980). *Network prime time violence tabulations for 1978-1979 season.* New York: CBS.

Comstock, G. (1989). *The evolution of American television.* Newbury Park, CA: Sage.

Douglas, W., & Olson, B. M. (1995). Beyond family structure: The family in domestic comedy. *Journal of Broadcasting & Electronic Media, 39,* 236-261.

Douglas, W., & Olson, B. M. (1996). Subversion of the American family? An examination of children and parents in television families. *Communication Research, 23,* 73-99.

Fernandez-Collado, C., Greenberg, B., Korzenny, F., & Atkin, C. (1978). Sexual intimacy and drug use in TV series. *Journal of Communication, 28*(3), 30-37.

Gerbner, G., Gross, L., Morgan, M., & Signorielli, N. (1980). The "mainstreaming" of America: Violence profile no. 11. *Journal of Communication, 30*(3), 10-29.

Greenberg, B. S., Edison, N., Korzenny, F., Fernandez-Collado, C., & Atkin, C. K. (1980). In B. S. Greenberg (Ed.), *Life on television: Content analysis of U.S. TV drama* (pp. 99-128). Norwood, NJ: Ablex.

Greenberg, B. S., Stanley, C., Siemicki, M., Heeter, C., Soderman, A., & Linsangan, R. (1993). Sex content on soaps and prime-time television series most viewed by adolescents. In B. S. Greenberg, J. D. Brown, & N. Buerkel-Rothfuss (Eds.), *Media, sex and the adolescent* (pp. 29-44). Cresskill, NJ: Hampton.

Kubey, R., Shifflet, M., Weerakkody, N., & Ukeiley, S. (1996). Demographic diversity on cable: Have the new cable channels made a difference in the representation of gender, race, and age? *Journal of Broadcasting & Electronic Media, 39,* 459-471.

Lichter, L. S., & Lichter, S. R. (1983). *Prime time crime.* Washington, DC: The Media Institute.

National Television Violence Study. (1996). *Scientific report.* Thousand Oaks, CA: Sage.

NCTV says violence on TV up 16%. (1983, March 22). *Broadcasting Magazine,* p. 63.

Potter, W. J., & Ware, W. (1987). An analysis of the contexts of antisocial acts on prime-time television. *Communication Research, 14,* 664-686.

Sapolsky, B., & Tabarlet, J. (1990). *Sex in prime time television: 1979 vs. 1989.* Unpublished manuscript, Department of Communication, Florida State University, Tallahassee.

Schrag, R. (1990). *Taming the wild tube: A family guide to television and video.* Chapel Hill: University of North Carolina Press.

Schramm, W., Lyle, J., & Parker, E. B. (1961). *Television in the lives of our children.* Stanford, CA: Stanford University Press.

Signorielli, N. (1990). Television's mean and dangerous world: A continuation of the cultural indicators perspective. In N. Signorielli & M. Morgan (Eds.), *Cultivation analysis: New directions in media effects research* (pp. 85-106). Newbury Park, CA: Sage.

Smythe, D. W. (1954). Reality as presented on television. *Public Opinion Quarterly, 18,* 143-156.

Turow, J. (1992). *Media systems in society.* New York: Longman.

Vande Berg, L. R., & Streckfuss, D. (1992). Prime-time television's portrayal of women and the world of work: A demographic profile. *Journal of Broadcasting & Electronic Media, 36,* 195-208.

Williams, T. M., Zabrack, M. L., & Joy, L. A. (1982). The portrayal of aggression on North American television. *Journal of Applied Social Psychology, 12,* 360-380.

Further Reading

Cantor, M. G. (1980). *Prime-time television.* Beverly Hills, CA: Sage. (143 pages, including index)

Written by a sociologist who spent 10 years interviewing actors, writers, and producers, this book explains how decisions about content are made in the television industry. Cantor presents a model to show that there are many forces that shape the development of any television program. The examples in the book are dated, but the principles still apply.

Greenberg, B. S. (1980). *Life on television.* Norwood NJ: Ablex. (204 pages, including index)

This is a classic content analysis of American television drama in the mid-1970s. Each of the 13 chapters addresses a different content topic, such as the demography of fictional characters, sex role portrayals, antisocial and prosocial behaviors, family interaction patterns, sexual intimacy, and drug use.

Lichter, S. R., Lichter, L. S., & Rothman, S. (1994). *Prime time: How TV portrays American culture.* Washington, DC: Regnery. (478 pages)

This is a look at what is on television, written from a critical humanistic perspective. There are few statistics but many examples from programs to illustrate the authors' main point that the world of television is very different from the real world of families, work, sex, crime, and the like.

National Television Violence Study. (1996). *Scientific report.* Thousand Oaks, CA: Sage. (568 pages with index)

The National Cable Television Association funded this $3.3-million project to examine the prevalence and context of violence on American television; the effects of warnings and advisories placed before violent programs; and the effect of public service announcements advocating the avoidance of violence. Some of the chapters are very technical and contain many statistics, but the overall report is the most comprehensive analysis of the issue of violence on television to date.

Quiz   Patterns in Television Entertainment

In answering the questions below, think about the television world in general. Try to think beyond your few favorite characters and focus on the entire television landscape.

Patterns With Characters

What percentage of all characters . . .

1. are female?   _____

2. are African American?   _____

3. are 65 years old or older?   _____

4. are wealthy or ultra-wealthy?   _____

5. have a professional or managerial job?   _____

6. are portrayed as having health problems requiring treatment?   _____

7. are overweight?   _____

Patterns With Plots

During a typical hour of television . . .

8. How many acts of sex (including kissing, hugging, etc.)   _____
   are there?

9. How many instances of talking about sex are there?   _____

10. How many acts of violence are there?   _____

Themes

List two themes that are prevalent behind television shows.

11. _____

12. _____

Exercise 8.1   Analyzing the Content of Television Entertainment

1. Write a definition for sexual behavior in a TV show. This is not as easy as it might first seem. You must consider such issues as what the characters must do for the behavior to be sexual, what the characters' intentions would have to be (a kiss or a hug is not always sexual). What about talk—if a character talks about what he or she wants to do, does that count?

2. Watch two different situation comedies and count how many acts occur that meet your definition. Note the gender, age, and ethnic background of the characters.

3. Discuss your results with others in class who did their own content analyses of sexual behavior.
   a. What is the range in the numbers of acts found? Can this range be attributed to differences in definitions or to differences in shows?
   b. Profile the types of characters who were most often involved in sexual activity.
   c. Are there any noticeable differences in character profiles across types of situation comedies?

4. Now try using your definition to analyze the content in soap operas, music videos, and action/adventure dramas.
   a. Do you see any big differences in the number of sexual acts across different types of shows?
   b. Do you see any big differences in the profiles of characters involved in sexual activity across shows?

5. Now think about how sex is portrayed in the television world.
   a. What types of activity are the most prevalent?
   b. How responsibly is sex portrayed in the television world—that is, how often are the physical and emotional risks discussed or considered? Is sex portrayed as a normal part of a loving, stable relationship or is it portrayed more as a game of conquest or as a source of silliness?
   c. Did you find anything in the patterns that surprised you?

6. What do you need to know about how sex is portrayed in the media and the role of sex in the real world in order for you to build a strong knowledge structure on this subject?

CHAPTER 9

Development of the
Mass Media Industries

KEY IDEA *The development of media industries generally moves from the innovation stage to growth, peak, decline, and then adaptation.*

This chapter views the media industries from a historical perspective. Why is this relevant for media literacy? It is important for you to understand the factors that have shaped the development of the media as competitive industries, so that you can better appreciate the messages they produce.

In this chapter, I ask you to think like a historian. This does not mean that I want you to memorize lots of names, facts, and dates. Instead, I want you to focus your attention on the broad patterns of how the media have developed over time and the factors that have shaped that development. In illustrating those patterns, I must present facts and dates, but these individual information bits are less important than the way they are arranged in patterns. Focus on the patterns and you will be able to organize good knowledge structures about the development of the mass media industries. With such knowledge structures, you will be able to continue your reading and thinking about the media industries much more efficiently.

Patterns of Development

Each of the mass media industries began as an innovation—that is, someone invented a technological means to disseminate information better. Business entrepreneurs then took that technology and marketed it. When the marketing was successful, the medium grew in popularity as more and more consumers spent time and money on exposure. After maturing, the popularity of each medium leveled off and then went through a period of decline. As is true of living organisms, each medium had to adapt to its environment in order to survive.

The life cycle metaphor provides a useful framework for examining the media industries, because it places focus on how they have developed. The life cycle metaphor contains five stages: innovation (or birth), penetration (or growth), peak (maturity), decline, and adaptation.

The innovation stage of a medium's development is characterized by a technological breakthrough that makes a channel of transmission possible or makes the transmission mass-like in its capacity to disseminate information. All mass media industries are initially influenced by technological innovations that create and improve their capabilities. Without certain technological inventions and developments, the mass media would not exist.

The innovation stage also requires successful marketing, or the medium will not be used by consumers and will not grow beyond this stage. A technological invention can create a channel of communication, but an entrepreneur with a vision must market that channel in order for it to be considered a mass medium. The entrepreneur must have a mass-like orientation, that is, he or

179

she must exploit the channel's potential to reach very large and broad audiences. For example, the shifting of individual newspapers away from being political newsletters for small readerships, toward a mass orientation to provide news to everyone, was a marketing innovation that transformed newspapers into a mass medium.

The penetration stage of a medium's development is characterized by the public's growing acceptance of that medium. As each medium grows, it is influenced by factors that shape its growth. These factors include the public's need and desire for the medium, additional innovations that change the appeal of other competing media, political and regulatory constraints, and the economic demands of the private enterprises that own and operate the mass media.

The public's reaction to a new medium is based on the medium's ability to satisfy an existing need or to create a widespread need that it can then satisfy. Once an innovation has created a new mass media channel, that channel needs to appeal to a very large, heterogeneous population if it is to be effective as a mass medium. This is called penetration. Television, as compared with other media, was the fastest to penetrate the American public. Acceptance was rapid and widespread as measured by the number of households buying a television set.

A medium can grow in three ways. First, it will grow if it can fulfill the needs of the public better than is currently being done by competing media. Television is so popular today, because it fulfills public needs better than the other media do. It has replaced radio as the general medium of entertainment, offering both a visual and an aural element to its messages. It is replacing the traditional distribution of films in theaters by giving the public the chance to see a wide range of current films (as well as older, classic films) in the comfort of the viewers' homes. It is trying to replace newspapers as the preferred medium of information on current events by offering more frequent, on-the-spot coverage of news events.

A second method of growing is based on fulfilling an existing need more efficiently (in terms of time and money) than other media. People with relatively low needs for information will turn to television news because, since they already own a television, it saves them the cost of subscribing to newspapers and magazines. Further, the news presented on television is fairly easy to grasp in a short time. Newspapers and magazines, while presenting more detailed information, require far more work on the part of the receiver in terms of the time and effort required to process and comprehend the message. It is relatively easy for people who watch a great deal of television to include news shows in their viewing schedules. Also, people with low reading skills favor television because of the time and effort they save by having someone read the news to them.

Third, a medium will grow if it can generate a new need or increase an existing need. Television is credited with increasing the American public's appetite for entertainment. The amount of viewing has steadily increased since television was first introduced, until now the average household has the set on for over 42 hours per week, most of which is entertainment programming.

The peak stage is reached when the medium commands the most attention from the public and generates the most revenue compared to other media. This usually happens when the medium has achieved maximum penetration; that is, when a very high percentage of households has accepted a medium and it cannot grow any further in penetration. Of course, it can continue to absorb a greater proportion of an audience member's time and money.

Eventually, the medium will be challenged by a newer one and will go into a decline. In the decline stage, the medium is characterized by loss of audience acceptance and therefore by a loss in revenues. A decline in audience support results not from an atrophied or shrinking need but by audience needs being satisfied better by a competing medium.

A medium enters the adaptation stage of development when it accepts the challenge of redefining its position in the media marketplace. Repositioning is achieved by identifying a new set of needs that the medium can meet, since the old set of needs it used to fulfill is now met better by another medium.

The Mass Media Profiled

This section provides a very brief sketch of the development of each of the nine major mass media. Remember, the organizing principle for each medium is the life cycle metaphor. Notice that there are several media that do not fully fit this metaphor, mainly because they have not experienced a peak stage.

Book Industry

The book publishing industry is currently in the adaptation stage.

Innovation: Book publishing was in its innovation stage in the mid-1400s when the printing press with moveable type was invented by Gutenberg. Book publishing was already well developed when this country was colonized. Until the 19th century, however, books were not a mass medium, because they were purchased and read by only the educated and the affluent.

Penetration: During the late 1800s, there were several developments that transformed books into a mass medium. First, paperback books began to be published in the late 1800s, and this made books more affordable for the masses. Second, public schools were widespread by 1900, and literacy was commonplace. Third, large publishing houses were being established, so many more books were being published and marketed.

Peak: It can be argued that book publishing has never reached a peak; that is, it has yet to achieve dominance among the mass media. However, it is still a successful industry, and it continues to grow. There are about 1,500 book publishers, each of which publishes five or more titles a year. About 2 billion books are sold each year.

Adaptation: The book industry competes well alongside the other mass media. To survive, it is sub-divided into niches to meet the specialized needs of different types of readers. Each year, about one third of published titles are mass market type publications; 24% are trade books; 20% are textbooks; 10% are for book clubs; and the rest are religious, professional, and specialty books.

Newspaper Industry

Newspapers have been a mass medium for over a century. They reached their peak in the period from 1900 to 1920 and have since adapted to being a local mass medium.

Innovation: The innovation stage for newspapers dates back to before the United States was founded. In the 1500s and 1600s in Europe there were printing presses and distribution processes that made newspapers a mass medium. As far as this country's history is concerned, the innovation in the newspaper industry came about through marketing rather than technology.

In looking back over the development of America's newspapers, it has been business decisions (more than technological innovations) that have shaped the industry's development. In the colonies, publishers made the decision to use the newspaper medium as a way to shape political opinion. These early newspapers were more like propaganda leaflets, and each had a very small circulation. By 1776 there were already 30 weekly newspapers in the colonies, and these newspapers went into a total of 40,000 homes. These newspapers were run by political parties that dictated their content. The parties used their own newspapers to present their version of the news.

By the 1830s, a big shift in the purpose of newspapers was taking place. Publishers became much more interested in making money with their newspapers. To increase revenues, publishers needed to build large circulations. They were no longer interested in appealing to a small, select group of political partisans. Instead, they needed to broaden their base, so they began hiring professional editors who could produce a product that responded to broader social needs and human interests rather than to narrow political ideologies.

Penetration: By the 1870s, newspapers had truly become a mass medium and the only one. The telegraph linked the newspapers instantaneously to far away locations where news was happening. New developments in printing presses made printing the papers faster and cheaper. By 1900, improved transportation allowed distribution to larger territories.

Newspapers were being run in a more business-like fashion. They used economies of scale to lower their unit costs, so that even though they were selling copies for a penny a piece, their profits were increasing dramatically, because their volume was growing so fast. Between 1880 and 1900, the number of newspapers in America more than doubled—from 850 to 1,967. In 1870, about 2.6 million copies were circulated daily to the 7.6 million households in America (1 out of every 3). By 1900, 93% of all households subscribed.

With the decline of political partisanship, more and more readers found a broad range of newspapers interesting and useful. Advertisers also found the medium very useful.

Peak: In 1919, newspapers reached their peak of penetration with the average household receiving about 1.4 newspapers per day. Also, the number of daily newspaper organizations was at a peak at almost 2,500 firms.

Decline: Newspapers began to decline as "the" mass medium in the 1930s and 1940s as radio then television took away newspapers' functions of providing information and entertainment. Even more devastating was that the newer media eroded the base of advertising, especially among the national advertisers. The number of daily newspapers declined to about 1,750 in 1945 and has remained at about that level ever since.

Adaptation: Since the 1950s, newspapers have redefined their role as a local medium for audiences and advertisers. Although the newspaper industry has experienced overall growth, most of that growth has not been in big cities; the circulation of city newspapers has remained static. Most of the growth in circulation has been in the daily and weekly newspapers of smaller communities.

Magazine Industry

Magazines are like newspapers in their pattern of growth. Currently, the magazine industry is in the adaptation stage and doing very well.

Innovation: The magazine industry began in the United States in 1741, but until 1800, no American magazine lasted more than 14 months. Advertising support was hard to find, so magazines struggled to stay in business. Circulations were very small, with the average circulation for a magazine being about 500 copies, and large-circulation magazines selling between 2,000 and 3,000 copies. Yet people kept beginning new magazines, and by the time of the Civil War, there were about 700 magazines published in this country.

Penetration: In the late 1800s, two things occurred that helped the penetration of the magazine industry. After the Civil War, education of children was made mandatory by most states, and the percentage of the population that could read grew dramatically. Also, in 1879 the U.S. Postal Service made low-cost mailing available. The magazine industry began a boom. By 1885 there were about 3,300 magazines, many with large circulations in the 100,000 range. In the 1890s, magazines cut their prices to below production costs to increase circulation, and advertising revenue became very important. By the end of the 19th century, magazines were a mass medium; that is, there were more than 50 well-known national magazines, each with a circulation above 100,000.

Peak: Magazines have never reached a "peak" in the sense that they became the dominant mass medium above all others. However, they did reach a peak of general popularity during the first several decades of this century. Throughout this time, the magazine industry continued to grow because of three important factors. First, people's incomes generally grew, so people had more money for discretionary spending. Second, people had more leisure time. Third, the spread of popular education greatly reduced the illiteracy rate and made people want to read more on a wider range of topics.

This peak is a different type of peak than that experienced by newspapers, because it is based on a unique set of characteristics that differentiate magazines from newspapers. Because magazines do not have to carry up-to-the-minute news, they can rely more on leisurely delivery systems. Also, they are capable of offering advertising to a national audience, because they are mailed out to subscribers all over the country. Newspapers have circulations limited to small geographical areas, such as their home cities.

Decline: The magazine industry declined between 1930 and 1960 primarily because of heavy competition from radio and then television for advertising dollars. National magazines had the hardest time surviving, not only because of the loss of advertising revenue but also because of steep rises in postal rates. In 1950, there were 40 magazines with a circulation of more than one million; within 25 years, all but 10 had gone out of business.

Adaptation: To survive, magazines became more specialized. They changed from trying to achieve a mass appeal audience and instead targeted narrow, specialized audiences. The 10,000 magazines that exist today do not really compete with each other for readers or advertisers. For example, *Boy's Life* does not compete with *Forbes,* and *Newsweek* does not compete with *Cosmopolitan.* Instead, each magazine tries to create a distinct audience base that it can rent to its own special set of advertisers. Magazines are niche oriented: They aim less at *quantity* of circulation and more for a *quality* audience. Within a niche, there is usually a small number of magazines that do compete against one another. For example, *Newsweek* competes against *Time* and *U.S. News & World Report* for essentially the same readers and the same national advertisers.

As an industry, magazines have adapted very well. Both the number of magazines and circulation are up. The number of magazines and other periodicals has increased steadily, from 5,500 in 1900 to 6,900 in 1950 to more than 10,000 today. Now, more than 50 magazines have circulations greater than one million. Still, the newspaper industry has a higher total circulation than the magazine industry. Monthly circulation of magazines is 350 million copies; newspapers, however, have a total circulation of 2 billion copies every month.

Today, the magazine publishing business is highly competitive, with easy entrance. An entrepreneur with a good editorial concept and a clear conception of an audience niche can be successful. Most new magazines fail unless the owner can afford to stay with it for several years until the magazine finds its audience and begins to make money.

Film Industry

Film as a mass medium reached its peak of popularity and productivity in the early 1940s. Then all indicators displayed a sharp decline until a bottoming out in the early 1960s. Since then, there has been an increase on most indicators.

Innovation: The film camera and projector were invented in the 1880s by Thomas Edison, who owned the early patents and therefore had a monopoly. By 1900, however, there were three companies marketing film equipment. These three companies also provided films and sold them outright to users as a way to encourage the sale of equipment. The stars of those early films were chosen not for their acting skill but for their contribution toward making a profitable picture. Films had self-contained plots, and theaters began to be alternatives to the live entertainment of vaudeville shows. In 1902, film exchanges were established so theaters could share films. Small producers consolidated their resources and formed studios for production and distribution.

Penetration: By 1905, there were over 100 film exchanges, and the producer-wholesaler-retailer chain in the film industry became institutionalized. Five years later there were 10,000 small theaters, each run by entrepreneurs who parlayed low investments into quick profits.

By 1912, producers were making full-length feature films. The Hollywood star system was devised as a way to lure people to the movies by attaching identifiable names to an otherwise unknown film and by merchandising the star as an important part of the distribution process. During this time, audiences began to regard movies less as a novelty and more as a habit.

Peak: The film industry's peak was reached in the 1920s and lasted into the late 1940s. Sound movies were introduced in 1927, and color was introduced in the late 1930s. In 1927, an average of 60 million people attended motion pictures *every week.* By 1929, this figure was over 110 million people. The number of commercial films released to theaters grew to a peak of 497 films in 1941. In the 1940s there were about 20,000 theaters. The number of movie seats, including car spaces at drive-ins, reached a peak of 11.1 million in 1935.

Decline: Starting in the late 1940s, the industry went into a decline. The federal government regarded some of the very large film companies as monopolies and forced them to sell parts of their operations. For example, it became illegal for a single film company to produce, distribute, and exhibit films, so the large film studios sold off their theaters.

After divestiture, film production companies lost some of their incentive, because they no longer owned their own theaters. Production dropped. The number of commercial films released to theaters declined steadily from the 1941 peak of a record 497 films to a low of 203 films released in 1963. Costs skyrocketed. Massive advertising and marketing campaigns were necessary to build audience interest for each picture.

Adaptation: Film studios adapted first by reducing their workforces and selling off their property. Not until 1970 did the production-distribution sector turn around financially.

Film studios now survive by producing films for television showing and by exporting films to foreign countries. Film companies began making films primarily for television showing in 1965, and have experienced steady growth since then. The United States is the world's largest film market, and for more than 50 years has been the world's largest exporter of filmed entertainment.

The exhibition sector of the film industry did not turn around financially until later, when it went into multiple ownership of theaters and to multi-screen theater complexes.

The film industry now has more establishments than newspaper and broadcast stations combined, due mostly to the large number of theaters. However, the number of motion picture theaters has decreased from about 12,000 to 10,000 (a multi-screen complex is counted as one theater). The number of companies involved in film production, distribution, and allied services increased from about 2,800 in the early 1960s to over 4,500 in the late 1990s.

Recording Industry

Innovation: Thomas Edison invented the original technology for recording and playback of sound in the 1880s.

Penetration: Several advances in technology helped to transform the recording industry into a mass medium. For example, in 1925 Joseph Maxwell invented the jukebox, which allowed recordings to compete with radio music. In 1947, the long-playing record was marketed. In the early 1950s, the sound quality of recordings was dramatically improved with high fidelity. In 1960, 34 million units were sold, and this climbed to almost 59 million in 1970.

Peak: Like book publishing, the recording industry never became a dominant mass medium.

Adaptation: The recording industry is still growing and competing well with the other mass media. There are now about 1,300 recording and tape production companies, 125 record processing plants, and 250 tape duplicating plants. Each year, the industry ships about 500 million units—CDs and tapes.

Technological advances keep changing the industry. Records were replaced by tapes (first eight tracks, then cassettes), then by CDs (compact discs). Advances in recording techniques (digital) and playback (boom boxes, car stereos, Walkmans, etc.) keep people buying new equipment, and the fast turnover in music styles and recording artists keeps people buying new recordings.

Radio Industry

Radio reached its peak of influence in the 1940s when it was the dominant national medium relied on for entertainment and information. In the 1950s, television began taking away radio's audience and advertisers. Radio adapted by identifying new needs in the audience, and it has survived. In fact, it is prospering once again.

Innovation: Radio broadcasting began in 1920 with the combination of the new technology and old content forms from vaudeville and the dramatic stage. In 1921 there were only five AM radio stations and only about 1% of all the households in this country had a receiver.

Penetration: Almost overnight, hundreds of radio stations sprang up. By 1923 there were more than 500 stations; almost half were owned by manufacturers of radio receivers who initiated the stations as a way of stimulating sales of receivers to the general public. Other kinds of organizations then started radio stations. Newspapers and other publishers had about 70 stations; educational institutions owned about 70, and retail stores owned over 60.

Radio evolved from a novelty into a business as it developed the concepts of stations, sponsorship through commercial advertising, and networks. Advertising was first introduced in 1922 as a way of supporting an increasingly expensive industry. Initially, advertising was of an institutional nature with price not being mentioned and the hard sell being avoided. More obtrusive types of advertising were not fully accepted until the late 1920s when advertising moved toward dominance. In 1927, 20% of radio network time was sponsored; by 1940, more than half was. Sponsors wanted to know how many people were being exposed to their ads, so by the 1930s, the use of standardized ratings research became a common practice.

Peak: Radio reached its peak in the 1930s and 1940s. In 1930, 50% of all households had at least one radio, and by 1947, this had increased to 93%. By 1936, there was an average of one receiver per household—in 10 years, this had doubled.

Decline: Until the 1950s, radio had the structural characteristics that television now has; that is, it had a distinctly national orientation for both entertainment and advertising. The radio networks played a crucial role in creating and maintaining this national orientation. Radio ceased being a general national medium around 1950, when national advertisers began shifting their business to television.

Adaptation: To survive, radio replaced its full-service, mass-oriented, family-type general entertainment format with specialized music formats designed to appeal to unique target audiences. By 1970, 300 radio stations were programmed to appeal primarily to African Americans; over 800 carried foreign language programs; and over 1,000 carried country-and-western music. They replaced their national advertising revenue with local ad revenue.

Also, to survive the competition with television, radio became more mobile. With car radios and portable radios, people could listen to music and news anywhere—especially places they could not take a television set. Between 1950 and 1970, radio set production almost doubled although the U.S. population increased by only one third.

Despite the dominance of television, the radio industry has adapted well and is very successful. The number of radio stations has grown dramatically from about 2,000 stations in 1948 to almost 12,000 today. They employ about 112,000 people.

Broadcast Television

Commercial broadcast television is in the later years of its peak stage. During its development, it was especially affected by minimal governmental regulation and a maximum profit motive on the part of owners. Commercial broadcast stations are licensed to provide service to local communities, but they can meet this requirement even if they affiliate with national networks or syndication services that feature national programming.

Innovation: By the 1930s, the technology had been developed to make the transmission and reception of television signals possible. The first television stations went on the air in 1941. These were commercial stations on the VHF (Very High Frequency) band. The first receivers were marketed in the New York City area where the first broadcast signals were. As stations began broadcasting in other metropolitan areas around the country, receivers were marketed in those additional areas. By 1948, 2.5% of all households owned a receiver.

Penetration: By 1950, there were 107 television stations; all of these early stations were on the VHF band (channels 2 through 13). By 1953, the first UHF stations (channels 14 through 83) went on the air. The number of stations grew to more than 500 by 1960.

By 1953, 50% penetration was reached; that is, half of all the households in the country had a television set that could receive a signal. Television was catching on even though few homes had much choice in viewing alternatives—only one third of television households could receive as many as four channels. By 1960 the average household had at least one set, and more than three quarters of sets were able to receive at least four broadcast channels.

During its penetration stage, television had a very strong impact on other media. It quickly became *the* entertainment medium, thus reducing movie attendance and radio listenership. Over time it also became a primary source of information, thus reducing readership of newspapers and magazines. The public accepted this medium so quickly because television was seen as fulfilling the audience's need for entertainment as well as information better than any other medium. Advertisers, especially national advertisers, were aware of this shifting media preference among audiences, and they too shifted their support to television. This resulted in severe reductions in national advertising support for magazines, newspapers, and radio.

Peak: By 1960, commercial television was the dominant mass medium. It accounted for a larger share of audience and advertising dollars than any other medium. Almost every area within the entire country had local television stations. The average household owned at least one set, it could receive about seven channels, and it was turned on over 5 hours per day. By 1980, 99.5% of all households had at least one television set; over 90% had color sets; over 50% had two or more sets.

Television was the dominant mass medium from the 1960s to the early 1990s. To maintain its peak, it had to attract the largest general audience and to generate the most revenue. In 1960, the television industry already had an annual revenue of more than $1 billion, with the profit before taxes about 20%. Revenues continued to climb, and profits stayed high as broadcast television created the largest audiences ever. Unless a prime-time program could generate an audience of at least 20 million viewers every week, it was canceled.

Because penetration is complete in this country and because the size of the U.S. population is not growing very much, the broadcast television industry can no longer substantially expand its audience. In fact, it must now work very hard just to hold on to the audience it does have as competing media (especially cable television) offer alternatives to broadcast television. Competition is very strong, and it will get even stronger. To appeal to as wide an audience as possible, programmers are very careful to present material that will not incur rejection or restriction. Stations therefore attempt to show the least objectionable programming. To determine what is least objectionable, television relies upon proven formulas. This is why programming is becoming both less diversified and more limited. When a particular program becomes very popular, programmers try to develop similar shows in an effort to share in the popularity. Because a popular show generates a great deal more revenue than an unpopular one, programmers are unwilling to take a chance on new types of shows for fear that they might be held responsible for losing money for the station or the network.

Perhaps in the future, stations will not try to achieve so broad an appeal and instead choose a particular target group for their programming and advertising. If this happens, then programming will become more specialized and diversified.

Present character: Broadcast television is still the dominant medium. It has a higher reach than any other medium: TV reaches 88% of the U.S. population, radio 71%, newspapers 56%, and magazines 34%. There are now about 1,600 broadcast television stations, and they generate revenue of more than $21 billion each year.

But there are the beginnings of trouble for broadcast television. The networks and stations are losing viewership. Until the late 1970s, they got 95 share. The combined viewing of TV networks (ABC, CBS, and NBC) during prime time dropped to 61% in the 1991-1992 season (*Multichannel News,* 1993) and is expected to dip under 50% by 2000. People are finding alternatives to broadcast television. Cable television is expanding, and with VCR penetration at 74%, viewers are renting tapes or are re-programming the shows of broadcast television, which reduces the power of station programmers who try to create the habit of viewing. In addition, there is competition from pay channels and computer delivered services.

Cable Television

Cable television is the newest of the mass media. It grew rapidly through the penetration stage and is entering its peak stage as it begins to eclipse broadcast television.

Innovation: The growth of cable was slow at first. It began in the 1940s as a means of delivering television signals to areas unable to receive broadcast signals because of distance or interference. Until the 1950s, cable systems were quite small; each had a few hundred homes as subscribers and carried only three or four broadcast signals from the closest stations. The systems were generally confined to mountainous areas with little or no reception.

The ownership of a cable system was typically a small local company, often in some related primary line of business like selling TV receivers. The cable systems were marginally successful as businesses. By 1952 there were only 70 systems, and they served a combined total of 14,000 subscribers, which represented less than 0.1% of all television households at the time. Growth was slow. Not until the late 1950s was 1% of television households reached by cable.

Penetration: By 1960, there were 640 systems with a total of 650,000 subscribers, which was 1.4% of all households for an average of 1,016 subscribers per system. Until the mid 1960s, cable was primarily a retransmission service offering only the few signals from the closest stations. By the mid-1960s, cable began expanding into areas that already received clear broadcasting signals without help, such as the urban areas of Los Angeles and New

York City. Cable systems also began adding channels to make their services more attractive to potential subscribers. In 1970, 3% of the systems offered more than 12 channels; by 1976, 26% of the systems did. By the late 1960s, some cable systems were even originating programming of their own.

In the early years of cable, broadcasters welcomed cable systems as a means of extending their broadcast viewership into areas their signal could not reach. Then cable systems began using microwave relays to bring in more distant signals, such as broadcast stations from far away markets, as well as signals from some superstations such as WTBS in Atlanta and WGN in Chicago. These new channels were in direct competition with local broadcasters, and the local broadcasters began to resent cable systems. Broadcasters began complaining that cable was receiving payment from subscribers but not giving any money to the broadcasters who originated and paid for the production of the programs. Cable systems were no longer viewed by broadcasters as expanders of audiences but as direct competition. So in 1962, the FCC (Federal Communications Commission) began to regulate the selection of programming on cable systems. The FCC decided to allow cable systems to continue to use microwave relays and to bring in distant signals. If a cable system did this, it would also have to carry all the local signals; that is, it could not ignore a local broadcast affiliate and instead bring in a station from another market in its place. Many other regulations were added during the next decade until 1972 when a period of deregulation began.

By 1985 there were 6,600 cable systems serving a total of 32 million subscribers, which represented 37.7% of all television households. The 50% penetration mark was reached in early 1988.

Peak: It looks like cable television may be entering the peak stage. By the mid-1990s, cable's total revenues—$27.5 billion—surpassed those of the broadcast television industry. Most of that revenue is from subscriptions. Cable is now competing with broadcast for advertising dollars and is being very successful. In 1990 it generated $2.4 billion in advertising revenue, and predictions are that that will increase dramatically (Koplovitz, 1990).

Cable systems now rival the networks in programming power. With more than 11,000 cable systems operating, there are about seven systems for every broadcast station in this country. Unlike the networks, there are no limitations on ownership. A cable company may buy one or many other cable systems. Such a conglomerate is called an MSO (Multiple System Operator). The number of MSOs is growing, and some of the larger ones rival the commercial television networks in terms of the size of the audience controlled through programming. With about 130,000 employees, cable supports more people than broadcast television.

Computers

Computers are in the penetration stage and growing rapidly at 30% per year (*Hoover's Guide,* 1996). There are now 40 million personal computers in U.S. homes; and half of all home computers have a compact disc (CD) player (Maney, 1995). More than 97% of the country's schools have computers—1 for every 11 students, which is up from 1 computer for every 63 students just 10 years ago (Intelligence Infocorp, 1996).

One of the important reasons for computers moving quickly and successfully through the penetration stage is the digitization of information and images. Once a message has been digitized (translated into a standard computer-readable code), it can be moved seamlessly across all media—print, audio, visual, and motion. For example, a picture can be copied from a magazine and inserted into a home video. What controls the manipulation of these digital packets is a computer. This is why the computer is such an important technology and why it can be regarded as a medium. It also represents a fundamentally different type of medium from everything that came before. All media up to this point were channels to deliver uniform, intact messages from senders. Now, with a computer, each of us can customize messages by cutting and pasting from a wide range of sources and media, then send these messages out for display to a particular friend, to a great number of people simultaneously through e-mail, or simply make them available on the World Wide Web where millions of people can come and visit the messages and even download them to their own computers where they can undertake further manipulation.

With a computer, a person can access information as never before. In the United States there are more than 12,000 electronic information services that offer consumers everything from complex electronic legal libraries to reports on local surfing conditions, and almost everything imaginable in between. These services are offered by hundreds of different providers, including newspapers, cable TV companies, broadcasters, database services, start up entrepreneurs, and many more (Black, 1992).

A recent study has found that about 26% of adults in the United States (or 51 million people) have access to the worldwide computer network known as the Internet (Bimber, 1996). The Internet is a network of computer networks designed to move information around among users. It has no centralized controlling body or mechanism. It was originally set up by the Pentagon in 1969 as a decentralized structure so as to make it resistant to breakdown by attack. A bit of information sent across the country has many alternative paths it can take, so if one path is blocked (or down), the information can take one of the many other alternatives and arrive just as quickly. The Pentagon originated the system by linking up government computers with those at universities across the country. Since that time, many other networks from all over the world have attached themselves to the Internet. Since 1975, its cost has been supported by the National Science Foundation, but that responsibility is now being turned over to businesses who want to use the Internet to advertise their products and services.

Anyone with a personal computer (PC), a modem, and some accessing software can get onto the Internet. Once on the Internet, people can cruise around the different parts, by sending e-mail to specific people, posting messages on bulletin boards, entering chat rooms where interactive conversations on a particular topic take place, playing games, and downloading information, images, or software that others have made available. These services have become very popular and are attracting new audience members constantly. Every minute, 40 novices log on to the Internet for the first time. Every year, the number of users doubles. In 1996 there were 40 million users worldwide. Also, every 10 minutes a new corporate or academic network is added; by 1996 up to 100,000 networks were linked. Data traffic increased over 300 times in the past few years (Simons, 1996).

A popular part of the Internet is the World Wide Web, which is like a notebook. Any user can create his or her own "Web page," which is usually a billboard with graphics. Many businesses have created Web pages to display their services. Users who visit a Web page can usually click on one of the displayed icons and get more information about that person, service, or product.

This new industry hopes to take customers and revenues away from such other industries as catalog houses and book clubs that do $350 billion in revenues; video stores that rent 3.6 billion videos a year; and video games that sell at 73 million units per year (Kantrowitz, 1993). Lots of money must be spent to provide the infrastructure to make this new medium financially successful. Fiber-optic cables expand the conduit of information into American households. In 1991, 5.6 million miles of fiber optics had been completed, and by the year 2000 there will be 40 million homes connected (Kantrowitz, 1993). Local phone companies are spending about $100 billion to build networks to connect all homes and buildings with fiber-optic cable—a job that is expected to be completed by 2010 (Maney, 1995). Fiber-optic cable is able to carry a tremendous amount of information. Old phone lines can transmit a few pages of text per second, but a single hair-thin fiber-optic line can transmit about 5,000 pages per second.

Clearly, the computer medium is doing very well in the penetration stage. Many companies are successfully selling hardware and software services. Whether computers grow to a peak and replace television as the dominant medium remains to be seen.

General Employment Trends

Related to the growth and development of the media industries are the questions, "How large are the various mass media industries in terms of employees?" and "What are the characteristics of the people who work in the mass media?" You may be surprised to find that even though the media are so pervasive, less than 1% of the U.S. workforce is employed by a media company. You should have some sense of the gender of the people who create the messages and control their distribution.

Overall Size of the Workforce

The media are healthy and expanding in terms of employment. The total workforce across the media industries generally grows about 3% each year. What might surprise you is that the number of people who work in these industries is rather small, given the high visibility and powerful influence of the industries (see Table 9.1).

Newspapers are by far the largest employer; they also have the largest number of establishments of dailies and weeklies. There is a big drop to cable TV, where most of the employers are very small companies with only a handful of workers, mostly cable installers and maintenance people. The large MSOs also have sales and administrative staffs in addition to their maintenance people.

Radio and broadcast television stations are organized in a similar fashion with departments for sales, production, engineering, and administration.

Table 9.1 Employment Patterns

Medium	Number of Establishments	Number of Employees
Newspapers	8,644	416,000
Cable TV	4,468	128,963
Magazines	4,695	117,000
Radio	6,956	112,385
Broadcast TV	1,593	109,370
Books	2,503	84,000

SOURCE: Figures from *Statistical Abstract of the United States, 1995.*

Demographic Patterns

Looking at the total labor force in this country, we can see a trend toward more and more women becoming employed outside the home. Now about 45% of the labor force is female. With the mass media industries, there has been a growth in the number of females employed, but there are many more males working in the mass media than there are females.

The media industries that employ the highest percentage of females are magazines and books, where women make up more than 50% of the labor force. The greatest growth in terms of percentage of females employed has been in the newspaper industry. In 1960, only 20% of all people working on newspapers were female, but this percentage has been growing each year. A major reason for this increase is because newspapers have been moving away from the traditionally male-oriented press jobs and into more clerical and technologically oriented jobs. In broadcasting, 23% of all employees were female in 1960. This remained fairly static until 1972, when the federal government began monitoring hiring practices in businesses. Since that time there has been a gradual increase to the current figure of about 30%.

In motion pictures, about 40% of all employees are female, but this changes depending on the sector of the industry. In the large exhibition sector, about 45% of all employees are female. In the production sector (actors, directors, producers and writers), however, 95% are men.

A popular profession within the media industries is journalism. In this journalistic community, there are about 67,000 reporters and correspondents, 23,000 writers and editors, and 67,000 radio and television announcers and newscasters. Most are male, white, and young. About one third of working journalists are women; this despite the fact that about two thirds of students in journalism schools in the 1990s were women. Only about 8% are minorities (3.7% are African American, 2.2% Hispanic, 1% Asian American, and 0.6% Native American). More than half of U.S. journalists are under 35, and only 10% are 55 or older. Almost all have a college degree, with a major in either the skill of journalism or in another content-based area, such as English, American studies, political science, or others. In this country there are more than 300 universities with journalism/mass communication programs, and each year they grant about 20,000 bachelor's degrees.

According to the American Association of Advertising Agencies, there are about 100,000 people currently employed in advertising agencies in this country: about 24% in creative, 15% in account management, 10% in media, 10% in financial, 8% in special support services, and the rest are clerical workers (i.e., about 33%). Employment in ad agencies grows at about 3% each year.

Women account for 34% of people in advertising, but only 17% of top executives (those making over $200,000 per year). Characters such as Heather Locklear's Amanda on *Melrose Place* are very rare in the real advertising world ("Ad Agency Women," 1996).

Men make higher salaries than do women. On newspapers, salary discrepancies exist even after the differences in education, experience, and newspaper size are taken into consideration.

Females who are employed in the media industries are usually in positions of lower status, earn less money, and have less education. For example, in newspapers, women hold about 120 managing editorships in this country's 1,700 daily newspapers. As far as policy-making positions on newspapers, women hold about 361 (11%) positions while men hold 3,057 (89%). In book publishing, about 64% of editors, vice presidents, and professionals are men; however, there is better representation of women in the smaller publishing houses.

Summary

This chapter is designed to help you start building a strong knowledge structure about the mass media industries. The framework of your knowledge structure should be that there are nine major mass media industries: book, newspaper, magazine, film, recording, radio, broadcast television, cable television, and computer. Each of these industries was born out of a combination of technological developments that made its channel of communication possible and a mass marketing orientation that drove it, as an industry, to provide messages for as large and broad an audience as possible.

After an innovation stage, each industry entered a stage of penetration in which it increased its appeal to more and more people. Acceptance of a medium is based on its ability to satisfy an existing need or to create a widespread need that it can then satisfy.

A peak stage is reached when the medium commands the most attention from the public and generates the most revenue compared to other media. This usually happens when the medium has achieved maximum penetration.

Eventually, the medium will be challenged by a newer one and go into a decline. In the decline stage, the medium is characterized by a loss of audience acceptance and therefore by a loss in revenues. A decline in audience support results not from an atrophied need but by needs being satisfied better by a competing medium.

A medium enters the adaptation stage of development when it accepts the challenge of redefining its position in the media marketplace. Repositioning is achieved by identifying a new set of needs that the medium can meet, since the old set of needs it used to fulfill is now met better by another medium.

Most of the mass media are currently in the adaptation stage, where they share audiences and advertisers by serving a different function from the other competing media. There is reason to believe that they will continue refining their messages and services and thereby continue to survive in a healthy manner.

The media industries employ fewer workers than most people would guess, and those workers do not reflect the demographics of the population of the country. Although the media have been trying to hire a larger proportion of women and minorities, those groups are still very much under-represented in the media workforce.

Take your media industries knowledge structure into the next two chapters to help you organize the information there. While reading those chapters, think about elaborating this knowledge structure by adding information about the economics and control of the media industries.

 References

Ad agency women hit TV stereotypes. (1996, May 20). *Los Angeles Times,* p. 10.

Bimber, B. (1996, December 3). Study: 51 million Americans have Internet access. *93106 News-paper,* p. 3.

Black, C. (1992, January). Fair and equal access. *Link,* p. 43.

Hoover's guide to media companies. (1996). Austin, TX: Hoover's Business Press.

Intelligence Infocorp. (1996, May 22). *Nando.net release.* La Jolla, CA: Author.

Kantrowitz, B. (1993, May 31). An interactive life. *Newsweek,* pp. 42-44.

Koplovitz, K. (1990, March 12). Cable's cutting edge. *View,* p. 22.

Maney, K. (1995). *Megamedia shakeout: The inside story of the leaders and the losers in the exploding communications industry.* New York: John Wiley.

Multichannel News. (1993, July 19). p. 42.

Simons, J. (1996, December 30). Waiting to download. *U.S. News & World Report,* p. 60.

U.S. Department of Commerce. (1995). *Statistical abstract of the United States.* Washington, DC: Government Printing Office.

CHAPTER 10

Economic Perspective

KEY IDEA *The businesses in the media industries are in strong competition with each other to acquire limited resources, play the high-risk game of appealing to audiences, and achieve a maximum profit.*

The media produce products that are bought by the public for large sums of money. American consumers spend about $56 billion per year on media products; $5.4 billion of this is at the movie box office, $15.3 billion on music videos, $12 billion on recorded music, and $23.1 billion on cable television (Federman, 1996). How much of your money do you personally contribute to the media? Before you read on in this chapter, take a few minutes to complete Exercise 10.1 at the end of the chapter.

If you are in an average household, you spend about $570 annually—buying books, recordings, and movie admissions; subscriptions to magazines and newspapers; and purchasing hardware, such as TVs, VCRs, tape players, and other media products; this money goes directly to a media company. But you also support the media indirectly by buying advertised products. For example, every time we buy a can of Coke, some of that money goes into Coke's advertising budget; those advertising expenditures also support the media industries. The average household in this country contributes $1,630 each year to the media in indirect costs.

Where does all that money go? It might seem to go to all the well-known entertainers who have huge incomes. According to *Forbes Magazine,* Steven Spielberg was the highest paid entertainer in 1994-1995 with an income of $285 million. Oprah Winfrey was in second place with $146 million; then the Beatles with $130 million. The highest earning actor was Sylvester Stallone at $58 million, then the two-time Oscar-winner Tom Hanks at $52 million. The highest paid television actor was Bill Cosby at $49 million, and the highest earning writer was Stephen King at $43 million.

Clearly, there is a great deal of money being exchanged for services in the mass media industries. To understand how the industry acquires and uses its resources, we need to learn to think like economists. This chapter is designed to introduce you to that way of thinking by first defining some fundamental terms and concepts, then examining how five key economic principles influence how people in these industries negotiate for resources. Then the chapter presents a brief economic sketch of each of the media industries.

 ## Basic Terms and Concepts

Economics is concerned with resources. With the media, some of those resources are tangible, such as money, ink, paper, cameras, and microphones, to name a few. Many other resources are intangible, such as acting talent, station loyalty, name recognition, and brand image. When we look at the media from an economic point of view, we are most concerned with how resources are used in the constant process of negotiation and exchange. People continually face decisions about which of their resources to give up in order to get other resources that they want more.

Who are the key players in this ongoing negotiation process? The four major groups of players are (a) the people who control and own the media vehicles, (b) employees of the media companies, (c) advertisers, and (d) audiences. Each of these groups has a different set of resources and needs. The owners want to maximize profits by increasing their revenues and decreasing their costs. Employees want to increase their income and benefits for each hour worked. Advertisers want to rent time and space in the media vehicles so that they can get their messages to as many audience members as possible at the lowest cost to them. Audiences want to increase the value of their exposure by focusing on more useful information and entertainment while avoiding boring messages and ads for products they don't want.

Notice that the goals of these four groups are at odds with one another, so there is a situation of constant negotiation. A determining factor in these negotiations is the balance between supply and demand. For example, a newspaper wants to minimize its costs. Let's say you are an employee of the newspaper, and you want a raise in pay and benefits. If you are a receptionist or a secretary, the negotiating power is with the newspaper, because there is a very large supply of people with your skills relative to the demand. If, however, you are an investigative reporter with extensive contacts in your city and a track record of writing shocking exposés that increase your newspaper's sales, you have a rare talent. There is a very high demand for this talent and a very small supply of it—therefore you will have the negotiating power.

Let's look at another, and bit more complicated, example. A radio station wants to attract more advertisers so it cuts the price of its ads by 20% in its highest rated show. Advertisers fight to buy those ad times (called avails), so demand for the avails at this station increases. The station, which used to air 9 minutes of ads during an hour, decides to air 20 minutes of ads, thus increasing its supply of avails to meet the increasing demand. The station likes this, because even though it has cut its income per ad by 20%, it is now selling more than twice as many avails; the station has almost doubled its total revenue. The audience notices this change and becomes upset that there are so many ads and not nearly as much music. Most of the audience switches stations during the ads and never comes back. The station's ratings drop dramatically, and advertisers become unhappy because it's no bargain to get a 20% discount on ads if the audience they expected is almost gone. Advertisers begin feeling they are wasting their money, so they stop buying the ads.

There are many possible examples to illustrate the point that these four groups are in constant negotiation to satisfy their conflicting needs and wants. Everything is linked in the complex economy.

There are three other characteristics that make this inter-relationship even more complex. First, the situation is highly dynamic and inter-related. When a person at one media company makes a decision, the decision can often have an impact on other companies in the same industry and perhaps in other media industries. Returning to the radio station example above, when advertisers flocked to the station to get the discounted price for the avails, other radio stations (as well as television stations, newspapers, and local magazines) most likely lost advertising revenue. So when the revenues of one vehicle dramatically increase in the short term, the revenues of other competing vehicles are affected and usually go down. The same ripple effect can be seen with media company expenses. For example, if several media companies started paying writers more money, then the better writers would be attracted to those companies, and the other companies would either have to pay more or else make do with writers of lesser talent, which would lower the quality of their shows and result in losing audience size, which would lower revenue. When something changes in a tightly linked industry, that change ripples outward and affects other players.

Second, sometimes decision makers are conflicted, because they are experiencing cross-purposes; that is, a decision maker might be a member of more than one group—each with a different economic goal. Let's say you work at a small newspaper and also own half of the newspaper company. As an employee you might want a raise in salary, but this would increase expenses and therefore reduce profits, making your investment less valuable. On a different scale, let's say you work for a large newspaper and own stock in the company that owns the newspaper. A raise in your wages will benefit you a great deal more than a non-raise would benefit shareholders, so your needs as an employee greatly outweigh your needs as an owner.

Third, media vehicles compete in different markets. A market is a segment of the audience to which you offer your product or service. Markets differ in size, with the largest market in this country being the national one. Only a few vehicles, such as television network prime-time broadcast programs, *USA Today* newspaper, *TV Guide* magazine, and major Hollywood movies, see themselves as competing in a national market. More typically, vehicles carve out a special niche. Geography is one way of identifying a niche; this is the case with newspapers, radio stations, and broadcast television stations. Media vehicles in these industries have their own geographical locale, such as a city or a limited region. Another way of identifying a niche is by audience interest, which is common with magazines, books, and radio. For example, *Surfer* magazine appeals to a very different audience niche than does *Ladies' Home Journal.* College texts are marketed very differently than religious books. Country-and-western formatted radio stations appeal to a very different audience than does a rap station.

Clearly, the economics of the mass media industries are complex. The complexity is traceable to the fact that there are many different components, each with its own needs and wants that are most often in conflict with the needs and wants of other components. This requires a constant negotiation process, and as decisions are made, effects ripple out and influence the decisions of others. All parties are profoundly interlinked.

People who are at low levels of media literacy are likely simply to blame the media for actions they don't like, such as when their favorite television show is canceled, or when the subscription rate for cable increases, or when a radio station changes its format. They feel anger that the media don't understand their needs and wants.

People who are at higher levels of media literacy try to analyze changes to understand the degree of good that will come to them as consumers. They compare current changes to past changes to evaluate what the short-term and long-term implications will be. They consider who will benefit and who will be hurt by the shift in resources. From this information, they synthesize a reasoned opinion. The result of this thinking might be an emotional reaction of anger—much like the anger of the person with a low level of media literacy. Yet people with a higher level of media literacy will have a clearly reasoned perspective on their anger, and this perspective can be used to help them do something about it personally, such as changing their attitudes and behavior, or to do something about it in society, such as boycotting or putting pressure on the media organization. In order to increase the effectiveness of your actions, you need to understand clearly what the problems are and the influences that led to those problems.

 ## Key Economic Characteristics

Sorting through all the economic complexity in the media industries reveals five important characteristics that appear industry-wide. These are: profit motive, first copy costs, direct versus indirect support, the principle of relative constancy, and the competitive nature. An understanding of this set of principles will help you comprehend how the negotiation for resources takes place.

Profit-Making Motive

Almost all mass media are profit-oriented enterprises. As businesses, they are run to make as large a profit as possible. Profit is what a company has at the end of the year after paying all its expenses. Profit is the difference between revenue, which is the total amount of income for the business, and expenses.

To make large profits, a business needs to keep expenses low while increasing revenue. A medium generates revenue only by appealing to some need for information or entertainment and thus building an audience. This can generally be done in one of two ways. A media business can be either (a) oriented toward a *quantity* goal, that is, attracting as large an audience as possible; or (b) oriented toward a niche, that is, attracting a special kind of audience.

The dominant mass media are always ruled by the law of large numbers. Therefore they must present whatever content they feel will attract the greatest number of consumers. For example, commercial television is the dominant mass medium today. In order for it to stay in its dominant position, it must present programming that appeals to as large an audience as possible. A small shrinkage in audience size can mean a substantial reduction in revenue. To illustrate, a television network would lose more than $90 million dollars over the course of one television season for every average rating point a particular show drops.

In contrast, the radio and magazine industries are oriented toward crafting an appeal to a particular type of audience. The audience may be relatively small compared to an audience for broadcast television, but small, highly targeted audiences have great value to many advertisers. Special groups of people have special needs. Businesses that market products for a special audience will pay a premium to the media vehicles that attract that special audience. For example, joggers as a group have a special need for information on running practices, equipment, and training techniques. They support several magazines that publish nothing but this type of information. Manufacturers of jogging equipment pay a premium to place ads in these magazines, knowing that buying advertising space in these magazines is a very efficient purchase, because the ads placed there will reach their most likely customers.

One of the largest expenses across all the media industries is personnel, which can be sub-divided into two broad categories: talent and clerical. Talent is the ability to generate revenue, as well as artistic mastery. Some people have sales talent and can sell advertising space and time. Some people have writing talent and have large followings of readers who buy their books, magazines, or newspapers. Some have musical talent and continually produce records that go platinum. Some have acting talent and generate huge sales at theater box offices or high ratings for television programs. There is never enough talent to meet the demand, so media companies bid up the prices for the services of people who have talent. The few talented people at the tops of their industries make large sums of money.

However, most of the positions in the media industries are fairly low-level jobs that entail routine assignments that can be done by many different people with little training: the secretaries, receptionists, ticket takers, and low-level craftspeople. A bit higher than this are the assistant producers, camera operators, disk jockeys, and the like. Some of these people have special talent and quickly move up to the top of their industry, but most of them do not.

The media pay the people with a lot of talent a lot of money, because these people are required in order for a company to generate large revenues. To counterbalance the large payments to talent, companies reduce expenses by paying clerical people as little as possible. Because the supply of potential workers for entry-level positions is so much larger than the demand, media companies can pay near minimum wage and get good workers.

Principle of First Copy Costs

The principle of first copy costs states that the cost of producing the first copy of something is much higher than the cost of the second or any subsequent copy. To illustrate, let's say you are a newspaper publisher and your daily cost of operation (cost of paying all your reporters, editors, salespeople, office staff, rent on building, depreciation on all your equipment, supplies, phones, other utilities, etc.) is $6,000. This is your fixed cost. If you print only one copy of the newspaper, you will have to sell it for $6,000 just to cover your fixed costs. If you print two copies, you will have to sell each for $3,000; your average fixed cost per copy is cut in half. If you print 60,000 copies, your average fixed cost per copy is only 10 cents. Thus, your average fixed costs keep going down as these costs are spread over more and more copies.

When you print more copies, however, the costs of paper, ink, and distribution increase; these are your variable costs, because they vary according to the number of copies you print. The more copies you print, the more paper and ink you will need, although the price you pay for a roll of paper or a gallon of ink will go down because you can buy these materials in bulk and get big discounts. While your total cost for ink and paper will go up when printing more copies, your *average* variable cost for these will go down. This is known as economies of scale. The bigger the scale of your business, the more likely your costs will go down, either through your ability to demand greater discounts or because you are able to operate more efficiently beyond a certain point.

The more copies you print, the more your distribution costs will go up—both in total and on average. To illustrate this point, imagine that you publish only 1,000 copies of your newspaper. You could hire 10 youngsters to deliver 100 papers each after school and pay them a nickel for each paper delivered. Thus your average distribution cost is 5 cents per newspaper. But let's say you want to publish 50,000 newspapers. You would need to hire 500 youngsters, and this would require you to develop a whole new layer of administration to recruit, train, and keep track of all these paper carriers. You would have to buy some trucks and hire drivers to get the newspapers out to these 500 carriers quickly every afternoon. You would also have to hire some bookkeepers to keep track of all the subscriptions and billing. So the average variable cost might increase from 5 cents to 15 cents per newspaper as you go from 1,000 to 50,000 in circulation.

Media companies, like any business, want to keep their expenses down, so they find the point at which the combination of their average fixed costs and their average variable costs are lowest. Beyond this point, distributing more copies only serves to increase unit costs and thus reduce profit. Newspaper, magazine, book, and recording companies each seek the point where their average total costs (the sum of average fixed costs plus average variable costs) are lowest.

On this principle of first copy costs, broadcast television and radio are different from the other media. They have no variable costs, only fixed costs. For example, with broadcast television there is no cost to the station for adding an additional viewer to the audience. Viewers pay for their own television receivers, and they pay for the electricity to run them. The station has no distribution costs other than the electricity for the broadcast signal, and the power used to broadcast a station's signal is the same whether 100 or 100,000 sets are tuned in. It is fixed. With no variable costs and with a very high first copy fixed cost, broadcast television stations keep dropping their average total costs with each additional audience member added. For this reason, the broadcast media (both radio and television) are strongly motivated, more than any other medium, to increase the size of their audiences.

Direct and Indirect Costs

Consumers of the mass media support the industry by paying both direct and indirect costs. When you write a check to your cable television provider for your monthly bill, you are paying money directly to a media company. That is a direct cost. Other examples of direct costs include paying admission to a movie or buying a magazine, book, recording, or computer software. When you buy hardware (TV set, VCR, computer, etc.) that is required to receive media messages, you are also contributing to direct costs.

In contrast, you also support the media indirectly. Let's say you spend $5.00 for lunch at McDonald's. Some of that money (let's say $1.00) will find its way into McDonald's advertising budget and is sent on to a television network. That $1.00 of your lunch payment is an example of your indirect support of the media. The payment originated with you, but it did not go directly from you to a media company. Had you not bought lunch at McDonald's, that $1.00 would not have gone to the television network. Every time you buy an advertised product or service you are indirectly supporting the media.

The media of books, films, recordings, and computers are supported almost entirely by direct costs to the consumer. There are a few examples of ads being stuck in books or displayed before films or in computer programs, but the revenue from these ads is minor compared to direct costs. With magazines, newspapers, and now cable TV, the costs are split between direct (subscription or newsstand selling price) and indirect (advertising). With broadcast television and radio, there is no direct cost for exposure to a program, but there is a high cost for purchasing the means to receive a program, in addition to indirect costs in the guise of advertising.

The balance between direct and indirect support is shifting from direct to indirect payment. In the 1930s, 72% of media support was paid *directly* by consumers; by 1958, there was a 50%-50% split; now, about 75% is paid *in*directly by consumers.

Principle of Relative Constancy

The consumer's proportion of direct economic support for the mass media is a constant percentage of the general economy. While the size of the economy usually grows each year, the percentage of the economy that supports the mass media stays the same. This is the principle of relative constancy.

Mass media products have become staples of consumption in our society, much like food, clothing, and shelter. As staples, they receive a fixed, constant share of the economic pie, a relatively fixed proportion of all expenditures. This was true in 1929 and has been true every year since then, through years of inflation and depression. It is still true 70 years later, even though there are more media and more media vehicles.

Although the percentage of direct consumer spending on the mass media has remained constant at around 3% of GNP (Gross National Product) since 1929, that money breaks down differently year by year, depending on the media available and the relative attractiveness of their messages. The percentage of media expenditure for newspapers and magazines peaked in 1933; movie admission peaked in 1945; books peaked in 1970. Expenditures for radio, television receivers, recordings, and computers are still growing.

Nature of Competition

Most mass media operate in a market of monopolistic competition. *Monopolistic,* because each firm is large relative to the size of the market for its products; also, there are very high barriers to entry in most media industries. *Competition,* because firms in an industry compete.

Unusually high profits in a industry typically attract new firms, which results in greater competition, expanded output, lower prices, reduced profits, and greater consumer benefits. This trend is not apparent in most mass media industries (especially broadcasting), however, because the cost of entry is so high. Therefore the few existing firms in a market tend to monopolize their markets.

All media must compete in two markets simultaneously. In one market, the medium must act like a seller of services to the largest possible audience. In the other market, the medium must be a buyer of information and entertainment for the lowest possible cost. There is a big overlap in each market within the media and among the media.

Another characteristic of the competition is that within a market all products are relatively indistinguishable; that is, the messages are not identical but are very similar. For example, the stories in *Newsweek, Time,* and *U.S. News & World Report* are very similar in terms of content, depth, and perspective. A situation comedy on ABC is very similar to one on CBS; the characters have different names, but the stereotypes, settings, and plot points are very similar. With computer software, all spreadsheet application programs are pretty much the same; also, Web browsers are almost identical in features. The key to competition is making the audience in the market believe that your product is different from the others. Competition does not take place as much in the marketplace with product features; instead, it is designed to take place in the minds of audience members. This is why advertising is so important; it is an essential tool of this type of competition.

How Profitable Are the Individual Media?

Profit can be simply defined as the payoff or reward for doing business. This reward can be conceptualized in several different ways. First, it can be regarded as the difference between a company's revenue (total income) and expenses (total costs)—usually expressed as a percentage of revenues. For example, let's say I run a small magazine and at the end of the year I total up everything and find that my revenues (all income through subscriptions and advertiser's fees) came to $100,000. My expenses (paying writers, editors, photographers, printers, distribution, taxes, office supplies, utilities, etc.) sum to $90,000. That means I have $10,000 left over after having paid all my expenses for the year. This is my reward. I get to keep 10% of all my revenues—that is, my ROR (return on revenues) is $10,000 divided by $100,000.

Table 10.1 Comparison of Profits Across Media Industries

Industry	Revenue (Billions)	ROR (%)	ROA (%)
Broadcasting (radio and television)	$42.4	18	18
Newspapers	$44.2	17	26
Cable and pay television	$29.0	17	9
Magazines	$13.2	11	24
Films	$32.5	11	9
Books	$16.7	10	14
Audio recordings	$11.0	7	14

SOURCE: Format adapted from Picard, 1989, p. 89; data from Standard & Poor's *Index to Surveys,* 1996.

A second way of computing my reward is to compare my profit to my assets, which is the money I have invested in the business. Let's extend the same example above where I had a $10,000 profit at the end of the year. If I had $50,000 invested in the business (office furniture, computers, printers, fax machines, and other equipment), then my ROA (return on assets) would be 20%, which is very good.

Both ROR and ROA are very important indicators of the reward of doing business, but they look at reward in different ways. For example, let's say I bought a radio station for $1 million and at the end of the year I had generated a profit of $10,000 on revenues of $100,000. That 10% ROR is pretty good, but the ROA is only 1%, which is terrible! I could have invested the $1 million in a passbook savings account at the bank and done much better! To use another example, let's say I start a small weekly newspaper and my only assets are a computer and a few pieces of furniture, totaling $4,000. My newspaper generates revenue of $50,000, but my expenses are $49,000 so my profit is only $1,000. My ROA is very high at 25% ($1,000 profit divided by assets of $4,000), but my ROR is only 2% ($1,000 profit divided by revenues of $50,000).

Let's look at the ROR and ROA of the mass media industries (see Table 10.1). Newspapers appear to be the best of the mass media industries, because they have very high percentages on both ROR and ROA. Remember, these are industry-wide averages; some newspapers do much better than these figures, and others have been losing money.

On the weaker end is the audio recording industry, with the lowest ROR. However, 7% is still better than the average for all industries in the United

States. As for ROA, the cable television and film industries are the lowest, but both of these industries have huge asset bases, and this is what tends to make their ROA percentages appear smaller.

Now let's look at economic profiles of the media. Remember that the companies in these industries are businesses that are driven to maximize their profits. When you read the profiles below, think about how the five basic economic principles outlined earlier are illustrated in the way they try to maximize revenue and minimize expenses. Unless otherwise indicated, the information in the profiles below is from the July 1996 Standard & Poor's *Index to Surveys,* and the profit figures are ROR.

Book Industry

The book industry now has an annual revenue of about $16.7 billion by publishing 50,000 new titles each year. This revenue is more than all ticket sales to movie theaters ($4.9 billion) and sales of pre-recorded music ($11 billion) combined. The revenues have been climbing steadily year to year. Annual revenues did not break the $1 billion mark until about 1960, and by 1980 the revenue was $4 billion. This is an economically healthy industry and it continues to grow each year in terms of both revenues and titles produced.

The industry is segmented according to the type of book produced and the type of audience (see Table 10.2). The largest segment is the adult trade book, which includes general interest fiction and non-fiction, advice, and how-to books. These are the books typically found in the bookstores in malls. Most books are sold through retail book stores (see Table 10.3). Most of the sales in this segment are through the very large chains, such as Waldenbooks or Barnes & Noble.

There are many elements that go into the expense of book publishing. Let's take a typical example of a hardbound trade book that lists for $19.95 in a retail bookstore. When this sells, the store keeps about 48% for its own expenses and profit, and sends the remaining $10.37 to the publisher. It costs the publisher about $2.00 to manufacture the physical copy of the book (composition, typesetting, jacket design, paper, ink, printing, binding, etc.). Another $3.00 is for overhead, which includes the expense of editors, office staff, marketing, and so forth. The author gets about $2.00 in royalties. The remaining $3.37 is profit, unless the stores return the unsold copies—a common practice—and wipe out the potential profit. Only one book in five is successful, meaning it makes money for the publisher after all the expenses and returns are subtracted from sales. The small number of successful books, in essence, subsidizes the industry and makes it possible for publishers to take chances on all sorts of "risky" books and new authors.

Table 10.2 Book Industry Revenue Broken Down by Type of Book

Type of Book	Percentage of Industry Revenue
Adult trade	21.5
Elementary & high school texts	21.2
College texts	18.6
Mass market paperbacks	11.8
Technical/scientific/business	10.3
Juvenile trade	5.1
Other	11.4

SOURCE: 1994 data from Standard & Poor's *Index to Surveys*, p. M26.

Table 10.3 Book Industry Revenue Broken Down by Type of Outlet

Type of Outlet	Percentage of Industry Revenue
Sold directly to the public through retail stores	38
Sold through book clubs	21
Sold in college book stores	17
Sold to schools for use as texts	15
Sold to libraries and other institutions	10

SOURCE: 1995 data from Standard & Poor's *Index to Surveys*, p. M32.

Because of the economic risks in the industry, publishers are continually searching for books they think the public wants, rather than searching for what they think are the best or most literary books. Publishers believe the public likes books on scandal and celebrities. This is why there have been so many books on O. J. Simpson in the past few years. Another example is Dick Morris, who was a political consultant and a close political advisor to President Clinton and unknown to the public. No publisher was interested in a book deal with him until he was discovered to have frequented a $200-an-hour call girl and the scandal made the front page in all the newspapers. His wife divorced him, but publishers scrambled to sign him to a "kiss-and-tell" book about how he liked to suck on a prostitute's toes while telling her about his private conversations with the president. The negotiations ended with Morris signing a $2.5 million deal to write one book. Obviously, the publisher thought that all the free publicity about Morris's disgrace would make the book high profile and a best seller.

Book publishing is very competitive. If a bookstore doesn't think a book will sell, it won't even take a chance and stock it. The average bookstore carries about 20,000 titles at any given time. Remember that the industry publishes 50,000 new titles each year. Bookstores can handle only a small fraction of the new titles produced each year, especially when you consider that they need to keep in stock many "old" books, such as the Bible and other classics, reference books, last year's best sellers, and so on.

Newspaper Industry

Newspapers have two major streams of revenue. One is through subscriptions and newsstand sales, which generated $9.8 billion in 1996. The much bigger revenue stream is advertising, which brought in $34.4 billion in 1996. Over time, the advertising stream has grown much faster than the sales stream. In 1880, the average newspaper received 25% of its revenue from advertising; by 1910, advertising accounted for 50% of all revenue; now it accounts for almost 80%.

Historically, newspaper publishers have been reluctant to increase their prices to readers, so they have been asking advertisers to bear most of the increases in expenses. This has been changing recently. Throughout the 1980s and into the 1990s, there was a consistent shift of revenue burden to readers in the form of higher subscription rates and the selling price of an issue at the newsstand (Blankenburg, 1995).

The biggest expense for newspapers is personnel costs, which account for about 60% of all expenditures. While this cost goes up each year, it has been doing so at a slow rate of about 3% to 4% a year.

The average profit margin for a newspaper company is about 17%, which is more than triple the median profit margin (4.8%) for companies in the Fortune 500.

Chain-owned newspapers are even more profitable. The primary purpose of a chain-owned newspaper is to maximize the profits of the parent company. Therefore, chain-owned newspapers have a strong incentive to increase revenues (by eliminating competition) and reduce expenses (by using economies of scale). Of course, non-chain-owned newspapers also have a similar profit motive, but chains have more economic power. Their (a) first copy expenses are amortized over larger circulations, thus resulting in a lower per unit cost (first copy costs are fixed and these are very large in small circulation newspapers, as high as 40% of total revenue, so the more papers sold, the lower the per unit cost); (b) reproduction costs decline as circulation goes up (additional pages do not cost as much as the first few pages), and (c) the distribution process is more efficient the denser the circulation pattern, though this works against multiple deliverers of multiple papers.

Magazine Industry

The magazine industry also has two primary streams of revenue. About 60% of the revenue comes from advertising—$7.9 billion in 1994. The other 40% comes from subscriptions and newsstand sales. There has been a generally steady growth in sales for more than 50 years. The industry did not break the $1 billion mark in revenue until the mid 1950s and now it is over $13 billion per year.

There is a growing trend toward more support from customers, especially through subscriptions. Single-issue newsstand sales have been decreasing over time because the cost of magazines has been steadily increasing to the current level of an average of $3.10 for a copy. Subscriptions, which average $30.50 a year, are increasing in popularity, because they are more convenient and more economical for consumers than buying individual issues at the store.

As with newspapers, the biggest expense for a magazine is personnel, but this has not been climbing very fast. In contrast, expenses for paper and mailing have been increasing rapidly over the past decade.

Film Industry

Recall that the film industry has three sectors: production, distribution, and exhibition. The production sector is the most risky for several reasons. First, a Hollywood feature film takes about 18 to 24 months between the inception of the idea and the actual theatrical release. In television it takes 3 months. This means there is a danger that a film might miss the changing tastes of audiences.

Second, the cost of making a feature film is very high, and it continues to escalate. The average cost of films, including their marketing, doubled between 1991 and 1996. The average film now costs $35 million to make and another $15 million to market. This means that a film must gross more than $100 million at the box office before it begins to make money for the studio. The average movie, however, makes only about $33 million. For example, in 1994, Hollywood released 332 feature length films. Only about 60 of these films generated revenues of even $20 million, and only about one third made any profit.

The most dramatic increase in the cost of making films can be traced to the rising fees of stars—even lesser known stars. In 1929, the highest paid silent film star was John Gilbert, who made $520,000 a year or about $8 million in 1997 dollars. Clark Gable at his peak, the year he made *Gone With the Wind* and *Mutiny on the Bounty,* was making $208,000. Jean Harlowe made $78,000 at her peak. When Greta Garbo was the highest paid actress, in the

1930s, she made $250,000 a picture, and in the 1940s Barbara Stanwyck was the highest paid at $225,000 a picture (LaSalle, 1996).

The box office mega-stars in 1996 were: Harrison Ford, Jim Carrey, Tom Cruise, Mel Gibson, Arnold Schwarzenegger, and Sylvester Stallone, who each got about $20 million per film. Second-tier people made about half that figure; for example, Demi Moore made $12.5 million per film and Kurt Russell, $10 million. Third-tier actors such as Charlie Sheen got $5 million. Unknown actors can quickly increase their fees if their early movies are successful. For example, Sandra Bullock's fee climbed from $600,000 for *Speed* to $1.2 million for *While You Were Sleeping;* she now gets over $10 million per film. Also, known actors can make a quick comeback with a successful film or two. John Travolta was down to $150,000 for *Pulp Fiction,* then bounced up to $10 million. Big name directors also command high fees (usually about $3 million), but not as high as actors. Even bit players make a decent fee. Scale salary for the members of the Screen Actors Guild (SAG) is $522 *a day,* which is much better than the U.S. average for salaried workers at $500 *per week* (Weinraub, 1995). However, a very small percentage of the 95,000 members of SAG are working during any given day.

The central sector of the film industry is distribution, which is controlled by the Hollywood studios. The studios have several major revenue streams. First, there are domestic movie rentals to theaters, which is the income to the studios from the theater owners. In 1995, this was $2.7 billion. Second, there are foreign rentals, which was another $2.7 billion in 1995. A third stream is sales of videos and the licensing of films to television outlets. This adds $10 billion.

The exhibition sector is composed of the theaters, with their total of about 26,000 screens (DeFleur & Dennis, 1996). This year, theaters will sell between 1 and 1.3 billion tickets for total revenues of about $5 billion. The revenues increase from year to year but not due to more people attending the movies; instead the increases come from higher ticket prices. About 70% of this revenue is sent to the film distributor. Movie theaters generate revenues of about $7.8 billion through their two revenue streams: (a) the portion of the ticket sales they get to keep, and (b) high-margin concessions, such as popcorn, soda, and candy, that account for about 30% of their revenue.

Recording Industry

Revenue from pre-recorded music sales is now about $11 billion per year. A high percentage (70%) of this total is due to the sales of compact discs (CDs). A recording that sells 10 million copies is a huge success; there are only one or two recordings per year that reach this milestone, however (Standard & Poor, 1996, p. L38).

In the recording industry, the cost of manufacturing CDs is coming down, while the cost of signing artists is going up. In the early 1980s it cost $3 to $4 to manufacture one CD, but now the cost has been reduced to less than 75 cents, including the jewel box container. The big costs are for the artists and for promotion. It now costs about $500,000 to sign a name band.

Producers must sell at least 300,000 to 500,000 copies of a CD before covering their costs. About 80% of all recordings lose money. In general, the revenue in the recording industry is divided as follows: 35% goes to the retail store, 27% to the record company, 16% to the artist, 13% to the manufacturer, and 9% to the distributor (Strauss, 1995).

Radio Industry

Radio is very profitable and, except during the 1950s, it has been profitable throughout its history.

When radio began broadcasting in 1922, it received its income through the sale of home receivers. This continued to be a source of revenue to radio stations until the mid-1930s. Throughout the 1920s, stations realized that the sale of receivers would not bring in enough revenue to support the growing industry, so stations began selling advertising.

Revenues increased each year until television began taking away advertisers in the late 1940s and early 1950s. Radio hit bottom in 1955 when revenues dropped to $554 million and only 2,669 stations were broadcasting. By the early 1960s more than 4,000 stations were broadcasting, and revenues were up to $700 million per year. By 1980, total revenues had climbed to $3.2 billion, and now total revenues are $10.7 billion—all from advertising. The economic recovery of the radio industry can be traced to radio's shifting from a national medium to a local one. Now 80% of a station's revenue comes from local advertising. Thus radio stations compete primarily in local markets with newspapers for advertisers.

Because of the profitability of well-run radio stations and because of the limited number of stations available (about 12,000), large companies want to buy weaker stations and transform them into moneymakers. Each year about 1,000 radio stations change owners. The average sale is for about $1 million.

Broadcast Television

The television industry began strong and grew rapidly. By 1957, commercial television had gone over $1 billion in revenue per year, and now it generates about $32.4 billion a year. The revenue stream is from advertising, over half of which is national (Standard & Poor, 1996, p. M36).

The total number of television commercials more than doubled from 1967 to 1975, largely because of the reduction in the length of an average spot from 60 seconds to 30 seconds. Over the past decade, the average spot has been reduced down to 15 seconds, and the number of television ads continues to grow each year.

Television networks do not produce much of their own programming; instead, they license broadcast rights from the producers. The fee to broadcast a program is not large enough to cover the producer's costs. These deficits are usually between $50,000 to $300,000 per episode. Producers hope that the series will run long enough for them to make about 100 episodes and then sell the series through syndication. The most successful syndicated show thus far is the *Cosby Show,* which got $4 million per episode in licensing fees to television stations (Standard & Poor, 1996, p. L30).

A program's survival depends on its reaching a large audience, especially one of women between the ages of 18 and 49, because they buy the most of the commonly advertised products. A show does not usually survive unless it gets at least a 10 rating. A rating is the percentage of people in the U.S. population who watch a particular show. Thus a rating of 10 means that 10% of the country's population, or about 26 million people, watched the show. A rating of 20 is very high, and a rating of 15 will put a show in the top 10 most popular shows (Standard & Poor, 1996). Yet things are changing for broadcasters, because they are losing much of their audience to cable. Throughout the 1980s, broadcast networks' viewership slipped from 71% to 53% of total viewing and from 91% to 63% in prime time (Howard & Carroll, 1993).

Cable Television

Cable operations are increasingly profitable, with revenue growing faster than assets. In 1992, cable surpassed broadcast TV for the first time, with revenues of over $21 billion from a combination of subscriber fees and advertising. Subscription revenues are now about $25 billion per year and ad revenues bring in another $4 billion (Standard & Poor, 1996).

Computers

There are three components to the computer media industry. Each has its own stream of revenue. First, there is the hardware component of PCs and peripherals. This accounts for about $100 billion per year. Second, there is software, which had sales of $86 billion in 1995. Third, there are on-line services, which in 1996 accounted for about $1 billion per year but are growing at an annual rate of 27% (Standard & Poor, 1996, p. C102). Profit margins run about 20% to 25% annually on software and about 10% to 15% on hardware (Standard & Poor, 1996, p. C127). Consumer spending for all kinds of computer hardware and services is increasing at about 20% per year, from about $6 billion in 1994 to a projected $14 billion in 1999 (*Hoover's Guide,* 1996).

Summary

When you add the economic information from this chapter to your knowledge structure about the media, you develop a deeper understanding of how decisions are made. The media industries are composed of businesses that are run to make profits. They do this by attempting to maximize revenues and minimize expenses. Each of the media industries does this well, and each earns a profit much higher than the average of all the industries in this country.

There are some key economic characteristics that set the media industries apart from other types of industry. First, the cost of the first copy of their messages is usually much higher relative to subsequent copies, so there is a strong motivation to increase the size of their audiences. Second, almost all the media industries have several streams of revenue, from both direct costs to the consumer and indirect costs through advertising. Third, the media consistently seem to account for about 3% of the GNP. However, expenditures shift around among the media, depending on the relative attractiveness of the services and products the different industries provide. Fourth, most of the media industries compete in monopolistic markets. The barriers to entry are fairly high, and once a company gets into a market, it must compete for audiences, production talent, and advertisers with the other companies in that market. An interesting part of this challenge is that the products and services offered by the companies in a given market are fairly similar, so each company must convince target audiences, prospective employees, and desired advertisers that it is somehow superior to the other competing companies.

References

Blankenburg, W. B. (1995). Hard times and the news hole. *Journalism & Mass Communication Quarterly, 72,* 634-641.
DeFleur, M. L., & Dennis, E. E. (1996). *Understanding mass communication: A liberal arts perspective.* Princeton, NJ: Houghton Mifflin.
Federman, J. (1996). *Media ratings: Design, use and consequences.* Century City, CA: Mediascope.

Hoover's guide to media companies. (1996). Austin, TX: Hoover's Business Press.

Howard, H. H., & Carroll, S. L. (1993). Economics of the cable industry. In A. Alexander, J. Owers, & R. Carveth (Eds.), *Media economics: Theory and practice* (pp. 245-266). Hillsdale, NJ: Lawrence Erlbaum.

LaSalle, M. (1996, July 7). Why overpaid stars aren't worth it. *Santa Barbara News-Press,* p. D9.

Picard, R. G. (1989). *Media economics: Concepts and issues.* Newbury Park, CA: Sage.

Standard & Poor. (1996, July). *Index to surveys.* New York: Author.

Strauss, N. (1995, July 10). Why do CDs cost so much? *Santa Barbara News-Press,* pp. B5, B9.

Weinraub, B. (1995, September 20). Hollywood deep in the age of mega-salary. *Santa Barbara News-Press,* p. B13.

Further Reading

Alexander, A., Owers, J., & Carveth, R. (Eds.). (1993). *Media economics: Theory and practice* Hillsdale, NJ: Lawrence Erlbaum. (391 pages, with glossary, indexes, and appendices)

There are 15 chapters in this edited volume. It contains a good deal of technical economic information that is presented in a readable manner. A 13-page glossary defines the key terms presented throughout the book.

Picard, R. G. (1989). *Media economics: Concepts and issues.* Newbury Park, CA: Sage. (136 pages, with index)

This is a short introduction to the major economic principles that underlie the media industries.

Exercise 10.1   Estimating Your Personal Media Expenditures

1. Before you go any farther, stop and make a general estimate of how much money you spent on all forms of the media over the past year.

   Write your estimate here: $_____

2. Now, itemize those expenditures. Think back to one year from today and try to remember how much money you spent on each of the following over the past 12 months. If you want to do this accurately, get out your checkbook register and credit card receipts.

   $_____   Cable subscription (multiply monthly bill by 12)

   $_____   Magazine subscriptions

   $_____   Buying individual issues of magazines

   $_____   Newspaper subscriptions

   $_____   Buying individual newspapers

   $_____   Text books

   $_____   Other books (pleasure reading, gifts, reference books, etc.)

   $_____   Movie theater admissions

   $_____   Rental of movies from video store

   $_____   Buying videotapes (blank and pre-recorded)

   $_____   Buying CDs, tapes, and other recordings

   $_____   Buying blank audio tapes

   $_____   Buying video (Nintendo, etc.) or computer games

   $_____   Playing video games at arcades

   $_____   Buying computer software and/or manuals

   $_____   Subscription to computer services (America Online, Prodigy, etc.)

   $_____   Buying hardware: radios, televisions, VCRs, Walkman, computer, etc.

   $_____   Repairs on media equipment

   $_____   TOTAL (sum of all the figures down the column)

3. How close are your figures in #1 and #2?

4. Does the amount of money you spent surprise you? Why?

Exercise 10.2   Financial Analysis

1. Go to the library and get a list of media companies. Try *Hoover's Guide to Media Companies* or get your reference librarian to help you. Find two media companies that look interesting to you.

2. For each company, do a brief financial analysis by answering the following questions:

   a. How much revenue did the company have last year?

   b. What were the major sources of that income?

   c. Given the sources of income, would you say that the company is primarily concerned with media businesses, or are media businesses really a sideline to other more important businesses?

   d. What were the company's expenses for the year?

   e. What was the company's profit margin? (Can you get both ROR and ROA?)

   f. What did the company do with its profits? Did it disperse all or part to the shareholders who invested in the company? Or did the company keep all or most of the profits for investing in additional media properties or other businesses?

3. Given your analyses of two the companies, in which would you rather invest your money? Why?

CHAPTER 11

Who Owns and Controls the Mass Media?

KEY IDEA *Ownership patterns show a strong movement toward concentration and away from localism.*

Ownership and control are not always the same thing. If you own a computer, you can decide who you will allow to use it and when. You control it as well as own it. If you own 10 shares of stock in a large media company, you are a part owner but in no real sense can you control it. Almost all of the powerful media corporations are owned by thousands of shareholders, but the control of each of those companies is in the hands of one person, the Chief Executive Officer (CEO). While the CEO is accountable to the shareholders, the amount of power he or she has in comparison to any one of the shareholders is enormous. Even if you were able to round up 100 of your closest millionaire friends and invest a total of $100 million in one of these powerful companies, your group as a whole would still own only a small percentage of the company.

When we think about the control of the media companies, we should not think of the owners, we should instead think of the decisions the CEOs have been making. The primary goal of CEOs is to maximize profits. This goal is accomplished most efficiently when a company is very large and is powerful enough to control all phases of the production of messages and their distribution in very large markets where it has very little or no competition. Thus, media businesses become more efficient and wealthy through the concentration of power.

In American society, however, there is a strongly held value that power should be dispersed to as many people as possible. The Founding Fathers thus created a democratic form of government rather than a more efficient, totalitarian one. Over time, American society has retained its value of dispersion of power and has kept pressure on government regulators to prevent any one person or company from becoming "too powerful." The idea of "too powerful" is impossible to define objectively; instead, it is a matter for debate.

Competing Forces

An essential tension between dispersion of power, called localism, and concentration of power can be seen clearly in the development of the media industries. Consumers favor localism; they want a marketplace with as many voices as possible so they have many choices for satisfying their various needs for information and entertainment. CEOs favor concentration; they focus on the capitalistic business environment where the goal is maximizing profits.

These key forces of localism and concentration operate in opposite directions. The localism force strains toward diversifying decisions by getting more people involved. The concentration force strains toward efficiency by consolidating resources and putting the power into the hands of a few people. In the section below, let's examine how these two forces have been competing.

Localism in American Culture

Localism is a populist perspective. It is based on the belief that control of important institutions should be in the hands of all of the people and that the best way to do this is to keep control decentralized, that is, at the local level where it is closest to individuals.

Localism is a part of the American tradition. This country was founded on the belief that the individual is more important than institutions or governments. This belief states that when government is necessary, it should be decentralized so as to be closer to the people's needs and more accountable to them.

Localism is not just an abstract philosophy. It has been put into practice, and it can be seen in the way people have organized schools, property taxes, land use, public health, business regulation, and many other political and social activities. Although the national government is very centralized and very pervasive in its powers, it does leave some powers to state and local governments, of which there are many. There are 18,000 municipalities and 17,000 townships in the United States. Within these, there are 500,000 local governmental units directly elected by local residents, and 170,000 of them have the power to impose taxes. Clearly, localism is a strong force in this country.

Concerning the mass media, there is also a strong feeling by many that the media voices should be kept local if they are to best serve the needs of individuals and society. The media started as innovations at the local level. When government was called upon to regulate them, the governmental agencies usually favored this localism ethic in their policy making. A good example of this is how the federal government handled the development of the broadcasting industries. If you want to broadcast a radio or television signal, you must send your signal out on a frequency. If you and I want to use the same frequency to broadcast our different signals, we will interfere with each other, and audiences will receive a garbled signal. There are only so many frequencies available in what is called the electromagnetic spectrum. Someone has to decide who gets to use which frequencies, then enforce these decisions so that others don't come along and interfere. The federal government decided that it was the one to make the decisions, reasoning that the electromagnetic spectrum belonged to all Americans, much like a national park or any other resource that should be shared by all citizens.

In the early days of radio broadcasting, the federal government decided to require individuals to apply for a broadcast frequency with the Federal

Communications Commission (FCC). The FCC was immediately flooded with applications for AM radio frequencies, but the AM band on the electromagnetic spectrum allowed for only about 117 frequencies. The FCC could have chosen 117 applicants and awarded each of them their own frequency. This would have led to 117 AM radio stations, each using its own frequency to broadcast its signal to the entire country. But that is not what the FCC did. Instead, the FCC divided the country into many local market areas and awarded some frequencies to each market. Also, each radio station was limited in the amount of power it could use to broadcast its signal so that the signals would not go beyond the local markets. This allowed the FCC to assign the same frequency to many different markets without having to worry about signals interfering with one another. The FCC chose this alternative because it wanted to spread the limited resource of broadcast frequencies around to as many different people as possible.

By keeping ownership of radio licenses at the local level, the FCC believed it was setting up a system whereby the stations would be operated in the best interests of their local communities. Private businesses were allowed to broadcast on these frequencies provided they operated "in the public interest, convenience, and necessity." Therefore, the rationale for regulation in broadcasting is based on the following points: spectrum scarcity, localism, public interest, promoting diversity of content, and the prevention of monopolies.

Now the country has grown to about 215 broadcasting markets with about 11,400 radio stations, including those on both the AM and FM bands of the electromagnetic spectrum. When television came along in the 1940s, the FCC used the same procedure of allocating broadcasting licenses to local stations in the local markets. Now we have about 1,500 regular broadcast television stations and another 1,400 low-power broadcast stations.

Concentration as a Goal of American Business

Straining against this ethic of localism is a very strong trend toward concentration, consolidation, and centralization. Although almost every media company began as a small, local operation, they take on the characteristics of big business as they grow. Big businesses are complex organizations that market many different products and services and do so under a strong, centralized system in order to achieve a more efficient operation. Big businesses grow by claiming a larger share of the markets in which they compete. They accomplish this by acquiring control of more resources, and this often leads to buying—or at least investing in—other companies.

General industry-wide trends show that fewer and fewer people own more and more of the media. This trend will probably continue as the cost of buying and operating a media voice keeps going up and as entry into the industry becomes more difficult. Today, a person needs a great deal of money and expertise to attempt to buy a mass media voice. Because of this, only companies that already own media voices are successful in acquiring new voices. This is no longer a place for the amateurs who were so instrumental in the innovation stage.

As media companies grow larger and more centralized, there is a danger that they will narrow the range of voices that will be heard. For example, if you send a letter to the editor of a newspaper with a circulation of 1,000, there is a good chance that your letter will be published. Yet if you send the same letter to a newspaper with a circulation of one million, your chance of being published is much smaller. Thus, the larger and more powerful the media company is, the less access you have to make a contribution to its messages or to influence the way it makes decisions. Larger companies must filter out more requests, and in this filtering out process, there is a danger that some voices will not be heard.

Critics of this trend toward concentration are alarmed that so few companies have control of the majority of each medium in the United States. Only 11 companies now control most of the daily newspaper circulation. In magazine publishing, a majority of the industry's total annual revenues now goes to two firms. Five firms control more than half of all book sales. Five media conglomerates share 95% of the recordings market, with Warner and CBS between them controlling 65% of that market. Eight Hollywood studios account for 89% of U.S. feature film rentals. Three television networks earned over two thirds of the total U.S. television revenues (Bagdikian, 1997). These figures within an industry *underestimate* the degree of concentration, because the powerful companies own properties in more than one media industry. For example, a newspaper corporation might own several radio and television stations and perhaps a magazine or two.

With all the recent mergers and acquisitions in the media industries, ownership patterns change rapidly, but the one constant is the trend is toward even greater concentration. Bagdikian (1997) conducted an analysis of media ownership patterns in 1983 and found that the control of the media was essentially in the hands of 50 people—the CEOs of the largest media companies that in combination controlled over half of the revenues and audiences in their media industries. Bagdikian found that less than a decade later the number had shrunk to 23 CEOs of corporations who control most of the business in the country's 25,000 media businesses (see Table 11.1).

As the media become more concentrated, so too does the advertising industry. The large, national agencies are becoming larger in order to deal better with the larger media companies. As ad agencies grow bigger, they become much less interested in local retailers and local markets, favoring instead the

Table 11.1 The Most Powerful Media Companies in the United States

Below is an alphabetical list of the 23 companies that control most of the media audience in the United States. Each of these companies is a conglomerate that owns businesses across several media industries. Next to each of the companies is a brief, partial list of some of the main media properties for which that company is known.

Company	Media Properties
1. A. G. Bertelsmann	Doubleday, Bantam Books, and other book publishers
2. Capital Cities/ABC	Newspapers, broadcasting
3. Cox Communications	*Atlanta Journal* and 19 other newspapers; cable TV
4. CBS	Broadcasting
5. Buena Vista Films	Disney motion pictures
6. Dow Jones	*Wall Street Journal* and 22 other newspapers
7. Gannett	*USA Today* and 87 other daily newspapers
8. General Electric	Owns RCA, which in turn owns the NBC television network
9. Paramount Communications	Book publishers, Paramount Motion Pictures
10. Harcourt Brace Jovanovich	Book publisher
11. Hearst	*San Francisco Examiner* and 13 other newspapers; magazines, including *Good Housekeeping, Cosmopolitan*
12. Ingersoll	37 newspapers
13. International Thomson	120 daily newspapers, book publishers
14. Knight Ridder	*Philadelphia Inquirer, Miami Herald,* and 27 other newspapers
15. Media News group	*Dallas Times Herald* and 17 other newspapers
16. Newhouse	26 newspapers, Conde Nast magazines, Random House
17. News Corporation, Ltd. (Murdoch)	*Boston Herald* and 2 other newspapers; magazines, including *TV Guide, Seventeen, New York;* 20th Century Fox motion pictures; Fox television network
18. New York Times	*New York Times* and 26 other newspapers
19. Readers Digest Association	Books

Table 11.1 Continued

Company	Media Properties
20. Scripps-Howard	23 newspapers
21. Time Warner	Magazines, including *Time, People, Sports Illustrated, Fortune;* book publishers; Warner Brothers television and motion pictures
22. Times Mirror	*Los Angeles Times* and 7 other newspapers
23. Tribune Company	*Chicago Tribune, New York Daily News,* and 7 other newspapers; magazines

SOURCE: This table was assembled with information from Bagdikian (1997) and *Hoover's Guide* (1996).

much larger national market where they can make bigger deals and more money. Thus, most of the advertising today is for national brands. For example, when most people think of hamburgers, they think of McDonald's, Burger King, and Wendy's—not the local restaurant run as a family business. The trend toward concentration is not just within the media industries; it is also taking place with retail stores and advertising agencies.

Concentration Within Media

In this section, a brief profile is presented for each of the nine media industries. Notice that while the indicators of concentration can vary across these industries, the key indicator is market share, which is the percentage of revenue in an industry that goes to a particular company.

Book Industry

While there are 3,000 companies that publish books, 5 produce most of the revenue (Bagdikian, 1997). Book publishing is a segmented field with different sets of publishers specializing in certain sub-markets. Even within these sub-markets, there is a trend toward concentration. For example, in mass market paperback publishing, the top seven firms account for more than 80% of all sales.

Consolidation is taking place in book publishing with big companies both merging with and acquiring smaller companies. For example, The Penguin Group recently acquired The Putnam Berkley Group, a U.S. subsidiary of

MCA, for $336 million. The Penguin Group publishes primarily classics and reference type books (Lyall, 1996). The Putnam Berkley Group is known for its successful best sellers from such authors as Tom Clancey, Dick Francis, Patricia Cornwell, and Amy Tan. The merged company will account for about 12% of all book sales in the United States.

There is a strong trend toward concentration in the bookstore segment of the industry. In 1958, companies that owned more than one bookstore (chains) accounted for only 28% of all sales, and there were no chains with more than 50 stores. Now there are chains such as Barnes & Noble and Borders that own more than 1,000 bookstores. Chain-owned bookstores generate over two thirds of all the revenue in the book industry.

Newspaper Industry

Almost all of the 1,500 daily newspapers printed in this country have a local orientation; that is, they circulate to readers in their home city and the immediately surrounding suburbs. There are only a small number of newspapers (such as *USA Today, Wall Street Journal, Christian Science Monitor*) that have national circulations. In this way, America is unique in newspaper localism compared to other industrialized countries in the world. In most foreign countries, newspaper circulation emanates from a few large cities and spreads out across the entire country. For example, Tokyo has 11% of Japan's population, but daily newspapers from Tokyo account for 70% of the total newspaper circulation in that country. London, with 14% of England's population, accounts for 70% of circulation. In America, New York City and Washington, D.C., combined have 7% of the population but account for only 10% of the country's daily newspaper circulation. Clearly, in this country, newspaper publishing is done at the local level.

While publication takes place on the local level, the ownership of newspapers is becoming more and more concentrated; that is, fewer people are controlling more and more newspapers. The trend toward greater concentration is evidenced in two ways: reduction in competition among newspapers and an increase in ownership by chains.

Competition among newspapers has been greatly reduced. For example, the number of cities with competing daily newspapers is decreasing. In 1900, over 65% of all U.S. cities had competing newspapers but now less than 1% do.

Two reasons have been cited for the decline in newspaper competition. First, political parties no longer support newspapers as they once did, and there has been a decline in the partisanship of the U.S. press. Second, advertisers are demanding large circulations without duplicate readership. As a result, the larger newspaper in a two-newspaper town gets the advertising and continues to grow. The newspaper with the smaller circulation loses advertising and eventually goes out of business.

Chains have increased in size and number. In 1909, there were only 13 chains, and they owned only 2% of all newspapers. Chains grew slowly until 1970, when the majority of newspapers were owned or controlled by small private groups—often a single family. Now 75% of all newspapers are chain owned (Picard, 1993).

There are several reasons why chains keep buying: (a) Newspapers are a profitable investment; (b) they are a scarce commodity because there are no new places to start a newspaper; (c) the use of professional management techniques can convert marginally successful papers into moneymakers; and (d) newspaper firms generate large amounts of cash while they usually carry low debt in relation to invested capital (Compaine, 1979).

As for control of circulation, the eight largest newspaper chains accounted for only 10% of daily circulation in 1900, but by the 1990s, chains controlled a total of 85% of the nation's newspaper circulation. However, no single newspaper or chain dominates the nation's news dissemination. For example, the two largest chains are Gannett Co., whose 82 newspapers have a combined circulation of about 6 million, and Thomson, whose 125 newspapers have a combined circulation of about 4 million. Together, these two chains control more than 200 newspapers but less than 16% of the nation's circulation (Picard, 1993). In contrast, the three television networks have a far greater control of the news flow than any combination of newspaper chains.

With concentration of newspaper control, access by individuals becomes harder. In 1900, there was one newspaper for every 36,000 people in this country, but now there is only one newspaper for about every 170,000 people. While people have many newspapers to read, those newspapers are spreading themselves thinner and thinner. Access is much more difficult.

Magazine Industry

The magazine industry is also a very concentrated mass medium. This can be seen in terms of both ownership patterns and sales. As for ownership, most magazines are published independently. There are about 4,700 firms publishing the 11,000 magazine titles in this country, but most of the circulation and revenue is controlled by three firms.

The magazine industry is subdivided into niches as follows: consumer magazines (such as *Reader's Digest, TV Guide*), news (*Time, Newsweek*), sports (*Sports Illustrated, Runner's World*), opinion (*National Review, New Republic*), intellectual (*Commentary, American Scholar*), men's interest

(*Esquire, Gentleman's Quarterly*), women's interest (*Cosmopolitan, Better Homes and Gardens*), humor (*National Lampoon, Mad*), sex (*Playboy, Playgirl*), and business (*Forbes, Money*). Within each of these sub-markets there is usually a small handful of magazines that account for most of the sub-market's circulation. Typically, these high-circulation magazines are published by the large companies, and these companies publish magazines in many of these sub-markets. For example, Time-Warner publishes *Time, Sports Illustrated,* and *Money.*

Film Industry

The film industry is composed of producers, distributors, and exhibitors. Each of these segments is very concentrated. There are no formal barriers to entry such as a franchise fee or licensing procedures. There are many small independent producers, distributors, and exhibitors, but power is concentrated in the hands of a few huge conglomerates that have diversified holdings beyond the film industry.

While there are about 175 film distribution companies, the industry is dominated by the seven major film studios. These seven typically account for 75% of all distribution.

Typically, the top 10 films each year account for between one third and one half of the industry's total annual receipts. About one third of national admissions comes from nine major metropolitan areas. The 17 weeks of summer, Christmas, and Easter provide 40% to 50% of theater receipts (Guback, 1978). Also, while American firms produce only 10% of the films in the world each year, those films occupy half of the world's screen time.

The four largest film exhibition companies account for about 20% of all receipts from the nation's 26,000 movie screens. The largest exhibition chain, Carmike Cinema, controls 2,401 of these screens (Standard & Poor, 1996, p. L18).

Because of the profitability of film exhibition, the film distribution companies are getting back into exhibition. Until the early 1940s, the major Hollywood studios controlled production, distribution, and exhibition, until the federal government engaged in anti-trust proceedings and forced them to divest themselves of part of their holdings. The studios sold off their theaters. Now, with deregulation and with a more complex business environment, distributors are getting back into exhibition. For example, MCA Inc., which owns Universal Films, also owns 40% of Cineplex Odeon, a large chain of theaters. Viacom, which owns Paramount Pictures, also owns Cinamerica. In total, major movie studios now have ownership stakes in about 2,300 screens nationwide (Standard & Poor, 1996, p. L19).

Recording Industry

The recording and tape industry is very concentrated, with its powerful distributors on one end and the chains of retail music stores on the other end. Distribution is dominated by six major companies: Columbia, Warner Brothers, Capital, MCA, Elektra, and Epic. These six control 80% of recording sales each year. Music retailing is dominated by the major chains. With over 800 outlets, Musicland Stores Corp. is the largest (Standard & Poor, 1996, p. L39).

Retailers that can't sell all of a company's tapes and CDs return them to the company. The major recording companies each run their own record club; the returns are offered to club members at deep discounts. As a group, the clubs account for about 11% of all sales (DeFleur & Dennis, 1996).

There are also thousands of independent record producers. These producers find talent, rent a recording studio to produce a recording, and get copies manufactured. Then they persuade one of the six major recording companies to distribute and market the recording. This is a high-risk endeavor; independent producers account for only about 20% of all hit recordings (DeFleur & Dennis, 1996).

Radio Industry

Recall from the beginning of this chapter that in the 1920s, the federal government favored localism when it awarded radio licenses to local owners. The local stations were mandated to serve the needs of the communities in which they were going to broadcast. Yet almost from the beginning, radio broadcasters began moving away from their mandate and instead made decisions that have helped their businesses to function more profitably. They have done this primarily through network affiliation and group ownership.

Instead of generating local programming, most broadcasters have chosen to affiliate with one of the large commercial networks. These affiliates get their programming from the networks, and this programming is national in content. Network affiliation began in 1927 when 6% of available radio stations became affiliated with one of the four radio networks: ABC, CBS, MBS, and NBC. The peak period of affiliation was reached in 1947 when 97% of the country's 1,062 radio stations were affiliated with one of the four national radio networks.

Now radio stations are not likely to affiliate with national networks, or if they do affiliate, they usually get only news and features from the network. However, this does not mean that radio stations now exhibit a wide variety of programming that reflects the local needs of their communities. Instead, radio stations are likely to affiliate with a certain type of programming such as Top 40, Golden Oldies, Album Oriented Rock, Country and Western, all news/talk, and so on. For example, most radio markets have a Top 40 station, and these stations sound the same all over the country, regardless of the locale in which they broadcast. They all play the same songs on the same rotation, play the same lead-in and lead-out for the news, cover the same types of news stories with the same kinds of formulas, and have the same kinds of contests and promotions.

There has been a steady increase in group ownership of radio stations. In 1929, only about 3% of the country's 600 existing radio stations were group owned. By the late 1960s, the figure had climbed to about one third of all stations, and that figure is even higher today.

Today there are about 11,400 radio stations in this country. In 1992, the federal government loosened restrictions on ownership so that now a person (or a corporate entity) can own up to 20 FM and 20 AM stations. This has stimulated a lot of buying and selling. Over the past few years about 1,000 stations have changed ownership each year at an average price of $1 million (Standard & Poor, 1996, p. M36). Then in 1996, the federal government loosened ownership regulations even more.

Broadcast Television

Television broadcasting has followed the same pattern as radio. The FCC attempted to reaffirm its perspective of localism as its guiding principle on licensing when it awarded television broadcasting licenses in the 1940s and 1950s. This decision required the establishment of hundreds of local stations, and the FCC had to find new spectrum space in order to provide these stations with their own broadcasting frequencies. As a result, the UHF band (channels 14 through 83) was set aside for television use in addition to the already used VHF band (channels 2 through 13).

Commercial broadcast stations are licensed to provide service to local communities. Over the years, however, the FCC has done very little to ensure that the stations do in fact provide responsible service to their communities. Television stations have been permitted to affiliate with national networks and to buy syndicated services, both of which feature national programming.

From the beginning, local stations affiliated with national television networks. In 1954, network affiliates were already getting 50% of their total programming from their networks. Within two decades, they were producing only about 10% of their own programming.

There are strong economic incentives for networking. Affiliates are able to share the production costs as well as the risks of a program. If something is to be produced locally, it must be inexpensive and very popular compared to the alternative program from the network. Therefore, the affiliates air most of the network programming, which is aimed at a national, not local, audience.

Perhaps network affiliation will decrease as audiences fragment. The three big television networks (ABC, CBS, and NBC) have been losing audience share for the past decade. They used to control 91% of the prime-time audience as recently as the mid-1980s, but their share has now dropped to 57% (Standard & Poor, 1996, p. M38). Counter to this trend is the recent start up of several new national television broadcast networks by Fox, Warner Brothers, and others. It will be interesting to see whether networks survive, and if so, in what form.

Concentration in station ownership was initially limited by FCC regulations that restricted ownership to 7 television stations, but this limit was raised to 12 stations in the 1980s and since then has been raised even more. By 1995, 75% of all TV stations in the top 100 markets were licensed to multiple owners. About one quarter of these were owned by publishers of newspapers, although it is rare for a newspaper and TV station in the same market to be owned by the same company. In total, there are 210 groups that own more than one TV station. Twelve of these groups own 10 or more stations each (Howard, 1995).

The advertising on commercial television is concentrated in the hands of a few very large advertisers who can afford to buy great amounts of time each year. For example, 20 companies account for more than half of all advertising on broadcast television.

Cable Television

Cable systems are treated as natural monopolies—like utilities such as electricity and water companies. They are extremely concentrated, because there is almost never cable competition within their area of coverage. They are franchised on the local level and must therefore meet the requirements that the local community writes into the contract, such as time requirements for wiring the community, control of rates, and percentage of profits. Entry is controlled by economic cost, which requires capital-intensive construction and franchise requirements. Once entry is achieved, however, the system typically has sole rights to the market for 10 to 15 years. Thus, it becomes a monopoly.

There are no ownership limits on multiple system ownership (MSO) size. The top four firms in 1965 accounted for only about 20% of all cable subscribers. In the past 30 years, the major MSOs have continued to consolidate so as to build efficient clusters. The top four MSOs (TCI, Time Warner,

Continental Cablevision, and Comcast) now have a combined share of 50% of all cable subscribers (up from 38% share just since 1993), and the top eight MSOs now have a combined 64% share (Chan-Olmsted, 1996).

The MSOs will continue to grow by buying up smaller cable systems or by trying to put some out of business in those rare markets that are overbuilt and where there is competition. Barrett (1996) examined the business practices of MSOs in two overbuilt cable markets and found that they used a variety of tactics—especially price cutting and litigation—to deter entry by rivals.

Computers

The computer industry is very new, and there is great flux in the way companies grow quickly, get bought by larger firms, or go out of business. Even so, there are some trends that reveal evidence of concentration. For example, the top six hard drive manufacturers account for 90% of the total market of 60 million units per year. Within the software component, Microsoft is the largest company, with sales larger than the next two companies combined (Standard & Poor, 1996, p. C107). Microsoft is the creator of the MS-DOS and Windows operating systems, which run 80% of all PCs. Also, Microsoft has created a great deal of software, such as Word, that accounts for about half of all software sold. The company has annual revenues of about $5 billion and spends about $600 million each year on research and development. It has 15,000 employees (Maney, 1995).

Cross-Media Ownership and Control

Types of Concentration

There are three different trends in concentration. One is the horizontal merger, in which one media company buys another medium of the same type. An example is a newspaper chain buying another newspaper. This pattern was very popular during the 1980s when newspapers were being gobbled up by chains at the rate of 50 to 60 per year.

Another is the vertical merger, in which one media company buys suppliers or distributors, or both, to create integration in the production and distribution of messages. An example is a book publisher buying a printing plant and some book stores.

A third is the conglomerate merger, in which a media company buys a combination of other media companies and/or companies in a non-media business. An example is a film studio that buys a newspaper, several radio stations, a talent agency, and a string of restaurants. Paramount Communications owns Paramount studios, which is one of the leading producers of motion pictures, television shows, and cable programming. It also owns Simon & Schuster—the world's largest book publishing company. Paramount is a major maker of entertainment video cassettes, and it controls 1,100 movie screens in the United States and 11 foreign countries (Bagdikian, 1997). In 1994, Viacom, which owns such cable television services as MTV, VH1, and Nickelodeon, took over Paramount Communications Inc. for $9.6 billion.

From the business point of view, cross-media ownership is very attractive. Not only is it very profitable, but the arrangement allows for cross-promotion of products. For example, when Paramount released its movie *The Brady Bunch,* Viacom put on several weeks of *Brady Bunch* TV reruns on its Nickelodeon cable channel as a way of promoting the movie.

Mega-Mergers

In the 1990s, the industry has become much more concentrated through a series of mega-mergers. For example, Westinghouse Corp. bought CBS in 1995 for $5.4 billion, giving the new company 15 TV stations and 39 radio stations that, combined, give it direct access to one third of the nation's households.

In 1990, Warner Communication Inc. merged with Time Inc. for $14.4 billion to make it the largest media company at the time (Lorimer, 1994).

In August 1995, Walt Disney Co. acquired Capital Cities/ABC Inc. for $19 billion, making it the largest media company. ABC had been concerned about the fragmentation of television audiences due to cable so it diversified and now owns the ESPN and Lifetime cable channels as well as the Disney channel.

Then, in the summer of 1996, Time Warner bought Turner Broadcasting making it once more the world's biggest media company with annual revenues of more than $20 billion (Roberts, 1996).

Companies outside the media area have been buying media properties, too, because they are so profitable. In 1986, General Electric bought RCA Inc. In the same year, Capital Cities bought ABC. Seagram Co. now owns about 80% of MCA, which owns Putnam publishing, films, records, and theme parks (Lyall, 1996).

Phone companies keep looking for entertainment companies to buy. For example, GTE has 17 million phone lines and $20 billion in revenue annually. BellSouth is the biggest regional phone company, with 19 million phone lines that bring in a total of $16 billion per year. With all their cash, the phone companies are looking to invest in profitable businesses, especially those that would give them access to customers who want to buy information and entertainment. In May 1993, US West, a telephone company, paid $2.5 billion for 25.5% of Time Warner (Maney, 1995). The new company plans to integrate the technologies that would provide a service allowing people to order instantly whatever programming they want (movies on demand), to shop for products, and to do their banking, listen to CDs, watch live sports and concerts, make travel plans, play video games, and more (Powell, 1993).

During the 1980s, there were 2,308 mergers and acquisitions involving media companies for a total of $214 billion (Ozanich & Wirth, 1993). This activity served to consolidate resources into fewer companies. Thus the CEOs of these newer, larger companies hold an even greater concentration of power as they manage those resources.

Look at the sampling of media companies profiled in Table 11.2. Notice that almost all are conglomerates with both media and non-media holdings.

International Perspective

Foreign companies have been buying American media properties, especially film studios, over the past decade. For example, Pathe, a French-Italian firm, bought MGM and United Artists. Sony, a Japanese electronics manufacturer, bought Columbia Pictures from Coca-Cola.

Foreign companies buying or investing in American media companies is not uncommon. In one year, companies from the United Kingdom made 188 deals totaling $23.6 billion to buy U.S. media companies; Japanese companies made 45 transactions for $11.9 billion; Canadian companies, 46 deals for $9.7 billion; French companies, 26 deals for $3 billion; and German companies, 27 transactions for $1.2 billion.

An example of how American companies attract foreign investors is Rupert Murdoch, who is from Australia where he owns newspapers in most of that country's major cities, including Australia's only national daily, as well as television stations, publishing houses, record companies, and a major airline. He went to Great Britain and bought the *London Times;* two sex and scandal sheets with a combined circulation of over 8 million; a string of magazines; a string of provincial newspapers; and companies for manufacturing paper, printing, and distributing newsprint. He came to the United States and bought the *New York Post, New York Magazine,* the *Village Voice,* the *Chicago Sun-Times,* two other daily newspapers, and 17 suburban weeklies. He bought Metromedia's seven television stations in New York, Boston, and other major cities, giving him access to 21% of the total television audience. His empire earns over $1 billion a year. Recently, Murdoch's Australian firm, News Corp., took over the American film giant, 20th Century Fox.

Table 11.2 Profiles of Six Large Media Conglomerates

Sony Corporation had 1996 sales of $44.8 billion, making it the largest media company in the world. Headquartered in Tokyo, Japan, it employs 138,000 people. It manufactures televisions, VCRs, Walkmans, Discmans, and Apple Powerbooks, among other electronic devices. It owns CBS Records and Columbia Pictures. It is in partnership with Microsoft to make SEGA video games. Its profit margin is about 12%.

Time Warner Inc. is the second largest media company in the world with 1996 sales of $17.7 billion and 65,500 employees. It owns magazines (*Time, Money, Sports Illustrated, Life, Discover, Fortune, People, Entertainment Weekly, Martha Stewart Living, In Style*), book publishing houses (Time-Life Books; Little, Brown and Co.; Book of the Month Club; as well as large interests in publishing firms in Germany, France, Mexico, and Japan), comic books (*Batman, Superman, Bugs Bunny, Mad*), newspapers (Pioneer Press, which publishes suburban Chicago newspapers), television networks (WB, Courtroom Television, HBO), broadcast television stations, Warner Brothers movie studio (with its recent successful films *Twister* and *Eraser,* along with TV shows *Friends* and *ER*), Looney Toons (which alone produces retail sales of $3.5 billion in cartoon merchandising), Time Warner Cable system (second largest cable operator in the country), recording companies (Atlantic, Warner Brothers), and Six Flags Entertainment. It also owns Turner Broadcasting, which includes the Cartoon Network, TNT, CNN, Turner Pictures, the MGM film library, Hanna-Barbera cartoon stars (Flintstones and Yogi Bear), and the movie studios of New Line Cinema and Castle Rock. In addition, it owns a marketing data company, video games (Atari), Inland Container Corporation, American Television and Communications Corporation, and Temple Industries, which is one of the largest landowners in the country.

The Walt Disney Company has annual revenues of $12 billion. It owns film studios (Disney, Touchstone, Miramax, Hollywood Pictures), the ABC television network, theme parks, record companies, book publishing houses, and television production studios. It employs 71,000 people.

Viacom Inc. has revenues of $11.7 billion and employs 81,700 people. It owns movie theaters, radio and television stations, production studios (Paramount Pictures, Spelling Entertainment, Worldvision), Blockbuster Video, book publishers (Simon & Schuster, Macmillan, Prentice Hall), and cable networks (Comedy Central, MTV, VH1, Nickelodeon, Showtime, The Movie Channel, Sci-Fi Channel, USA Network, and All News Channel).

Cox Enterprises, Inc., owns the fifth largest cable system in the country, 19 newspapers, 17 radio stations (including 3 in Los Angeles), 6 television stations, companies in the industries of farming, timber, cattle, paper manufacturing, direct marketing, auto auctioning, and publishing. It has annual sales of $3.8 billion and employs 38,000 people.

Barnes & Noble, Inc., was begun by a 24-year-old who borrowed $5,000 to start a college bookstore; it has grown to annual sales of $2 billion and employs 21,400 people. It owns more than 1,000 bookstores (including B. Dalton) in 49 states, as well as Doubleday, Scribner's, and Marlboro Books.

SOURCE: All information from *Hoover's Guide to Media Companies*, 1996.

Issues of Concern

We have seen that the media industries have been moving steadily toward greater concentration in two ways: within each industry and, especially, across media industries. Critics fear that this trend has already put too much power into the hands of a very few people. They feel that consumers are now worse off because of (a) less competition and (b) less access to the media. Let's take a close look at each of these two criticisms.

First, critics argue that as competition decreases, the quality of media products declines. But has the quality of the media products declined? There is no evidence that it has. A study done on newspaper content concludes that content does not change (e.g., see Picard, Winter, McCombs, & Lacy, 1988). When newspapers are acquired by chains it does not appear that their newshole changes, that the stories change, or that the editorial page expresses a narrower range of opinions.

Also, it does not appear that radio station content is changed when a station is bought by a group. Lacy and Riffe (1994) looked at the news content of radio stations, comparing group ownership effects. They found group ownership had no impact on the financial commitment or on the local and staff emphasis of news coverage.

This criticism—that concentration of ownership reduces competition in a market—seems valid on the surface, but it breaks down when analyzed. To illustrate, let's say a city has two newspapers. A chain buys one of those newspapers. The chain-owned newspaper cuts subscription costs and ad rates. Readers and advertisers switch to the chain newspaper because it is less expensive. Eventually, the other newspaper goes out of business. The degree of concentration in that market goes up, but this does not mean that the newspaper has no competition simply because it is the only newspaper in the market. The newspaper must compete for audiences and advertisers with the radio, television, and cable stations in the market. Thus, if the newspaper degrades its news product, people will drop their subscriptions and turn to other sources of news. With lower circulation rates, the newspaper will need to drop the rate it charges advertisers, and this will produce less revenue. With less revenue, the newspaper will need to lay off reporters, and the news product will degrade further. This downward cycle continues until the newspaper is out of business. This almost never happens, because chain-owned newspapers are driven by making large profits, and to do that, they must do everything they can to expand their circulation.

Newspapers, as well as all the other media, expand their revenues only by providing more and better services to consumers. How do they know what consumers want? They are constantly doing market research to test new ideas.

Also, they carefully monitor the public's reactions, verbal as well as monetary, to their messages. When the public's tastes or wants change, the media know this, and they offer new types of products and messages.

Second, critics argue that as concentration increases, the individual's access to the media is reduced. "Access" here can mean two different things. One meaning is ownership. It is still possible for an individual to buy an existing media company or to start one as a sole owner. There are comparatively low barriers to entry in the magazine, book publishing, newspaper, and computer industries. With several thousand dollars, a desktop computer, and a strong initiative, most people could begin a company in one of these media industries. Of course, the person should be prepared to face very stiff competition to gain the attention of an audience and to gain the confidence of advertisers. In contrast, barriers to entry are much higher in the radio, television, cable, and film industries; and the conglomerate mergers over the past several decades have raised those barriers even higher, almost to the point of being prohibitive for anyone except the wealthiest individuals. Yet because almost all of these media companies are public corporations, you can buy a share of any of them. However, while buying one share of a large media company makes you a part owner, your one share out of the total of millions of shares owned would not give you much access to the workings of the company.

Access can also mean the ability to get your particular point of view heard through someone else's media property. This is still fairly easy to do at the local level, such as newspapers and small-circulation magazines. Most still print letters to the editors, and most buy articles from people with little journalistic experience. Most markets also have call-in radio programs where you can get your voice heard. In contrast, getting your voice heard in national media properties, such as *Newsweek* magazine or a TV or cable network, would require a great deal of skill and good connections, because the competition to use those channels is so strong.

Summary

Media critics are wary of the degree of concentration in the media industries. Their concern is focused on the central issue of which is more important: efficiency (brought about by industry integration and economics of scale) *OR* independence (diversity of content and easier entry into the market, thus allowing alternative voices).

This is an issue about which you should have an opinion. To synthesize a good opinion, you need to build it up from an analysis of the situation. This chapter provides just such an analysis to start your thinking. You should begin by considering which ethic you think should be dominant in the formulation of the media industries. Do you favor localism with its focus on the power of society—through citizen activism and government regulations—to make the media responsive to the different needs of the broad spectrum of people in the society? Or do you favor concentration as a goal of businesses driven to operate more effectively and efficiently and thus generate as large a profit as possible for the owners?

Once you become interested in this issue and begin formulating your opinion, you need to monitor changes in this dynamic situation and continually update your knowledge structure. Over time, the government has been relaxing regulations, and as a result businesses have been moving strongly toward concentration. Even so, there is still a great deal of competition among the media industries as they try to claim more of our attention and a greater share of the advertisers' dollars.

References

Bagdikian, B. (1997). *The media monopoly* (5th ed.). Boston: Beacon.

Barrett, M. (1996). Strategic behavior and competition in cable television: Evidence from two overbuilt markets. *Journal of Media Economics, 9*, 43-62.

Chan-Olmsted, S. M. (1996). Market competition for cable television: Reexamining its horizontal mergers and industry concentration. *Journal of Media Economics, 9*, 25-41.

Compaine, B. (Ed.). (1979). *Who owns the media?* White Plains, NY: Knowledge Industry Publications.

DeFleur, M. L., & Dennis, E. E. (1996). *Understanding mass communication: A liberal arts perspective.* Princeton, NJ: Houghton Mifflin.

Hoover's guide to media companies. (1996). Austin, TX: Hoover's Business Press.

Howard, H. H. (1995). TV station group and cross-media ownership: A 1995 update. *Journalism & Mass Communication Quarterly, 72*, 390-401.

Lacy, S., & Riffe, D. (1994). The impact of competition and group ownership on radio news. *Journalism & Mass Communication Quarterly, 71*, 583-593.

Lorimer, R. (1994). *Mass communications: A comparative introduction.* New York: Manchester University Press.

Lyall, S. (1996, November 27). Penguin's deal to buy Putnam will create major publishing force. *Santa Barbara News-Press*, p. A6.

Maney, K. (1995). *Megamedia shakeout: The inside story of the leaders and the losers in the exploding communications industry.* New York: John Wiley.

Ozanich, G. W., & Wirth, M. O. (1993). Media mergers and acquisitions: An overview. In A. Alexander, J. Owers, & R. Carveth (Eds.), *Media economics: Theory and practice* (pp. 115-133). Hillsdale, NJ: Lawrence Erlbaum.

Picard, R. G. (1993). Economics of the daily newspaper industry. In A. Alexander, J. Owers, & R. Carveth (Eds.), *Media economics: Theory and practice* (pp. 181-203). Hillsdale, NJ: Lawrence Erlbaum.

Picard, R. G., Winter, J. P., McCombs, M., & Lacy, S. (Eds). (1988). *Press concentration and monopoly: New perspectives on newspaper ownership and operation.* Norwood, NJ: Ablex.

Powell, B. (1993, May 31). Eyes on the future. *Newsweek,* pp. 39-41.

Roberts, J. L. (July 29, 1996). Mergers main men. *Newsweek,* pp. 42-48.

Standard & Poor. (1996, July). *Index to surveys.* New York: Author.

Further Reading

Bagdikian, B. (1997). *The media monopoly* (5th ed.). Boston: Beacon. (288 pages, with index)

Bagdikian has had to update his book, originally published in 1983, four times to keep up with the trend of consolidation in the media industries. He argues that the media are in the hands of too few corporations, claiming that this is an unhealthy condition, because it focuses decisions too much on profit and not enough on quality or diversity of messages. Profits are maximized when corporations increase revenues, which means that program producers must not offend advertisers. He shows how advertising has pressured journalism to change the way it reports stories.

Maney, K. (1995). *Megamedia shakeout: The inside story of the leaders and the losers in the exploding communications industry.* New York: John Wiley. (358 pages, including index)

This is a well-written description of the major players in the end-technologies landscape in the mid-1990s. There are many anecdotes and stories about what has been happening in the telephone, cable, computer, wireless, and entertainment industries. The book is full of facts and personal descriptions of the personalities involved. Unfortunately, things are happening so fast in these industries, with new roll-outs and buy-outs, that the book will soon be dated.

Exercise 11.1   What Is the Concentration of Media Ownership in Your Local Market?

This exercise asks you to be a detective and search out information in your local media market. See how creative you can be in coming up with strategies to get the answers to the following questions.

1. How many movie screens are there in your market?
   a. How many theaters control those screens?
   b. Are the theaters owned by chains? If so, how many chains control the total number of screens?

2. How many radio stations are there in your market?
   a. How many are group owned?
   b. How many of the stations are owned by companies that also own other media businesses in your market?

3. How many broadcast television stations are there in your market?
   a. How many are group owned?
   b. How many of the stations are owned by companies that also own other media businesses in your market?

4. Is your local newspaper owned by a chain? If so, does it own other media businesses in your market?

5. Are there any magazines published in your market that are distributed only in your market? If so, does the controlling company also own other media businesses?

6. What is the name of the company that provides your market with cable TV service? Is that cable company an MSO?

7. In total, how many different media outlets (voices) are there in your market? How many individuals or companies control these voices?

8. If you wanted to express yourself through the media in your market, how hard do you think it would be to gain access to one of these outlets?
   a. For example, assume that you wanted to criticize some new governmental regulation or tax policy in your local area; which outlet would be most likely to give you space or time to speak out?
   b. Which outlet(s) do you think would be the least likely to do so, or impossible?

9. Given your answers to the questions above, how concentrated do you think your market is—that is, do you think the outlets are in the control of too few individuals?

CHAPTER 12

What Is an Audience?

KEY IDEA *We are members of many different niche audiences as defined by where we live, as well as our demographic and psychological characteristics.*

W e are constantly exposed to all sorts of media messages, and with many of them, we are unaware of being exposed to them until we carefully pay attention. Remember the exercise in Chapter 2 on becoming sensitized to message saturation? Now that you have built a good knowledge structure about the media industries from the information in Chapters 9, 10, and 11, let's revisit this issue of exposure. This time, let's look at it from the media's side; that is, how do the marketers view you as audiences?

Mass Audience?

What is an audience? At first, this question may seem very simple with an obvious answer. Up until several decades ago, most people treated it like a simple question. We were all believed to be part of a mass audience, so we had terms like "mass media" and "mass communication." The term *mass communication* came into use about 100 years ago when early social philosophers argued that newspapers, magazines, and books communicated their ideas to all audience members in roughly the same way. Once a writer perfected his or her message, it would affect everyone the same way.

The term *mass* did not refer to a *large* audience as much as it referred to a certain *type* of audience. Early sociologists focused on the way people in industrialized societies felt about themselves and others in social networks. They felt that people in the modern mass society were becoming both isolated and alienated from other members of society, because increasing technology was making people machine-like.

In order to be a "mass," an audience needs four characteristics. First, the audience composition has to be heterogeneous. This means that the audience is composed of people of all kinds, and no one is excluded. Second, the audience members are anonymous. The message designers don't know the names of anyone in the audience nor do they care to, because the designers regard everyone as being the same and interchangeable. Third, there is no interaction among the members in the audience. People don't talk to each other about the media messages, so the messages are not modified in conversations. Instead, the messages will have a direct effect on each person in a uniform manner. Fourth, there is no leadership. The mass is very loosely organized and is not able to act with the concertedness or unity that marks a crowd (Blumer, 1946). Blumer also pointed out that a mass has no social organization, no body of custom and tradition, no established set of rules or rituals, no organized group of sentiments, and no structure or status roles.

You may be thinking: That idea of mass audience is silly. How could anyone really believe that an audience was like that?

Yes, that conception of audience does sound rather silly now as we look back on it from our present society. But at the time, this was the accepted way of thinking about audiences in this and other countries. Our thinking on this point has changed dramatically. Use this insight to alert yourself to the fact that there are likely to be current beliefs that will be found to be silly when we look back on the late 1990s in future decades. How can we protect ourselves from current faulty beliefs? We need to develop strong knowledge structures and carefully analyze our existing opinions and our experiences. In short, we need to be highly media literate.

Support for "Mass Audience"

Starting with the industrial revolution in the mid-1800s, the United States and countries in Western Europe were regarded as having mass societies. Because these countries were heavily industrialized, it was believed that the technological progress had shaped the lives of people. Less industrialized countries did not have mass societies, because people there were tightly integrated into social networks in which they interacted continually with others on a daily basis. Thus the United States was regarded as having a mass society but India was not, even though the population of India was much larger than that of the United States.

Because it was believed that communication did take place in a mass-like fashion, it was assumed that a message reached everyone in the same way and was processed by everyone in the same manner. It was also believed that the processing itself was very simple: that is, people were vulnerable—they had no psychological defenses against messages, because they did not discuss messages with other people.

As evidence for this position, social critics pointed to the way Adolph Hitler used the mass medium of radio in the 1930s to mobilize the German population to support him. Kate Smith's radio telethons for war bonds, in which she raised millions of dollars, were also offered as evidence that people were highly susceptible to media messages. Another often cited example of the public's seeming lack of defense against media messages is provided by the widespread reaction to Orson Welles's 1939 Mercury Theater presentation of "War of the Worlds." Some listeners actually believed that Earth was being invaded by Martians.

Sociologists of the 1930s and 1940s were very vocal in their warnings about the dangers of mass communication. A more careful analysis of the three examples mentioned, however, reveals that most people were not affected by those messages (Cantril, 1947). Further, it was later shown that the people who were affected were not all affected in the same manner nor did they all react in the same way.

Rejection of the Idea of "Mass Audience"

By the 1950s, it became apparent to many scholars that the assumption of the audience as a "mass" was incorrect. Friedson (1953) was the first to criticize this view of the audience. He felt that people attend movies, listen to radio, and watch television within an interpersonal context. Discussions of media material frequently take place before, during, and after exposure. There is a well-developed web of organized social relationships that exists among audience members. This social environment influences what audience members will expose themselves to and how messages will affect them. Media behavior is merely a part of their more general social behavior. Friedson warned that "the concept of mass is not accurately applicable to the audience" (p. 316). Since Friedson made this point, many other researchers have supported this position (Bauer & Bauer, 1960; Brouwer, 1964).

Today, we look back on such thinking and find it rather naive. Were earlier days really more simple? Was life more innocent and easy? No. That is not the reason. The reason is that sociologists at the end of the 1800s used too simple an explanation to describe the media and its audience. This is not a criticism of sociologists. In social science, simple explanations are usually better than complex ones that no one can understand. An explanation must also be useful, however, and this idea of a mass audience was found not to be useful, because when sociologists carefully observed how people behaved, they realized that some of the elements of the definition of *mass* did not fit. For example, people did interact with each other and did talk about media messages. Also, there was a leadership structure in which certain people were regarded as opinion leaders who influenced the attitudes of other people.

Today, the term *mass communication* is still used, but rarely is there a time when everyone is exposed to the same message. Even with events like the Superbowl, only about 60% of people watch. More important, those who do watch the Superbowl do not all experience the same thing. Some viewers are elated as their team is winning; others are depressed as their team is losing; some are happy there is a reason to party and have no idea who is playing; and many are bored as the game becomes one-sided. There is no common experience. Also, people talk to each other during the viewing and help each other interpret events.

There is no "mass" communication, because there is no "mass" audience. Instead, there are many audiences, some with structures and leadership and others without these characteristics. Some audiences last for only a few hours (Superbowl viewers) while others last for a whole season (diehard football fans). Some audiences are based on a need for immediate information (viewers of CNN), some on in-depth information (readers of news magazines), some on a need for a religious experience (viewers of the *PTL Club*), some on a need for political stimulation, musical entertainment, romantic fantasy, and on and on.

Marketers know that there is no mass audience. Therefore, they almost never attempt to sell a product, service, or media message to *everyone*. Instead, they try to determine how the total population can be divided into meaningful segments. Then marketers identify a segment or two with people who would want or need their product. They then target these audiences for their messages and ignore other people.

Each of us is a member of multiple audiences. You are a member of a local community that the local newspaper and cable TV franchise targets. You are a member of virtual communities when you are on the Internet—communities that quickly form and may last for only one evening. You are a member of certain hobby groups that are targeted by certain magazines, although other members of your audience segment are spread out all over the world and will never meet you in person.

Conceptions of Segmented Audiences

All media produce content to attract certain types of audiences. Some of those media (newspapers, magazines, radio, and television) rent those audiences out to advertisers who want to put their messages in front of certain types of people. For example, a classical music radio station will play only a certain type of music and present interviews and news only about certain artists in order to attract an upscale, highly educated, older audience. The station then rents this audience out to such advertisers as luxury car dealers, jewelers, and travel agencies.

Identifying audience segments is an important task for media organizations and advertisers. Over the years, audience segmentation schemes have become more complex in an effort to generate more precise groupings. This is illustrated below by showing the development of thinking over five types of segmentation methods: geographics, demographics, social class, geodemographics, and psychographics.

Geographic Segmentation

Geographic segmentation schemes are most important to newspapers and local radio and television stations, because there are geographical boundaries to their coverage areas. They have also been useful to other media in thinking about getting their messages out to certain regions of the country.

This is the oldest form of segmentation, and it worked well when regions of the country were culturally diverse. A company would begin a business in a certain locale and produce products that the people in that locale wanted. Because of limits on distribution, that company would do business only in that one area and advertise only in that one area. If that company wanted to expand, it would move out from its home locale to other places in the region where the product met a need. If there was a nationwide need, then the company could expand into national distribution and advertising—but then there would be no need to do geographic segmentation. As many businesses took their products into the national market, regional differences eroded.

Geographic segmentation is becoming less useful as the country becomes more geographically homogenized. We are a mobile society. Each year, about 20% of the population moves to a new home. Regions are therefore not as insulated as they once were, and there is a sharing of foods, music, clothing, and other cultural elements across regions.

Demographic Segmentation

Demographics focus on the relatively enduring characteristics of each person, such as gender, ethnic background, birth year, income, and education. While some of these can be changed (such as education and income), the change takes a great deal of effort. These are therefore fairly stable characteristics and have been quite useful in classifying us into meaningful audience segments.

The usefulness of demographics as an audience segmentation device has been diminishing. Decades ago, when adult women stayed home and raised children, it made sense to market household and child care products to women only. Also, radio and television presented programs targeted to women during the daytime hours when women were home. Now that the percentage of women in the labor force is the same as that for men, gender is less useful as a segmenter.

Ethnicity also used to be a stronger demographic than it is today because the range of income, education, political views, and cultural needs is much greater *within* any ethnic group than it is *across* ethnic groups. With the tremendous growth of credit, household income is no longer as useful a segmenter as it once was. In addition, some demographic groups, such as teenagers, have greatly increased their spending. American teenagers spent $109 billion in 1995—up 10% from 1994. A hefty portion ($41 billion) of that was money earned by their parents. Males spent an average of $67 per week and females $65 ("Teen Spending Up Again," 1996).

Educational level is also less useful. Fifty years ago, having a college degree put you in an elite grouping—the top 5% of the population. Now, almost 20% of American adults have at least one college degree and another 20% have earned some college credit.

Social Class

We could think of social class solely in terms of level of household income, but then social class would mean the same thing as the demographic of income. Why would we need both types of segmentation schemes if they put the same people into the same groups? Instead, social class is a mix of characteristics. One of those characteristics is income, but psychological characteristics are also part of the mix. For example, being in the lower class of course means a low income, but you as a college student have a very low income. Do you consider yourself lower class? No, there is more to the definition. Being in the lower class means taking the psychological perspective that what happens in life is not under your control. You feel that you were born into a situation with little opportunity and that you must struggle to maintain your existence. Because Fate has put you in this situation, all you can do is to try to make the best of it when you can. Therefore, when you get a windfall of money, have as much fun as you can before someone takes it away from you. There is no point in saving for a better tomorrow that will never come.

Being middle class means holding the value that it is good to put off immediate pleasures for more important, longer term goals. Thus middle-class people have a strong work ethic, believing that work is good for them and for society in general. The fact that you are in college is a good indication that you hold a middle-class perspective. You believe that it is a good idea to make economic, time, and lifestyle sacrifices for 4 years now, so that you will later receive much larger rewards for your efforts. You believe that your current actions influence your future. You believe that you control your fate—not the other way around.

Being upper class does not simply mean having more money: It means being able to control more resources—yours and those of others. It means having the ability to raise large sums and wield lots of power.

Geodemographics

A recent innovation in consumer segmentation, geodemographics is a blend of geographic and demographic segmentation. It is based on the assumption that we choose to live in neighborhoods where other people are like us. This means that neighborhoods tend to be homogeneous on important characteristics and that these characteristics change across neighborhoods.

One example of geodemographic segmentation is the PRIZM scheme, which was developed by Claritas Corporation in 1974. PRIZM is based on a complex analysis of U.S. census data. It began with a study of the 35,000 zip code neighborhoods, and concluded that there were 40 different kinds of neighborhoods in this country. It gave the clusters memorable (and trademarked) nicknames such as "Sun Belt Singles" (which are southern suburban areas populated by young professionals), "Norma Rae-ville" (named after the movie about a working-class woman who unionized factory employees), "Marlboro Country" (evoking a western rural area with rugged men on horseback), "Furs and Station Wagons" (typified by new money living in expensive new neighborhoods), and "Hard Scrabble" (which represents areas in the Ozark mountains, Dakota Badlands, and south Texas border).

Psychographics

Psychographics is the current cutting edge of segmentation schemes. It is not limited to one or two characteristics of people but uses a wide variety of variables to create its segments. A typical psychographic segmentation scheme will use demographics, lifestyle, and product-usage variables for segmenting consumers. There are many examples of psychographic segmentation. Two stand out as being very influential.

Twelve American Lifestyles. William Wells, director of advertising research at Needham, Harper & Steers in Chicago, developed the 12 American lifestyles, which include Joe the factory worker and his wife Judy; Phyllis the career woman and her liberated husband Dale; Thelma the contented homemaker; and Harry the cigar-chomping middle-aged salesman. Each of these creations represents a different lifestyle. For example, Joe is a 30s, lower-middle-class male who makes an hourly wage doing semi-skilled work. He watches a lot of television, especially sports and action/adventure programs; he rarely reads. He drives a pickup truck and knows a lot about automotive parts and accessories. In contrast, Phyllis is a 30s career woman with a graduate degree. She reads a lot and when she watches television, it is usually news or a good movie. She likes fine food, dining out, and travel.

VALS Typology. VALS was developed at SRI (Stanford Research Institute) in Menlo Park, California. After monitoring social, economic, and political trends during the 1960s and 1970s, Arnold Mitchell constructed an 85-page measurement instrument that asked questions ranging from people's sexual habits to what brands of margarine they ate. He had 1,635 people fill out the questionnaire, and the answers became the database for his book *Nine American Lifestyles,* published in 1983. In the book, Mitchell argues that people's values strongly influence their spending patterns and media behaviors. So, if we know which value group a person identifies with, we can predict a great deal about the products and services that person will want. For example, one of the groups is called Experientials. The people in this value grouping like to try new and different things to find out what they are like. They like to travel. They are early users of new types of products—and they are constantly looking for something different.

Over the years, Mitchell's scheme has been updated as our culture changes, but the VALS typology has made SRI very successful, with an income of more than $200 million per year. By the mid-1980s, SRI had 130 VALS clients, including the major TV networks; major ad agencies; major publishers such as Time; and major corporations such as AT&T, Avon, Coca-Cola, General Motors, Procter & Gamble, RJ Reynolds, and Tupperware. For example, Timex, a giant corporation best known for its watches, wanted to move into the home health care market with a selection of new products including digital thermometers and blood pressure monitors. It decided to focus on two VALS segments: the Societally Conscious and the Achievers. Everything about the packaging and the advertisements was chosen with these two groups in mind. Models were upscale, mature, and shown in comfortable surroundings with plants and books. The tag line was, "Technology where it does the most good." Within months, all of Timex's products were the leaders in the new and fast-growing industry.

Media Exposure

The amount of time people spend with the media continues to grow. Now, according to the *U.S. Statistical Abstracts* (1996), Americans spend on average 3,297 hours with the media every year—this is more than 42 hours per week. About 70% of this is watching television, which includes broadcast, cable, pay, and movie rentals. The other 30% is spread out over newspapers, magazines, books, and films. The amount of television that Americans watch continues to climb throughout the 1990s.

We each have our own pattern of exposure to the media. Seldom is there an overlap in patterns across all individuals, which is one reason why there is no mass audience. Each of us constructs our own pattern to satisfy our personal needs. Although we have a wide variety of media and messages available to us, we usually select a small sub-set of the ones that tend to serve our needs best. We each have our preferred media and our preferred vehicles, and we use these preferences to develop our habits of media exposure. For example, most of us watch television, but we do not watch all of television. Only when the number of channel choices is low (around three or four) will we expose ourselves to a high proportion of available channels. When there is a large number of channels available (such as the 50 or more on most cable services), we tend to select only one or two types of programming (such as news, drama, comedy, education/information, talk, soap operas, music, game shows, etc.) and limit our viewing to the channels with this type of programming (Youn, 1994). Each of us thus has our own channel repertoire of between three and six channels; rarely do we check out the options available beyond this repertoire.

Having a VCR or a remote control does not substantially increase our channel repertoire. In cable households the repertoire is a bit larger (between five and eight channels), even though the number of channels available to viewers is much higher (Ferguson, 1992).

Television viewing is inertial. The best predictor for a program's rating is the rating of its lead-in and lead-out programs (Cooper, 1993). For this reason, television programmers will put similar type programs together (like four situation comedies back to back) to hold on to their audience. If they interrupted the block of situation comedies with a game show, they would lose all the viewers who did not have game show programs in their viewing repertoire.

While we form media habits in terms of our repertoires and inertial flow through a block of time, the habits do not hold day after day. This was revealed through research that showed that repeat viewing of any particular program is low (Barwise & Ehrenberg, 1989). For programs shown every day, only 50% of the people who watched one day would watch the next. There is the same drop off for viewing of weekly shows. The drop off is lower with news and soap operas, because viewers of these types of programs exhibit a stronger daily habit. The loss of audience is not due to choosing a new show but to not watching TV. If people are watching the next day, they will probably watch the same show. Therefore the decision to watch TV is different than the decision about what to watch.

Awareness of Exposure

Do we really know how much TV we watch? Probably not. For example, parents often overestimate how much TV their children watch—they include time when the children say they are playing with their toys (Alexander, Wartella, & Brown, 1981). Large discrepancies were also found by Anderson and colleagues (Anderson, Field, Collins, Lorch, & Nathan, 1985). The amount of attention given to the television screen varies with age. At one year of age there is 10% attention; at age 3, 50%; at age 13, 80%; and with adults, attention averages 60% (Anderson, 1985). Children may appear to be exposed to the set in the judgment of parents or other observers, but children's attention is usually very low—even to the point that they do not consider their activity viewing.

Adults also might have the television set on and be in the same room, but not pay much attention to it. Attention to the show varies by genre with movies, children's programs, and suspense shows having the highest concentration (attention given 76% of the time). Commercials, sports, news, and daytime soap operas have the lowest (attention only 55% to 60% of time) (Comstock, 1989).

Blurring of Mass Media Channels

To most people, messages are much more important than channels; many people don't even know the difference between channels. For example, most people who are watching television do not know if they are watching a broadcast station (whether network affiliate or independent) or a cable channel. Some won't know if they're watching a pay movie on a premium channel, a Hollywood rental movie, or a made-for-TV movie on a network. As consumers, we care more about selecting a particular kind of message—not about choosing a channel—so we do not make distinctions among channels.

Differences across media are also blurring over time. Newspapers are becoming more like magazines in their editorial outlook by featuring more soft news and human interest pieces that are not time-sensitive and that appeal more as entertainment than as information. Trade books are becoming shorter and less literary, and computers with their games, encyclopedias, and Web pages are becoming more like films, books, magazines, and newspapers. Given the focus on messages and the convergence of channels, the content is becoming much more of a concern than the delivery system.

Some futurists argue that we are moving toward a convergence where all the media will be one—"a single, high capacity, digital network of networks that will bridge what we now know as the separate domains of computing, telephony, broadcasting, motion pictures, and publishing" (Neuman, 1991, p. x). Just as the cotton gin and the assembly line symbolized the onset of industrialization and mass society, the personal computer may come to symbolize the onset of de-industrialization and the decentralization of information processing (Neuman, 1991, p. 1).

This is an exciting time in our culture. There are so many messages being made available, and the new technology of computers will allow us to access them all and arrange them in any manner that suits us. This opportunity requires that we become more media literate in order to make the most of its positive aspects and avoid its potential harm.

 **Summary**

Think of audiences as the layers in a pyramid. At the top of the pyramid we are all the same—certain messages (like coverage of the Gulf War) bring us all together. At the bottom of the pyramid, we are all unique individuals. At each layer in the pyramid, there are audience segments. Media marketers continually search for the right segment to which to pitch their message. The marketers who are successful at this build meaningful audiences by giving people what they want and need in the form of particular kinds of entertainment and information. Once the marketers have constructed their niche audiences, they rent them out to advertisers.

Over time, thinking has moved away from trying to group us all together into one general mass audience and toward a mid-level model of putting us into meaningful segments in terms of our media message preferences. Accompanying this is a change in thinking, away from channels and more toward types of messages. Thus, companies who own television stations have diversified by buying magazine companies, book publishing houses, cable systems, and more, so as not to be bound by the limitations of any one channel in the new media environment. They no longer think in terms of being the most powerful newspaper chain, for example, but of being the most powerful media conglomerate. The goal is no longer to construct the one message that will attract the greatest number of people. Instead, the game is to construct a constellation of audience segments by crafting special messages for each segment. Thus, when all exposures across all segmented audiences are totaled, the conglomerate is considered powerful if it achieves a huge audience in the sum.

We group ourselves into audiences through our exposure patterns. We all have a great deal of exposure to the media, but there are profound differences in patterns across people. Each of us has preferences for certain kinds of messages, so we actively seek those. Our active seeking results in regular patterns of exposure to certain media and certain vehicles, because we can depend on them to satisfy our needs best—this is our media exposure repertoire. At the same time, we are also being constantly bombarded by all sorts of messages from outside our repertoire. Because we have not sought out those messages, we tend not to perceive them; we think they don't exist. Being media literate means being more aware of the messages that are being aimed at you as a target of some marketer. We should be thankful and increase our appreciation for some of those messages. For others, we should be skeptical and increase our analysis of them. These tasks are accomplished better when we understand something about how markets assemble us into audiences.

 ## References

Alexander, A., Wartella, E., & Brown, D. (1981). Estimates of children's television viewing by mother and child. *Journal of Broadcasting, 25,* 243-252.

Anderson, D. R. (1985). Online cognitive processing of television. In L. F. Alwitt & A. A. Mitchell (Eds.), *Psychological process and advertising effects: Theory, research, application* (pp. 177-199). Hillsdale, NJ: Lawrence Erlbaum.

Anderson, D. R., Field, D. E., Collins, P. A., Lorch, E. P., & Nathan, J. G. (1985). Estimates of young children's time with television: A methodological comparison of parent reports with time-lapse video home observation. *Child Development, 56,* 1345-1357.

Barwise, P., & Ehrenberg, A. (1989). *Television and its audiences.* Newbury Park, CA: Sage.

Bauer, R. A., & Bauer, A. (1960). America, mass society and mass media. *Journal of Social Issues, 10*(3), 3-66.

Blumer, H. (1946). Collective behavior. In A. M. Lee (Ed.), *Principles of sociology* (pp. 185-186). New York: Barnes & Noble.

Brouwer, M. (1964). Mass communication and the social sciences: Some neglected areas. In L. Dexter & D. White (Eds.), *People, society and mass communications* (pp. 547-568). New York: Free Press.

Cantril, H. (1947). The invasion from Mars. In T. Newcomb & E. Hartley (Eds.), *Readings in social psychology* (pp. 619-628). New York: Holt.

Comstock, G. (1989). *The evolution of American television.* Newbury Park, CA: Sage.

Cooper, R. (1993). An expanded, integrated model for determining audience exposure to television. *Journal of Broadcasting & Electronic Media, 38,* 401-418.

Ferguson, D. A. (1992). Channel repertoire in the presence of remote control devices, VCRs, and cable television. *Journal of Broadcasting & Electronic Media, 36,* 83-91.

Friedson, E. (1953). The relation of the social situation of contact to the media in mass communication. *Public Opinion Quarterly, 17,* 230-238.

Mitchell, A. (1983). *The nine American lifestyles: Who we are and where we're going.* New York: Macmillan.

Neuman, W. R. (1991). *The future of the mass audience.* New York: Cambridge University Press.

Teen spending up again (1996, March 31). *Parade Magazine,* p. 6.

U.S. Statistical Abstracts (1996). Washington, DC: Department of Commerce.

Youn, S.-M. (1994). Program type preference and program choice in a multichannel situation. *Journal of Broadcasting & Electronic Media, 38,* 465-475.

Further Reading

Neuman, W. R. (1991). *The future of the mass audience.* New York: Cambridge University Press. (233 pages)

Neuman begins with a good, balanced discussion of the difficult idea of post-industrialism and with the conflict between fragmentation and homogenization. He argues that education contributes to fragmentation, because people with better educations are more able to peruse their specialized interests. Family life is also changing as women enter the workforce in large percentages. He also shows that media use is fragmenting.

Neuman says the central question is whether or not the proliferation of new communications channels will lead to fragmentation of the mass audience. He says that this is not a new issue but is a continuing and central problematic of political communications. The key issue is that of balance: balance between the center and the periphery, between different interest factions, between competing elites, and between an efficient and effective central authority and the conflicting demands of the broader electorate (p. 167). In other words, the conflict between community and pluralism.

Exercise 12.1   Segmentation

1. Think about the students at your college or university. Are they all identical? Or are there segments—several different groups of students that are clearly identifiable by how they dress, act, and talk?

   a. Segment the student body. Try to identify between four and seven segments.

   b. For each segment, come up with a catchy name. Then describe the students in each segment demographically and psychologically.

2. Think about the different media and vehicles that would appeal to each group. For example, which groups would prefer film over books, and so on.

   a. What would be the favorite television show(s) of each group?

   b. Which radio format would each group prefer?

   c. Which magazines would each read?

   d. Which CDs would each buy?

   e. Can you think of other media differences?

3. Let's say you are interested in starting a campus newspaper. Pick one of the above groups as your primary target.

   a. What kind of news and entertainment would you want to feature in your newspaper in order to build a strong appeal among your target audience?

   b. What advertisers would be most interested in getting their messages in front of your target audience?

CHAPTER 13

Broadening Our Perspective on Media Effects

KEY IDEA *The media exert a wide range of effects—immediate and long term, positive and negative, across five levels.*

Three-Dimensional Perspective on Media Effects
Timing of Effects
Immediate
Long Term
Level of Effects
Cognitive
Attitudinal
Emotional
Physiological
Behavioral
Direction of Effects

A Broad Listing of Media Effects
Immediate Cognitive
Temporary Learning
Extensive Learning
Intensive Learning
Long-Term Cognitive
Hypermnesia
Generalization
Exposing Secrets
Framing Life

Summary

Suzanne is baby-sitting her two younger brothers, ages 4 and 6. She is reading a magazine while they are watching the Ninja Turtles on television. She sees an ad for a new shampoo and tears out the coupon in the magazine ad, making a mental note to buy some of this brand when she is out shopping later today. Her brothers are starting to shout at the television screen, so she puts on her headphones and turns on the radio. She really likes the song she is hearing and wonders, "Who is singing this? I've never heard it before." She begins to daydream about her date tonight. "I hope Tim takes me to another horror flick. It's so much fun to scream my lungs out and to attack him during the bad parts."

When the song on the radio is over, the DJ goes right into an ad, not telling her the song's title or artist. She is frustrated, so she tries to remember the melody by humming it so she can ask one of her friends later.

Suddenly her thoughts are interrupted as her brothers begin screaming at each other, then wrestling around on the floor. Suzanne runs into the TV room and breaks up the fight. "You guys better behave yourselves or I won't let you watch *Ninja Turtles* anymore! Get back in your own chairs now."

Peace restored, Suzanne picks up a newspaper and notices a story about a drive-by shooting where a gang of youths imitated some action in a recent movie. She thinks, "The media have such a bad effect on young kids. My brothers are going to end up in jail if they keep watching those shows. Thank goodness the media don't have any effect on me!"

Many of us have a narrow view of media effects. We look for high-profile tragedies as evidence of a media effect and use those isolated incidents to conclude that all media effects are like them.

We look for startling changes in our behaviors or attitudes and when we don't find such changes, we conclude that the media don't really affect us. But they do.

What is the effect? Or rather, what are all the effects? An understanding of the full range of media effects is an essential ingredient in media literacy. Knowing what to look for helps us monitor the effects the media have on us. The purpose of this chapter is to make you sensitive to the wide range of probable media effects so that you will know what to look for in your everyday lives.

Three-Dimensional Perspective on Media Effects

Let's begin with a metaphor. Media effects are like the weather in many ways. Weather is always there, and it can take many forms. Sometimes it makes you shiver, sometimes it makes you wet, and sometimes it gives you a painful sunburn—but it is all weather. Also, it is very difficult to predict the weather with any precision, because the factors that explain the weather are large in number and their interaction is very complex. Supercomputers are used to try to handle all those factors in highly complex models. The weather models help increase the predictive accuracy on the broad level, that is, they can tell us how much rainfall and how many sunny days a particular locale will have this year, but they cannot tell us with accuracy who will get wet on which days. The Weather Bureau cannot control the weather, but we can control the weather's effect on us. We can carry an umbrella, use sunscreen, or close ourselves off from elements we don't like, and we can run outside to embrace a beautiful day.

Like the weather, the media are pervasive and always around us. Also like the weather, media influences are difficult to predict, because the factors that explain the effects are large in number and their interaction is very complex. We use powerful computers to examine large sets of variables in trying to make predictions, and we have learned much about media effects. We know in general that certain types of messages will lead to certain kinds of opinions and behaviors, but we cannot predict with any precision whose opinion or behavior will be changed. As individuals, we do not have much power to control the media, but we do have a great deal of power (if we will use it) to control the media's effects on us. In order to know how to use this power, we must be sufficiently literate.

However, there is an important difference between the weather and the influence the media have on us. With the weather, we all recognize its different forms and know when they are happening. It's fairly easy to tell the difference between rain, fog, and snow, because there is so much tangible evidence whenever these occur. With media influence, however, the effects are very difficult to perceive until someone points them out. Then they become easier to spot. The purpose of this chapter is to broaden your thinking about media effects. Let's begin by thinking about effects on three different dimensions: timing, level, and direction.

Timing of Effects

Media effects can be either immediate or long term. This distinction focuses on when the effect occurs, not on how long it lasts.

Immediate Effects. An immediate effect is one that happens during exposure to the media message. If it does not happen during the exposure, the opportunity is lost. If the effect does happen, it might last for only a short period of time (such as becoming afraid during a movie) or it might last forever (such as learning the outcome of a presidential election), but it is still an immediate effect because it changed something in you during your exposure to the message. For example, when you watch a news program, you learn about the events of the day; when you read a newspaper, you learn that your favorite sports team won an important game. If, while you watch an action/adventure film, you begin jumping around in your seat and wrestling with your friends, this clearly is an immediate effect. It is triggered by the film, your reaction happens during the film, and your behavior stops shortly after the film ends.

Long-Term Effects. Long-term effects, on the other hand, show up only after many exposures. Neither a single exposure nor a single type of message is responsible for the effect. Instead, it is the pattern of repeated exposure that sets up the conditions for a long-term effect. For example, after watching years of crime programs and news reports, you might come to believe that your neighborhood is a high-crime environment. No single exposure or event "causes" this belief; the belief is slowly and gradually constructed over years of exposures until one day it occurs to you that you better buy another set of locks for your doors.

Level of Effects

Most of the concern about the media focuses on behavioral effects. For example, there is a belief that watching violence will lead people to behave aggressively; that watching portrayals of sexual activity will make people engage in illicit sex acts; and that watching crime will make people go out and commit those crimes.

There are five levels (four levels in addition to behavior) in which media have demonstrated effects. They are: cognitive, attitudinal, emotional, physiological, and (of course) behavioral.

Cognitive. Media can immediately plant ideas and information into our minds. Learning is the acquisition of facts so that they can be recalled later. Oftentimes we seek out facts in the media, such as by reading a newspaper or magazine or by listening to the news on radio or television. There are also times when we do not search for facts but learn them just the same. For example, we might watch a movie merely to be entertained but learn facts about the country in which the movie takes place. Thus, we can learn without consciously seeking out information.

Learning can be formal, such as when a person intentionally seeks out particular content in order to learn something specific. For example, you read the morning paper to learn about which sports teams won their games yesterday, you watch a cooking show to copy down a new recipe, you listen to your car radio driving to work to learn how to get tickets for a concert. The information does not need to be extremely important. Also, it need not be remembered for more than a few minutes in order for an effect to have occurred. Every day there are hundreds of examples where you use the media to pick up a fact that you can use—if only for a few minutes.

One important distinction with learning is to consider the difference between formal learning and incidental learning. Sometimes people will formally seek out information from the media, especially newspapers, magazines, and books. But other times, people will expose themselves to the media (especially true with television, radio, musical recordings, and film) in order to be entertained. Even when people are not motivated to seek out information, they can still learn. This type of learning is called *incidental learning*. Incidental learning happens when people expose themselves to the media without intending to learn anything, but during their exposure they pick up some information anyway. In order for incidental learning to take place, the learner must be passive, not actively involved in the message. This is what makes incidental learning a dangerous thing in the eyes of many television critics. When you are a passive viewer, your defenses are down. You are not aware that you are learning anything, so you are not actively evaluating and processing the information.

Another important distinction is between factual and social information. Factual information is usually acquired through formal learning. Social information is usually acquired in a process of observational learning, which refers to any learning that takes place through a vicarious experience from observation of some model, either living or symbolic. Observation of social models accounts for much of the information communicated to children, and the media provide an enormous number of models and actions from which children might learn. Given the large amount of time children spend with the media, characters in film and television exert a strong influence on their learning about social situations.

Attitudinal. The media can create and shape our opinions, beliefs, and values. Attitudes can also be learned immediately. We might watch a political candidate give a speech and decide that we like her. If we had no attitude about that candidate prior to the viewing of her speech, then this immediate effect is one of opinion creation. It is also possible that the immediate effect converted us to this candidate and away from liking her opponent. We have known for a long time that the media's major effect on attitudes is the reinforcing of already existing opinions and beliefs (Berelson & Steiner, 1964; Klapper, 1960), but the media can also create and change attitudes (McGuire, 1973).

The media influence what we believe about the world in general. Over time, we come to believe that the world is mean and violent. The media can also create and reinforce general political orientations such as liberalism or conservatism (Gerbner, Gross, Morgan, & Signorielli, 1994). In addition, over a long period of exposure to advertising messages, we can have our attitudes shaped about drugs (Adler et al., 1980), nutrition (Atkin, 1982), and beauty (Tan, 1981).

Emotional. The media can make us feel things. They can trigger strong emotions such as fear, rage, and lust. They can also evoke weaker emotions such as sadness, peevishness, and boredom. Emotional reactions are related to physiological changes. In fact, some psychological theoreticians argue that emotions are nothing more than physiological arousal (Schachter & Singer, 1962; Zillmann, 1991). If we feel a very high level of arousal and don't like it, we might label it hate. If we like it, we might label it love.

Physiological. Media can influence our automatic bodily systems, which are usually beyond our conscious control. These include such reactions as the contraction of the irises of our eyes when we look at a bright object. We cannot control the degree to which our irises contract or dilate, but we can look away from the object and thus prevent the iris from contracting.

With the media, there are many physiological effects that usually serve to arouse us (Zillmann, 1991). A suspenseful mystery serves to elevate our blood pressure and heart rate. A horror film triggers rapid breathing and sweaty palms. Hearing a patriotic song might raise goose bumps on our skin. Viewing erotic pictures can lead to vaginal lubrication, penile tumescence, and increased heart rate (Malamuth & Check, 1980). A farce might make us laugh and be unable to stop even when the laughing becomes painful. Listening to peaceful music can calm and relax us by reducing our heart rate and bringing our breathing down to a regular, slow rate.

Behavioral. Media can trigger actions. For example, after seeing an ad for a product, we might leave the house and go buy the product. Or we read about something in a magazine and call a friend to talk about it. Or we watch a violent movie and as we file out of the theater afterwards, we act aggressively by elbowing people out of the way so we can get out the door first.

Direction of Effects

The effect can be in either a constructive or destructive direction. These terms are value laden. Who is to decide what is constructive and what is destructive? The answer can be approached in two ways: the individual or society. From the individual perspective, a constructive direction is one whose effects lead you toward some valued goal. If your goal is to get some information in order to satisfy your curiosity, then finding facts in a book, newspaper, or on television can be very satisfying. This can move you toward your goal of having more information and achieving a higher level of knowledge.

We can also look at this from a broad, societal point of view. If the media teach people how to commit crimes and trigger criminal behavior, then the media are exerting a destructive influence.

Let's put all these ideas together and use this as a structure to display the many different effects of the media. Table 13.1 is constructed from the two dimensions of timing (two columns) and level (five rows) of effect. The 10 cells contain a total of 20 effects. The third dimension—the direction of effect—is not shown, but it is implied. When you look at the table, imagine a range from positive to negative on each of these 20 effects. For example, opinion creation can be positive or negative depending on the person's viewpoint.

A Broad Listing of Media Effects

Now let's take a closer look at each of the 20 media effects shown in Table 13.1.

Immediate Cognitive

Temporary Learning. We use the media to learn about the particular events of the day. Much of this information stays with us for several hours, then we forget it. Certain advertising messages (such as jingles, sale prices, key selling appeals, store hours, etc.) also stay with us for a short period of time to allow us to act on that information, then we forget them.

Extensive Learning. Our learning can be extensive or intensive. Extensive learning refers to the acquisition of something new. For example, you could learn a new fact or behavior or have an attitude created. The acquisition of each new fact or attitude serves to broaden your base of knowledge, attitude set, or behavioral repertoire.

Searching out and finding some particular piece of information to broaden your knowledge structure results in a positive effect, because it adds something of value to your existing knowledge structure. If the information is not accurate and you add it to your existing knowledge structure, the effect is negative.

Table 13.1 Overview of Media Effects

Type	Immediate	Long Term
Cognitive	Temporary learning	Hypermnesia
	Extensive learning	Generalization
	Intensive learning	Exposing secrets
		Framing of life
Attitudinal	Opinion creation	Sleeper effect
	Opinion change	Reinforcement
		Internalization
Emotional	Temporary reaction	Sensitization
Physiological	Temporary arousal	Increasing tolerance
Behavioral	Imitation	Habit formation
	Activation	Disinhibition

Intensive Learning. In contrast, intensive learning is the acquisition of another example of the same thing that you already have. To illustrate, imagine that you like a particular soft drink and see an ad for that product. You don't learn a new reason to like that soft drink, and you don't learn anything more about the product, but the ad still has the immediate effect of making you feel better about using the product; that is, your favorable attitude and behavioral habits are reinforced. The ad gives your existing attitude and behavioral set greater weight. This greater weight is evidence of an immediate effect even though nothing seems changed on the surface—you have not been converted to another product. This greater weight for your existing attitudes and behaviors makes it harder for competitors to convert you to using their products.

Long-Term Cognitive

Hypermnesia. This effect appears to be the opposite of forgetting. Instead of being less able to recall information from a message as time goes by, we become more able to recall that information (Wicks, 1992). For example, you read a story in a magazine about forest fires but are not able to recall many of the facts after reading it. Then, during the next few weeks, the media cover several big forest fires in your area, and you begin to recall more of the facts from the magazine story. This is hypermnesia. It seems very strange that a person could know less immediately after reading something compared to much later. We are more used to thinking that the opposite occurs, that our learning is highest right after an exposure and then we gradually forget facts.

How is hypermnesia possible? The key to understanding hypermnesia is to recognize that we can't demonstrate everything that we have learned if we have a problem with recall. When we are exposed to information, the facts are recorded somewhere in our brains. If we don't catalog new information well, it will be very hard to find it when we try to recall it. However, on topics where we already have a good deal of knowledge, the recording of new facts is done in a highly organized manner by cataloging them quickly and accurately in the knowledge structure that we have previously developed on that topic. When we are asked about that information, we have no trouble retrieving it.

When a topic is new to us, we don't have a knowledge structure for it. The new facts may be stored haphazardly inside other knowledge structures, and this makes those facts very difficult to retrieve. As we begin to learn more about the new topic, we construct a new knowledge structure on that topic and sort through our older knowledge structures to bring all the facts on that topic together in one place. During periods of rest (such as sleep), our minds sort out the facts and move them around to where they can be more efficiently catalogued. Once all the facts on the new topic are assembled into a new knowledge structure, they are much easier to recall.

Generalization. A person watches a local news program and hears a story about a house that was vandalized in an area near his apartment. Then he hears a story on the radio about a local bank being robbed. Next he reads the newspaper and sees that there was an assault in his town last night. He has learned three facts—one from each message. Later that night he might generalize from these three facts and draw the conclusion that crime has become a real problem in his town. This conclusion was not given to him by the media; the media just provided him with some facts that could set him up to jump to this conclusion.

Let's consider another example. A person watches a situation comedy in which several teenagers are very witty and joke their way out of trouble. She then watches a stand-up comedian who wins the admiration of his audience. Then she watches a romantic comedy in which the characters are attracted to each other because of their sense of humor. She has learned facts about how these televised characters behave and the consequences of their behaviors, and she generalizes to a conclusion that humor is a very useful tool that can get her whatever she wants.

The mass media have been found to stimulate many different kinds of generalizations about the amount of crime and violence in society, the structure of families, the nature of gender roles, the behavior of the elderly, and the workings of certain professions—especially the legal, law enforcement, and medical professions (Hawkins & Pingree, 1982). The media also influence generalized knowledge about stereotypes, especially gender, ethnicity, family, and occupational roles (Greenberg, 1982), health and nutrition (Gerbner, Morgan, & Signorielli, 1982), sexual mores (Comstock, 1982), and about fashion, hair care, and facial care that generalize to an overall conception of what it means to be beautiful (Tan, 1981).

Sometimes this generalization process results in a conclusion that is very much unlike the real world. When this happens, one of three conditions exists: (a) we have acquired false information from the media, (b) we have been exposed to an imbalance of information (extreme depth in one narrow area but no breadth) and this gives a distorted picture, or (c) we have accumulated a great number of facts and have not properly sorted or organized them.

Exposing Secrets. For many people, the media, especially television, are devices that expose secrets about how the world works. The media, especially the electronic media, do this by restructuring social arenas. Meyrowitz (1985) argues that the media affect us not through their content, but by changing the "situational geography" of social life. One of the reasons Americans may no longer seem to know their place is that they no longer *have* a place in the traditional sense. For example, Meyrowitz says that we all change the way we act depending on whether we are in public or private. When we are in public we perform on stage in front of others, such as colleagues at work. In contrast, we have "backstage" or private behaviors that we reserve for intimates, such as very good friends or spouses.

The media expose important social secrets by taking viewers into the backstage. For example, parents act like authority figures when they are on stage in front of their children. Parents hide their shortcomings from their children by keeping their shortcomings in the backstage. Yet when children watch situation comedies on television and see parents as buffoons, and when they watch talk shows and see all the problems that some adults have, children lose the belief that adults have superior wisdom and experience. It becomes much harder for parents to establish a sense of authority over their children. It is not necessary for TV to reveal all the secrets of adults; children already know a great deal about traditional adult roles just by knowing for certain that adults consciously conspire to hide things from children (Meyrowitz, 1985, p. 247).

Another example is in the political arena where much of the president's life used to be kept backstage. Now all of the backstage information about a president's sexual indiscretions, overeating problems, draft avoidance, previous banking practices, and more, are brought into the foreground, and it is much harder for that person to appear presidential—like a person who possesses the superior qualities necessary to make all the decisions that must be made.

The electronic media are especially powerful at being able to destroy the place of backstage, because electronic media such as television present "expressive" information that was once accessible only in intimate, face-to-face encounters. Through TV, viewers have access to the personal expressions—information that was once available to only a few people—of people from all over the world. Television undermines the behavioral distinctions between foreground and background, because it provides all kinds of information to all kinds of people. It leaves no secrets.

Framing Life. This effect can be seen in three ways: agenda setting, spiral of silence, and narrative closure. By choosing certain images and themes, the media focus our attention on particular things while telling us to ignore other things. Called agenda setting, this effect was first observed in the political arena where the media were found to be very influential in telling us what to think *about* (McCombs & Shaw, 1972). By putting certain issues, attitudes, and images before us constantly, the media tell us what is important. By ignoring other issues, attitudes, and images they teach us that those are unimportant. This agenda-setting effect is not limited to telling us what to think about politics and current events. It is much broader. It also tells us what kind of music we should listen to; what kinds of people we should regard as beautiful, smart, or successful; and what kinds of events are important.

Thus the media, without intending to do so, can be very persuasive simply by bringing certain kinds of people to our attention and maintaining them as celebrities. The media confer status on certain people, and we continue to hear what these people have to say even when they don't have anything important to say. Non-celebrities are not given status, so we don't hear what they have to say, even if it is something potentially important. This is the agenda-setting effect.

When the media ignore an issue, people stop talking and thinking about it. Noelle-Neumann (1984) refers to this as the spiral of silence.

As for narrative closure, the media translate most ideas into neat little stories with a clear beginning, middle, and end and a driving force of conflict. This is the frame used for telling us about the world. Thus elections are not primarily about issues; they are about who will win the race. Governing is not about cooperation and synthesis of ideas; it is about who will wield the power and get the credit. In advertisements, problems are quickly identified and neatly resolved. Relationships must also fit this frame. We learn that everything is moving quickly to an end, but the end is then quickly replaced by the beginning of a new story.

Immediate Attitudinal

Opinion Creation. The media provide information or images that can trigger the creation of a new opinion or attitude in you. This is most likely to happen the first time you see an ad for a product about which you were previously unaware. Also, the first time you see an actress or actor on the screen, you immediately develop an attitude about her or him.

Opinion Change. Media can change a person's attitudes and feelings about something. For example, after watching a teenage character insult her parents and be rewarded for this by the admiration of other characters, a child could acquire the attitude that it is okay (and even desirable) to insult one's parents. Or a person who watches a political debate might not just acquire new information on an issue, but might also adopt the opinion of one of the debaters; or the viewer might acquire a favorable attitude about one of the debaters.

Long-Term Attitudinal

Sleeper Effect. This is an effect that takes a relatively long time to occur. During an exposure to a message, a person discounts the message because of a dislike for the source. Then, over time, the person forgets the source and the negative feeling about the information goes away and is replaced by a positive feeling.

To illustrate, let's say you listen to a news commentator deliver an analysis of the problem of illegal immigration. You don't like or respect the news commentator, so you don't agree with the analysis. However, you remember the conclusions of the analysis and the facts that support it. Several weeks later, you are in an argument about illegal immigration and cite many of the facts that you learned from the commentator; you even argue for the same conclusion as the commentator. Yet you don't remember the experience of being exposed to the arguments of the news commentator; that is, you have forgotten the source of the information but remembered the information itself. This is an example of the sleeper effect, which is the immediate learning of information linked with a negative attitude about the source of the information; then, over time, forgetting the negative attitude and the source but retaining the information.

Reinforcement. When we think of media effects, we usually look for some change even though the primary media effect is reinforcement of the status quo. For example, the media will usually strengthen our existing attitudes rather than wipe out an old attitude and replace it with a new one. This effect is often overlooked because we have been conditioned to think of effects in terms of change. The very powerful effect of reinforcement is evidenced by non-change. The media can reinforce already existing attitudes and thus make them more resistant to change.

Internalization. In this long-term process, people acquire certain attitudes and beliefs by internalizing the major themes in society as exhibited through the mass media. Throughout this long-term exposure to all kinds of messages (news, ads, movies, cartoons, talk shows, etc.), we infer patterns across the individual facts, events, and character portrayals. These inferences become our beliefs about how the world is constructed.

The internalization effect is especially powerful when there is overlap among the various media in presenting the same themes. The media have been found to present consistent messages about violence, family structures, interpersonal mistrust, fear of victimization, traditional sex roles, family values, images of older people, attitudes about doctors, and concern about racial problems.

Repeated exposure to the cultural and social stereotypes seen on TV (particularly those portraying gender, race, family, and occupational roles) substantially alters people's beliefs by contributing to stereotyped perceptions. However, media can establish new perceptual sets when non-stereotypical content is introduced. Being exposed to TV programs affects children's occupational aspirations and their evaluations of occupational roles. This even holds for adults and is especially true when viewers are personally unfamiliar with the portrayed occupations and thus have little real-world information on the topic.

Sometimes we internalize myths about our culture and how life works. Thomas (1995) points out that television creates myths. She defines *myth* as something that represents

> any belief in a culture that is so ingrained in and pervasive among members of the society that, for the most part, what the belief asserts goes without question. In other words, the accuracy of the information contained in a myth is not, on an everyday level, very important. A myth is accepted as a given. (p. 446)

One of these myths is that spending money is a good way to defeat depression. When female TV characters are depressed, they go shopping and are shown as feeling better. Another myth is that more consumption leads to better service in restaurants, stores, hotels, and other places, and that people who are cheap are the butts of jokes. Another television myth is that anyone can achieve. Most of the successful or wealthy people on television are shown working their way up from being poor and doing so very quickly.

One of the primary messages of the mass media is this: In order to be happy, we must own things and avail ourselves of commercial services. These things improve our lives. Over time we become obsessed with acquiring material goods and overlook the things in life that do not cost money (inner peace, harmony, strong relationships, family, respect for others, etc.).

A corollary of this is the belief that new is better and that old things wear out, lose their usefulness, or both. New is better, because new is improved—so your old friends are not as good as potential new ones. Your spouse is not as good as a potential new romantic attachment. We thus lose a sense of security, because we do not believe in permanence.

The media use templates for time and action. We are told that certain things happen in a certain order. As for velocity, the media foster in us a need for immediate gratification. The media themselves are so varied and available that they offer us the possibility of immediate gratification for anything we could possibly want. Also, with cable offerings of all kinds and RCDs (remote control devices), we can immediately increase our gratification. Have you ever been watching a sporting event in real life and found yourself trying to fast forward through the slow parts to get to the action? Have you ever listened to one of your friends tell a story and wished you could push a button to speed through the boring parts to get to the "good stuff"? If so, you have been conditioned to believe that you can make time move faster.

In relationships, do you wish you could meet that "special someone" right away? Do you feel that there is something wrong with you if you haven't been swept away by love in the past several months? When you are excited by someone, do you wish things would progress more quickly? Then, after you have developed a relationship with that "special person," have you ever quickly become bored, wishing that someone better (or just newer) would come along to sweep you away again?

In our careers, we have come to expect very high rewards very quickly without much work. It comes as a surprise how difficult it can be to get even a mediocre job—then how much work is required to keep it. In real life, the speed of success is unexpectedly slow, because in the media, the velocity of success is very fast.

Immediate Emotional

Temporary Reaction. People, especially children, can become frightened by certain media content (Cantor, 1994). This fear, though intense at the time, is short lived. After watching a horror movie, children may look under their beds and in their closets to make sure their environment is safe, then lie awake in bed hoping they will not be attacked (Wilson & Cantor, 1985). By the next day, the fear has usually passed, even though it can last up to several weeks with some children (Cantor, 1994).

Long-Term Emotional

Desensitization. Some things within the media are presented so often we can no longer treat them with wonder or awe. Our tolerance has been increased so that things that used to entertain us or impress us no longer do.

This is especially important with the issue of violence. Viewing TV violence leads to lowered sensitivity to aggression and violence. Among children, even watching a single violent film can make them temporarily less aware of and less concerned about aggressive acts in others. There is a relationship between the amount of exposure to TV violence and the willingness to use violence, to suggest violence as a solution to conflict, and to perceive violence as effective (Liebert, Neale, & Davidson, 1973; Tan, 1981). This effect has also been found in adults who have been exposed to strong violence against women (Linz, Donnerstein, & Penrod, 1984, 1988) or even to relatively mild forms of violence (Thomas, 1982).

Another form of media desensitization results from the superficial treatment media give to certain issues. This superficial treatment by the media cloaks our apathy as an audience by allowing us to feel that by knowing about a problem, we are doing something about it.

Desensitization can have positive effects in a therapeutic setting. People who fear something (such as dogs, heights, air travel) can be gradually desensitized (Dorr, 1981; Foa & Kozak, 1986; Goranson, 1970; Rushton, 1979).

Immediate Physiological

Temporary Arousal. Certain content (especially violence and erotica) can temporarily arouse people physiologically. This type of arousal dissipates, usually within an hour after exposure.

Long-Term Physiological

Increasing Tolerance. Your body builds up a resistance to certain experiences. For example, the first time you see a horror film, your body responds with a fight-or-flight reaction by substantially increasing your heart rate and blood pressure. As you continue to view horror films over the years, your body's reaction to this stimulus is not as strong. Your heart rate and blood pressure still increase, but not as much. You are building up a higher physiological tolerance to this type of message. In an extreme case, with massive exposure to this type of message, you might even extinguish all physiological reactions to horror.

Immediate Behavioral

Imitation. Children as young as 2 have been found to imitate behaviors they see in the media (Comstock, Chaffee, Katzman, McCombs, & Roberts, 1978; Tan, 1981). In a survey of young children, 60% said they frequently copied behaviors they had seen on television (Liebert et al., 1973).

Copying need not be identical to the action seen on the screen—it can be generalized to similar actions. For example, children may watch Superman jump off a building and fly across town to rescue someone. Children will imitate this by jumping up and down with their arms outstretched as they run across the backyard. If they watch two kickboxers beat each other to death, they will imitate this by spin-jumping around, kicking, chopping at each other with their arms, shouting, and grunting. Seldom will they actually hit each other. By fantasizing, the "hitting" is in their minds as they imagine they are inside the kickboxing world they saw on television.

This kind of play is usually harmless, but because so much of it is triggered by violent messages, the potential for actual physical harm is present. Once in a while, when a real weapon is available, the resulting physical harm is very great.

Activation. The media can exert a triggering effect on our behavior. For example, when watching an ad, we might jump out of our chair and rush to the store to buy the product. Another example would be of children watching a cartoon and trying to imitate the action.

Activation is different than imitation. With imitation, viewers take it upon themselves to emulate or copy a specific behavior seen in the media. In contrast, with activation viewers react to a suggestion to do something, such as go to the store to buy an advertised product; viewers don't see the behavior portrayed.

Long-Term Behavioral

Habit Formation. The media have changed the way we spend our time. The media consume us by consuming our time. The *Statistical Abstract of the United States* (U.S. Department of Commerce, 1995) says that the average person spends 3,297 hours with the media each year—that's about 9 hours every day (p. 572). Over half of this time is spent watching television.

Only a small portion of our media exposure is exclusive of other activities. For example, while we are watching television, we might also be talking on the telephone, or doing the dishes, or reading a magazine. If we were to add up all the time we spend engaging in different activities during a day, it would total more than 24 hours. Thus, the media exposure figures can be misleading if we think of that time as displacing other activities.

Acknowledging this overlapping of exposure is important, because it reveals something about the nature of our exposure—much of our exposure to the media does not command our full attention. The media are often only a background to other activities, which means that the exposure shapes our mood subconsciously. The media can be like a powerful drug. The first exposure to a new magazine, CD, TV show, or the like, can bring a rush of excitement so we go back to it to get the same feelings again. It is habit forming. For example, people can get hooked on the media, especially on computers. Only 6% of households are on-line, but there are already on-line junkies who are addicted. Addicts show a compulsion to check for e-mail 20 to 30 times a day; to give their computer a higher priority than anything else; or to spend time away from important real-life activities such as talking to spouses or kids. Therapists are already developing 12-step plans to help these people (Vranizan, 1995).

When we build up a tolerance to an effect, we want more. Each time we go back, we require more from the media to get the same rush. With entertainment, we want a more outrageous story line, more attractive characters, more visual effects. If the media can give us only the same kinds of messages, we do not feel the rush. Over time our expectations become very high, and we find ourselves flipping through 50 channels and saying, "There's nothing on!" What we mean by this, of course, is that TV is no longer able to exceed our expectations and to significantly arouse us in a surprising way. We keep exposing ourselves to the TV anyway, because, for many of us, that's better than not watching.

This narcotizing effect works with news content, too. At first we are excited to find out what is happening. Then, over time, we don't want to hear the same old news. We want stories that will surprise us, so we look for more bizarre happenings, more dramatic confrontations, and more arousing debates. Our tolerance for these increases and our expectations grow beyond what news stories can provide. We continue to watch—fearing that we will miss something important or something truly arousing.

There is also a concern that exposure to the media—especially to escapist fare—will prevent people from using their time more productively. This is especially an issue with children and their schoolwork. Although the media have been found useful in stimulating interest in some topics (Schramm, Lyle, & Parker, 1961; Weiss, 1969), they have not generally been found to be either a positive or a negative factor—that depends on what is exposed.

There is a concern that, for very young children with the habit of watching television, playtime is pre-empted (Singer, 1982). When TV structures children's lives, children spend less time creatively making up their own games and situations.

Disinhibition. This is the process of gradually wearing down the inhibitions that prevent us from behaving in certain ways. We may not like to dance in front of others, but after several months of watching dance programs, our resistance wears down and we find ourselves dancing in a club. Also, most of us have been raised to solve our problems in non-aggressive and non-violent ways, but after years of exposure to violent portrayals in the movies and on television that show attractive characters successfully using violence to get what they want, our aversion to using violence gradually wears down. One day, when someone steals the parking place we wanted, we find ourselves screaming and pounding on the offender's car; inhibitions that prevented us from behaving violently have been worn down and no longer prevent us from behaving in an antisocial manner.

The mass media can influence behaviors not just in a specific action, but in a general, long-term manner (Comstock et al., 1978). The more violence a person watches over a long period of time, the more willingness there is to use violence (Liebert & Schwartzberg, 1977; Tan, 1981). This is also true in a positive direction; that is, the more a person watches constructive behaviors, the more likely the person is to perform prosocial activities (Rushton, 1979; Tan, 1981). Some people have an aversion to behaving in a prosocial manner—the media can wear down those inhibitions too.

Summary

A key step in increasing your media literacy is to expand your perspective about what media effects are. Don't think that the media affect only others, such as young children who don't know any better or the criminal types who claim they copy what they see in the media.

We live in a media saturated environment, and are constantly being influenced by media effects as they shape our knowledge patterns, attitudes, emotions, and behaviors. They even trigger physiological reactions, such as heart rate, blood pressure, and other bodily functions. We don't even need to experience a change in order to see that the media have had an effect on us, because the most prevalent effect is reinforcement—that is, solidifying our existing beliefs and behaviors.

For example, in our everyday lives the immediate and long-term processes work together. The immediate process gives us a new fact that either extends our learning (it is extensive) or adds weight to our already existing structure (it is intensive). In the long term, we look for patterns across these facts and infer conclusions about how the world operates. These generalized conclusions then form our knowledge structures, which guide our search for facts in subsequent exposures to media messages.

Being media literate requires that we understand the full range of media effects. We need to recognize when those effects are having a negative influence on us so we can protect ourselves, and we need to recognize when the effects are having a positive influence on us so we can appreciate and enhance their power.

 References

Adler, R. P., Lesser, G. S., Meringoff, L. K., Robertson, T. S., Rossiter, J. R., & Ward, S. (1980). *The effects of television advertising on children.* Lexington, MA: Lexington Books.

Atkin, C. K. (1982). Television advertising and socialization to consumer roles. In D. Pearl, L. Bouthilet, & J. Lazar (Eds.), *Television and behavior: Ten years of scientific progress and implications for the eighties: Vol. 2. Technical reviews* (pp. 191-200). Rockville, MD: U.S. Department of Health and Human Services.

Berelson, B., & Steiner, G. A. (1964). *Human behavior: An inventory of research findings.* New York: Harcourt, Brace, and World.

Cantor, J. (1994). Fright reactions to mass media. In J. Bryant & D. Zillmann (Eds.), *Media effects* (pp. 213-245). Hillsdale, NJ: Lawrence Erlbaum.

Comstock, G. A. (1982). Violence in television content: An overview. In D. Pearl, L. Bouthilet, & J. Lazar (Eds.), *Television and behavior: Ten years of scientific progress and implications for the eighties: Vol. 2. Technical reviews* (pp. 108-125). Rockville, MD: U.S. Department of Health and Human Services.

Comstock, G. A., Chaffee, S., Katzman, N., McCombs, M., & Roberts, D. (1978). *Television and human behavior.* New York: Columbia University Press.

Dorr, A. (1981). Television and affective development and functioning: Maybe this decade. *Journal of Broadcasting, 25,* 335-345.

Foa, E. B., & Kozak, M. J. (1986). Emotional processing of fear: Exposure to corrective information. *Psychological Bulletin, 99,* 20-35.

Gerbner, G., Gross, L., Morgan, M., & Signorielli, N. (1994). Growing up with television: The cultivation perspective. In J. Bryant & D. Zillmann (Eds.), *Media effects* (pp. 17-41). Hillsdale, NJ: Lawrence Erlbaum.

Gerbner, G., Morgan, M., & Signorielli, N. (1982). Programming health portrayals: What viewers see, say and do. In D. Pearl, L. Bouthilet, & J. Lazar (Eds.), *Television and behavior: Ten years of scientific progress and implications for the eighties: Vol. 2. Technical reviews* (pp. 291-307). Rockville, MD: U.S. Department of Health and Human Services.

Goranson, R. E. (1970). Media violence and aggressive behavior: A review of experimental research. In L. Berkowitz (Ed.), *Advances in experimental social psychology* (Vol. 5). New York: Academic Press.

Greenberg, B. S. (1982). Television and role socialization: An overview. In D. Pearl, L. Bouthilet, & J. Lazar (Eds.), *Television and behavior: Ten years of scientific progress and implications for the eighties: Vol. 2. Technical reviews* (pp. 179-190). Rockville, MD: U.S. Department of Health and Human Services.

Hawkins, R. P., & Pingree, S. (1982). Television's influence on social reality. In D. Pearl, L. Bouthilet, & J. Lazar (Eds.), *Television and behavior: Ten years of scientific progress and implications for the eighties: Vol. 2. Technical reviews* (pp. 224-247). Rockville, MD: U.S. Department of Health and Human Services.

Klapper, J. T. (1960). *The effects of mass communication*. Glencoe, IL: Free Press.

Liebert, R. M., Neale, J. M., & Davidson, E. S. (1973). *The early window: Effects of television on children and youth*. Elmsdale, NY: Pergamon.

Liebert, R. M., & Schwartzberg, N. S. (1977). Effects of mass media. *Annual Review of Psychology, 28,* 141-173.

Linz, D., Donnerstein, E., & Penrod, S. (1984). The effects of multiple exposures to filmed violence against women. *Journal of Communication, 34*(3), 130-147.

Linz, D., Donnerstein, E., & Penrod, S. (1988). Effects of long-term exposure to violent and sexually degrading depictions of women. *Journal of Personality and Social Psychology, 55*(5), 758-768.

Malamuth, N. M., & Check, J. V. P. (1980). Penile tumescence and perceptual responses to rape as a function of victim's perceived reactions. *Journal of Applied Social Psychology, 10,* 528-547.

McCombs, M. E., & Shaw, D. (1972). The agenda setting function of the mass media. *Public Opinion Quarterly,* 176-187.

McGuire, W. J. (1973). Persuasion, resistance, and attitude change. In I. DeS. Pool, W. Schramm, F. W. Frey, N. Maccoby, & E. B. Parker (Eds.), *The process and effects of mass communication* (Rev. ed., pp. 216-252). Urbana: University of Illinois Press.

Meyrowitz, J. (1985). *No sense of place: The impact of electronic media on social behavior*. New York: Oxford University Press.

Noelle-Neumann, E. (1984). *The spiral of silence: Public opinion—Our social skin*. Chicago: University of Chicago Press.

Rushton, J. P. (1979). Effects of prosocial television and film material on the behavior of viewers. In L. Berkowitz (Ed.), *Advances in experimental social psychology* (pp. 321-351). New York: Academic Press.

Schachter, S., & Singer, J. E. (1962). Cognitive, social, and physiological determinants of emotional state. *Psychological Review, 69,* 379-399.

Schramm, W., Lyle, J., & Parker, E. B. (1961). *Television in the lives of our children*. Stanford, CA: Stanford University Press.

Singer, D. G. (1982). Television and the developing mind of the child. In D. Pearl, L. Bouthilet, & J. Lazar (Eds.), *Television and behavior: Ten years of scientific progress and implications for the eighties: Vol. 2. Technical reviews* (pp. 39-52). Rockville, MD: U.S. Department of Health and Human Services.

Tan, A. S. (1981). *Mass communication theories and research.* Columbus, OH: Grid Publishing.

Thomas, M. H. (1982). Physiological arousal, exposure to a relatively lengthy aggressive film, and aggressive behavior. *Journal of Research in Personality, 16,* 72-81.

Thomas, S. (1995). Myths in and about television: Entertainers and economics. In J. Downing, A. Mohammadi, & A. Sreberny-Mohammadi (Eds.), *Questioning the media* (2nd ed., pp. 444-459). Thousand Oaks, CA: Sage.

U.S. Department of Commerce. (1995). *Statistical abstract of the United States.* Washington, DC: Government Printing Office.

Vranizan, M. (1995, June 5). On-line junkies hooked on his screen. *Santa Barbara News-Press,* p. A11.

Weiss, W. (1969). Effects of the mass media of communication. In G. Lindzey & E. Aronson (Eds.), *The handbook of social psychology* (2nd ed.; Vol. 5, pp. 77-195). Reading, MA: Addison-Wesley.

Wicks, R. H. (1992). Improvement over time in recall of media information: An exploratory study. *Journal of Broadcasting & Electronic Media, 36,* 287-302.

Wilson, B. J., & Cantor, J. (1985). Developmental differences in empathy with a television protagonist's fear. *Journal of Experimental Child Psychology, 39,* 284-299.

Zillmann, D. (1991). Empathy: Affect from bearing witness to the emotions of others. In J. Bryant & D. Zillmann (Eds.), *Responding to the screen* (pp. 135-167). Hillsdale, NJ: Lawrence Erlbaum.

Exercise 13.1 Broadening Your View on Media Effects

Think about the differences between immediate and long-term effects. Also, think about the differences among cognitive, attitudinal, emotional, behavioral, and physiological effects.

On a blank sheet of paper, make two columns. Label one Immediate Effects and the other Long-Term Effects. Then divide the page into five rows, labeling them for the effects: Cognitive, Attitudinal, Emotional, Behavioral, and Physiological.

This will result in 10 blocks on the page. For each block, write in one example of how the media has affected you or someone you know.

Use the outline below to guide your thinking.

I. Immediate Effects

　1. Cognitive: Media can immediately plant ideas and information.

　2. Attitudinal: Media can influence attitudes and feelings about things.

　3. Emotional: Media can trigger an immediate emotional reaction, such as fear, attraction, sadness, laughter, or others.

　4. Behavioral: Media can trigger behavior.

　5. Physiological: Media can cause arousal or calming. Exposure to communication, especially entertainment, is likely to provide escape by disrupting the rehearsal process that would perpetuate states of elevated arousal associated with negative affective experiences. Exposure is thus likely to produce feelings of relief and escape.

II. Long-Term Effects

　1. Cognitive: Oftentimes people will not expose themselves to the media with the purpose of learning anything. Rather, they will be interested in seeking escape or entertainment. This is especially true with television, radio, and film. However, acquisition of information and attitude change does take place. This type of learning is called "incidental learning."

　2. Attitudes: Erosion or building up of certain attitudes.

　3. Emotional: People can build up a tolerance for emotional reactions over time and thus become desensitized.

　4. Behavioral: New behaviors can be learned in the short term, though not performed until much later.

　5. Physiological: Increased tolerance for certain content; physiological dependency on the medium or on certain content.

Exercise 13.2 What Have You Internalized From the Media Culture?

1. When you are driving and listening to your car radio, do you switch the station, looking for something else even when you are satisfied with the song you are currently hearing—thinking that maybe a better song is on another station now? Do you flip through the channels on the television set looking for something better?

2. In romantic relationships, which is more important to you: commitment or perfection?

   When you are in a romantic relationship, are you happy when you make a lasting, strong commitment to the other person? Or do you worry that this person may not be the absolute best one for you and perhaps there is someone a little better out there?

3. In college, which do you value more: learning or efficiency?

   Do you make a commitment to each course and attend every session and try to get all you can from it? Do you take a wide range of courses (some you know nothing about) in order to expand your experience?

   Or, do you look for ways to spend your time better during class, such as going on a job interview, finishing a term paper for another course, catching up on sleep, and so on? Do you look for courses on the basis of which ones require the least amount of work for the highest grades?

4. In your career, which will be more important to you: loyalty or success?

   Will you find a job and build your entire career there to repay your employer for your first big opportunity? Or will you take the first job as a stepping stone to something better and leave as soon as you have learned all you can in that job?

5. When you have a major problem, are you upset if you cannot solve it in a short period of time?

CHAPTER 14

HOW Do the Effect Processes Work?

KEY IDEA *There are many factors about you and the media messages that in combination increase the probability that the media will have an effect on you.*

A group of boys goes to the movies and watches *The Deer Hunter,* a film in which American prisoners of war in Vietnam are forced by their captors to play the game of Russian roulette. Russian roulette is a game where one chamber in a revolver contains a bullet while the other chambers are empty. Each player in the game takes a turn pointing the gun at his head and pulling the trigger. If he is lucky and the chamber is empty, the gun does not fire and the player is not killed. If he is unlucky, the chamber contains the bullet, which is then fired into his brain, killing him instantly.

Several days after watching this movie, the boys are playing in the bedroom of the parents of one of the boys and find a revolver under the bed. They decide to play Russian roulette. Eventually the gun fires, killing one of the boys.

Should the media portrayal be blamed for this death? This is a very important question. Some people would argue that the boy caused his own death. Some would argue it is the fault of the parents for having a loaded gun available. Some would blame the producers of *The Deer Hunter.* Still others would generalize this example into an argument for how irresponsible all media are. Sorting through all these attributions of blame is at the heart of the issue of media effects. This chapter presents some tools that you can use when trying to understand the complex issue of media effects.

Cause and Effect

When we attribute effects to the media, we raise the issue of causation. After all, if the media do not cause the effect, how can we say that the media have had an influence? There are several ways of thinking about causation. One way is to think about the media *determining* (or *causing*) an effect. Another way is to think about the media *influencing the probability* of an effect.

Deterministic Causation

Causation has a special meaning for social scientists. In order for an argument for a causal relationship to be convincing, it must demonstrate three conditions. First, there must be a relationship between the hypothesized cause and the observed effect. Second, the cause must always precede the effect in time. Third, all alternative causes for the effect must be eliminated.

The problem with making a strong case for the media causing certain effects lies with the second and third conditions. To illustrate, let's consider the hypothesis that television violence causes aggressive behavior in viewers. Because a great deal of research has been conducted to test this hypothesis, researchers are generally able to meet the first condition by showing that there is a relationship between exposure to violence and a person being more likely to exhibit aggressive attitudes and even behaviors. However, researchers have a great deal of difficulty meeting the remaining two conditions. Except for short-term experiments, it is very difficult to argue convincingly that viewing violence on TV really preceded a person's aggression. Aggressive behavior (which is the presumed effect) often precedes the TV viewing (which is the presumed cause). It is often the case that aggressive people seek out violent content. Viewing the content then reinforces their aggressiveness, which leads them to watch more violence. At best, the relationship is reciprocal— each of the two factors is (to a certain extent) the cause of the other.

The requirement of ruling out alternative explanations is also a problem for social scientists. Returning to our example of the Russian roulette game, perhaps the boys were raised in households that strongly valued competition and the ridiculing of people who were afraid of challenges. Perhaps one of the boys was severely depressed and saw this game as a way to commit suicide. Or, perhaps the boys had played with the gun many times before, thinking that it was not loaded. Each of these conditions could be responsible for the death. Unless we can rule out all these (and all other) alternative explanations, we cannot conclude that the media exposure *determined* the shooting.

Probabilistic Causation

There is another way of thinking about causation—probabilistically. As we have seen above, deterministic causation seeks to explain influences in a simple manner, that is, arguing that one thing (the media) caused the effect (the shooting). But our world is very complicated. It contains many competing influences. Some of these come from the media, while others come from institutions, interpersonal interactions, and within ourselves. At times, many of these influences may act in unison to push us in a particular direction. When this happens, none of these individual influences can be regarded as causing or determining the outcome by itself. Instead, each of the factors contributes its own special push; that is, each increases the probability of an effect.

Media effects are almost always probabilistic, not deterministic. There are many factors about the audiences, the messages, and the environment that rachet up the probability that an effect will occur. What are these factors? The major ones are listed below.

Developmental Level. The developmental level of the person is a very important factor in the media effects process (Dervin & Greenberg, 1972; Hawkins

& Pingree, 1982; Murray, 1980; Roberts, 1973; Singer & Singer, 1981). *Developmental level* refers to a person's level of ability for cognitive functioning—for making sense of the world. Recall from Chapter 5 that Piaget showed that infants operate at a very low level of cognitive functioning. As infants grow older their minds mature, and they move up one level at a time until by age 12 their minds have developed to a point that they can function like adults. For example, pre-schoolers have difficulty in understanding and making use of the order of isolated events in a plot. They lose track of the order in which things happen and of relationships among events separated in a plot. They have difficulty making inferences about the causes and meanings of actions, and they have difficulty understanding characters' motives and the consequences of their actions. When pre-schoolers watch television, they focus their attention on the micro elements of particular sound effects, voices, bits of music, and small segments of motion or color. As they age, they are able to organize these individual elements into meaningful chunks. This conceptual chunking allows them to begin to understand plot and character development (Roberts & Bachen, 1981).

Because of differences in cognitive development, children learn different things from the media at different ages. Younger children are not able to follow the narratives in news stories or dramatic plots, so they construct less meaning from them. Thus they cannot engage in much generalization, and this protects them from constructing false images of the world or internalizing many of the themes in the culture. Yet they are more susceptible to the claims of advertisers, because they are not skeptical of that information. Also, young children are more likely to be frightened by monsters and scary sound effects. As they age, children develop the ability to protect themselves from certain kinds of messages, but they become vulnerable to the negative effects of others (Roberts, 1973).

Motivations. When people have a conscious need for a particular kind of information, they will actively seek out this type of information in the media, and the chance of them learning from this experience is high. When people are passive, learning can still occur, but it is not as likely.

People who are more highly educated and more intelligent are more motivated to seek out information from the media (Roberts, 1973). These people select the information that has the greatest utility for them.

Personal Information. People with the largest amount of knowledge learn the most from media (Comstock, Chaffee, Katzman, McCombs, & Roberts, 1978; Rice & Wartella, 1981). When people have a great deal of knowledge on a particular topic, they have a strong, well-developed knowledge framework. They are usually motivated to acquire more information on various topics and thus seek out media that will provide them with this information. When they see a new message on the topic, they are able to integrate that new information quickly and efficiently into their existing knowledge structure.

If a person's knowledge structure is composed primarily of information from only the media, then this structure may be dominated by media-stimulated generalizations and by internalizations from the media world. With many topics, we have no choice but to rely primarily on media information. This is what makes the media such a powerful socializing influence—we cannot check out the media information by comparing it to information from other sources, like real life. For example, almost no one knows what it feels like to be a professional athlete. We are given some insights about what the life of a professional athlete might be like, but almost no one has an opportunity to check out those insights for him- or herself. This is true for almost all news content. The same is true for much fictional programming. Viewers do not know what it feels like to be a multimillionaire, or a detective, or many other portrayals on TV. Because viewers do not have an opportunity to check them out in real life, it is impossible to prove the messages false or inaccurate. When people are asked if TV entertainment is credible and is a reasonable representation of the way people live, most people say yes. As you increase your amount of viewing, your perceptions of the reality of TV entertainment programs increase. This is especially true among children and those who have the least amount of variety of real-world experiences.

Content of Media Messages. People who expose themselves to news are likely to learn about current events, while people who expose themselves to soap operas will learn what the characters have done that day. Both types of content result in learning, but the type of learning is different.

Content differences also influence long-term effects. If you watch a lot of television in general, you will likely come to believe that the world is a mean and violent place, because there is so much crime and violence across the television landscape (Gerbner, Gross, Signorielli, Morgan, & Jackson-Beeck, 1979). This is especially true if you watch mostly crime and action/adventure programs (Potter, 1991). If you watch only prosocial programming, such as *Mister Rogers' Neighborhood, Sesame Street,* and similar shows, you will likely internalize a very different attitude about the world.

When the media present a relatively constant picture of a social world, their effect is more powerful, because all the content points to the same type of effect. When the media present messages that are the same as those presented by other institutions—family, education, religion, the legal system—then all of the messages reinforce one another, but when there are differences across messages, the media messages are often regarded as the most important. This is especially true for people who spend more time with the media than other institutions and for people who like, trust, or are aroused more by media messages than by messages from other sources.

Context of Portrayals. People will generalize about behaviors as a function of the characteristics of the model and whether the model's behavior was successful. If the behavior is successful and rewarded, the viewer will learn that that behavior is good and useful. If the behavior is punished, the viewer will learn that the behavior is bad and should not be tried (Bandura, 1994).

Observation of social models, that is, watching how people act, accounts for much of the information communicated to children, and the media provide an enormous number of models and actions from which children might learn. Given the large amount of time children spend with the media, those mediated models exert strong influence on children's learning about social situations.

Degree of Identification. This is also a key factor in the effects process, because people will pay more attention to characters with whom they identify. We become involved in the media-depicted events through a psychological relationship with the characters through a two-step process. First, we make a judgment about how much we are attracted to the character and how much the character is like us—or what we would like to be. Second, we engage in an "as if" experience in which we imagine ourselves in the role of the character.

We identify with characters who have characteristics like our own but who also have qualities that we would like to possess but do not. Generally, there is a greater liking (positive affect and emotion) for characters who are more similar in age, gender, ethnicity, or interests (Himmelweit, 1966; Weiss, 1971). While most of us tend to select same-gender characters, girls often choose male characters as role models; boys rarely choose female characters. Girls look for physical attractiveness in their selections for role models; boys look for physical aggressiveness. Usually, identification is with a positive object, but it can also be induced through negative sentiment.

Viewers form strong attachments to certain characters, depending on what those characters do and say (Hoffner & Cantor, 1991). The stronger the attachment, the stronger the probability of an effect (Bandura, 1986, 1994).

Arousal. When viewers are aroused, their attention is more concentrated, and the experience is more vivid for them. They will remember the portrayals better and will be more likely to act while aroused (Comstock et al., 1978; Zillmann, 1991).

Certain production techniques tend to arouse viewers. These techniques include fast cuts, quick motion within a frame, loud music, and sound effects.

Also, certain narrative conventions (such as suspense, fear, life threatening violence, and erotica) can lead to arousal.

Sociological Factors. The effects of the mass media are influenced by messages from society and its institutions. If you hear a fact that is counter to your political and religious beliefs, you are likely to discount the fact and forget it or to remember it as an example of a falsehood. Thus the degree to which you are socialized influences the degree to which the media can have an effect (Comstock, 1980; Murray, 1980).

With children, parental involvement in media exposure serves to influence learning. Children increase their understanding and recall of both central and incidental program content when adults provide comments to guide their children's attention and understanding during viewing. However, most parents do not usually provide critical insights while watching TV with their children (McLeod, Fitzpatrick, Glynn, & Fallis, 1982; Roberts, 1973).

People with strong interpersonal ties will use them to filter media messages (Comstock, 1980; Liebert & Schwartzberg, 1977). The more a person identifies with a peer group and the more cohesive the group is, the more the person will be influenced by the group and the less effect the media will have by itself.

The degree of prior socialization is also related to the amount of influence the media will have. Parental support for aggression as a means of problem solving has been found to have a greater influence on attitudes that favor the use of aggression than the viewing of TV violence does (Comstock, 1980; Hawkins & Pingree, 1982; McLeod et al., 1982).

Existing Value Structure. If a person's, especially a child's, set of values is well developed, it will be used as a standard to judge the media messages, and the person will not be as influenced by those messages (Himmelweit, 1966). Your existing values serve as an anchor. When you see something that goes against your values, you are offended and you resist the message, but when messages continually challenge your values, you will slowly drift to a new attitude over time.

Lifestyle. People who have active lifestyles and who interact with many people and institutions are less affected by the media. People who have fewer real-life experiences because of lack of money, education, or vitality are more likely to have a much higher exposure to media that is not counterbalanced by other experiences. This is why people who are poor, who are in a low SES (socio-economic status), who belong to an ethnic minority, and who are elderly are particularly susceptible to influence by the media, especially television, because they expose themselves to a great deal of TV due to their sociological and psychological isolation. TV becomes their window on the world and their primary source of information.

Countervailing Influences. Sometimes two different media effects will take place at the same time, each canceling the other out—these are countervailing influences. One example of this is the issue of children's creativity and day-dreaming. Some people argue that TV *stimulates* daydreaming, because TV is so exciting that viewers will want to relive those episodes. Other people argue that TV *reduces* daydreaming and imagination, because television has such rapid pacing that it leaves children no time to stop and reflect or daydream. TV's ready-made images don't engage the imagination the same way a book does. Also, TV presents so many fantasies that the viewer can access with so little effort, why bother to expend the creative effort needed to daydream?

Does television exert these two countervailing influences on children's imaginations? Valkenburg and Van der Voort (1995), in a Dutch study of elementary school children, looked into the effect of television viewing on daydreaming. They found that there was an important interaction between type of daydreaming and type of TV program. There is more than one type of daydreaming: positive-intense (characterized by vivid, pleasant, and child-like daydreams), aggressive-heroic (action characters acting violently), and dysphoric (escapist). A positive-intense daydreaming style was found to be stimulated by watching non-violent children's programs and to be inhibited by watching violent dramatic programs. An aggressive-heroic daydreaming style was stimulated by watching violent dramatic programs and inhibited by watching nonviolent programs.

Another example of a countervailing effect is exposure to television violence. Some theorists say that exposure to high amounts of explicit violence is bad, because it can trigger a learning effect. Other theorists say that exposure to high amounts of explicit violence might be good, because it can sensitize people to the brutal nature of violence and therefore make people more sympathetic to its victims and less likely to perpetrate violence themselves. The two effects of disinhibition and sensitization may happen simultaneously, thus canceling each other out so that on the surface it appears that there is no effect.

Other Issues of Effect

While causation may be the most important issue we need to understand about media effects, there are other issues. These include the idea of thresholds, linear relationships, contingent conditions, necessary conditions versus sufficient conditions, and direct effects versus indirect effects. They might

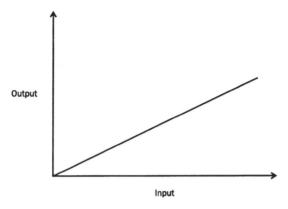

Figure 14.1. Linear Relationship

sound complicated at first, but they are actually simple ideas that will help you develop a much richer appreciation of the nature of media effects.

Thresholds

There are some effects that do not show up until media exposure exceeds a certain point. For example, viewing television generally does not have a negative influence on academic performance until it reaches a point of about 30 hours per week—then it really begins cutting into study time (Potter, 1987). A student who increases television viewing time from 10 hours to 20 hours per week usually will not show a decrease in academic performance. A student who increases TV viewing from 30 to 35 hours per week will show a drop in grades.

Non-Linear Relationships

The effect process is rarely linear. A linear process is in evidence when one unit of input is associated with one unit of output. Figure 14.1 illustrates a linear relationship, because one unit of reading a book is associated with one unit of learning. In contrast, Figure 14.2 shows a non-linear relationship, where the amount of reading needs to be considerable before the reader achieves the first unit of learning. However, readers who keep working at the task of learning will eventually get to a point where the learning will increase relative to the work. When they reach a point on the right-hand side of Figure 14.2, they are receiving *more than one* unit of learning for each hour of reading. This particular non-linear relationship has been referred to as the

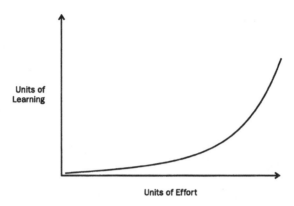

Figure 14.2. Learning Curve

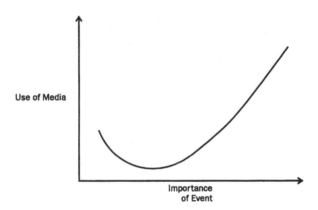

Figure 14.3. J Curve

"learning curve." It is a graphic representation of the principle that the more you know about a given topic, the more efficiently you will be able to learn more about that topic.

There are many other non-linear relationships possible, and several have already been discovered in media effects research. Figure 14.3 presents the J-curve, which expresses the relationship between the use of the mass media and the importance of an event. Figure 14.4 presents the S-curve, which expresses the rate of diffusion of innovations in a society over time. Other examples are the bell curve (Figure 14.5), the advertising exposure plateau curve (3 to 10 exposures optimal; Figure 14.6), and the sine curve (Figure 14.7).

All of these figures have smooth lines. Another form of a non-linear pattern is the catastrophic event. Figure 14.8 represents a person who adds to his

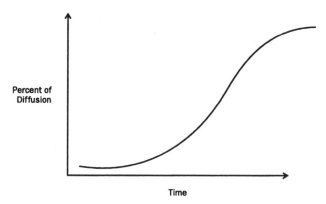

Figure 14.4. S Curve

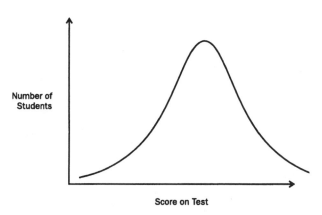

Figure 14.5. Bell Curve

or her television exposure for 5 years with no change in aggressive behavior, then suddenly something happens and the person's aggressive behavior increases enormously. The catastrophic event could be something in the exposure, but it could also be something in the viewer's life, such as a severe injustice, a chemical imbalance in the brain, or the loss through violence of a loved one.

Contingent Conditions

When we expose ourselves to the media, we bring into play our own motives, expectations, and emotions. Each of these can contribute to or take

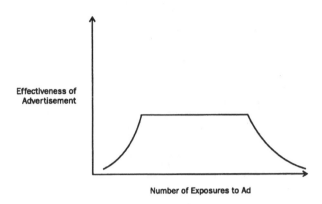

Figure 14.6. Plateau

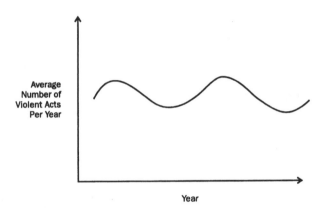

Figure 14.7. Sine Curve

away from the effect. Also, as we interpret the meaning of messages, our skills come into play. For example, if Greg watches a violent fight on television and sees that the perpetrator was attractive and rewarded, he is likely to begin behaving aggressively. Here, the violent message leads to aggressiveness. If Cindy has poor attention skills as she watches the same violence, she might not understand the meaning of the violence and become confused, not aggressive. The violence in this case leads to confusion. Marcia watches the same violent message but laughs at it, because she thinks it is farcical and unrealistic. In this case the violence leads to laughter. From these three examples, can we say that violent messages lead to aggressive behavior? In general, there isn't a consistent pattern—it depends on the message and the person.

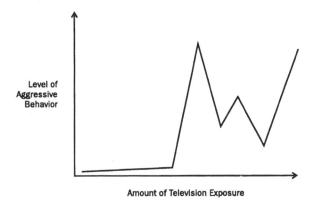

Figure 14.8. Catastrophic Change

When we use an approach that takes all these simultaneous factors into consideration, we discover that *under certain conditions* violent messages can cause aggressive behavior. In short, the effect is contingent on certain conditions.

Necessary Conditions Versus Sufficient Conditions

To illustrate this distinction, I will use the metaphor of starting a fire. In order to start a fire, you need fuel, oxygen, and heat. Having only oxygen is not sufficient to create a fire; you must have all three. To start a fire, none of the three elements is sufficient, but each is necessary—that is, you cannot have a fire if any one is missing.

With the media, there are no sufficient conditions; that is, no single factor is sufficient to guarantee an effect. An effect is the result of many factors acting in concert. Some of the factors may be necessary, that is, the effect could not occur if one of these were missing. However, many of the factors aren't even necessary; factors can be substitutable. For example, let's return to the Russian roulette example. Among the many factors that led to the death of that teenage boy were the revolver, exposure to the movie *The Deer Hunter,* and the peer pressure among the group of friends. None of these factors could be regarded as sufficient, and only the loaded revolver could be regarded as a necessary condition; without it there would have been no game of Russian roulette. Exposure to the movie was an influence, but we could have substituted something else to give them the idea (a book, an interpersonal conversation, etc.). Peer pressure was also an influence, but we could have substituted depression—if the boy were alone and severely depressed, he might have played the game by himself.

Direct and Indirect Influences

The media effect process is not always direct. The effect *can* be direct—we read something and learn it, or we see an ad on TV and it changes our existing attitude. The effect can be indirect, through others. A friend watches the news and tells us about an event. The friend tries to change our attitudes using persuasive techniques gained through watching television.

The effect can be indirect through institutions. The media have changed the way families are structured, so we are raised in a different manner than we might have been. The media have changed the way politics are conducted, so we live under the decisions of a different type of leader.

 ## Summary

Making a clear case for what a media effect is, is difficult because the nature of the effect is almost never a simple causal one. Instead, we must think about necessary and sufficient conditions; about probabilistic influence; about both indirect and direct influences; about non-linear relationships; about thresholds; and about patterns of simultaneous conflicting effects that appear to cancel each other out and make it appear on the surface that no effects are taking place.

A key step in increasing your media literacy is to expand your understanding about how media effects work. This means to avoid looking for a simple causal influence. Instead, there are many factors in the influence, and each factor increases the probability of an effect occurring.

The effects process is complex. That is why it requires a person of relatively high media literacy to appreciate the situation. People who are at low levels of literacy will either believe there is no effect because they do not know what to look for, or they will focus on artifacts that might not be attributable to the media. Either way, a low level of media literacy misleads people into a false sense of awareness of effects.

Despite the complexity in determining what is a media effect, we do know there is a wide range of them, from minor effects to serious, widespread effects. Knowing the factors that increase the probability of an effect is the first step in the process of controlling their influence on you.

 ## References

Bandura, A. (1986). *Social foundations of thought and action: A social cognitive theory.* Englewood Cliffs, NJ: Prentice Hall.

Bandura, A. (1994). Social cognitive theory of mass communication. In J. Bryant & D. Zillmann (Eds.), *Media effects* (pp. 61-90). Hillsdale, NJ: Lawrence Erlbaum.

Comstock, G. A. (1980). *Television in America.* Beverly Hills, CA: Sage.

Comstock, G. A., Chaffee, S., Katzman, N., McCombs, M., & Roberts, D. (1978). *Television and human behavior.* New York: Columbia University Press.

Dervin, B., & Greenberg, B. S. (1972). The communication environment of the urban poor. In F. G. Kline & P. J. Tichenor (Eds.), *Current perspectives in mass communication research* (pp. 195-233). Beverly Hills, CA: Sage.

Gerbner, G., Gross, L., Signorielli, N., Morgan, M., & Jackson-Beeck, M. (1979). The demonstration of power: Violence profile no. 10. *Journal of Communication, 29*(3), 177-196.

Hawkins, R. P., & Pingree, S. (1982). Television's influence on social reality. In D. Pearl, L. Bouthilet, & J. Lazar (Eds.), *Television and behavior: Ten years of scientific progress and implications for the eighties: Vol. 2. Technical reviews* (pp. 224-247). Rockville, MD: U.S. Department of Health and Human Services.

Himmelweit, H. T. (1966). Television and the child. In B. Berelson & M. Janowitz (Eds.), *Reader in public opinion and communication* (2nd ed.). New York: Free Press.

Hoffner, C., & Cantor, J. (1991). Perceiving and responding to mass media characters. In J. Bryant & D. Zillmann (Eds.), *Responding to the screen* (pp. 63-101). Hillsdale, NJ: Lawrence Erlbaum.

Liebert, R. M., & Schwartzberg, N. S. (1977). Effects of mass media. *Annual Review of Psychology, 28,* 141-173.

McLeod, J. M., Fitzpatrick, M. A., Glynn, C. J., & Fallis, S. F. (1982). Television and social relations: Family influences and consequences for interpersonal behavior. In D. Pearl, L. Bouthilet, & J. Lazar (Eds.), *Television and behavior: Ten years of scientific progress and implications for the eighties: Vol. 2. Technical reviews* (pp. 272-286). Rockville, MD: U.S. Department of Health and Human Services.

Murray, J. P. (1980). *Television and youth: 25 years of research and controversy.* Boys Town, NB: Boys Town Center for the Study of Youth Development.

Potter, W. J. (1987). Does television viewing hinder academic achievement among adolescents? *Human Communication Research, 14*(1), 27-46.

Potter, W. J. (1991). Examining cultivation from a psychological perspective: Component subprocesses. *Communication Research, 18,* 77-102.

Rice, M., & Wartella, E. (1981). Television as a medium of communication: Implications for how to regard the child viewer. *Journal of Broadcasting, 25,* 365-372.

Roberts, D. R. (1973). Communication and children: A developmental approach. In I. DeS. Pool, W. Schramm, F. W. Frey, N. Maccoby, & E. B. Parker (Eds.), *The process and effects of mass communication* (Rev. ed., pp. 596-611). Urbana: University of Illinois Press.

Roberts, D. R., & Bachen, C. M. (1981). Mass communication effects. In P. H. Mussen & M. R. Rozenzweig (Eds.), *Annual review of psychology* (pp. 307-356). Palo Alto, CA: Annual Reviews.

Singer, D. G., & Singer, J. L. (1981). Television and the developing imagination of the child. *Journal of Broadcasting, 25,* 373-387.

Valkenburg, P. M., & Van der Voort, T. H. A. (1995). The influence of television on children's daydreaming styles: A 1-year panel study. *Communication Research, 22,* 267-287.

Weiss, W. (1971). Mass communication. In P. H. Mussen & M. R. Rozenzweig (Eds.), *Annual review of psychology* (pp. 309-336). Palo Alto, CA: Annual Reviews.

Zillmann, D. (1991). Empathy: Affect from bearing witness to the emotions of others. In J. Bryant & D. Zillmann (Eds.), *Responding to the screen* (pp. 135-167). Hillsdale, NJ: Lawrence Erlbaum.

Exercise 14.1   Profiling the Probability of an Effect

1. Analyze a particular media effect along with its pattern of factors that would influence the probability of the effect actually occurring. For example, choose the viewing of a violent movie and its potential effect on your behaving aggressively immediately after viewing the film.

   a. Look at the list of 11 factors in this chapter and use them to write a profile of the characteristics that would need to be present in both the film and yourself in order to increase the probability of your behaving aggressively. For example, in the context of portrayals, what contextual characteristics would need to be in the film in order to increase the probability of an aggressive effect.

   b. Now, using the same 11 factors as a guide, write a profile that would keep the probability of an aggressive effect as low as possible.

   c. Look at the two profiles. Which one is closer to what you experience in your life? Are there factors about you, personally, that put you at risk for this type of effect? Are there characteristics about the films you typically see that increase your risk?

2. Do this exercise again, using a different effect. Refer to Table 13.1 for choices.

3. Think about the possible effects of the media on your life and try to apply the following ideas:

   a. *Thresholds:* Have you noticed no effect in some area until you passed a certain level of exposure? What was the effect and the threshold level of exposure?

   b. *Non-Linear Relationships:* Can you think of a non-linear relationship in your life between media exposure and some effect? Can you draw a diagram of the shape of that non-linear relationship?

   c. *Contingent Conditions:* Can you think of something that had an effect on you but not on your friends or family? What was the contingent condition that put you at risk but not the other people?

   d. *Necessary Versus Sufficient Conditions:* Think of a particular media effect, such as newspaper political advertising changing viewers' voting opinions. Are there any sufficient conditions? Are there any necessary conditions?

   e. *Direct and Indirect Effects:* Can you think of any effects the media have had on you indirectly? For example, have your friends formed an opinion from media messages, then gotten you to adopt that opinion without you ever being exposed to the original media messages?

CHAPTER 15

Media Influence
on Institutions

KEY IDEA *The media, especially television, have fundamentally changed many of our institutions.*

Family
Decline of the Traditional Family
Television Content
Television Exposure
Parental Control
Other Contributing Factors

Politics
Primaries
Nominating Conventions
Campaign Spending
Content of Advertising
Campaign Staffs
News Coverage
Agenda Setting

Religion
Religion on Television
Money
Television's Influence on Individuals' Religious Experiences
Television's Influence on the Institution of Religion
Television as Religion

Sports
Focus on Money
Sports and Television
Sports Marketing
Event Sponsorship
The Olympic Games

Society

Summary

In Chapters 13 and 14, we examined how the media affect individuals. The media also profoundly influence our institutions. Some institutions, like politics, have fundamentally changed due to the direct influence of the media, especially television. Some—such as the family, society, and religion—have changed because of many different social pressures, while the media have served to heighten these pressures. The media have brought about the emergence of other institutions such as sports.

In this chapter, we examine how the media have influenced these five institutions. The more you know about the present character of these institutions, the more you can appreciate the power of the media. This chapter also illustrates how the media can have an indirect effect on you through these institutions. The more you understand about these dynamics, the more media literate you will be.

Family

Decline of the Traditional Family

In the span of just one generation, the makeup of the American family has changed radically. The number of traditional two-parent families has shrunk, eclipsed by childless couples, single parents, and people living alone (Perkins, 1996). In 1970, married couples with children made up 40% of American households, but now the figure is 25%—the same number of households with people living alone. More married couples are waiting longer to have children or deciding not to have any. Now, 30% of all households are married couples without children. Today, twice as many children live in single-parent households as 20 years ago (Pipher, 1996).

One argument for the cause of the decline of the traditional family is that the rates of divorce are very high in this country, and they have been climbing since television first penetrated our culture. In 1960, 16% of first marriages ended in divorce, and by 1996, that figure had climbed to 40% (Whitman, 1996).

The steep rise in the divorce rate took place during the same time period that television went from an innovation to the dominant mass medium. However, this is only a pattern of covariation, that is, both things increased together. Recall from Chapter 14 that covariation is only one of the elements needed to demonstrate deterministic causation, which is what most people think of when they criticize the media for unwanted effects. Remember that with deterministic causation we also need the elements of (a) the cause preceding the presumed effect in time and (b) the ability to rule out all other explanations for the effect, leaving the media as the only explanation. Yet when it comes to the media causing the changes in family structures, we cannot present a convincing argument for either of these two elements.

Remember, too, that there is also probabilistic causation, which allows for many contributing causes of an effect. Using this perspective on media effects, the important question becomes: Are the media, especially television, one of the contributing factors to the fundamental changes in the American family? The answer to this question appears to be yes for the following reasons.

Television Content

Critics point out that television too frequently portrays divorce, single-parent households, and alternative lifestyles. These portrayals presented over many different kinds of shows and over many years tend to be internalized by viewers. Over time, people become dissatisfied with their own marriages and seek adventure with other partners.

Television Exposure

Television affects the family as a group in terms of how its members spend their time and how they interact with one another. For example, much of television viewing in families is done by individuals viewing by themselves. More than two thirds of all households have more than one TV set, so individual viewing is possible in most homes. Also, with 65% of households having cable, and the average cable service providing more than 35 channels, individual viewing is desirable so family members do not have to compete for the television. Each family member can watch what she or he wants by viewing a separate TV in a separate room.

Families differ in the centrality of television in their homes (Medrich, Roizen, Rubin, & Buckley, 1982). This is a continuum with television being the center of life at one end, and the TV either muted or rarely on at the other end. Centrality is related to exposure. Children raised in a house where TV is central will watch more, because the TV is so important to all family members.

Also, the layout of the house influences television viewing patterns. Families who live in traditional homes with a closed floor plan (lots of walls and doors dividing the living space into private rooms) are more likely to view TV individually. Families in community-oriented homes (lots of open space and few doors) prefer communal viewing (Pardun & Krugman, 1994).

Even when family members view television together, there is less interaction than if the television were off and the family members had to entertain one another. For example, more than a third of families have TV on during meals, and this reduces the conversation among family members.

Television viewing also slightly reduces the amount of time parents devote to child care, because it serves as a baby-sitter and substitutes for reading bedtime stories (Comstock, 1989). Parents and children tend to talk less to one another when viewing television, but they are often in close proximity—so there is more touching, hugging, and the like.

Parental Control

Most parents exercise little overt control over the amount or kind of television their children watch. Instead, viewing conventions develop based on power structures in the household. For example, when the members of most families view together, the power is with those who have the status—usually the father, followed by the mother, then the older children. Also, viewing control patterns have been found to differ significantly across different types of families. McLeod and Chaffee (1973) have identified four kinds of families:

- Laissez faire: Parents leave children and each other alone; everyone decides for themselves what they do. Television viewing is usually done individually, with each person deciding what to watch and for how long.
- Protective: Parents set up lots of rules and impose them on the family. Rules are constructed "for everyone's good." There are strict rules for media use.
- Pluralistic: Lots of discussion and debate; uniqueness of individuals preserved. Each person, unhampered by others, seeks out media messages.
- Consensual: Lots of discussion and debate; strong motivation to agree and conform. In these households, there are rules for media use, but the rules are developed by the family as a unit.

Even more important than rules is the example set by parents in their own media exposure habits. Television habits are formed early. The amount of television viewed is quite stable from age 3 onward, probably because it depends on family patterns that do not change much over time. Parental example is the best influence on children's television uses and abuses.

Also important is how parents interact with their children during exposures. Parents who watch television with their children and help them to understand and critique the messages are extremely valuable in helping their children develop higher levels of media literacy. Unfortunately, parents in the 1990s spend 40% less time with their children than parents did in the 1950s (Pipher, 1996).

When it comes to the media, parents have found their roles changing dramatically. For example, Pipher (1996) points out,

> Good parents used to introduce their children into the broader culture; now they try to protect their children from the broader culture. Good parents used to instill the values of the broader culture; now they try to teach their children values very different from the ones the world at large teaches. (p. 11)

She argues,

> Rapidly our technology is creating a new kind of human being, one who is plugged into machines instead of relationships, one who lives in a virtual reality rather than a family. (p. 92)

> When people communicate by e-mail and fax, the nature of human interaction changes. (p. 88)

The conveniences of technology serve to cut us off from others. We depend less and less on others (at least face to face). People become things or services, not human beings. Pipher says that 72% of Americans don't know their neighbors, and the number of people who say they have never spent time with the people next door has doubled in the past 20 years. Children are losing social skills as they grow up in a consumer-driven, electronic community.

Other Contributing Factors

Even if we accept the argument that television has influenced the trend toward the breakdown of the traditional family, we must realize that there are also other influences, such as economic ones. For example, it takes more money to support a family. The median household income is now just over $30,000 and both adults are likely to work, which makes it harder for them to have children and raise them at home. The percentage of females in the labor force has been steadily climbing, until now about 58% of all females 16 years old and older have jobs (DeFleur & Dennis, 1996).

Another reason for the change in family structures is that careers have become more important to many people than their families. Wage earners work longer hours, and this takes them away from their homes for a higher proportion of their waking hours. There are strong stressors of time, money, and lifestyle that make people regard the home as a place to recover from the workplace, not a place where they have high energy. Family is no longer of paramount importance in most people's lives (Pipher, 1996).

Clearly, family structures and interaction patterns have been changing since the late 1950s. There are many reasons for this. Television is a key element in this change, but not the only one. The additional elements of economic demands, rise in the importance of careers, and changes in lifestyle preferences have all contributed to the probability of change in the institution of family.

Politics

The mass media have always had an influence on shaping the way politics have been conducted. Ever since the founding of this country, candidates for political office have relied on coverage of their campaigns in newspapers and magazines, and they have bought ads in these media in order to get their messages out to the electorate and to create an image for themselves. When William Henry Harrison ran for U.S. president in 1840, he wanted to change his image so he would appeal more to the voters, who were mostly common people who distrusted the rich. He was afraid of being perceived as an aristocrat because he was the wealthy son of a governor and the owner of a palatial Georgian mansion on a 2,000-acre estate worked by tenant farmers. Instead, he wanted to be perceived as a farmer and backwoodsman in order to increase his appeal to the electorate. In his newspaper ads, he was shown wearing a coonskin cap and drinking cider by a log cabin. This image was everywhere during the campaign.

Later, Daniel Webster created the first political pseudo-event for the press. He camped out in the woods with Green Mountain boys and challenged to a fist fight anyone who called him an aristocrat.

Harrison won his election, but Webster lost his. Using the media might not guarantee victory, but not using the media can guarantee defeat. Candidates for public office—from city council to president of the United States—must establish name recognition among the electorate; along with a recognized name, they must instill a positive image. The media are the channels that make it possible for candidates to achieve these goals quickly and across many people.

As radio came along, politicians used it to reach more of the electorate. In the 1930s, Thomas Dewey, a crusading New York City district attorney, ran for governor. On the final day of the campaign, he was on the radio from 6 a.m. until midnight, inviting people to phone in and ask him questions. Most of the calls were from one of his assistants, who spent the day in a phone booth with a pile of coins.

When television came along in the 1950s, politics began to change dramatically. Since that time, there has been a gradual and continual erosion of the amount of influence the political parties are able to exert. No longer do we have to be members of a political party and go to its functions in order to feel informed and involved. Primary elections are now much more important, and the party's nominating conventions are much less important, but the biggest change is in the cost of campaigning, because it is essential to use television, and television is very expensive.

Primaries

Television has increased the importance of primary elections for presidential candidates. The nomination of presidential candidates used to be decided in party caucuses and conventions. In 1940, primary elections were held in only 13 states. By 1976, 30 states had primaries. Now, almost every state has either a primary election or a caucus.

Today, someone who wants to run for U.S. president must do well in the early primaries to get press coverage. Candidates who do not do well are not put on the press's agenda, and the public rarely hears about them. Those candidates who do well get a great deal of coverage, which is free publicity for their campaigns.

Nominating Conventions

The media have changed the presidential nominating conventions of our political parties by focusing so much of the public's attention on them. The historical purpose of these conventions was for the loyal party members to gather at a national meeting to cut deals and wield power. The result of all this negotiation was to select a candidate to represent the party in the presidential election. Now the candidates are known well in advance of the "nominating" conventions, so those meetings have been transformed into advertising platforms for the parties. Thus the delegates are instructed to portray a favorable impression of the party to the public. This means showing harmony and togetherness rather than debating important issues.

Campaign Spending

Television's increasing importance in political campaigns has resulted in great increases in campaign spending. Between 1952 (the early days of television) and 1974, expenditures on the media for political advertising increased 600% (adjusted for inflation) (Comstock, 1980). By 1972 spending was way out of control, with McGovern spending $30 million and Nixon $60 million. The reason for the increase was a major shift in the way the campaigns allocated their money. For example: In 1956, 85% of presidential campaign expenditures were for setting up rallies for in-person speeches by the candidates. Three elections later, with total expenditures four times greater, more than half the money was spent on television ads (Comstock, 1989). The television budget continued to increase dramatically, resulting in smaller budgets for field operations like setting up rallies and local campaign offices, and for making buttons, bumper stickers, and so on.

Shortly after the 1972 presidential election, in which the candidates spent $90 million, Congress passed some campaign reform legislation that placed strict limits and regulations on spending. In the 1976 election, each candidate spent about $9 million.

Despite the limits imposed by Congress, however, the money required to run for president is increasing dramatically again, and a good deal of it is being spent very early in the campaigns. Candidates must spend huge amounts of money early for name recognition. For example, in 1984, the Democratic front runner Walter Mondale spent over $30 million to win a single primary. His two challengers (Jackson and Hart) spent a total of more than $21 million in a losing effort—that adds up to more than $55 million spent by Democratic candidates in a single state! The Republican candidate, Ronald Reagan, who was the incumbent president at the time and running unopposed in the primaries, spent $18 million. When the primary campaigns were over, Mondale was nominated as the Democratic candidate and Reagan as the Republican candidate. During the general election that fall, the two presidential candidates were each allowed to spent $40 million, which was the limit imposed by Congress. However, political action committees (PACs), which were not regulated, were allowed to raise as much as they could and to spend it any way they wanted. The wealthy right-wing National Conservative Political Action Committee spent $14 million to campaign for Reagan.

The high cost of campaigning is not limited to presidential races; it is also very expensive to run in gubernatorial and congressional races. In 1970, candidates for governorships spent an average of 9¢ to 10¢ per vote; candidates for the U.S. Senate spent an average of 8¢ to 9¢ per vote; and candidates for the U.S. House of Representatives spent an average of 1¢ to 2¢ per vote. Those figures are much higher today, with candidates for all levels of office generally spending at least $1 per vote. For example, candidates in the 1986 congressional elections spent $450 million. By 1994 in California, $31.8 million was spent on the race for governor.

Expenditures for political ads are on the increase at the state and local levels, because campaign managers now believe that the amount of advertising may determine the election outcome. For example, in Alabama, the gubernatorial candidate who had the most ads in both the electronic and print media did win the election. It is interesting to note that in that election, as the size of ads in print media or the length of ads in electronic media increased, so did the number of issues presented in those ads. Instead of dealing with fewer issues in depth, new issues were added as a result of more advertising.

When people say that "too much" is spent on political advertising, it is not clear what they mean by the "correct" amount. This is the point made by the columnist George Will (1996), who says that the annual sum spent on political campaigning is less than that spent on yogurt. Also, when you take a 2-year period and include all the money spent by all candidates campaigning for state and federal offices—$700 million—it equals the amount spent in 2 years by the nation's two largest commercial advertisers—Procter & Gamble and Philip Morris. This $700 million works out to be a combined total, across all elections, of $1.75 per eligible voter per year.

The issue of concern now is that a very rich person who doesn't have to raise any campaign funds and who therefore does not have to abide by campaign financing laws can buy an office. For example, in one campaign, Jay Rockefeller spent $11 million of his own money to win a second term as governor of West Virginia. This does not always work, however: In 1992, Ross Perot spent $60 million of his own money and lost the election for U.S. president.

Content of Advertising

Critics also complain that much political advertising is either fluff (non-informational) or negative. Roger Ailes, the media consultant who produced the "new Nixon" in 1968, agrees, saying that television is only good for covering three things: visuals, attacks, and mistakes. As a result of this reasoning, there have been high proportions of negative ads in presidential campaigns. As an example, 70% of the ads in the 1988 presidential campaign were negative.

Campaign Staffs

The increase in television involvement in political campaigns has altered the makeup of campaign staffs. The most important person in a campaign used to be the campaign manager, who had extensive contacts among party workers so he or she could pull in favors and get many members active in setting up rallies, passing out bumper stickers, and going door to door to hand out party literature. Now the most valued people in the campaign are the public opinion polling expert and the media consultant.

The polling expert finds out what the public wants in a "leader"—that is, how the person should look, how the person should act, and what stand the candidate should take on important issues. The media consultant then crafts ads and pseudo-events for the media to make the candidate appear like that ideal image.

News Coverage

The press usually presents campaigns as horse races. An analysis of more than 1,300 election stories carried by ABC, CBS, and NBC during the 1988 primaries found that more than 500 dealt with who appeared to be winning and another 300 dealt with campaign strategies, for a total of more than 60% of the coverage clearly exhibiting the horse-race mentality. In contrast, only about one story in six covered the issues ("Election '88," 1988).

The "front runner" is the candidate who wins the very first primary. The press then creates expectations for candidates and the campaign outcome. Throughout the campaign, the press reports polls to set up these expectations about who is winning and by how much. When something different than the expected occurs, it is deemed newsworthy.

Media coverage fluctuates, depending on the performance of the candidate in the preceding contest. The most attention generally goes to the candidate who was the winner or who has emerged surprisingly as the challenger. Candidates who falter become progressively less able to compete, because they begin slipping off the agenda (Patterson, 1980).

There is a trend toward using new sources of information on politics—such as on MTV and talk shows (*Larry King Live* and *Donahue,* for example). Hollander (1995) found that attention to MTV and late night shows is not related to gains in political knowledge, but attention to talk shows is.

Agenda Setting

Media can directly affect how people process information about political events, and this priming effect influences behavior (Iyengar & Kinder, 1987). By focusing on certain issues and ignoring others, the media set the agenda for the campaign. The agenda alters the public's priorities. The high-priority issues then are what the public focuses on when examining the stance of candidates. Thus, if a candidate is strong on many issues and weak on one, and the press makes that one issue a priority, then the public will think that particular issue to be very important and therefore rate that candidate low.

In summary, television has made it possible for candidates to build name recognition quickly and to plant a favorable image in the minds of the voters, but this comes with a high price. Television advertising is very expensive and thus requires candidates continually to raise large sums of money. There is also a price to the institution of politics, which has been forever changed. There are also some key benefits to this change. As voters, we are given much more information about candidates, and significant coverage of campaigns begins earlier. Also, with this additional information and the opportunity to vote in primaries, we are given more power to select the candidates who will run in the general elections. There is also a down side—the information we are given about the candidates is usually very superficial and often negative; and the mainstream media set the agenda, thus channeling our interest to a few selected topics and away from all others. We can counteract this down side by being careful to analyze the information we do get and to seek out more extensive and intensive information, and to build stronger knowledge structures about the political process and its players.

Religion

Commitment to religious institutions has been dropping in this country, especially among younger people such as the 76.5 million baby boomers, people born between 1946 and 1964. About two thirds of these baby boomers dropped out of organized religion during the past several decades, although some of them are starting to return (Woodward, 1990). About 80% of Americans consider themselves religious and believe in life after death, but only 57% (43 million people) of these religious people attend a church or synagogue on a regular basis.

Religion on Television

Religious programs have been on television ever since its earliest days in the 1950s, but it was not until the 1970s that this type of programming became very visible. There is a controversy about how large the viewing audience is for religious television. The televangelists claim that the audience is very large. In contrast, Fore (1987) says that the audience for the electronic church is far smaller than claimed. According to surveys, about 71 million people say they have watched one of these programs each week, but Nielsen diaries put the figure at about 24.7 million a week for a duplicated audience;

the unduplicated figure is about 13.3 million who watch at least 15 minutes of religious programming a week. The number who watch for an hour or more is less than 4 million. Only the top religious programs draw an audience of more than 2 million viewers (Horsfield, 1984). Demographics show that this audience tends to be female, older, less well educated, in lower paying jobs, and probably in blue-collar occupations (Hoover, 1988; Horsfield, 1984).

The best predictor of religious program viewership is whether a person is affiliated with a church. It is churchgoers who watch religious TV. Thus, religious programs are "preaching to the converted" and do not serve to convert non-churchgoers (Horsfield, 1984). Hoover (1988) found viewing of religious television to be associated with church attendance, giving, and private religious behaviors like prayer and Bible reading. Therefore, the effect of these shows is possible reactivation of inactive members or channeling members from one church to another.

Religious programming on television is shaped by the same forces that shape television content in general (Horsfield, 1984). The three major forces are:

1. Sensationalism: There is a strong emphasis on producing material that will quickly capture and hold viewers' attention.
2. Instant gratification: Programmers strive to provide immediate answers to easily defined problems.
3. Oversimplification: Programming avoids in-depth, demanding analyses of issues, events, and human relationships and instead relies heavily on stereotyped characters, plots, and relationships.

Money

A big theme on all religious programs is the appeal for money. In 1983, Abelman (cited in Fore, 1987) conducted a content analysis of the 40 leading religious shows and found that in an average hour, the viewer was asked to donate $328; a person who watches 2 hours a week is subject to direct appeals for about $31,500 a year. Most of these appeals are to allow the televangelist to stay on the air, not to fund missions for helping to clothe or feed people.

Figures for yearly contributions in the late 1970s were: $60 million to Oral Roberts, $46 million to Christian Broadcasting Network, and $20 million to Jimmy Swaggert (Horsfield, 1984). By 1983, Pat Robertson's CBN brought in $101 million, of which $89 million came in as donations. In 1985, Jim Bakker's *PTL Club* had an income of $72.1 million, with $42 million in direct contributions and the rest earned from a new $30-million Victorian-style hotel and biblical theme park, the 2,500-acre Heritage USA. PTL's expenses that year were $89.7 million. Jimmy Swaggert generated about $45 million a year, 80% of which was spent to keep his show on the air (Fore, 1987).

Television's Influence on Individuals' Religious Experiences

What do viewers get from watching religious television programs? Hoover (1988) argues that the electronic church has had a revitalizing effect by recognizing individuals' experiences of dissonance, frustration, and cultural crises. By depicting the culture as out of control, religious programs present themselves as offering stability and a clear purpose. They have done this by developing a total, universal explanation of life that proposes to resolve the dissonances felt in contemporary life.

What is the appeal of the electronic church? Fore (1987) explains that the electronic church appears authoritative at a time when authority appears to be in disarray. It highlights competition between God and the devil. It places emphasis on individuals as the basic societal unit and charges them to act. It is also generally affirming of the social values most people hold, and it reinforces this belief system with attractive personalities.

Television's Influence on the Institution of Religion

Some social critics, such as Hoover (1988), argue that the main effect of the electronic church is not in changing people's beliefs. Instead, the main effect of the electronic church is that it has changed the institution of religion in America. How has religious television done this? It has broken down denominational boundaries and brought evangelicals and fundamentalists into the mainstream, and it has changed the way we see politics and religion—the electronic church has taken on a political prominence.

Television as Religion

Some scholars think of television as becoming a dominant institution that has taken over some of the functions of religion (Gerbner & Gross, 1976). They say that television implicitly communicates values and interpretations of the world by presenting lessons about success, power, and dominance. By conveying status to certain people, television identifies those people as being much like priests who guide our thinking.

Television is seen by some as the new American religion:

> Television is the new "cultural storyteller," an agent of norms and values as much as of news and information. Television fulfills this function very much in the way traditional storytellers did—by a process of dialectic, not didactic— where the stories evolve with the culture, retaining most, but not all, of their

formal integrity by changing to suit its audiences and new contexts of expression. (Hoover, 1988, p. 241)

Fore (1987) says that television is

beginning to replace the institution that historically has performed the functions we have understood as religious. Television, rather than churches, is becoming the place where people find a worldview which reflects what to them is the ultimate value, and which justifies their behavior and way of life. Television today, whether the viewer knows it or not, and whether the television industry itself knows it or not, is competing not merely for attention and dollars, but for our very souls. (p. 24)

Television is itself becoming a kind of religion, expressing the assumptions, values, and belief patterns of many people in our nation, and providing an alternative worldview to the old reality, and to the old religious view based on that reality. (p. 25)

These writers are very critical of the idea that television is becoming the dominant religion in this society.

The values, assumptions, and worldview of television's "religion" are in almost every way diametrically opposed to the values, assumptions, and worldview of Christianity and the historic Judeo-Christian tradition in which the vast majority of Americans profess to believe. (Fore, 1987, p. 25)

Also, Hoover (1988) cautions that contemporary religion is at odds with many of the messages of television—the messages of materialism rather than sharing and asceticism; of force and violence dominating the value systems instead of love and cooperation; and of classes of people being objectified and manipulated, not encouraged and cared for. Many evangelists see TV as secular humanism, that is, as competing with the values they espouse; therefore, TV is the enemy.

Critics fear that the technological worldview poses three threats to religion (Fore, 1987). First, that it is diverting a major portion of the world's interests, motivations, satisfactions, and energies away from a religious center. Second, that it is robbing genuine religious vocabularies of their power as people know more about TV characters than about religious symbols and figures. Third, that the new technological environment encourages the growth of religious concern that rejects or ignores organized religion. People spend more time with electronic devices than they do with people. With increasing numbers of channels and content options, people can pick only those things that reinforce their already held beliefs. This puts the development of beliefs into the hands of individuals rather than the institution of religion. Thus, communication is treated more as a commodity to serve an individual's immediate needs, rather than as a broad cultural phenomenon that brings us together into a large community where the needs of the community are more important than the needs of any individual.

Fore (1987) contrasts the central myths of television with the central values of religion. He says television presents five myths: (a) The fittest survive (social Darwinism); (b) Power and decision making start at the center and move out (Washington is the center of political power; New York the center of financial power; Hollywood the center of entertainment power); (c) Happiness consists of limitless material acquisition (corollaries include that consumption is inherently good and that people are less important than property, wealth, and power); (d) Progress is an inherent good (it is good to keep moving, it is less important to have a goal); and (e) There exists a free flow of information (this is a myth because there is almost no chance for non-establishment information to get a wide hearing).

Television is forcing churches to adapt. Comstock (1989) says, "In the case of cultures in which traditional religious observances have a visible and important place, television is one of the central components of modernization that channels public energies toward secular pursuits" (p. 246). As people become more secular, religion has to adapt, either by fighting against the trend of secularization and thus becoming less relevant to people's everyday lives, or by changing its values. For example, in Israel, television took time away from participation in celebrations and activities associated with Jewish religious practice, so television broadcasting was outlawed on the Sabbath; but the public demanded that the prohibition be lifted, and it was (Katz & Gurevitch, 1976).

In summary, the key benefit of religious messages in the media is that they provide more experiences for worship for people who are already religious. Yet critics are concerned that television itself has become a religion as evidenced by the ritualized viewing of many people. This has critics worried, because the values presented on television are very different from the values presented by organized religion.

Sports

Focus on Money

Sports have changed dramatically since the late 1950s. The reason is big money. Not only have the revenues been skyrocketing; now the focus of sports is almost exclusively on money.

To illustrate this trend, in 1959 Red Sox star Ted Williams returned his contract unsigned to management, that is, he was rejecting their $125,000 offer. Coming off a year in which he hit "only" .259, he felt he was not worth that much money so he asked for a pay cut of 25%, which was the maximum pay cut possible.

Those days are gone. Over the past 30 years, salaries for baseball players have been increasing rapidly. In 1995, the average salary was $1,110,766 per player. In total, baseball clubs spent $924 million for players. The range is pretty wide across clubs, with the New York Yankees at the top with their average player making $2,000,271. Montreal had the lowest average salary at $411,142 ("Average Baseball Salaries," 1995).

Football salaries are also high. In the 1995 NFL season, the salary cap was $37.1 million per club, and 26 of the 30 teams in the league went over that maximum. Dallas spent the most at $62.2 million; Jerry Jones spent almost $40.5 million in signing bonuses, including $13 million to Deion Sanders. Seattle had the lowest payroll at $33.3 million ("NFL Teams," 1996).

Michael Jordan earned $4 million for the 1995-1996 season when he led the Chicago Bulls to their fourth championship in professional basketball in the past 6 years. He was named the most valuable player of the year, and many regard him as the best basketball player of all time. Yet his salary ranked him the 27th highest paid player in the league. After becoming a free agent, he was signed for $18 million for one year, making him the highest paid player in the league—temporarily. How high can salaries go? Several years ago, the NBA instituted a salary cap per team. The 1996-1997 salary cap for the Bulls was $24.3 million, but the Bulls can pay Jordan whatever they want because the salary cap does not apply to the re-signing of a team's existing players (Rhodes & Reibstein, 1996).

The owner of the Chicago Bulls, Jerry Reinsdorf, could afford this because the value of his franchise has climbed from $17.5 million in 1985—Jordan's rookie year—to $178 million in 1996. The owner has a huge yearly income from broadcast rights, merchandising, and ticket sales. The Bulls play at the new United Center where there are 216 suites, each selling for $175,000. All are sold out and there is a waiting list. There is also a waiting list of more than 17,000 fans for season tickets.

Players have been demanding higher salaries and getting them. Owners have been cultivating additional revenue streams, such as luxury skyboxes at stadiums, apparel merchandising, and very lucrative television contracts. When players ask for more money, the owners must pay it. The owners then raise the prices of tickets, concessions, parking, and apparel and other souvenirs. For example, Superbowl tickets sell for between $200 and $350 a seat—that's the list price.

Sports and Television

The biggest increase in sports revenue is from television. Without a television contract, no sports league could survive. The American Football League (AFL) got started in the early 1960s with a TV deal of $1.7 million. In 1965, CBS got the National Football League (NFL) rights for $14.1 million. Now, 30 years later, the NFL sells a year's broadcasting rights for $500 million. This sum is so large that it is shared by five networks: ABC, NBC, ESPN, Fox, and TNT.

Television broadcasters pay these huge fees to sports organizations because broadcasters know that large numbers of us will watch. Broadcasters then rent us out to advertisers willing to pay huge sums for the opportunity of getting their commercial messages in front of us. The list of the most popular sports on television is headed by the NFL with an average rating of 16; major league baseball is second with an 11.1 average rating. The cost of a 30-second ad in football is about $130,000, and $80,000 in baseball. Golf and tennis are the least popular sports, with average ratings of about 4.5 and 3.8, respectively. These sports deliver a high-quality audience, however, one that is very affluent and hence very attractive to companies who advertise luxury products.

With television and advertisers putting so much money into these sports, they demand that the sports be exciting, so they have forced some changes in the games themselves. For example, basketball now has a shot clock that requires players to shoot the ball much more often. Basketball now has a 3-point play, which is much riskier and hence more exciting. Football has the 2-minute warning (new in the mid-1960s) and television time outs. Uniforms are more colorful. All of this is to increase viewer interest and thereby provide advertisers with a better audience.

They also want the coverage to be more entertaining. For example, the coverage of a football game is more than 3 hours, although the game itself takes 60 minutes, and there is less than 10 minutes of action on the field during the 60 minutes that the clock is running. This means the announcers must provide lots of anecdotes, statistics, and color commentary. The director must provide lots of replays, slow motions, shots of the crowd and cheerleaders, and so on.

Sports Marketing

Sports marketing has really grown by focusing on product endorsements by athletes. By 1983, $25 million was spent on endorsements; by 1988 the amount had doubled to $50 million. Now Michael Jordan alone makes more than $40 million per year in product endorsements.

Companies are willing to spend huge fees on athletes who endorse their products, because such endorsements work to increase sales. For example, in 1985, when Boris Becker signed a multi-million dollar deal to promote Puma tennis shoes and rackets, the company's sales increased 25%. John McEnroe's endorsement of Bic disposable razors increased the company's market share from 12% to 23% of total razor sales.

Event Sponsorship

Event sponsorship is also very big. By 1986, more than 2,100 companies were sponsoring sporting events and spending a total of more than $1 billion a year on all kinds of sports. This money bought some companies the leverage to change the names of some sporting events. The Boston Marathon was re-named the John Hancock Boston Marathon and the Sugar Bowl football game was re-named the USF&G Sugar Bowl. This advertising money gives sponsors a stronger presence at particular sporting events, and sometimes their ads can overwhelm the sporting event itself. For example, Budweiser sponsored the Marvin Hagler-Sugar Ray Leonard middleweight fight in 1987. For $750,000, Budweiser got the right to cover the ring mat and the ring posts with its logo.

The Olympic Games

In 1964, NBC paid $1.5 million to broadcast the Tokyo Summer Olympics. By 1980, the cost had skyrocketed to $85 million when NBC acquired rights to the Moscow Summer Olympics, despite the fact that the Soviets wanted $210 million plus $50 million in production equipment to be left behind. The broadcast was never made, though, because of the boycott by the American government. ABC paid $225 million for the Los Angeles Summer Games in 1984, and $91 million for the Winter Games in Sarajevo. Despite losing money on the Winter Games, ABC came back with an even higher bid of $309 million for the 1988 Winter Games in Calgary. NBC got the 1988 Summer Games in Seoul, Korea, for $300 million. NBC paid $456 million for the 1996 Atlanta games, while CBS bid $375 million to broadcast the 1998 Nagano games in the Winter Olympics. NBC broke its record by bidding $705 million for exclusive U.S. rights to broadcast the 2000 Summer Games in Sydney, Australia and another $545 million for the 2002 Winter Games in Salt Lake City. The total NBC package is worth about $1.3 billion—none of the other U.S. networks entered a bid (Nelson, 1995). NBC bid $2.3 billion for the rights to the Olympic Summer Games in 2004 and 2008 and the Winter Games in 2006, even before the sites were decided ("NBC Gambles," 1996).

Where does this money go? It is paid to the Olympic Committee, which also sells rights to broadcast the games to media in other countries. When ABC paid $309 million for the 1988 Winter Games, the EBU (European Broadcast Union, which represents 32 countries and a population of several hundred million) paid $5.7 million, and the Soviet Union, along with its Eastern European allies, North Korea, and Cuba, paid a combined total of $1.2 million. Thus it is clear that the United States (or rather advertisers on U.S. television) really support the Games—without them, the Olympics would be very different.

The broadcast rights are just one expense. Production is another big expense. The United States sent 500 athletes to compete in the 1984 Los Angeles Summer Olympics; ABC sent 3,500 people (1,400 engineers, 1,800 support personnel, and 300 network production and management people). To produce 188 hours of coverage, they used 205 cameras, 660 miles of camera cables, four helicopters, three houseboats, 26 mobile units, 35 office trailers, and 404 hardwired commentary positions. There were microphones on basketball backboards, underwater in the diving pool, in boxing ringposts, and in equestrian saddles. The cost of covering the games was $100 million.

In 1984, the Olympic Games in Los Angeles became the first to be supported entirely by commercial sponsorship, and they made a big profit. VISA alone spent $25 million on the rights and on promotions, and 146 corporations were official sponsors of various events. One by one, all major sporting events are turning to sponsorships for funding.

In summary, sports have become more exciting and entertaining to the general viewer over the past several decades. The public is showing increased interest in sporting events and personalities of all kinds, but the price for this continues to climb. As a viewer, you pay the price in the form of higher cost of admission to games as well as more frequent interruptions of televised games in the form of advertising messages.

 Society

The same forces that are fragmenting politics, religion, and the family are also fragmenting society. There is irony in this situation, because on the surface the media appear to be a unifying force. The mass media give us the illusion that we are all experiencing the same messages. When we see a show on TV or hear a song, we often assume that everyone else has also seen or heard it. When we read about a national figure in a newspaper or magazine, we assume every one else in our society also knows who that person is. To a large extent, this holds true—at least for popular cultural messages. People get the feeling that everyone else is tied into the same things that they are, but this is an illusion.

Instead, the media are serving to fragment us; that is, we are becoming more different from one another, and we have a smaller and smaller set of shared experiences over time. Why? Although we all have *access* to the same messages, we cannot possibly *expose* ourselves to them all. For example, you probably have access to 50 different television stations, but you can watch only one at a time. You must make choices. It's our choices that fragment us. Because each of us has a different set of interests, we are all screening out a different set of messages. While our *access* to the media may be the same, everyone is paying attention to a different set of messages. Over time, our information bases develop very differently; we have very little of a shared set.

This information base is what we use for context when interpreting new messages. Because our contexts are so different from one another's, our interpretations differ. These differences remind us of how little we have in common. This trend toward differences continues as more messages are made available and we screen in only a very small sub-set of them.

When we look at this fragmentation phenomenon from the media point of view, we see an irony. The mass media are driven to appeal to as many of us as possible. For example, programmers at ABC, CBS, Fox, and NBC, as well as Hollywood producers and the publishers of general magazines and best-selling books, want to construct messages that will appeal to as wide an audience as possible. So, they strip away as much context as possible so that the messages don't require much in the way of interpretation from their audiences. For example, when you watch a situation comedy on prime-time television, you don't need much contextual information. You are not required to know anything about the history of situation comedies, or their economic nature, or the political environment of getting one on the air. You don't even have to know what the characters did in the last episode in order to follow this episode. Very little is asked of you as a viewer, compared to what is asked of you if you were to watch a documentary of Egypt or a Shakespearean play, for example. With situation comedies, you don't need to bring much context to the viewing. The viewing of situation comedies does not contribute much to the contexts you already have, so this common viewing along with millions of other people does not really build a common context.

Donnelly (1986) describes this fragmentation of society when he says that we are currently living in an Autonomy Generation that will soon change to a Confetti Generation. The Autonomy Generation people believe that each individual is the center of all relevant values:

We are responsible only to ourselves, and we alone can decide which activities and ways of behaving have meaning for us and which do not. We live subjectively according to our own feelings with little need for outside reference. . . . We interpret life in terms of what's in it for us, seek authenticity by transcending society and external value systems, and insist on being ruled only by the laws of our character. . . . We live in the present, responding to momentary perceptions, relationships, and encounters. To us, what is most important is how outside events are perceived and understood by the individual. (p. 178)

He says we experience what Durkheim called *anomie*, the peculiar pain derived from individuals' inability to identify with and experience their community.

Donnelly says that the new electronic media have five characteristics that will affect society: quantity (in terms of availability and use), speed (delivery and satisfaction), weightlessness of images (no context), remoteness (bringing faraway information close), and choice (huge increase in number of alternatives). Because the present generation does not possess the cultural tools to absorb such an explosion of information, we will become the Confetti Generation. The Confetti person is inundated by experience but not grounded in any cultural discipline for arriving at any reality but the self. "We will witness an aggregated version of today when all ideas are equal, when all religions, life-styles, and perceptions are equally valid, and equally indifferent, and equally undifferentiated in every way until given a value by the choice of a specific individual" (Donnelly, 1986, p. 181-182).

Whether Donnelly is overstating the problem remains to be seen. He may be right if the literacy of the people in society does not keep up with the changes in our world.

Summary

The media—especially television and especially since the late 1960s—have changed institutions. Because these institutions affect us, the media exert an indirect effect on us through these institutions.

The family has changed from the traditional two parents, with one working outside the home and the other staying home to take care of the children. Television has been blamed for making people more materialistic so more people have to work longer hours to get the means to buy all the new products that have become necessities: multiple cars, multiple TV sets, stereos, computers, cellular phones, and on and on. Thus people spend more time in the workplace and less time with family members. When the family is together, its members are likely to watch TV in separate rooms. Parents are less likely to watch with their children and to talk with them about the shows. With little adult supervision over television viewing, video game playing, and computer usage, children experience worlds apart from their family and the shared experience is disappearing.

Politics has changed from a process of interpersonal persuasion, speech making, and back room power deals to one of opinion polling, broad-scale negative television ads, and images that look good on television. The power of the primaries has greatly increased, while the purpose of nominating conventions has evaporated. Now more than ever the campaigning process is driven by big money so that candidates can produce slick ads and saturate television audiences with them. Spending lots of money will not guarantee a victory, but having little money to spend will guarantee a loss.

Religion has moved onto television to provide messages to the already religious. Without advertising, these religious programs depend on the donations of viewers, and they are able to raise a great deal of money each year. For many people in this society, television is becoming a religion. People search out messages, take great comfort in the entertainment and news, structure their time around those messages in a ritualistic manner, and learn fundamental lessons about life from their exposure.

Sports have made changes in order to become more entertaining and thus appeal to more viewers. With more viewers, television stations charge advertisers more. Stations pay higher sums of money to team owners for the right to cover their sports. The owners become more wealthy and the players demand higher salaries and get them. This circle of money is an upwardly moving spiral as prices, revenues, and salaries all jump dramatically each year. Television coverage makes this spiral possible.

Society is fragmenting. Television has the ability to bring everyone in society together by giving us all common, shared experiences every day. In the early days of television broadcasting this was perhaps the case. Now, however, with most households able to access 50 or more channels, no two people's viewing habits are the same. We each have an incredible variety of messages at our fingertips. In the pursuit of this variety, we lose the sense of shared community.

Although the media, especially television, have influenced these changes, we must be careful not to think that they are the only influence. We live in a complex society where the family, sports, religion, politics, the economy, and many other forces are constantly working, often at cross purposes. The media are important players in all this, because they transmit information about change so quickly and broadly. The pace of life is accelerating. Those who are media literate can have an influence on the direction of that pace—at least for themselves.

References

Average baseball salaries take rare dip. (1995, November 29). *Santa Barbara News-Press*, p. B1.

Comstock, G. A. (1980). *Television in America*. Beverly Hills, CA: Sage.

Comstock, G. A. (1989). *The evolution of American television*. Newbury Park, CA: Sage.

DeFleur, M. L., & Dennis, E. E. (1996). *Understanding mass communication: A liberal arts perspective*. Princeton, NJ: Houghton Mifflin.

Election '88: The media aftermath. (1988, November 14). *Broadcasting Magazine*, pp. 35-37.

Fore, W. F. (1987). *Television and religion: The shaping of faith, values, and culture*. Minneapolis, MN: Augsburg Publishing House.

Gerbner, G., & Gross, L. (1976). Living with television: The violence profile. *Journal of Communication, 26*(2), 173-199.

Hollander, B. A. (1995). The new news and the 1992 presidential campaign: Perceived vs. actual political knowledge. *Journalism & Mass Communication Quarterly, 72*, 786-798.

Hoover, S. M. (1988). *Mass media religion: The social sources of the electronic church*. Newbury Park, CA: Sage.

Horsfield, P. G. (1984). *Religious television: The American experience*. New York: Longman.

Iyengar S., & Kinder, D. (1987). *News that matters*. Chicago: University of Chicago Press.

Katz, E., & Gurevitch, M. (1976). *The secularization of leisure: Culture and communication in Israel*. Cambridge, MA: Harvard University Press.

McLeod, J. J., & Chaffee, S. H. (1973). Interpersonal approaches to communication research. *American Behavioral Scientist, 16*, 469-499.

Medrich, E. A., Roizen, J. A., Rubin, V., & Buckley, S. (1982). *The serious business of growing up. A study of children's lives outside school*. Berkeley: University of California Press.

NBC gambles on the future. (1996, January 22). *Santa Barbara News-Press*, p. A11.

Nelson, J. (August 8, 1995). NBC gets Olympic TV rights in coup. *Santa Barbara News-Press*, p. A12.

NFL teams dodge salary cap. (1996, January 2). *Santa Barbara News-Press*, p. B5.

Pardun, C. J., & Krugman, D. M. (1994). How the architectural style of the home relates to family television viewing. *Journal of Broadcasting & Electronic Media, 38*, 145-162.

Patterson T. (1980). *The mass media election*. New York: Praeger.

Perkins, K. (1996, November 27). Statistics blur image of American family. *Santa Barbara News-Press*, pp. A1, A2.

Pipher, M. (1996). *The shelter of each other*. New York: Putnam.

Rhodes, S., & Reibstein, L. (1996, July 1). Let him walk!!! *Newsweek*, pp. 44-45.

Whitman, D. (1996, September 30). The divorce dilemma. *U.S. News and World Report*, pp. 58-60.

Will, G. F. (1996, April 15). Civic speech gets rationed. *Newsweek*, pp. 80, 78.

Woodward, K. L. (1990, December 17). A time to seek. *Newsweek*, pp. 50-56.

Further Reading

Bianculli, D. (1992). *Teleliteracy: Taking television seriously*. New York: Continuum. (315 pages)

David Bianculli was a TV critic/columnist for 15 years before writing this book, which is a defense of television. Admitting that 90% of TV content is "crap," he feels that there is still a great deal of value there. He presents a manifesto of 10 points, all intended to get TV more respect. The most interesting part of the book is in the first section where he presents a 150-question literacy quiz (75 questions about TV and 75 about classic literature and music). The

TV questions are very easy to answer and the other questions are very difficult. His point here is that the population is very TV literate. He also presents a fascinating history of criticism of various forms of literature and music dating back to Plato; this clearly shows that there are people who think every new piece of art is bad and that every new medium is dangerous.

Donnelly, W. J. (1986). *The confetti generation: How the new communications technology is fragmenting America.* New York: Henry Holt. (329 pages)

Donnelly is a former ad-man and professor who retired from Young & Rubicam, a large advertising agency, to write this book. His main point is that people (especially Toffler and other futurists) who make predictions about new media focus on the technologies and ignore the audience. Because of this, their projections of media use in the future are way off (e.g., 200-channel cable by 1990).

Exercise 15.1 Becoming Sensitive to Changes in Institutions

I. Interview your parents by asking them the following questions. Ask them to think back to when they were your age or younger for their answers.

A. Family

1. What was the most important medium in their households?
2. How many television sets were in the house and who controlled them?
3. Were there viewing rules? Restrictions on kids?
4. Did family members ever read books or magazines to one another?
5. Did family members listen to radio or music together?

B. Politics

1. Where did people get most of their information about political campaigns? Conversations or media? If media, which ones?
2. Did they go to political events, such as rallies, speeches, meetings?
3. Can they remember any political ads? If so, what stands out in their minds about those ads? Images? Negativity?
4. Do they have any strong memories about news coverage of nominating conventions, the campaign, or election returns?

C. Religion

1. Did they listen to religious programs on the radio or watch them on television?
2. What was their opinion of religious leaders at the time?
3. Do they feel that religion has changed in the past several decades? If so, do they think the media had any influence?

D. Sports

1. Did they used to attend sporting events in person?
2. Did they follow sports through the media? If so, which sports and which media?
3. Are they aware of any changes in their favorite sports over the past few decades? If so, what is their reaction to those changes?
4. What is their reaction to the salaries paid to athletes today?
5. What is their reaction to the amount of advertising at the games and during media coverage?

II. Next, interview your grandparents and ask them the same questions.

III. Ask yourself the same questions.

IV. Compare the patterns of answers across three generations. Do you see any changes in attitudes, perceptions, or the way people live their lives? If so, can you attribute any of these changes to the media?

CHAPTER 16

The Importance of
Real-World Knowledge

KEY IDEA *The more primary knowledge we have about our world, the stronger the context we have for evaluating the accuracy and usefulness of information from the media.*

*Children recite jingles instead of poetry and they
know brand names instead of the names of presidents.
More students can identify Mr. Peanut and Joe Camel
than can identify Abe Lincoln or Eleanor Roosevelt.
They can identify twenty kinds of cold cereal but
not the trees and birds in their neighborhoods.*

Pipher, 1996, p. 94

Back in 1922, before the mass media became so dominant in our culture, the journalist Walter Lippmann wrote a book called *Public Opinion,* in which he said,

> Each of us lives and works on a small part of the earth's surface, moves in a small circle, and of these acquaintances knows only a few intimately. Of any public event that has wide effects, we see at best only a phase and an aspect. . . . Inevitably our opinions cover a bigger space, a longer reach in time, a greater number of things, than we can directly observe. (p. 79)

Our world is far more complex today, which makes his comments even more significant. Are our opinions and beliefs keeping pace with our world? Are we willing to search out more information from a wider variety of sources so that we can use the complexity to arrive at more reasoned opinions? Or do we uncritically accept partial sets of facts and infer simple conclusions? Being media literate is a far greater challenge today than it was 75 years ago.

Importance of Information

There is a great deal of information in our culture, and it is growing at an enormous rate. Today, the English language contains about 500,000 usable words—five times more than 400 years ago during the time that Shakespeare wrote (Wurman, 1989). The world's great libraries are doubling in size every 14 years, a rate of 14,000% every century. In the early 1300s, the Sorbonne Library in Paris contained only 1,338 books and yet was thought to be the largest library in Europe. Today, there are many libraries with more than 8 million books. This means that if you were to spend only one minute reading each book and never sleep or take a break, it would take you more than 15 years to get through them all. But by then you would still be behind, because about 1,000 books are published internationally every day, and the total of all printed information doubles every 8 years. More information was produced in the past 30 years than in the previous 5,000.

There are 10,000 magazines publishing information on every conceivable subject. Hollywood releases 350 films each year, and there are tens of thousands of independent, corporate, and educational releases. In a local media market, the radio stations pump out over 3,000 hours of messages every week and a cable television outlet puts out three times that amount.

With this constant flood of messages, we must face the fact that we live in an information society. We cannot avoid being bombarded by information every day, but all this information does not necessarily make us more knowledgeable. There is a difference between information and knowledge. Information is facts, data, impressions. Information becomes knowledge when it is arranged into structures that mean something to you. This requires screening out bad information and knitting together the elements of good information into a useful pattern. Unless we have good knowledge structures, all the information is nothing more than noise.

In order to be media literate, you need to develop strong knowledge structures on a wide range of topics—about the media and about the real world. This requires that you have a plan that identifies important topics. Then you must actively seek out information on these topics so you can build knowledge structures. Don't passively wait for the media to give you all the information you need.

What is a good plan for identifying real-world topics? This book cannot decide that for you, but it can give you some things to think about. It can also stimulate you to think about developing a plan for yourself.

This chapter is not a catalog of all the knowledge that a media literate person should have. Such a list would be impossible to provide in the space of one chapter. Several authors have made strong arguments for the importance of such a list, among them Bloom (1987) and D'Souza (1991). Also, a few scholars have attempted to build such a list (Hirsch, 1987; Hirsch, Kett, & Trefil, 1993).

While there is a core of information that arguably everyone should have, there are substantial differences across people in what information they will need to become media literate. People operate in different cultures and have different interests and different sets of experiences, so their needs for information differ.

Instead, this chapter presents an argument for the importance of a broad base of knowledge. Essentially, knowledge is a major tool in protecting media literate individuals from unwanted effects from the media. The broader and more accurate your knowledge bases are, the more you will be able to orient yourself toward positive effects and avoid the influence of negative effects.

Knowledge serves two functions in this process: an orienting function and a confirming function. When we are not very media literate, the media control these functions. Being highly media literate means that we have shifted the control of these functions over to ourselves.

Orienting Function

Seldom are messages complete enough for us to understand them without having to draw from some contextual information outside the message. For example, if we see a story that the United Nations has sent troops into Bosnia, at minimum we need to know what the United Nations and Bosnia are. It would also help to know what the intention of the United Nations is and why it would want to send troops into Bosnia.

It is helpful to think about any media message as a core cluster of facts that sit at the center of a set of progressively larger concentric circles. Each circle contains facts that help us to make meaning of the media story that sits in the middle of those circles. The more developed our knowledge structure, the wider is our context of understanding. Therefore we must carry around a good deal of general information in order to be able to make meaning out of any media story.

Where do people get this orienting knowledge? They need a liberal education. *Liberal* in this sense means broad. If someone has a very narrow education, no matter how deep it is, that person will have difficulty making meaning out of many media messages.

Confirming Function

Typically in our everyday exposure to the media, we acquire partial sets of facts on topics. The messages often leave out important elements, either because of time or space limitations or because producers assume we would not be interested in more detail. When we have only a partial set of information, we are in danger of inferring wrong patterns about the world. An example of this happens when we view the evening news and see a very partial set of the day's events. Because so much crime and harmful action is reported but is not balanced by stories about constructive events, we conclude that the world is a mean and violent place. When we are not given a useful context (such as actual crime rates), we are likely to infer patterns that are not correct.

Thus, when we are exposed to a fact, we need to compare it to a standard to judge its merit. If we do not make such a comparison, we simply accept the fact without evaluating it, and we accept all facts equally.

What can serve as a standard to judge new facts? There is no single place to go to get an objective standard. Rather, we must develop a strategy for searching for confirming information. There are two ways to do this.

First, we can go to credible sources of information. Typically, primary sources are more credible than secondary sources. For example, if we read an article about a political candidate's position, that article is a secondary source—the primary source is the candidate. The secondary source may have presented a complete and accurate account of the candidate's position, but maybe the reporter mis-stated something or left something out. The possibility of distortion is part of the risk of using secondary sources.

Second, we can search out multiple sources and compare the resulting accounts. Following through on the example of the political candidate above, we could search out other magazine, newspaper, and broadcast reports of the candidate's position. We can also ask the candidate's opponent and other people active in politics. From this set of resulting information, we can get a much more accurate fix on what the candidate believes. None of these sources by itself presents the full picture. Even the most primary source—the candidate herself—might be flawed, because she might not point out inconsistencies in her voting record or how her position has changed over time.

These strategies are especially important when dealing with facts illustrated through numbers and percentages. Percentages are the comparison of two numbers; that is, a figure is compared to some base number. Sources might faithfully report a percentage, using accurate numbers, but had they made a comparison to a different base number, the entire meaning of the situation would change. For example, in the summer of 1996 the Health and Human Services Department of the federal government released the results of a 16-year tracking study of the amount of drug use by the nation's adolescents (12 to 17 years old). The lead sentence in a story by the Associated Press was, "A 105 percent jump in teen-agers' drug use since 1992 instantly became a campaign issue" ("Teen Drug Use," 1996). In the ninth paragraph, the story explained that in 1992, 5.3% of adolescents said they had used an illegal drug in the past 30 days and in 1995, the figure was 10.9%. Thus, if we compare 5.3% to 10.9% we get an increase of 5.6%. But if we compare the increase of 5.6% to the 1992 base of 5.3%, the increase is 105%. Which percentage is accurate? They both are—but the two convey really different pictures about drug use.

Another example is the reporting of a survey about women and abortions (Leo, 1996). The Guttmacher Institute, which is strongly in favor of abortion rights, released a report that said that Catholic women have an abortion rate 29% higher than Protestant women, while one fifth of women having abortions are born-again or evangelical Christians. A closer look at the data indicate that Catholic women have an abortion rate right at the national average and that the rate for Protestant women is at 69% of the national average. When women are grouped by religion, the non-religious women have an abortion rate four times as high as the religious women. Again, which set of facts is accurate? They both are.

In sum, highly media literate people will, of course, rely on media messages as sources of information, but they will also seek out information from other secondary sources as well as primary sources. By assessing the relative credibility of the sources, they can then weigh the relative value of information from each source. By looking for patterns of consistency in the information across the sources, people can arrive at a more solid understanding of the topic.

 ## Types of Information

There are two types of information: factual and social. We use both the media and real-world institutions as sources for these types of information.

Factual knowledge refers to parameters about the world that are usually not in dispute (not open to individual interpretation). Examples include the size of the population of this country, names of political leaders, final scores of sporting contests, the distance between cities, and so on.

Social knowledge relates to shared understandings about human interactions. Examples include the way people should behave in certain roles (such as parent, professor, partier, stranger, colleague, etc.), and the moral themes within a culture or institution.

Need for Factual Information

Social critics have a lot of ammunition when they target the educational system in this country. For example, the National Assessment of Educational Progress monitors the learning of our nation's youth in public schools. The results of its recent testing were that the majority of America's high school seniors did not know basic facts about U.S. history, and they could not use what they did know to back up their opinions. Among 12th graders, only 43% attained at least the basic level, 11% were proficient, and 1% was advanced. Scores on math and science have been improving, but scores on reading and writing have been going down (Buzbee, 1995).

However, children don't seem to have trouble identifying the celebrities who get the most media coverage. When children ages 9 to 12 were asked to identify names of people, Michael Jordan and Michael Jackson topped the recognition list at 96% of respondents. Hillary Rodham Clinton was recognized by 82%. Boris Yeltsin got 21% and Nelson Mandela was low at 20% ("Names & Faces," 1995).

Thus, it seems that the media, especially television, are the dominant teachers of the nation's youth. Television, however, is largely focused on entertainment and popular culture. It does not teach literature, languages, history, mathematics, or other academic subjects that form the basis of a strong knowledge infrastructure. It does not teach useful skills (such as writing, critical reading, analysis, and problem solving) that are the essential tools of an educated person. The media could teach this type of knowledge and skills, but they prefer instead to focus on entertainment. They are, of course, only responding to what they think the public wants.

This would not be a problem if the public school system were providing a strong education of core knowledge and skills to all students, and television were used as minor diversion a few hours a week. However, this is not the case. The public's base of knowledge is very narrow, according to E. D. Hirsch, Jr. (1987), who wrote a book titled *Cultural Literacy*. He argues that there is a set of core information that the educational system needs to instill in every individual. Without this broad base of general information, individuals cannot be regarded as being educated; that is, they are not literate about the culture within which they live. He observes that the educational system is not fulfilling this function.

The public's level of higher order skills is also not very strong. For example, in a poll of 400 chief executives conducted by *Fortune* magazine, 77% rated the American public education system as fair or poor—the lowest ratings possible. These business leaders said that they needed an educated workforce that could think, write, analyze, and solve problems in order to function in the information age. They felt that the American educational system was failing in this task.

Social critics present a bleak picture, but what they fail to acknowledge is the enormous amount of learning that does take place every day. All of us have some very good knowledge structures. All of us have mastered the rudimentary skills of literacy and many of us operate at high levels of proficiency on the advanced skills. Of course, the population could be better, and the social critics perform a useful function in reminding us of this. Bringing this issue down to the personal level, it is important for you to realize that there is a range of knowledge and abilities in society. You must decide for yourself where you want to be in that range. To help you think through this issue, look at Exercise 16.1.

Need for Social Information

Social information is perhaps even more important than factual information. The media, especially in their entertainment messages, show how people behave, how they achieve success, how they form relationships, what they do when they are unhappy, and more.

Real life offers a wide latitude on these social lessons. This latitude includes many, if not almost all, of the media portrayals. However, the media portrayals do not cover the gamut of human experience; those portrayals tend to emphasize the unusual and the dramatic. Therefore it is not that media portrayals are not possible or that they are unrealistic—instead, the problem is on the aggregate level where people come to think that life should be more unusual and dramatic. To put their perspectives back into a real-life balance, people need to have real-life experiences in order to see a greater range of social lessons.

Examples of Mis-Inferences

There are many examples of public opinion being formed in a faulty manner, that is, where the media have presented a partial set of facts from which the public has generalized. Six examples are presented below. In each of these you can see that public opinion might have been different if people had been provided with a more complete set of information.

Crime

A major focus of news is on crime. Also, entertainment messages present us with many messages about crime. With all this vicarious exposure to crime, most of us generalize to a pattern that there is a great deal of crime in this country and that it continues to increase. A recent Gallup Poll commissioned for the White House Office of National Drug Control Policy found crime and violence to be the top national concern among adults (Ostrow, 1996).

Is this opinion an accurate generalization? Despite the public's thinking that crime is a top concern, it has been decreasing for 4 years in a row. In 1996, the murder rate fell by 8%, violent crimes dropped by 4%, and there was also a drop of 2% in serious crimes. Fewer than 24,000 people were murdered in 1996—this is only about 40% of those who were killed in traffic accidents. Cities with the largest populations showed the largest drop in crime.

However, homicide and suicide rates remain high for one group—young males. The combined homicide and suicide rate for males 15 to 24 years old was 63 per 100,000 people, compared to 22.1 per 100,000 in the general population. In 1994, there was a total of 23,730 homicides (16,000 with handguns) and 32,410 suicides. Homicides are the second largest killer for young Americans ages 15 to 24 and the third leading killer for young children ages 5 to 14. For young males, the suicide rate was up 26% in 1994 (Connell, 1995). Arrest rates among juveniles for violent crimes jumped 100% between

1983 and 1992, although the number of teenagers (10 to 17 years old) in the population grew only about 20%.

The media continually focus on the high-profile violent crimes, and this gives us the impression that crime is very prevalent and even growing. Once in a while there will be a story about overall crime rates or an analysis of the trends, but these are rare compared to the message that crime is everywhere.

Legal System

America has become a highly litigious society. The courts are clogged; more than 100 million cases were filed in state courts in 1990. In federal courts, filings have increased 69% since 1980. The number of lawyers more than doubled between 1970 and 1992 (from 355,000 to 805,000). America now has 70% of the world's lawyers (Will, 1991).

Why so much litigation? Samuelson (1992) argues that the dramatic increase in the number of lawyers and law suits has some legitimate reasons—such as increases in crime, divorce, regulations, and government—but there is something else. Glendon (1991) points out that until the 1950s the focus of Constitutional law was on the structure of our political regime—the allocation of powers among the federal government's branches and between the federal and state governments. Over time, the focus has changed to the individual and his or her rights. This change coincides with the rise of TV and its theme of satisfying the individual. Thus we have been conditioned to look out for our personal rights and to sue when we feel we have been wronged, as characters on television frequently do.

Government

Politicians have been running for president on a platform of reducing the size of the federal government ever since 1980. They promise to cut inefficiency and waste and to lower taxes. Have they done so?

Quinn (1996) says that it is a myth that the federal government has gotten smaller overall, although some aspects have gotten smaller. With the demise of the USSR, defense spending was cut in half between 1970 and 1997 when figured as a percentage of the Gross Domestic Product (GDP). The federal payroll peaked in 1990 and has been in decline since, and there are caps on discretionary spending.

Nevertheless, the overall size of the federal government has remained at about 22% of GDP. The growth has been in the areas of debt servicing, Medicare, and social security. In contrast, state and local governments are growing—up 23% since 1980. Most Americans are paying less (about 2% less compared to 1985) in federal income tax, but this is more than offset by increases in state and local taxes.

Another myth about the federal government is that it spends huge amounts of money on foreign aid. In 1996, the federal government spent about $12 billion in foreign aid. Most people think this figure is much higher. Most people also think that this money is simply sent to other countries. Not so. The Business Alliance for International Economic Development said that 80% of the foreign aid budget is spent in the United States, explaining that, "The livelihoods of hundreds of thousands of Americans–farmers, truckers, assembly line workers, software developers—depend on U.S. foreign assistance" (Rothberg, 1996).

Also, there is a controversy over whether the federal government should allow foreign-made products into this country to compete with American-made products. Some people argue that allowing foreign-made products into our market will take jobs away from Americans. This argument sounds reasonable on the surface, but let's look at it in more depth, using the automobile market as an example.

What is an American-made automobile? Did you know that Jaguar cars are made by a wholly owned subsidiary of Ford Motor Company? Lamborghini, the Italian sports car maker, is wholly owned by Chrysler Corporation. The Lotus is a General Motors (GM) product. The Mazda Navajo four-wheel drive vehicle is made in the Ford Explorer plant in Kentucky; and 50% of Saab is owned by GM.

Also, some purportedly American-made cars are not made by Americans. For example, the Ford Festiva is made by Kia of Korea. The Plymouth Laser is a Mitsubishi Eclipse, and vice versa. The Ford Probe is really a Mazda MX-6 made by Mazda in Flat Rock, Michigan, and the Geo Prizm, which seems to be a model of Chevrolet, is really a Toyota Corolla made in Fremont, California ("It's Pretty Hard to Tell," 1993).

The global economy is very interdependent, with overlapping ownerships. The idea of a purely American-made car is passé. Even if the automobile were assembled in an American plant, many of the parts would come from all over the world. Also, a foreign-made automobile sold in the United States benefits the U.S. economy, because the dealership supports Americans. The servicing, replacement of parts by local mechanics, the gasoline and oil are all purchased in this country. The taxes on the car (sales, gasoline, licensing, and tolls) all benefit local governments.

The idea that buying a seemingly foreign-made product does not benefit workers in this country is very superficial reasoning. Economists tell us that foreign trade does not lessen or add to jobs; instead, it shifts them from lower, unskilled positions to higher paid skilled jobs (Quinn, 1996).

Employment and Wages

The media continually present stories of corporate downsizing and lay-offs—3 million corporate layoffs were announced between 1989 and 1995 (Brenner, 1996). This leads people to feel insecure in their jobs. One third of American workers fear that someone in their household will lose a job during the year.

Also, people think the unemployment rate is high, but the unemployment rate has been going down and now is at 5.5%, which is a very low figure. The problem within this generally good picture is with young workers who have not been to college; their unemployment rate is 6.8% for whites, 11.0% for Hispanics, and 20.3% for African Americans. For teenage workers, the over-all unemployment rate is 15.8%. The opportunities for workers with only a high school education or less are growing smaller.

> The typical work-bound high school graduate can find entry level employment only in service-oriented jobs, offering poverty-level wages. . . . This marks a dramatic change from the time when the country's manufacturing industries of-fered satisfying careers and high wages for workers without college degrees. (Educational Testing Service, 1990, p. 3)

Although a very high percentage of the population is working, the earning power of families has not increased much since 1973. The Census Bureau shows that median family income was $38,782 in 1994, only up from $37,838 (adjusted for inflation) in 1973 despite the fact that during that time there was a 56% increase in the number of families with two working parents (Brenner, 1996).

Many people may be shocked at the low median income (the point at which half make more and half make less) when they see the salaries of some well-known people reported in the media. For example, in 1995, Neil O'Donnell, quarterback of the N.Y. Jets, made $5 million; Demi Moore made $12 million; Roseanne Barr made $19 million; Jim Carrey made $29 million. These sala-ries are highly visible and influence our thinking about wages, but they are so rare that they have almost no effect on the nationwide median income level.

Births and Deaths

We continually hear about increasing numbers of children on welfare and increasing numbers of children born out of wedlock to very young moth-ers. However, the birthrate for American teenagers dropped 2% in 1993. For every 1,000 women between 15 and 19 years of age, 59.6 gave birth.

As for death, the reporting of high-profile crimes makes us believe that most of us will eventually meet a violent death, but we are 10 times as likely to die a natural death (such as from heart disease, cancer, or even pneumonia) than a violent one. In the violent death category, we are more likely to die in an accident than to be murdered. We are even more likely to commit suicide than to be murdered. The suicide rate is 32,000 per year, compared to murders at 24,000 per year.

Risks

When we rely exclusively on the media for information, we come to believe we are at risk of being injured by the high-profile catastrophes that are frequently covered in the news. The things that are not covered make us believe that there is much less risk than there really is. For example, when we compare causes of death per 100,000 people, smoking accounts for 21,900; motor vehicle accidents, 1,600; diagnostic X rays, 75; lightning, 3; and asbestos in school buildings, 1. Among the things on this list, however, the public is most concerned about asbestos in school buildings, and when the media focused on this story in the late 1980s, the asbestos removal industry grew from almost nothing to a $4.2-billion enterprise (Matthews, 1992). There are people who feel uncomfortable about a dentist x-raying their teeth, but who feel much less uncomfortable about smoking, which is 293 times riskier.

Another way to compare risk is to look at how many days, on average, a behavior will cut from your otherwise normal life span. On average, smoking cigarettes cuts 2,500 days from a male's life and 800 days from a female's life; being overweight by 30% cuts 1,300 days; working as a coal miner, 1,100 days; being poor, 700 days; and nuclear reactor accidents, .02 days (Allman, 1985).

Some people are terrified of flying but feel no risk when riding in a car. Wurman (1989) says the number of passenger deaths per billion miles is 2,154 in an automobile compared to 214 in an airplane. Also, most people do much more traveling in an automobile so their risk is far higher in an auto than in an airplane.

We all feel an uncomfortable sense of risk at times. Perhaps when we drive through a "bad" neighborhood, or walk alone at night, or fly in an airplane. Where do we get these feelings of risk? For most of us, from the memory of a story of a mugging or a plane crash that we saw in the media. Those gruesome images, although very small in number, stay with us and lead us to unrealistic assessments of risk. The media are silent about many risky behaviors. If we depend exclusively on the mainstream media's messages for our information, we will generalize to a very unrealistic world in which our sense of danger will be very much misplaced.

Summary

The media can greatly expand our knowledge by giving us information on topics that we cannot experience for ourselves. They can take us deep under the sea, into outer space, back in history, and into the Oval Office, but the picture they give us of these places, events, and people is partial and often without much context. If we accept this information as is and do not check it, analyze it, or expand it, we get only a limited picture and may be inferring patterns and themes that are faulty.

How do we know how our government works and who has the real power? How do we know about historical figures? Most of our information comes to us through the media. We depend on this media information, because it is impossible for us to have firsthand exposure to historical events, or even to current events, so we are dependent on the media for information. Some of this information is good and some of it is not so good. We must develop the skills to know the difference. It is not always clear what is fact and what is faulty.

Being media literate means consciously processing the information in all messages as well as being able to recognize useless information and screen it out, then keeping the useful information and building a strong knowledge structure. This requires searching out multiple sources of information and determining the relative credibilities of the different sources, then evaluating the variety of claims. It requires analyses of the relevant positions, then synthesizing the worthwhile elements into a reasoned opinion that has been consciously derived and that can be defended. It is important that you develop a program of information acquisition that is balanced: read a national newspaper, a national newsmagazine, several general interest magazines, some reference books, some non-fiction, and some fiction.

References

Allman, W. F. (1985, October). Pesticides: An unhealthy dependence? *Science, 6*(8), 14.

Bloom, A. (1987). *The closing of the American mind.* New York: Simon & Schuster.

Brenner, L. (1996, June 23). What people earn. *Parade Magazine,* pp. 4-7.

Buzbee, S. (1995, November 2). U.S. students score poorly in American history. *Santa Barbara News-Press,* p. A3.

Connell, C. (1995, October 24). Homicide, suicide rate rises in '94 for young males. *Santa Barbara News-Press,* p. A3.

D'Souza, D. (1991). *Illiberal education: The politics of race and sex on campus.* New York: Free Press.

Educational Testing Service. (1990). *Beyond high school: The transition to work.* Princeton, NJ: ETS.

Glendon, M. A. (1991). *Rights talk: The impoverishment of political discourse.* Cambridge, MA: Harvard University Press.

Hirsch, E. D., Jr. (1987). *Cultural literacy: What every American needs to know.* Boston: Houghton Mifflin.

Hirsch, E. D., Jr., Kett, J. F., & Trefil, J. (1993). *The dictionary of cultural literacy* (2nd ed.). Boston: Houghton Mifflin.

It's pretty hard to tell what's what these days. (1993, July 31). *Washington Post,* p. A12.

Leo, J. (1996, August 19). The joys of covering press releases. *U.S. News & World Report,* p. 16.

Lippmann, W. (1922). *Public opinion.* New York: Harcourt, Brace.

Matthews, J. (1992, April 13). To yank or not to yank? *Newsweek,* p. 59.

Names & faces. (1995, September 11). *Santa Barbara News-Press,* p. B8.

Ostrow, R. (1996, May 6). Violent crime in U.S. fell 4% in '95, FBI says. *Los Angeles Times,* pp. A1, A11.

Pipher, M. (1996). *The shelter of each other.* New York: Putnam.

Quinn, J. B. (1996, April 1). Politics: Fable vs. fact. *Newsweek,* p. 62.

Rothberg, D. M. (1996, June 23). Group seeks increase in foreign aid budget. *Santa Barbara News-Press,* p. F2.

Samuelson, R. J. (1992, April 2). I am a big lawyer basher. *Newsweek,* p. 62.

Teen drug use soars. (1996, August 21). *Asbury Park Press,* p. A1.

Will, G. F. (1991, September 23). Too much of a good thing? *Newsweek,* p. 68.

Wurman, R. S. (1989). *Information anxiety.* Garden City, NY: Doubleday.

Further Reading

Bloom, A. (1987). *The closing of the American mind.* New York: Simon & Schuster. (392 pages with index)

This is a critique of the present state of higher education by a professor of social thought at the University of Chicago. His primary criticism is that universities no longer have a vision for what students should learn to become educated human beings. When curriculum decisions are left up to students, they decide to take easy, unchallenging courses, so they graduate without having an understanding of the past or a vision for the future.

D'Souza, D. (1991). *Illiberal education: The politics of race and sex on campus.* New York: Free Press. (319 pages with index)

In this criticism of higher education, D'Souza argues that the movement toward political correctness has led to an "anything goes" curriculum at most universities. As a result of this, students are not receiving rigorous educations.

Hirsch, E. D., Jr. (1987). *Cultural literacy: What every American needs to know.* Boston: Houghton Mifflin. (251 pages with index)

Hirsch points out that reading is more than recognizing words; it also requires the person to decipher the meaning in the words and stories. In order to do this, he argues, we need to educate students so they have a core knowledge of our world and our culture. He lays out a plan for doing this along with 63 pages of key terms and concepts that he feels every educated person should know.

Hirsch, E. D., Jr., Kett, J. F., & Trefil, J. (1993). *The dictionary of cultural literacy* (2nd ed.). Boston: Houghton Mifflin. (619 pages with index)

This is a dictionary of the "core concepts" of our culture. It is organized into 23 sections, such as life sciences, business and economics, world politics, technology, fine arts, and more.

Wurman, R. S. (1989). *Information anxiety.* Garden City, NY: Doubleday. (353 pages)

This book contains many intriguing ideas about how much information has invaded our culture and how that is effecting us. Wurman has written it in a non-linear manner so that the chapters and even the paragraphs can be read in any order.

Exercise 16.1 Thinking About a Plan for
Real-World Knowledge

I. Make an assessment of your knowledge structures of the world.

A. Start with a template of knowledge, such as Arts, Humanities, Social Sciences, or Physical Sciences. Fill in the knowledge areas under each by looking at your college catalog's list of academic departments and courses. Or, you could go to the library and look at how knowledge is organized there, whether by the Dewey Decimal System or the Library of Congress System. On a piece of paper, sketch a set of blocks to represent the different areas and sub-areas of knowledge organization. The big blocks (such as Physical Science) should be composed of smaller blocks (such as Physics, Chemistry, Biology, etc.). Some of these smaller blocks (such as Biology) may also be composed of sub-sets (such as Botany and Zoology). Don't spend more than an hour sketching this. The goal is not to include every detail, but to try to come up with a reasonable picture of how human knowledge is generally organized.

B. Think back over the past 2 years and try to remember significant learning experiences you have had during that time. A significant learning experience is something you remember as valuable to your learning, such as:

1. A course that really challenged you and made you think.

2. An interest in something that made you read a series of books (or search out information in other media) and want to discuss the issues.

Write these significant learning experiences in the appropriate content blocks in your template in red ink.

C. Now think back over the past 2 years and remember the "just okay" learning experiences. These may have been courses in which you learned something but not a whole lot. Or these could have been minor interests that led you to search out information in the media.

Write these "just okay" learning experiences in the appropriate content blocks in your template in blue ink.

D. Look at the patterns on your template.

1. Are there the blank areas where there is neither red nor blue ink? Have you been broadening yourself as a student in college or have you been playing it very safe so you don't experience new areas? What does this tell you about what you value in a college education and the kind of person you want to become as a graduate?

2. Where are the red areas? Are they clustered in one small part of the template or are they sprinkled all over? What does this pattern say about you as a learner and what it takes to make something a significant learning experience?

3. Where are the blue areas? What do these have in common? How do these blue areas differ from the red areas? What does this pattern tell you about yourself as a learner; that is, to what extent were these experiences less than optimal because of outside forces (such as the teacher, the course materials, etc.) or because of something within you (such as motivation, previous knowledge structures, etc.)?

II. Think about your goals for overall learning.

A. Do you have goals for depth? Are you building elaborate knowledge structures in a few particular areas so you can attain an expertise as a foundation for a career or for further study in graduate school?

B. Do you have goals for breadth? Are you building a string of knowledge structures across a variety of areas so you have strong contexts for interpreting the value of information throughout a wide range of topics?

PART IV

Putting It All Together

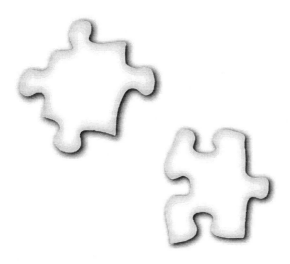

CHAPTER 17

The Media
Literacy Perspective

KEY IDEA *The journey to higher media literacy requires awareness and control.*

Awareness of Your Knowledge Structures

Awareness of How Your Mind Works
  Field Dependency
  Tolerance for Ambiguity
  Conceptual Differentiation
  Reflection-Impulsivity

Awareness of Effects Processes
  Factors Affecting the Immediate Effects Processes
    Need for Information
    Degree of Identification
    Arousal
    Content of the Messages
    Level of Development
    Sociological Factors
  Factors Influencing the Long-Term Effects Processes
    Sociological Factors
    Personal Information
    Existing Value Structure
    Content of the Messages
    Context of Portrayals
    Lifestyle
    Level of Development

Illustrations

Summary

Achieving higher levels of literacy is a life-long developmental process of building stronger and more elaborate knowledge structures by using a wide range of skills. How can we increase our literacy? This chapter and the next address this central question by synthesizing and extending the key points in the previous 16 chapters. This chapter asks you to be more self-aware by fully internalizing the media literacy perspective outlined in this book. The next chapter guides you in developing your strategies to increase your level of media literacy.

Increasing media literacy is best regarded as a journey to better perspectives from which to view the media. There is no one best perspective, so the journey does not have a single destination. Thus, becoming media literate is a continuous process. On your journey, you must take many steps. The steps alternate between awareness and control. The first step is to expand your awareness about some aspect. This expanded awareness gives you more options. The next step is control. With more options and with mindful decision making, you gain greater control over the effects. The exercising of this greater control leads you a higher awareness, and this in turn leads to even greater control. Thus, step by step—awareness and control—you make the journey to more and better perspectives on the media.

This chapter focuses on the awareness steps. Synthesizing from the information in the previous 16 chapters, the key domains for awareness are: your awareness of your own knowledge structures, awareness of how your mind works, and awareness of the key elements in the effects process. Each of these three is discussed in more detail in the following sections, and each presents an exercise to help you diagnose your current level of awareness. The chapter concludes with some illustrations of various levels of media literacy compared on the learning ladders of cognitive, emotional, moral, and aesthetic development.

Awareness of Your Knowledge Structures

Think back on the exercises in each chapter. How well did you do? Do you remember the main points of the previous chapters? Check this out by doing Exercise 17.1 now.

How did you do? How far along the media literacy journey are you in terms of having internalized some basic knowledge structures? If you have done well, then your exposure to more media messages will likely result in a more efficient acquisition of information. As your journey continues, you need to continue your critical assessment of those messages to decide if they are accurate, complete, and useful. If they are, then add them to your knowledge structures of the media and the real world. As your knowledge structures grow more elaborate, you will be developing more context and this will help you make more efficient and more in-depth evaluations of future messages. It is important that you continually work on your knowledge structures. In our information-rich, fast-paced society, it is impossible to stand still. Information is perishable. Every day, large pieces of information become obsolete as new facts replace old, as new research findings are reported, and as new perspectives emerge. Also, if you do not continually practice your skills, they will atrophy. If you do not work to improve, you will fall behind.

Awareness of How Your Mind Works

It is important to develop an awareness about how your mind works in order to be media literate. This, of course, means that you pay attention to how well you handle the generic-type, rudimentary skills as well as the more advanced skills of analysis, comparison/contrast, evaluation, abstracting, generalization, and synthesis.

In addition to the profile of using the skills above, we also have a unique profile of cognitive style. Your cognitive style is your approach to organizing and processing information (Hashway & Duke, 1992). We vary in our cognitive styles along the several key dimensions that are delineated below.

Field Dependency

People who are highly field dependent get stuck in the field of chaos—seeing all the details but missing the big picture, which is the signal. Field independent people, on the other hand, are able to sort quickly through the field to identify the elements of importance and to ignore the distracting elements.

The media present us with a lot of noise—that is, they do not always provide us with the information or emotional reactions we want. Dependent people are passive and float along in this stream of messages unable to do much of the conscious filtering that would help them focus on the signal and ignore the noise.

In contrast, field independent people will be able to identify the key information of the who, what, when, where, and why in media messages. To what extent are you field independent?

To estimate your position on the continuum, turn to Exercise 17.2.

Tolerance for Ambiguity

To help us in our encounters with people and situations that are unfamiliar to us, we have developed sets of expectations (schemas). What do we do when our expectations are not met and we are put in an ambiguous situation? That depends on our tolerance for ambiguity. People who have a low tolerance for ambiguity find such situations very disturbing so they tend to ignore those messages. In contrast, people who have a high tolerance for ambiguity do not feel frustration. Instead, they are willing to stay with ambiguous messages and follow them into unfamiliar territory that goes beyond their preconceptions.

During media exposures, we try to look for patterns so that we can make sense of the messages, but sometimes it is difficult to perceive a pattern. People with a low tolerance for ambiguity will become quickly frustrated by something different and will avoid messages that do not fit their preconceptions. There is no analysis, and there is no formal or systematic comparing or contrasting of the message elements with those of other messages, because these people seldom recall any of the discordant elements that would be required to make a contrast. Also, these people are not in a position to synthesize, because they are not motivated to create new perspectives.

People with a high tolerance for ambiguity do not have a barrier to analysis. They are willing to break any message down into components and to make comparisons and evaluations in a quest to understand the nature of the message.

Conceptual Differentiation

People who classify objects into a large number of mutually exclusive categories exhibit a high degree of conceptual differentiation (Gardner, 1968). In contrast, people who use a small number of categories have a low degree of conceptual differentiation.

Those people who have few categories for classifying things usually have broad categories so as to contain all types of messages (Bruner, Goodnow, & Austin, 1956). For example, if a person has only three categories for all media messages (news, entertainment, and ads), then each of these categories contains a wide variety of things. In contrast, someone who has a great many categories will have narrow ones, and all entertainment would not be the same—some would be comedy and some drama. Within the comedy category might be situation comedy, stand-up comedy, cartoon comedy, and so on.

Reflection-Impulsivity

How quickly do you make decisions about messages? How accurate are those decisions? People who take a long time and make lots of errors are regarded as slow/inaccurate; those who are quick and make few errors are fast/accurate; those who take a long time and make few errors are reflective; and those who are quick and make many errors are impulsive (Kagen, Rosman, Day, Albert, & Phillips, 1964).

In summary, being highly media literate means being highly field independent (so that we can quickly orient to the information and screen out the noise), having a high tolerance for ambiguity (so that we like new experiences and information and thereby continually expand our knowledge bases), being high on conceptual differentiation (so that we are driven to create more elaborate knowledge structures composed of a great deal of detail that is highly organized), and being fast/accurate (so that we are able to cover a great deal of information and process it efficiently and effectively).

Awareness of Effects Processes

The more you know about the effects the media can have on you, the more you can see the media influencing your own life; and the more you understand about what contributes to the effects processes, the more you can control those effects in your life. Listed below are the major factors that can contribute to an immediate effect and to a long-term effect. These have been synthesized from previous chapters to form a general list of factors.

Factors Affecting the Immediate Effects Processes

Recall that an immediate effect can be cognitive, attitudinal, behavioral, or physiological. The primary cognitive effect in the short term is the learning of facts. Oftentimes we seek out facts in the media, such as by reading a newspaper or magazine or by listening to the news on radio or television. However, there are also times when we do not search for facts, but we learn facts just the same. For example, we might watch a movie merely to be entertained but learn facts about the country in which the movie takes place. Thus, we can learn without consciously seeking out information.

Attitudes can also be learned immediately. We could watch a political candidate give a speech and decide that we like him. If we had no attitude about that candidate prior to the viewing of the speech, then this immediate effect is one of opinion creation. It is also possible that the immediate effect converted us to this candidate and away from liking his opponent.

Behaviors can also be changed immediately. A person might see a coupon in the newspaper, clip it out, and go to the store to buy the product. Or a person might hear a favorite song on the radio and begin singing it over and over.

As for physiology, certain content (especially violence and erotica) can make a viewer's heart rate and blood pressure temporarily rise. This type of arousal usually dissipates within an hour after exposure.

In general, there are six factors that together determine whether a person will be subjected to an immediate effect. These factors, discussed below, are need for information, degree of identification with characters, degree of arousal, content of the messages, level of development, and sociological factors.

Need for Information. When people have a conscious need for a particular kind of information, they will actively seek out this type of information in the media, and the chance of their learning from this experience is high. When people are passive, learning can still occur, but it is not as likely.

Degree of Identification. This is also a key factor in the short-term process, because people will pay more attention to characters with whom they identify. We become involved in the depicted events through a psychological relationship with one or another of the characters in a two-step process. First, we make a judgment about how much we are attracted to the character and how much the character is like us—or how similar the character is to how we would like to be. Second, we engage in an "as if" experience in which we imagine ourselves in the role of the character.

People identify with characters who have characteristics like their own but who also have qualities that the person would like to possess but does not. Generally, people have a greater liking (positive affect and emotion) for characters who are similar to them in age, gender, ethnicity, or interests. While most people tend to select same-gender characters, girls often choose male characters as role models; boys rarely choose female characters. Girls look for physical attractiveness in their selections for role models; boys look for physical aggressiveness.

People who identify with a character look longer at that character, remember more of his or her actions, report more emotional reactions to the crisis points for the character, and say they feel more emotions like those of the character. When those models are in danger, viewers are more likely to feel that danger and to become physiologically aroused.

The characters need not be fictional. People who identify with Rush Limbaugh are more likely to follow his arguments and remember what he says. Also, the characters can be in fictional situations. Viewers, especially children, select role models in their favorite entertainment shows.

Arousal. When viewers are aroused, their attention is more concentrated, and the experience is more vivid for them. They will remember the portrayals better and will be more likely to act while aroused.

Certain production elements tend to arouse viewers. These include fast cuts, quick motion in a frame, and loud music and sound effects. Also, certain narrative conventions (such as suspense, fear, life-threatening violence, and erotica) can lead to arousal.

When people become too aroused, they will seek ways to reduce the arousal. Exposure to communication—especially entertainment—is likely to provide escape by disrupting the rehearsal process that would perpetuate states of elevated arousal associated with negative affective experiences. Exposure to entertainment is thus likely to produce feelings of relief and escape.

Content of the Messages. Viewers have different expectations of different content, and this changes the exposure situation. For example, people who read a weekly newsmagazine expect to be informed about current events. Viewers who watch a soap opera expect to learn about what the characters have done that day. Both types of content result in learning, but the type of learning is different. When viewers' expectations are not met, they will lose concentration and eventually end the exposure.

Level of Development. The developmental level of the person is a very important factor in the effects process (Dervin & Greenberg, 1972; Hawkins & Pingree, 1982; Murray, 1980; Roberts, 1973; Singer & Singer, 1981). Infants are very limited in how they make sense of stimuli from the media. As they grow in experience and ability, they are able to extract more symbols and construct more meaning. By age 12, children's minds have developed to the point that they can function like adults. A child may not have the ability to understand a certain concept (such as conservation of matter) no matter how well someone tries to teach it to him, but almost overnight, when his mind has developed to a higher stage, he can figure it out for himself.

Young children have difficulty in comprehending and making use of the order of isolated events in a plot. They lose track of the order and relationships among events separated in a plot. They have difficulty in making inferences about the causes and meanings of actions, and they have difficulty understanding, let alone applying, dramatic characters' motives and the consequences of their actions.

Pre-schoolers and early elementary school aged children are often confused by TV narratives, and their failures of comprehension are reflected not only in their response to specific plots but in more general misrepresentations of the nature of reality and fantasy or in distortions of facts about the "outside" world. Young children have fairly high opinions about the reality of TV, that is, they see characters as being like themselves and their friends in real life. As children grow older, they develop a more sophisticated and complete cognitive schema that helps them evaluate whether occurrences are real events, fiction, or sheer fantasy.

Sociological Factors. The effects of the mass media are influenced by messages from society and its institutions. If people hear a fact that is counter to their political and religious beliefs, they are likely to discount the fact and forget it—or to remember it as an example of a falsehood.

For children, parental involvement in media exposure serves to influence learning. Children increase their understanding and recall of central and incidental program content when adults provide facilitating comments during viewing. Most parents, however, do not usually provide critical insights during TV viewing with their children.

Factors Influencing the Long-Term Processes

As with the immediate effects process, there are some key factors that can be used to predict the degree of influence of long-term processes: sociological factors, personal information, existing value structure, content of the messages, context of the portrayals in the messages, lifestyle, and developmental level. Notice that many are similar to the process of immediate effects.

Sociological Factors. People filter messages through their peer groups. The more a person identifies with a peer group and the more cohesive the group is, the more the person will be influenced by the group and the less effect the media will have by itself.

The degree of a person's prior socialization is also related to the amount of influence the media will have. Parental support for aggression as a means of problem solving has been found to have a greater influence on attitudes favorable to the use of aggression than the viewing of TV violence does (Comstock, 1982; Hawkins & Pingree, 1982; McLeod, Fitzpatrick, Glynn, & Fallis, 1982).

Personal Information. The extent of media influence is based on countervailing personal experience. Media entertainment is most likely to cultivate social beliefs in those areas where the least real-life information is available.

One of the most important characteristics that make the media so powerful a socializing influence is that most of the content cannot be disconfirmed in a person's real life, because it cannot be tested. For example, almost no one knows what a president of the United States does. The populace is told a version by the mass media, but almost no one has an opportunity to check it out. This is also true for almost all of the content of news broadcasts. The same is true for much fictional programming. Viewers do not know what it feels like to be—for instance—a professional athlete or a multimillionaire, or a detective, or any of the many other portrayals on TV. Because viewers do not have an opportunity to check this out in real life, it is impossible for them to prove the messages false or inaccurate.

Existing Value Structure. If a person's—especially a child's—set of values is well developed, it will be used as a standard to judge media messages and the person will not be as influenced by those messages (Himmelweit, 1966).

Content of the Messages. News and comedy programs have a weaker socializing influence than do dramatic programs. Also, if the values are presented in a dramatic form so they can evoke primary emotional reactions, their socializing effect will be greater.

The messages in the media are relatively constant. Because the same values and patterns appear from program to program, they have a greater influence. When the themes are the same as presented by other institutions, such as family, education, religion, and legal system, then they all reinforce one another. When there are conflicts, the media are only one of many of those conflicting influences. However, the media may be the most important among the set for people who spend more time with the media than with other institutions and for people who like, trust, or are aroused more by media messages than by messages from other sources.

The mass media restrict individual selective perception, and the more this happens, the more the dominant voice of the status quo is reinforced. If people did not choose to expose themselves to the media, then the constancy of the messages would have no effect; but people expose themselves to the media very much—continuously and constantly.

Context of Portrayals. People pay particular attention to whether or not the behaviors of characters are rewarded or punished. If a behavior is successful and rewarded, the viewer will learn that the particular behavior is good and useful. If a behavior is punished, the viewer will learn that the behavior is bad and should not be tried.

Observation of social models accounts for much of the information communicated to children, and the media provide an enormous number of models from which children might learn. Given the large amount of time children spend with television, the characters they watch have a strong influence on their learning about how to behave in social situations.

Lifestyle. People who have active lifestyles in which they interact with many people and institutions are less affected by the media. People who have fewer real-life experiences because of lack of money, education, or vitality are more likely to have much higher exposure to media that is not counterbalanced by other experiences. This is why people who are poor, in a low socio-economic level, part of an ethnic minority, or elderly are particularly susceptible to influence by the media, especially television, because they expose themselves to a great deal of TV due to their sociological and psychological isolation. TV becomes their window on the world and their primary source of information.

Level of Development. A person's abilities to process media messages cognitively, emotionally, morally, and aesthetically all affect the degree to which those messages will have an influence. But more importantly, the issue is control. People with highly developed abilities can exercise a great deal of control over the effects process—shaping it to accentuate the positive effects and greatly reducing the potentially negative effects.

In summary, there are many factors that can influence the immediate and the long-term processes of media effects. Each of these can contribute in a probabilistic manner; that is, none of these by themselves will trigger an effect. Rather, it is the combination of factors that increases the probability of an effect—either positive or negative.

To diagnose your understanding of these factors, do Exercise 17.3 now. This exercise will make you aware of the degree to which you can analyze a situation and assess the degree to which a person is susceptible to a media generated effect.

Illustrations

To help make you aware of differences in media literacy development, let's look at some examples of how people can react to different types of media content. These reactions are best understood when compared to positions on the learning ladders of cognitive, emotional, moral, and aesthetic development.

Learning Ladders

The learning ladders remind us that we can improve our degree of media literacy in four areas: cognitions, emotions, morality, and aesthetics. Progress up each of these ladders is accomplished by mastering the key skills of analysis, comparison/contrast, evaluation, and appreciation.

Cognitive Ladder. The first step is awareness, which is the ability to perceive information elements in media messages. This requires the use of the lower order skills. The next step is understanding. This is the ability to perceive the relevant components in any messages, then to compare and contrast them in order to see how those elements are related to each other. The third step is evaluation, which requires a good deal of contextual information in order to have templates with which to compare current messages. In order to do this well, a person needs a great deal of context in the form of elaborate knowledge structures. At the highest step, people are able to appreciate a message by comparing it to their understanding of the constraints and resources of the people who produced the message. The more elaborated a person's knowledge structure is about the media industries, the more the person will be able to appreciate how difficult it is to produce certain messages.

Emotional Ladder. At low levels of emotional development, people's emotions control them. They become aroused and angry without being able to stop or control the emotion. They experience fear so strong they cannot shake it, or they cry at a movie and cannot stop even though they are very embarrassed. Or, they are unable to feel any emotions, even though they long to do so.

At higher levels of emotional development, people can use the media to shape and control their emotions. For example, stressed women watch more game and variety shows as well as more television in total, while stressed men watch more action and violent programming (Anderson, Collins, Schmitt, & Jacobvitz, 1996). Depressed people especially use television to escape unpleasant feelings and real-world stimuli that could exacerbate those feelings (Potts & Sanchez, 1994).

If people are aware of what they are doing, then the use of media to manage moods is a sign of high levels of media literacy, that is, people consciously use the media as a tool to satisfy a particular need. If, in contrast, people are depressed and they don't know what to do, they may watch television by default until they are tired enough to fall asleep. This is not an example of people controlling their exposure; instead this is an indication of a low level of media literacy.

Moral Ladder. This requires the development of opinions about the acceptability of shows, people, and situations. Typically, we infer themes from shows by matching elements in the portrayals against our personal values. At the lowest level on this ladder, you develop your moral opinion of a message based purely on intuition or because someone else, whom you respect, gives you the opinion. You see the elements in the show as an undifferentiated mass or blur. You make quick intuitive reactions about whether the show feels right or not, according to your values. If there is a fit, you are happy; if there is no fit, you have a negative reaction. You really can't articulate your reaction very well, because it is primarily emotional. For example, if a respected friend tells you that *NYPD Blue* is a morally reprehensible program, you would likely accept this opinion without watching the show. If you accidently find yourself exposed to it, you immediately experience a negative reaction and turn it off.

At the middle levels of the moral ladder, you make a distinction among characters based on their values and find yourself identifying with characters who have the same values that you do. If those characters are portrayed positively (rewarded, successful, attractive, etc.), then you are happy.

At the higher levels, you think past individual characters to focus your meaning making at the overall narrative level. You separate characters from their actions: You might not like a particular character, but you still like his or her actions in terms of fitting in with (or reinforcing) your values. You do not tie your viewing to one character's point of view, but try to empathize with many characters so you can vicariously experience the various consequences of actions through the course of the narrative. During a narrative, you are able to assume different moral perspectives so you can more fully appreciate the action from all participants' points of view.

Aesthetic Appreciation Ladder. This development is oriented toward the cultivation of an enhanced enjoyment, understanding, and appreciation of media content. At lower levels on this aesthetic ladder, people have a very simple categorical opinion that the show is either good or it is bad. Not much reasoning goes into the intuitive decision, so they are not able to explain why they like something.

At the middle levels, people are able to distinguish acting from writing and directing. Viewers have the ability to perceive that one of these might be good while another is bad. Also, people are able to compare an artist's performance within a message with past performances and to infer a trend in the work.

At higher levels, there is an awareness of media content as a "text" that provides insight into our contemporary culture and ourselves. An awareness of artistry and visual manipulation is also needed. This is an awareness about the processes by which meaning is created through the visual media. What is expected of sophisticated viewers is some degree of self-awareness about their role as interpreters. This includes the ability to detect artifice (in staged behavior and editing) and to spot authorial presence (style of the producer/director).

Learning about visual conventions is not a prerequisite for interpreting visual messages. However, learning these conventions can help heighten our appreciation of artistry; it also provides us with the ability to see through the manipulative uses and ideological implications of visual images. This helps to enhance critical viewing.

Can you make a quick assessment of your position on each of these four ladders? If you can, then your awareness is fairly high. If you are unclear how to position yourself, think about these ladders as you watch television or read a newspaper. As you reflect on your media exposures while they are happening, you will develop more insights about the levels at which you normally operate. Remember, you will move your positions on the ladders depending on the type of message and your mood. If you are simply looking for fantasy to help you relax, you are likely operating at lower levels even though you may be capable of operating at higher levels at other times. As you are exposed to media messages over a long period of time, develop a sense of where your "home position" is, that is, at what level do you usually operate?

Now let's use these learning ladders as templates to examine some examples. This analysis will highlight the important differences across levels of media literacy.

Examples of Levels of Literacy

There are many different reasons why people expose themselves to different kinds of content, and there are many different benefits people can gain from any particular message. Because of this, it is not possible to analyze a message and assume that all those who are exposed to it will extract the same meaning or have the same experience. Below, we will explore several examples to illustrate this point.

Beavis and Butt-head. There has been a great deal of criticism of the television show *Beavis and Butt-head.* Many people find it offensive. However, it can be viewed in different ways depending on how literate you are.

At one level, you might really like the characters and identify with them. You feel that the characters see things the same way you do—something is either cool or it sucks. You think that finally there are characters who are not afraid to tell it like it is. You might watch them and realize that they ARE you. You use them as role models and feel confirmed because there are other people like you, so it is okay to be the way you are. This reaction to *Beavis and Butt-head* illustrates a low level of media literacy. The viewer demonstrates no real analysis of the show, so the cognitive level is low. There is no evidence of moral or aesthetic development, but there is a moderate emotional reaction of liking for the characters. Overall, however, the pattern on the learning ladders is at or near the lowest level.

At a higher overall level of literacy, people would be aware enough to regard the characters as simple stereotypes. By comparing and contrasting Beavis and Butthead with other characters on television, it is clear that these characters are less developed. This realization might lead to an emotional reaction of frustration because the characters never change or learn from their mistakes. Also, it might lead to a moral reaction that the characters are reprehensible.

At a level of literacy that is higher still, the show could be regarded as a satire on the insipid values of the X Generation. A greater cognitive effort of analysis, comparison/contrast, and evaluation would be required to construct this conclusion. It would also require a broader knowledge structure about what the X Generation is supposed to be. This might lead to a strong humorous emotional reaction; the laughter is *at* the characters, however, not with them. This stance on laughter is evidence of an awareness of a moral position that abhors the values of the characters and in so doing finds them funny in their fool's paradise. An aesthetic analysis of the program would reveal the characters to be very flat from an artistic point of view. This could lead to an admiration for the producer's ability to keep things so consistently flat. The artistic perspective is flat. The character development is flat; that is, the characters don't change or mature. The dialog is flat; it doesn't develop into deeper levels of insight. This consistent flatness is not easy to sustain over many episodes. At this level of reaction, there is a strong aesthetic appreciation, along with strong cognitive, emotional, and moral reactions.

Soap Operas. Soap operas as a genre can appeal to viewers at all levels of media literacy. At a low level of literacy, people feel some kind of unarticulated attachment to the program. They cannot explain why they like the characters or the show, because they don't analyze it; they just let it be.

At a somewhat higher level of development, people will watch soap operas, because they feel a personal identity with the characters and have substituted the soap opera world for their own barren existence. This leads to a strong emotional reaction. Other people will watch "soaps," because they want to learn how attractive characters dress and act; this leads to some cognitive processing and evaluation of how the characters look and act.

At a higher level, some people view soaps in groups so they can discuss the action as it unfolds, or they call their friends later and use the action as an important topic of conversation. These people use the viewing to maintain a community of friends that they would not have without the soap opera. This requires a considerable amount of cognitive processing and emotional attachment.

At a still higher level, the viewing becomes an in-depth analysis of the aesthetic and moral elements displayed there. Viewers marvel at the writing, directing, and acting challenges of mounting a multi-plotted program 5 days a week for an open-ended time period, sometimes stretching over decades. Also, the complexity of the changing moral sensibilities can be intriguing. It is a truly remarkable achievement that the creative people on these shows can sustain a sense of drama and suspense under such severe pressures in such a limited genre.

Nightly News. At a low level, looking at the news each night (whether in a newspaper, a magazine, on radio, or on television) can be nothing more than a mindless habit that provides people with a sense that they have been exposed to what is important each day. As a ritual, it provides structure to one's life, even if it does not provide any information of value to them.

At a higher level, people consciously monitor certain stories for new developments. They add new information to their existing knowledge structure of the story and feel some emotion as they derive a sense of satisfaction about learning more.

At the highest levels of media literacy, people use this regular exposure as a starting place for learning about the events of the day. They notice what is on the agenda and immediately use that information to elaborate their existing knowledge structures. Then they seek out alternative messages in other vehicles and other media to augment this information and to serve as a confirmation as to its completeness. They have a constant skepticism that there may be more to the story. They have developed a keen aesthetic awareness of the strengths and weaknesses of various reporters and news organizations and use these insights to evaluate the worth of each new story. Finally, they are very aware of the visual framing, the use of camera movement, and the use (or lack of use) of graphics and other production techniques that subtly construct the tone of the stories.

Remember, it is not the type of messages you watch that make you media literate or illiterate. Instead, literacy is keyed to what you think and how you feel while you are being exposed.

Summary

Media literacy is a perspective. In order to achieve this perspective, you need to increase your awareness and control. These are the two steps on the journey to higher media literacy. The exercises in this chapter are designed to help you make an assessment (and to continue this practice over time) of your awareness of your own knowledge structures, of how your mind works, and of your ability to apply your knowledge of the key elements in the effects process.

Media literacy is most clearly diagnosed when we compare people's patterns of thoughts and feelings to the positions on the learning ladders. Keep these ladders in mind during your exposures.

References

Anderson, D. R., Collins, P. A., Schmitt, K. L., & Jacobvitz, R. S. (1996). Stressful life events and television viewing. *Communication Research, 23,* 243-260.

Bruner, J. S., Goodnow, J., & Austin, G. A. (1956). *A study of thinking.* New York: John Wiley.

Comstock, G. A. (1982). *Television in America.* Beverly Hills, CA: Sage.

Dervin, B., & Greenberg, B. S. (1972). The communication environment of the urban poor. In F. G. Kline & P. J. Tichenor (Eds.), *Current perspectives in mass communication research* (pp. 195-233). Beverly Hills, CA: Sage.

Gardner, R. W. (1968). *Personality development at preadolescence.* Seattle: University of Washington Press.

Hashway, R. M., & Duke, L. I. (1992). *Cognitive styles: A primer to the literature.* Lewiston, NY: Edwin Mellen.

Hawkins, R. P., & Pingree, S. (1982). Television's influence on social reality. In D. Pearl, L. Bouthilet, & J. Lazar (Eds.), *Television and behavior: Ten years of scientific progress and implications for the eighties: Vol. 2. Technical reviews* (pp. 224-247). Rockville, MD: U.S. Department of Health and Human Services.

Himmelweit, H. T. (1966). Television and the child. In B. Berelson & M. Janowitz (Eds.), *Reader in public opinion and communication* (2nd ed.). New York: Free Press.

Kagen, J., Rosman, D., Day, D., Albert, J., & Phillips, W. (1964). Information processing in the child: Significance of analytic and reflective attitudes. *Psychological Monographs, 78,* 1.

McLeod, J. M., Fitzpatrick, M. A., Glynn, C. J., & Fallis, S. F. (1982). Television and social relations: Family influences and consequences for interpersonal behavior. In D. Pearl, L. Bouthilet, & J. Lazar (Eds.), *Television and behavior: Ten years of scientific progress and implications for the eighties: Vol. 2. Technical reviews* (pp. 272-286). Rockville, MD: U.S. Department of Health and Human Services.

Murray, J. P. (1980). *Television and youth: 25 years of research and controversy.* Boys Town, NB: Boys Town Center for the Study of Youth Development.

Potts, R., & Sanchez, D. (1994). Television viewing and depression: No news is good news. *Journal of Broadcasting & Electronic Media, 38,* 79-90.

Roberts, D. R. (1973). Communication and children: A developmental approach. In I. DeS. Pool, W. Schramm, F. W. Frey, N. Maccoby, & E. B. Parker (Eds.), *The process and effects of mass communication* (Rev. ed., pp. 596-611). Urbana: University of Illinois Press.

Singer, D. G., & Singer, J. L. (1981). Television and the developing imagination of the child. *Journal of Broadcasting, 25,* 373-387.

Witkin, H. A., & Goodenough, D. R. (1977). Field dependence and interpersonal behavior. *Psychological Bulletin, 84,* 661-689.

Exercise 17.1 Awareness of Your Knowledge Structures

A list of the chapters in this book appears below. Each chapter presents a knowledge structure on its topic.

1. For each chapter in the book, try to recall the structure of the content.
   a. Can you remember the key idea of Chapter 1? Can you remember major ideas or sections of the chapter?
   b. Now go back to the first page of that chapter and check your recall. If you remembered the key idea, give yourself 1 point, and give yourself another point for your recall of *each* major idea (the major points in the outline). Thus your score should be somewhere between zero and 5 for that chapter.
   c. Enter your score in the left-hand column, the one labeled "Book."
   d. Do the same procedure for each of the chapters listed below.

Book   *AddExp*   *INTRODUCTION*

Book	AddExp	
_____	_____	Chapter 1 What Is Media Literacy?
_____	_____	Chapter 2 Importance of Literacy

KNOWLEDGE ABOUT SKILLS

Book	AddExp	
_____	_____	Chapter 3 How Does the Human Mind Work?
_____	_____	Chapter 4 Importance of Skills
_____	_____	Chapter 5 Developmental Perspective

KNOWLEDGE ABOUT MESSAGES AND CONVENTIONS

Book	AddExp	
_____	_____	Chapter 6 What Is News?
_____	_____	Chapter 7 Commercial Advertising
_____	_____	Chapter 8 What Is Entertainment?

KNOWLEDGE ABOUT MEDIA INDUSTRIES

Book	AddExp	
_____	_____	Chapter 9 Growth of the Mass Media Industries
_____	_____	Chapter 10 Economic Nature
_____	_____	Chapter 11 Who Owns and Controls the Mass Media?
_____	_____	Chapter 12 What Is An Audience?

KNOWLEDGE ABOUT EFFECTS

_____	_____	Chapter 13 Broadening the Perspective on Media Effects
_____	_____	Chapter 14 *HOW* Do the Effect Processes Work?
_____	_____	Chapter 15 Effects on Institutions

REAL-WORLD KNOWLEDGE

_____	_____	Chapter 16 Importance of Real-World Information

2. Next, think about additional reading you undertook after studying each chapter.

   a. For each book or article you read from the Interesting Reading list or from the reference list, give yourself 2 points.

   b. For each additional book you have read relevant to the topic since studying the chapter, give yourself 1 point.

   c. For each significant experience you have had concerning that topic since studying the chapter, give yourself 1 point (a significant experience would be an extended conversation with someone on the topic of the chapter, consciously trying to apply the principles in that chapter, etc.).

   d. Record your point totals for each chapter in the column labeled "AddExp" for Additional Experiences.

3. Look at the pattern of numbers across the chapters. What does this tell you about the state of your current knowledge structures?

   a. Look down the Book column. If you have mostly 4s and 5s, you have a very strong set of knowledge structures. If you have mostly 3s, you have a good beginning set of knowledge structures. If you have any zeros, you need to go back and re-orient yourself to the structure of information in those chapters.

   Remember, having strong knowledge structures does not necessarily mean you have a great deal of knowledge on that topic, but it does mean you are aware of the main ideas. This will help you acquire additional knowledge much more efficiently.

   b. Look down the AddExp column. If you have 3s or above, you are showing a strong commitment to extending your knowledge and elaborating your knowledge structures. Notice where you have zeros and ask yourself why you were not willing or able to extend your knowledge.

   c. Look at the total pattern of numbers. Were you stronger on certain chapters than others?

   It is understandable that you may have more interest in particular topics than others, but remember that balance is important. Be proud of your accomplishments—now build on them to overcome your weaknesses.

Exercise 17.2 Awareness of How Your Mind Works

1. *Field Dependency:* Without looking back through this chapter, write down on a piece of paper the main idea of the chapter and several subsidiary ideas that amplify that main idea.

   If you were able to do this quickly, you are an active reader. You most likely previewed the chapter to determine its structure and main points. Then, with that structure in mind, you were able to navigate your way efficiently through the reading—adding detail to your structure at appropriate places. This is characteristic of a field independent cognitive style.

   If you instead struggled with this mini-exercise, you are less field independent. Perhaps you listed several points, but these were not the main points of the chapter. Perhaps you were able to list many relevant points (maybe 10 or 12), but were not able to decide which were more important—that is, which were superordinate to others. Perhaps you could not list any points, in which case you were forcing your eyes over each line of type as you read the chapter, but your mind was not distinguishing the ideas (signals) from the lines of type (noise).

2. *Tolerance for Ambiguity:* Expose yourself for 20 minutes to a television show on a topic about which you know nothing. For example, if you are *not* a sports fan, watch a hockey game. If you are *not* into high-brow art, watch an opera.

   During the exposure, did you continually look at your watch, wondering how time could go so slowly? Did you feel frustrated that you could not follow the action? If your answers to these questions are yes, then you probably have a low tolerance for ambiguity.

   Instead, did you find the new experience fascinating? Were you intrigued as you began to see some patterns? If your answers to these questions are yes, then you probably have a high tolerance for ambiguity.

3. *Conceptual Differentiation:* For this exercise, let's start with a general concept—like a newscast—and break it down into its component parts, such as news, weather, and sports, each of which can be broken down into their own sub-component parts. Think of this as a tree diagram. The trunk is labeled Newscast. The top of the trunk splits into three main branches labeled News, Weather, and Sports. Each of these main branches can split off into sub-branches, and the sub-branches can themselves split off into smaller branches, and so on.

   a. Now try drawing a tree diagram for Books. Draw a trunk and label it Book, then at the top split it into two branches labeled Fiction and Non-fiction.

Now you're on your own. Continue with the splitting of branches. Label each branch.

b. When you have finished, look at the overall pattern.

On average, how many sub-branches come from each split? In the Newscast example above, the split produced three sub-branches. But it could have produced more, say six: National News, International News, Local News, Features, Sports, and Weather.

How many levels did you pursue? In our newscast example above, there were only two levels: the Newscast level itself and the level with types of stories. But there could have been a third level. For example, Weather could have been sub-divided into Today's Weather and Forecast. It could have been further sub-divided into a fourth level; for example, Forecast could be broken into Precipitation and Temperature.

If in the Books example you have many levels and many branches at each split, then you are high on conceptual differentiation. This means that your cognitive style drives you to pay careful attention to structure and to acquire a good deal of information.

If, in contrast, you have only two or three levels and only a few branches at each split, then you are low on conceptual differentiation. Your knowledge structure about books is not as structured or as detailed as people who are high on conceptual differentiation.

Exercise 17.3 Awareness of Key Factors in Effects Processes

This exercise is similar to the one you did in Chapter 14. It is repeated here, because being aware of the factors that can increase the probability of an effect is so important. Also, this repetition will serve as a point of comparison with your performance several weeks ago to demonstrate how your learning has changed.

For each of the five scenarios below, think about the general factors synthesized in this chapter. Do not refer to them as you do this exercise; instead, see what you can recall and how you can apply what you recall.

For each scenario, write a brief profile that explains how the person is at risk for a negative media effect, that is, what factors are likely present to increase the probability of a negative effect. Also, make some specific recommendations for what this person should do to reduce the risk.

1. Bobby is a 5-year-old who loves to watch action/adventure cartoons on Saturday morning television. His mother is happy that the television serves as a baby-sitter for Bobby, freeing up time for her to work in another part of the house.

2. Jennifer is disgusted by watching political ads on television. She thinks all ads are negative and will not watch them. Also, she thinks all politicians are crooks, and refuses to vote or to pay attention to any news coverage of campaigns.

3. Cool Dude is a sophomore in college. For the past 4 years he has been closely following heavy metal and rap music. He also watches a good deal of MTV. He stays up partying all night, every night, and sees himself as the center of social life at the school because of his dress, his talk, and his style.

4. Four-year-old Alison is so grief-stricken because Bambi's mother died in the movie that she cannot take her nap.

5. Percy is a teenager who has seen every horror film made, but now the thrill is gone. He has recently lost the ability to be scared while at the movies. Still, he continues to go to every new horror film—hoping that there will be some awesome special effect or super-gruesome scene that can excite him.

CHAPTER 18

Postscript to Students

Strategies for Increasing Media Literacy

KEY IDEA *You have the power to develop media literacy strategies to influence society, other individuals, and yourself.*

Congratulations on having worked on your knowledge structures in the previous chapters. By now you should have a fairly good awareness of what it means to be media literate and what your strengths and weaknesses are in terms of media literacy skills and knowledge structures.

You should now be asking yourself: How can I preserve the skills and knowledge structures I already have so that they don't erode? How can I overcome my weaknesses? Is there anything I can do to help with media literacy among other people and in society in general? These are very important questions.

The answers to these questions require you to think about developing some key strategies. You've probably been thinking about such development as you were reading the book. If so, you have already started. In this chapter, I can help direct your thinking, but I cannot give you THE STRATEGIES. You must develop them for yourself in response to your particular needs; this last chapter of the book will not give you the definitive list of strategies. Instead, think of this last chapter as a platform—a jumping-off point for you to take greater control of the trajectory of your thinking as you glide through the rich atmosphere of media messages over the course of your life.

This chapter will attempt to stimulate your thinking in three areas: personal strategies, interpersonal strategies, and societal strategies. Use this information to guide the development of your own strategies to take control of your media exposure and the effects of those messages on you. Notice that this chapter does not include an exercise. It is time for you to begin developing your own exercises and to continue doing so as you execute your media literacy strategies from this point onward.

 ## Personal Strategies

The purpose of developing personal strategies is to shape the effects the media will have on you by mindfully viewing and actively discounting or amplifying messages. Below are nine suggestions for you to consider when developing your own personal strategies.

Develop an Accurate Awareness of Your Exposure

Periodically (maybe once a year) keep a diary of media usage for a week. Remember that you did this in the exercise in Chapter 2. By repeating this exercise over time, you can monitor your changing interests in media and their messages. As you monitor changes, ask yourself the following types of questions:

Am I broadening my exposure to different media or am I staying primarily with only one or two?

Am I broadening my exposure to different types of messages? (If you used to watch mainly sports and action/adventure on television, are you now spreading your viewing around to a wider range of genres such as news, reality programs, games, music, etc.?)

Am I planning my media exposures to serve specific goals of which I am aware, or am I just exposing myself to whatever comes along?

Variety and consciousness are important goals to achieve with exposure. Variety will broaden your interests and perhaps lead you to ask for different kinds of content from the media. Consciousness will lead you to move more of your exposure into the planned area, leaving less in the default area.

Acquire a Broad Base of Useful Knowledge

The key to knowledge is that it be useful; acquiring knowledge that is not useful does not help. This means you must be consciously aware of your needs for knowledge. When you see something unusual in the media, ask yourself: What additional information do I need in order to make sense of this? When you see something typical in the media, ask yourself: Is this really the way it appears?

There is always a gap between the knowledge we already have and the knowledge we need for understanding the world better. We can close the knowledge gap for ourselves, but we must do this on a topic-by-topic basis. The strategy for closing the knowledge gap on a topic is under our control, because the knowledge gap is influenced more by our interest in a topic than by our general level of education (Chew & Palmer, 1994). If we have high interest in a topic, we will search out information from many different media and many different sources. When we have low interest in a topic, we allow the media to determine for us how much information we get.

Continually Practice Literacy Skills in Mindful Exposure Sessions

Try to reduce your amount of mindless exposure. Remember, mindless exposure is not necessarily associated with a particular type of content—any content can turn your mind off, and any content can potentially have value and engage your mind. For example, a bland situation comedy can turn our minds off and so can a great work of literature—but for different reasons. If we watch a Shakespearean tragedy, we might find our mind wandering because so much mental effort is required to follow the Elizabethan language, the poetic expression, the historical settings, and the multiple-character plots.

It is important to develop active media use habits and not to practice bad habits. When you are passive, media effects are uncontrolled. Remember that active processing and high involvement with media reduces unwanted effects. People who are conscious of what they are exposed to and actively interact with the content will retain control over their learning process. Such people will consciously discount certain messages and carefully encode other information for memory storage. People who are not active processors of information will let the media, especially television, happen to them.

We can make viewing active for children by continually asking questions about meaning and structure, such as: Who did what to whom? and Why? This gets them practicing making connections. We can do the same for ourselves. Continually analyze messages, then move on to applying the other advanced skills. We should continually question the messages. What are the categories (schemas) we have for characters? Are they thin and two-dimensional or are they richly developed? What are our expectations for scripts? Are they simple or complex? How do we make judgments about what is relevant in the plot—can we see the subtleties in the sub-plots that provide more texture to the main plot?

The context of the exposure can also influence the activity of information processing. When watching a message, analyze the contextual elements. For example, with ads ask who is the spokesperson and is he or she credible and trustworthy? What are the product claims? With entertainment messages, look closely at the action. Is it rewarded? What are the characters' motivations? What appear to be the producer's motivations? What values underlie this portrayal?

Beware of factors that increase mindlessness in exposure. Factors that distract your attention during exposure serve to move you into a low involvement state. In this state you use peripheral modes of information processing, that is, your mind goes on automatic pilot. Advertisers rely on this to get their message into your subconscious without your defense mechanisms being aroused.

Focus on Usefulness as a Goal

There are different reasons for media exposure. All can be valid and highly useful, but uses vary. We need to be clear about what our goals really are during each exposure session. We should remember that we place ourselves at risk for unwanted effects if we expose ourselves mindlessly. With a little effort we could increase our control over the content—and perhaps even increase our enjoyment of the content by experiencing a stronger emotional reaction or aesthetic appreciation on a new level of understanding.

Continually ask yourself what you want to get from this media exposure. If you want facts and information, then process the material actively to select those facts and categorize them well. If instead you want to be entertained by establishing a parasocial interaction with a particular character who is attractive to you, then be aware of attraction and how it might be affecting you. Remember that this character lives in a world very unlike your own and is a product of a production system with particular goals and constraints.

Think About the Reality-Fantasy Continuum

Continually ask yourself the degree to which something is real or fantasy; this is a continuum. Some programs will be easy to spot as fantasy, such as *Looney Toons*. But other programs may not be so obvious. Some have a realistic setting and some realistic situations but are still fantasy, such as *Married With Children*. Others may have a fantasy setting but deal with situations in a realistic manner, such as *Star Trek*. Distinguishing reality from fantasy in the media is often a difficult task that requires you to think about the many different characteristics of a message. You must think analytically and break a message down into its component parts, then assess which parts are realistic.

The argument here is not to avoid fantasy. Exposure to fantasy can have many positive effects. Such exposure can be very entertaining because of its imaginative or humorous appeal. It can stimulate our thinking creatively; however, we must realize that it is a stimulating tool, not a model to imitate. The important thing is to know when you are being exposed to fantasy so that you can process those messages differently. If you aren't analytical, many messages with embedded fantasy might appear realistic.

Make Cross-Channel Comparisons

While media literacy is a generic concept that spans across all media, there are some special challenges presented by different channels. For example, reading a magazine article requires some skills not required when watching a situation comedy on television. This point, of course, is obvious, but the nature of the differences themselves are not so obvious. To illustrate this, watch a news story on CNN, then look for that story in your local newspaper. Analyze the similarities and differences—are they important?

These differences will become even clearer if you attempt to create a message for different channels. Try writing a news story for a radio station and for a magazine that comes out once a month. Try constructing a message that will make people laugh when they hear it in a song on a CD. Now translate that humor onto the computer screen for Internet browsers. Designing good media messages, especially humorous ones, is very difficult. Exercises such as these will help increase your aesthetic appreciation.

Increase Your Willingness to Expend Mental Effort

We all have expectations about the appropriate amount of mental effort necessary to read a book, listen to a lecture, or watch television. Compared to print, TV elicits lower expectations about mental effort. The amount of invested mental effort while viewing is a voluntary matter (Salomon, 1981). Because we can control our mental effort, we can also control the degree of our learning. The greater the mental effort expended, the higher our comprehension, learning, and eventual recall.

Examine Your Opinions

Ask yourself: Are my opinions well reasoned? For example, as Americans we say we are dissatisfied with materialism despite all the abundance. In a recent survey, 82% of Americans agreed that most of us buy and consume far more than we need, and 67% agreed that Americans cause many of the world's environmental problems, because we consume more resources and produce more waste than anyone else in the world (Koenenn, 1996). The United States has less than 10% of the world's population, but consumes nearly 30% of the planet's resources. Americans can choose from more than 30,000 supermarket items, including 200 kinds of cereal. Do we really need all these material products?

While people criticize television in general, their opinions are inconsistent. For example, The Roper Organization under the sponsorship of NBC in the early 1980s had respondents in a national survey express their reactions to 17 particular TV shows—16 of which had been the targets of complaints from religious organizations about sex and violence. Only 13% of respondents said there was too much violence on the *Dukes of Hazard,* and 10% said there was too much sex on *Dallas*—these were the most negatively rated shows! But when asked about television in general, 50% of the respondents said there was too much sex and violence on TV (The Roper Organization, 1981).

As can be seen in the above examples, we are not very systematic in gathering information or careful in assessing it when constructing our opinions. Instead, we operate fairly intuitively. As a result, we have a lot of superficial opinions.

Change Behaviors

Do your behaviors fit with your opinions? For example, if you think society is too materialistic, do you avoid buying many material goods? Or do you keep your behavior and change your attitudes—get honest with yourself.

You could boycott advertisers, cancel subscriptions, and write letters when you see something you don't like in the media. Unfortunately, such action will have very little effect on the media themselves, unless large numbers of other people feel as you and do the same things. However, that is not a reason to stop yourself from acting. By taking action, you give yourself a sense of gaining control over the media.

Changing your behavior to correspond to your beliefs demonstrates a commitment to the moral responsibility of following through on your beliefs rather than simply blaming someone else and doing nothing, which has become a popular strategy for many of society's problems. For example, let's examine what has been happening in the area of the environment and pollution. The media have put the issue of pollution on the public agenda, as the prominence and length of these stories has increased dramatically since the 1970s (Ader, 1995). During that same period, air pollution went down about a third, but solid waste went up about 25%. This shows us that as Americans become more concerned about pollution, we have put pressure on the government to clean up the air by regulating manufacturing plants and requiring emissions controls on cars. But reducing the volume of solid waste, which is under the control of individual citizens through voluntary recycling programs, has not been so successful. This means that individuals are not cutting back on their waste through lower consumption, through recycling, or both. Again, people are looking to the government or someone else to solve problems.

 Interpersonal Strategies

Interpersonal strategies orient you toward helping other individuals with their media literacy. You begin by identifying people who might be at risk for negative effects from the media and then work with them intensively. One example would be to work with children in a day care center, church, or other community group. Because of their young age, children are still at a low level of development and require special attention.

With young children, it is important that an adult guide their media exposure (Messaris, 1982). You can explain the meaning of words, pictures, narratives, and more. You can make viewing active for young children by continually asking questions about meaning and structure: Who did what to whom? Why? Questions such as these stimulate children to practice making connections. Be careful not to push a child too hard, before he or she is able to make the required connections to answer a particular kind of question. Remember, young children go through stages of cognitive development that cannot be rushed.

When parents actively mediate during television viewing, they can influence their children's interpretations (Austin, 1993). Parents should show children how to analyze both sides of an issue, in addition to encouraging that such an analysis take place. Categorizing, supplementing, and validating media messages may help children practice important skills that modeling of parental attitudes, behaviors, and communicative style alone cannot teach.

This type of interpersonal strategy is usually very successful. Children's responsiveness to (and understanding of) news, entertainment, and advertising messages can be significantly influenced by adult intervention. Even young children (kindergarten age) can be trained to understand the persuasive nature and techniques of commercials. This understanding then leads to increased skepticism. Unfortunately, in most households there is relatively little mediation of children's exposure and reactions to commercials.

These strategies can move beyond the cognitive and can also include emotional and behavioral aspects. Children who experience emotional media messages when they are among peers or adults will exhibit a reduced likelihood and intensity of immediate emotional effects, especially fear effects from scary movies. Also, the probability of a child behaving aggressively when watching violence can be reduced if adults verbalize comments and interpretations while observing with the child—such as pointing out unrealistic and inappropriate behavior in programs.

Children are likely to model their behavior after attractive characters they see in the media. This modeling can be shaped by interpersonal strategies. For example, Austin and Meili (1995) found that children use their emotion and logic to develop expectations about alcohol use in the real world when they see alcohol used by characters on television. When children rely on both real-life and televised sources of information, they are more likely to develop skepticism about television portrayals of alcohol use if they rely on parents as primary sources of information and behavioral modeling.

When you become a parent, you will need to be careful in monitoring your children's experience with the newest of the media—computers on the Internet. The Internet is a global network and is not governed by any entity. People can (and do) put out lots of questionable information and entertainment services.

There are no limits or checks on information—it is up to each of us to police ourselves.

There are primarily three types of risk for children or teens who use the Internet: One is exposure to inappropriate material such as sexual matter and hate speech. A second is developing inappropriate relationships with strangers. The third is harassment ("Is Your Child Safe," 1995). Parents therefore need to be careful in monitoring what sites their children visit. Children should never give out any identifying information such as address, phone number, school name, or anything similar. Never allow a child to arrange a face-to-face meeting with someone on-line. If you find information that may be illegal (such as child pornography or hate speech) report it to authorities. Remember that people on-line may not be who they seem; people can make up a personae in terms of gender, age, background, and so on. Be skeptical; not everything you read is true. Set time rules for access; too much contact can lead to addiction. Finally, surf as a family and discuss what you see; it can be fun, educational, and very rewarding.

Societal Strategies

With societal strategies, the focus is on exerting pressure on a particular part of the industry, the government, or some institution in order to increase public awareness about a problem or to bring about some particular change. To do this successfully, you will need a great deal of commitment, money, and contacts. Unless you stay with it for the long term, most of your short-term effort will be wasted. It will require many years of effort to effect a change. Also, it requires money. Often people will start a PAC (political action committee) or a consulting firm that will then apply for grants to support its work. Contacts are also extremely important. By linking up with other powerful people and groups, you could become part of something that could potentially have enough power to get the attention of the large media companies.

Changing media industry practices or content is very difficult. Remember, the industries have grown and developed in response to demands from the public. If an industry or a vehicle does not respond well to the demand, it loses money. Successful CEOs have confidence that their decisions will result in greater profits, so don't expect change just because you ask them to ignore their experience and to change their practices of content when that will likely cost them millions of dollars.

This is why the public concern about television violence has resulted in so little change over the past 40 years. A more modest goal than to expect a change of content or practices is to expect a change in perceptions among some decision makers in the media industries. In explaining this non-action, Stuart Fishoff (1988), a psychologist who writes for television and movies, said:

> Let's suppose the results, the conclusions were incontrovertible—TV and film modeling of aggression and other anti-social values has significant effects on the viewing audience. Would it really make any difference to the gate keepers of media fare in Hollywood and New York? I submit the answer is not on your life! (p. 3)

Fishoff cites an important principle in psychology for his conclusion:

> The more far-reaching and costly the consequences of accepting a message, the more facts needed before an audience will be persuaded as to the accuracy of the message—and the more energy will be expended in denigrating both the message and the messenger in order to maintain existing belief. (p. 3)

Therefore, the media industries have steadfastly refused to believe any of the research on negative media effects, although they use the research on positive effects to show that they are acting responsibly. This attitude has outraged many media critics and stimulated many average citizens to want to do something to remedy the problem.

Another example of a societal strategy is the concern over protecting very young children from the effects of television advertising. In the early 1970s, some consumer groups were formed to protect children from what was seen as abuses by broadcasters. Prominent among these groups was Action for Children's Television, which found examples of children's programs that contained as many as 16 minutes of ads per hour—far above the industry's self-imposed limit of 9.5 minutes—and the products advertised were largely non-nutritious snacks and deceptively presented toys. Many products were being pitched by characters from the programs, thus making the distinction between the show and the ad indecipherable, especially for young children.

The pressure influenced the Federal Trade Commission (FTC) to hold hearings throughout the 1970s. The FTC considered banning certain types of ads, but in the end, the FTC concluded that although there was evidence that television advertising created risks for children, there were no practical, effective remedies open to federal policy making. A primary problem was determining who is a child—that is, at what age is a person no longer a child? Also, there was the fear that regulating advertising on children's television might cause broadcasters to stop programming for children.

Still another example of a societal strategy took place in the fall of 1995 when some well-known political figures began a campaign to clean up talk shows on television. Headed by former Education Secretary William Bennett, Senator Joseph Lieberman (D-Conn.), and Senator Sam Nunn (D-Ga.), the campaign did not seek regulation of television content. Instead, it sought to influence public opinion and to shame certain television producers by characterizing the content of daytime talk shows as "lethal." These critics acknowledged that some of the 20 nationally syndicated talk shows dealt with serious issues of domestic abuse, drug abuse, and racism in a way that enlightened viewers. Then they pointed out that some shows had a circus atmosphere that included shouting matches, fist fights, foul language, and audience members yelling out unqualified advice. As an example of sleaze, they cited examples from Sally Jessy Raphaël's show where she talked to girls who were sexually active at the age of 10, and Jerry Springer who hosted a show about a 17-year-old who had four children with her 71-year-old husband whom she called "Dad" (Hancock, 1995).

There are many other examples of people and groups who have tried to influence the public's awareness of problems with media content and to bring about change in the media industries. These efforts have been more successful in raising public consciousness about the problems than they have been in bringing about changes in programming. This leaves us with the question: Should we continue to try? The answer, of course, is yes, but we should have modest expectations for what it means to have a successful societal strategy, and we need to have a long time frame. Societal change of this type moves at glacial speed—it takes decades to see change. Just remember that a glacier exerts constant pressure, and change happens constantly—we just can't see it happening, because it is happening so slowly. The same is true with societal campaigns. If we exert constant pressure, we will eventually be able to perceive changes. If you are impatient and want to see change happen more quickly, then try some interpersonal and personal strategies.

Summary

This book is now ending. What kind of an effect have you let it have on you?

Did you read it critically by analyzing the information and arguments? Did you compare and contrast the points made here with your existing knowledge structures? Did you evaluate my arguments and positions, agreeing with some and disagreeing with others? Did you synthesize the information you found most useful into your own perspective on media literacy and your own set of strategies to achieve that perspective? Can you abstract the main points in this book so that you could tell a friend in 100-200 words what the book is about? If you answered yes to these questions, then you had a favorable cognitive reaction to the book. The key to a high-quality cognitive reaction is not whether you agree with me and accept all this information. Instead, the key is that your mind was continually active as you read the book.

Did you have some strong emotional reactions while reading the book? For example, did you get upset with some of the information or arguments? Do you feel challenged and motivated to become more media literate? If you answered yes to these questions, then you had a favorable emotional reaction to the book. The key to a high-quality emotional reaction is not whether you have positive feelings about me or about the book. Instead, the key is that you are able to let your emotions become engaged by hating parts of the book and loving others.

Did you take moral positions throughout the book? For example, did you develop a sense of what is right with our culture (and what is wrong) because of the media? Did you make a strong commitment to yourself to do certain things to help yourself and others? If you answered yes to these questions, then you had a favorable moral reaction to the book. The key to a high-quality moral reaction is not whether you agree with my positions. Instead, the key is that you are able to perceive a sense of right and wrong about certain conditions and to take a stand for yourself.

Finally, were you aware of aesthetic reactions to the book? Were there times where you appreciated the way I structured a chapter or the way I illuminated an important point? Did you find certain examples useful and creative? Did you feel that certain sections could have been written better? If you are able to answer these questions, then you were sensitive to the aesthetic features of the book. I, of course, hope that your aesthetic reactions were favorable. But whether favorable or not, the more aesthetic reactions you had and the more aesthetic awareness you exercised, the better for your media literacy development.

Most important, I hope you can see that you have achieved a significant degree of media literacy. You have many useful knowledge structures and many useful skills. As you continue developing these knowledge structures and skills, remember to be aware of what you are doing and to stay in control of your progress. And make it fun!

References

Ader, D. R. (1995). A longitudinal study of agenda setting for the issue of environmental pollution. *Journalism & Mass Communication Quarterly, 72,* 300-311.

Austin, E. W. (1993). Exploring the effects of active parental mediation of television content. *Journal of Broadcasting & Electronic Media, 37,* 147-158.

Austin, E. W., & Meili, H. K. (1995). Effects of interpretations of television alcohol portrayals on children's alcohol beliefs. *Journal of Broadcasting & Electronic Media, 39,* 417-435.

Chew, F., & Palmer, S. (1994). Interest, the knowledge gap, and television programming. *Journal of Broadcasting & Electronic Media, 38,* 271-287.

Fishoff, S. (1988, August). *Psychological research and a black hole called Hollywood.* Paper presented at the Annual Meeting of the American Psychological Association, Atlanta, GA.

Hancock, E. (1995, October 27). Culture cops take on sleazy TV talk shows. *Santa Barbara News-Press,* p. A1.

Is your child safe in cyberspace? (1995, December). *USA Magazine,* pp. 28-31.

Koenenn, C. (1996, May 14). Let's get simple. *Los Angeles Times,* p. E1.

Messaris, P. (1982). Parents, children, and television. In G. Gumpert & R. Cathcart (Eds.), *Inter/media* (2nd ed., pp. 580-598). New York: Oxford University Press.

The Roper Organization. (1981). *Sex, profanity and violence: An opinion survey about seventeen television programs* (Conducted for the National Broadcasting Company). New York: Television Information Office.

Salomon, G. (1981). Introducing AIME: The assessment of children's mental involvement with television. In H. Kelley & H. Gardner (Eds.), *New directions for child development: Viewing children through television* (No. 13, pp. 89-112). San Francisco: Jossey-Bass.

Answers for
Media Literacy Quiz

Below are the answers for the Media Literacy Quiz. Check these answers against yours. Use this quiz as a diagnostic tool to tell you where you have stronger knowledge structures and where you need to do some work.

 Part I: The Media Industries

Scoring: Check your answers against the correct answers below. For each answer you get right, give yourself 1 point. Remember that some questions have more than one part. For example, Question 1 has 6 parts, so you could earn 6 points if you get them all right. Also, some answers, such as the answer to Question 4, require a number; if you guess close (plus or minus $20 billion) give yourself a point.

1. In which decade were each of the following media industries introduced into this country? *Broadcast television, 1940s; magazines, before 1880s; film, 1900s and 1910s; radio, 1920s; cable television, 1950s; and personal computers, 1980s.*

2. Which of the mass media is most dominant today? *Broadcast TV or Cable TV*

3. What is meant by "profit"? *Difference between a company's revenues and expenses.*

4. How much money was spent directly by consumers on the media last year? *$200 billion*

5. How much money was spent supporting the media indirectly through advertising? *$160 billion*

6. Which are the most economically concentrated media industries? *Film and Cable TV*

7. What is the largest media company? *Sony or Time Warner*

8. List the top five highest paid entertainers over the past 2 years? *The top 10 people and groups are: Steven Speilberg, $285 million; Oprah Winfrey, $146 million; the Beatles, $130 million; the Rolling Stones, $121 million; the Eagles, $95 million; David Copperfield, $81 million; Pink Floyd, $70 million; Michael Jackson, $67 million; Barbara Streisand, $63 million; Sylvester Stallone, $58 million. Give yourself a point for each one you named.*

9. What is the largest cable television company in this country? *TCI*

   What percentage of America's households are its customers? *About 20%*

10. How many theatrical movie screens are there in this country? *26,000*

11. What is the average profit margin across all industries in this country? *5%*

    Profit in book publishing, *10%*; magazine publishing, *11%*; newspaper publishing, *17%*; broadcast television, *18%*; cable television, *17%*; and radio, *18%*.

12. What percentage of the labor force works in some form of the media? *Less than 1%.*

When you are finished scoring this first part, write your score on the next line.

PART I SCORE: _____

Part II: Media Effects

13. Have the media had any effects on you? If so, list them.

Scoring: For each effect you have listed, give yourself 1 point and write your score on the next line.

PART II SCORE: _____

Part III: Media Content

14. On prime-time television, what is the percentage of all characters who are male? *75%;* African American? *10%;* 65 years old or older? *2%;* overweight? *5%,* and handicapped? *2%.*

Scoring: For each answer you got right, give yourself one point. If you are within several percentage points of the right answer, still give yourself one point. Then write your score for this section on the next line.

PART III SCORE: _____

Part IV: Perceptions of the Real World

Scoring: This is the section of tough questions. You may have had a good idea of some of these but had to make a wild guess on others. For each answer you got right, give yourself 1 point. If you are within several percentage points of the right answer, still give yourself 1 point.

Education

15. Percentage of adults who have not completed high school: *20%*

16. Percentage of adults who have a 4-year college degree: *16%*

17. Percentage of college graduates who earned their degree in 4 years or less: *43%*

Government Expenditures

18. What percentage of the total U.S. economy (Gross Domestic Product) is due to expenditures of the federal government? *17.5%*

19. Of the total expenditures of the federal government, what is the percentage spent on: national defense? *18%;* physical resources? *5%;* human resources? *60%;* interest on the national debt? *16%.*

Demographics

20. Population of this country: *265 million*

21. Percentage of the U.S. population 60 years old or older: *16%*

22. Median age of the population: *34 years old*

23. Immigrants to this country this year: *900,000 people*

24. Percentage of the immigrant total who will come from Mexico: *14%*

Families

25. Number of marriages this year: *2.4 million*

26. Number of divorces this year: *1.2 million*

27. Number of births this year in this country: *4.1 million*

28. Percentage of these births that will be to unmarried mothers: *28%*

29. Median household income: *$38,782*

Health

30. Per capita spending on health in this country: *$2,868 per person*

31. Percentage of health care paid for by Medicare: *16%*

32. Percentage of the total workforce employed in health care: *20%*

33. Percentage of medical doctors who are male: *74%*

34. Percentage of the U.S. population that has a disability that limits their ability to function: *17.5%*

Crime

35. Number of crimes reported to police last year: *13.3 million*

36. Percentage of crimes cleared by arrest: *21%*

37. Percentage of crimes that are violent: *28%*

38. Number of prisoners on death row: *2,482*

39. Average number of prisoners executed each year since 1930: *66*

Legal System

40. Percentage of lawyers who are female: *16%*

41. Number of cases filed in U.S. Supreme Court last year: *6,770*

PART IV SCORE: _____

Part V: Name Recognition

Scoring: We're almost done. For each person you knew, give yourself 1 point. If you wrote a lot of detail about a person (you know a lot about him or her), then give yourself 2 points. Write the number of points next to the person's name on the answer sheet.

42. Roone Arledge: *broadcast television executive; revolutionized television sports coverage in the 1970s*

43. Sandra Bullock: *movie actress*

44. Jim Carrey: *TV and movie actor–comedian*

45. Marcy Carsey: *TV producer*

46. Dan Conner: *name of the father character on TV show Roseanne*

47. Patricia Cornwell: *best-selling author of detective novels*

48. George Costanza: *name of character on TV show Seinfeld*

49. Kevin Costner: *movie actor and director*

50. Michael Crichton: *best-selling author of suspense thrillers*

51. Michael Eisner: *chairman and CEO of The Walt Disney Company*

52. Sandra Day O'Conner: *U.S. Supreme Court Justice*

53. Stephen Hawking: *eminent physicist*

54. Dean Koontz: *best-selling author of 60 books over the past 30 years; 160 million books in print*

55. Michael Irvin: *professional athlete; wide receiver for Dallas Cowboys*

56. Alan Greenspan: *head of the Federal Reserve Board*

57. Gerald Levin: *CEO of Time-Warner media company*

58. Heather Locklear: *TV actress*

59. Courtney Love: *rock singer, movie actress*

60. Nelson Mandela: *leader of the anti-apartheid movement in South Africa*

61. John Malone: *CEO of TCI cable company*

62. Reed Hundt: *chairman of the FCC (Federal Communication Commission)*

63. William Rehnquist: *Chief Justice of U.S. Supreme Court*

64. Janet Reno: *Attorney General of the United States*

65. Geraldo Rivera: *TV personality, talk show host, TV journalist*

66. Dennis Rodman: *professional athlete; forward on Chicago Bulls*

67. Bernard Shaw: *anchorman on CNN News*

68. James Waller: *best-selling author of Bridges of Madison County*

69. Who is the president of your college/university?

70. Name one of the U.S. Senators from your state.

71. Name the U.S. Congressperson from your home district.

PART V Total SCORE: _____

Now break this score down as follows:

_____ points for Knowledge of Personalities
(Add points from Questions 43, 44, 46, 47, 48, 49, 50, 54, 58, 59, 65, 67, and 68)

_____ points for Knowledge of Media Business People
(Add points from Questions 42, 45, 51, 57, and 61)

_____ points for Knowledge of Non-Media People
(Add points from Questions 52, 53, 55, 56, 60, 62, 63, 64, 66, 69, 70, and 71)

Index

A. C. Nielsen Co., 27*t*, 38
A. G. Bertelsmann, 226*t*
ABC, 237*t*
  advertising, 140*t*
  annual budget, 123
  audience share, 191, 233
  commercialism, 113
  competition, 208
  media properties, 226*t*
  mergers, 235
  news coverage, 307
  Olympic Games coverage, 315, 316
  programming, 317
  radio network, 231
  sports coverage, 314
Abelman, R., 309
Ability:
  crystallized, 93
  fluid, 93
Abstraction, 78
Access, 239
Achievers, 251
Acquiring Fundamentals stage, 13, 14*t*
Action for Children's Television, 375
Activation, 273
Active exposure, 25
"Ad Agency Women," 197
Adams, D. M., xii, xiii, xiv, xv, 4, 17, 94, 103
Ader, D. R., 377
Adler, R. P., 158, 159, 263, 276
Adults:
  cognitive development in, 93-97
Advanced skills, 13, 72-81
Advertisers, 142
  and news, 115
  responsibility of, 147
Advertising:
  business of, 139
  cigarette, 157

  commercial, 137-160
  deceptive, 147-149
  economic effects of, 150-153
  effects on children, 158
  effects on individuals, 153-158
  excessiveness of, 147
  immediate effects of, 154-155
  pervasiveness of, 139, 140*t*-141*t*
  political, 306
  popular criticisms of, 146-147
  side effects of, 157
  social criticisms of, 145-150
  socialization effects of, 155-156
  See also Marketing
Advertising agencies, 142
Advertising expenditures, 139, 141*t*
  shares by medium, 142, 143*t*
Advertising exposure plateau curve, 290, 292*f*
Advertising media, 144
Advertising research industry, 142-144
Advil, 151
Aesthetic appreciation ladder, 355-356
Aesthetic domain, 8
Aesthetic skills and knowledge, 126, 127*t*
AFL (American Football League), 314
African Americans:
  employment patterns, 196
  television characters, 163
Agenda setting, 268, 307-308
Ailes, Roger, 306
AIME (amount of invested mental effort), 371
Albert, J., 97, 103, 348, 359
Album Oriented Rock, 232
Alexander, A., 218, 252, 255
Allman, W. F., 334, 335
All News Channel, 237*t*
Alperstein, N. M., 157, 159
Alternative sources of information, 128-129

EDITOR'S NOTE: Page references followed by *t* or *f* indicate tables or figures, respectively.

385

A CENTURY OF
THE CATHOLIC ESSAY

A CENTURY OF
THE CATHOLIC ESSAY

Edited with Biographical Notes by

RAPHAEL H. GROSS, C.PP.S.
DEPARTMENT OF ENGLISH, ST. JOSEPH'S COLLEGE,
COLLEGEVILLE, INDIANA

J. B. LIPPINCOTT COMPANY
PHILADELPHIA   *NEW YORK*

Imprimi Potest

JOSEPH M. MARLING, C.PP.S.
Provincial

Imprimatur

✠ JOHN G. BENNETT, D.D.
Bishop of Lafayette in Indiana

Feast of the Patronage of St. Joseph
Lafayette, 1946

TO MY FATHER AND MOTHER

PREFACE

ONE hundred years ago, on October 9, 1845, John Henry Newman returned to the Faith of his fathers; one hundred years ago, on that day, began the resurgence of English Catholic life and culture. Younger, more vital, and more articulate than she had been for centuries, the Church in England (and in all English-speaking countries, for that matter) survived what Wilfrid Ward called a "state of siege." Today Newman's glowing prophecy of the Church's resurrection, so masterfully set forth in his sermon, "The Second Spring," is clothed in reality; today, likewise, Newman's other, despairing vision of materialism and irreligion rising like a tide "until only the tops of the mountains would be seen like islands in the waste of waters" is a menace to all Christian civilization.

But out of the Second Spring have come leaders, thinkers, and writers who, "like islands in the waste of waters," bring hope to a world deluged. Inspired by their rich Catholic heritage, they have brought forth a remarkable literature that may yet stem the rising tide. They have heeded the advice of Alice Meynell, "Let us be of the center, not of the province"; many of them have taken literally Louise Imogen Guiney's plea, "Let us crucify ourselves upon our pens."

Happily, the work of these Catholic writers is being each day more widely disseminated, appreciated, and studied. The story of the Revival has been well told by Thureau-Dangin, Maisie Ward, and others. In his *The Catholic Literary Revival,* Calvert Alexander wrote an enthusiastic study of the literature. Thomas William Walsh, Joyce Kilmer, Shane Leslie, Theodore Maynard and, latest, Alfred Noyes, have in

7

their anthologies made accessible the best poetry of the Revival. The short story was recently popularized by Mary Curtin and Sister Mariella. Catholic prose has been given place by Theodore Maynard and by Carver and Geyer's thin volume, *Representative Catholic Essays*. Both of these collections, unfortunately, have been out of print for some years.

The Catholic essay, as a distinct literary genre, is too important a contribution to present-day literature ever to be neglected. For out of the Second Spring have appeared some of the most accomplished essayists of English literature. Few will deny that Newman, Chesterton, and Belloc stand in the front rank of the English masters. So also Alice Meynell, Louise Guiney, and Agnes Repplier. Of Mrs. Meynell it has been said, "No woman has ever written an essay to compare with *The Rhythm of Life*." Christopher Morley has pronounced Miss Guiney "one of the rarest poets and most delicately poised essayists" America has produced. And Miss Repplier is still the recognized dean of American essayists.

To bring the work of these and of other Catholic essayists into focus for the general reader is the aim of this new collection. Catholics and non-Catholics alike, who are concerned with true cultural values, will (I trust) find here a point of view, at once eternally old and eternally new, together with freshness and artistic excellence. The book should prove valuable, too, as supplementary reading in any course on the essay or on Catholic literature. In so far as possible I have tried to assemble representative pieces of the authors included. I have given consideration, moreover, to variety of type and of theme. Part One is largely devoted to the informal essay, and Part Two to the more learned, formal essay. Within these main divisions are such examples of the short-story type of essay as Talbot's "A Date for Saturday Night" and Eden's "The Pensioner of the Pied Brothers"; such biographical essays as Daly's "Charles Waterton: Naturalist" and Martindale's "Hermann the Cripple." The book review essay is represented

by Windle's "The Everlasting Man," and the scholarly essay
by Sister Madeleva's "Chaucer's Nuns."

Not all the essays here gathered tend to indoctrinate or
to increase one's sense of world crisis. For the Catholic writer
frequently steps down from his high purpose to chat familiarly
with his friends on any and all subjects. Yet even in his "good
talk" he is in harmony with Catholic teaching: all that he
writes or speaks is governed, however indirectly, by his Catholic spirit and outlook.

Putting this book together has been something of a burden
light. My sorest disappointment is that I had necessarily to omit
many a choice piece—of men like Newman, Chesterton, and
Belloc, who rightfully have their own anthologies. Such essays
as Heywood Broun's "The Fifty-first Dragon," Agnes Repplier's "A Point of History," and Compton Mackenzie's "Ad-
ventures in Food" strongly sought admission. The work of
Shane Leslie, Maurice Francis Egan, Christopher Hollis,
Theodore Maynard, Michael Williams, and others seek an additional series. Reviewers, no less than readers, may be
tempted to score the anthologist for his omissions, but be sure,
I have tried genuinely to be a good host. To give here a general study of modern Catholic prose could only be, at best,
inadequate and, in view of the excellent chapters in Alexander's
book, perhaps superfluous. The essays speak for themselves.

The gladdest portion of my task remains—to thank all who
in any way contributed to the making of this book. First, there
are, besides the original authors, the publishers and the copy-
right holders, who have generously granted me permission to
reprint. There are, second, my fellow-members in the Society
of the Precious Blood, my colleagues on the faculty of St.
Joseph's of Indiana, and my friends—all of whom by their
interest made a greater contribution to this book than they
know. To some I owe a special debt of gratitude: to my former co-worker in the Department of English, the late Father
Paul F. Speckbaugh, a true scholar and a Christ-like priest, by
whose inspiration this book was first begun; to Father Clar-

ence Schuerman, Librarian of St. Joseph's of Indiana, and his assistant, Brother Philip, for their help in obtaining necessary books and references; to Fathers Edwin Kaiser, Rufus Esser, and Edward Maziarz, my associates on the faculty, for their gracious advice and suggestions; to Father Norman Koller, pastor of St. Augustine's Church, Youngstown, Ohio, and Father Marcellus Dreiling, of the St. Joseph's faculty, for their invaluable aid in preparing the manuscript; to Mr. Vincent Starrett, of The Chicago *Tribune,* for tracing a particular essay; to Mrs. Carl Caston, for typing portions of the copy; and to Miss Grace Guiney, Oxford, England, for sending me the emendated versions of Louise Imogen Guiney's "On the Delights of an Incognito" and "The Puppy: A Portrait."

R. H. G.

CONTENTS

PART ONE

The Texture of Life

Fellow-travelers

Length and Breadth

12 CONTENTS

Amenities

PART TWO

Culture and Education

Literature and Art